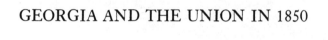

GEORGIA AND THE UNION IN 1850

GEORGIA AND THE UNION IN 1850

By

RICHARD HARRISON SHRYOCK

AMS PRESS
NEW YORK

AMS PRESS, INC.
New York, N.Y. 10003

To

M. H. S. and L. E. C.

PREFACE

This study was first submitted in partial fulfillment of the requirements for the degree of doctor of philosophy at the University of Pennsylvania. Additional material has since been incorporated and it has been considerably changed in form. It was prepared under the direction of Dean Herman V. Ames, to whom I am primarily indebted. Professor St. George L. Sioussat gave many valuable suggestions and he, with Professor A. E. McKinley, read and criticised the proof. My colleague, Professor W. K. Boyd, and Dean R. P. Brooks, of the University of Georgia, were also kind enough to criticise the study in proof. I owe much to the painstaking assistance of my colleague, Professor W. T. Laprade, Supervising Editor of The Duke University Press.

Professor Ulrich B. Phillips, of the University of Michigan, generously placed at my disposal his unsurpassed knowledge of the history of the ante-bellum South, and his papers relating to Georgia. Professor Arthur C. Cole, of the Ohio State University, made helpful suggestions on the general theme of the study. Professor Phillips, Professor Cole, and Professor J. S. Bassett, on behalf of the American Historical Association, gave permission to reproduce one of the maps in Professor Phillips' *Georgia and State Rights* (herein listed as Map No. 5) and a portion of one of the maps in Professor Cole's *The Whig Party in the South* (herein listed as Map No. 2). All maps, except Bonner's of 1849, and those noted, are copies of my own originals prepared by Mrs. J. R. Chamberlain of Raleigh.

Professor C. S. Boucher, of the University of Chicago, kindly placed at my disposal such of the unpublished Calhoun letters as related especially to Georgia. Mr. Warren Grice, of Macon, permitted me to examine several of his valuable papers relating to Georgia history. I am indebted to Miss Margaret A. Cosens, of Savannah, for permission to use the papers of her grandfather, Dr. Richard Arnold. Mr. William Harden and Mr. Alexander R. Lawton, of Savannah, and other members of the Georgia Historical Society, offered courteous assistance in the use of materials in that city. Mr. Wymberley W. De Renne, of Savannah, kindly permitted the use of valuable materials in the De Renne Library of Georgia History.

R. H. S.

Sachems Head, Conn.,
September, 1926.

TABLE OF CONTENTS

LIST OF MAPS

GEORGIA AND THE UNION IN 1850

INTRODUCTION

The period of promise in the ante-bellum history of the lower South was that of the generation following the War of 1812. This was no doubt due to the simple fact that the history of the lower South in this period was in large measure a part of a still greater story—the story of the growing West. It was the day of expansion, with dreams of still greater expansion just ahead. In the South, however, this great era was made possible only by the development of several institutions and circumstances peculiar to the section,—not one "peculiar institution," as is often stated, but several; namely, the plantation system, the system of slave labor and invested capital, and at last, but not least, the race question.

To say that the development of the lower South was made possible by these institutions—for even the Negro was in his way an institution—is to say that the very expansion of the section contained the germ of its own decline. This relative decline, as compared with the mounting prosperity of the North, may be dated roughly from the thirties and was becoming increasingly apparent through the forties. Far sighted southern leaders did not shut their eyes to the outstanding economic phenomena of their time and made strenuous efforts to revive the prosperity of their section. Unfortunately there were other factors involved in southern backwardness besides southern institutions. It happened that, when the economic life of the South was already threatened with ills from within, it was also subjected to criticism and attack from without.

First came the onslaught of the business men of the North, who demanded tariff protection for their growing industries at the expense of southern agriculture. Then came the attack of northern idealists, who demanded that the entire labor system upon which a large part of southern agriculture was based should be abolished,—and with it the whole social system with which that labor seemed inextricably associated. Either of these attacks might have been expected, under even the best of circumstances, to have elicited serious protest in the South. Coming as they did, however, when the southern leaders were already conscious of a relative economic backwardness, they were bound to result in the most bitter antagonisms. It seemed to southern men that the North, not content with its own growing prosperity, was intent upon destroying not only what prosperity there was in the South, but also the very civilization of the section itself. The motives of many northern antislavery idealists were of the highest, and their moral principles were coming to receive the commendation of the civilized world, but these facts could hardly have been expected, under the circumstances, to detract greatly from the resentment and the apprehension which their criticisms aroused in the South.

Now there were certain obvious remedies for the tariff and antislavery attacks of the North—at least there were expedients which seemed to promise a remedy. There was nullification, and, if this did not avail, there was secession from the union with the offending section. Certain southern leaders began to urge the employment of these expedients from 1828 on. It is at least a striking coincidence that the state which was most retrogressive in the lower South;

namely, South Carolina, was also the one whose leaders first and most insistently urged these radical remedies. This suggests the view urged by some northern critics at the time; namely, that the southern people who suffered most from the ills of their economic position were those most apt to blame all such ills upon northern attacks and the least apt to realize that many of their troubles might be inherent in their own insitutions.

This also suggests the significance of another fact that is so obvious as sometimes to be overlooked. All portions of the lower South were not equally backward in their economic life. In general, the newer lands, for obvious reasons, were more productive and prosperous than the older. Mississippi was better off than South Carolina. The outstanding prosperity of the section in 1850 was, however, to be found in Georgia, the "Empire State of the South"; which, after sharing in the general depression of the early forties, forged rapidly ahead towards the end of the decade, and by 1850 was renowned for its railroads and manufactures as well as for its agriculture. Here the property-holding classes tended to view their own prosperity as evidence that the South could yet make progress within the national Union. If Georgia could prosper, despite northern tariffs and criticisms, then the ills from which the neighboring "Palmettodom" suffered must be latent in the latter's own agricultural system rather than in the machinations of the Yankees.

Northern attacks, felt the conservative Georgia leaders, need not force the state to secede until they showed signs of developing into an ultimate menace to southern society. Until such time, so radical a measure as secession would only involve the nation in the danger of civil war, a danger that all, and especially the

property-holding classes, would wish to avoid as long
as possible. In a word, Georgians did not wish to run
a risk of civil war unless the risk involved in the maintenance of the Union proved an even greater one.
Sincere attachment to the "Union of the Fathers"
tended to strengthen this general attitude.

In 1847 came the first evidence which was apt to be
convincing to the mass of the people of the lower South
that the antislavery attack was about to become an
ultimate menace. In that year the antislavery forces
in Congress attempted to pass the Proviso denying to
the South what it considered its rightful share of the
territories of the new West. This seemed an earnest
of what was to come in the future—further restric-
tions and, finally, abolition and chaos. The lower South
as a whole began for the first time to think seriously of
secession. In 1850, however, the conservative North
rallied to the support of the conservative South, the
Proviso was finally defeated, and a "compromise"
achieved.

A serious secession movement, however, was by
this time under way, led as usual by South Carolina.
Georgia, it was hoped, would "lead off," with the secret
prompting and backing of the sister state. This hope
was destined to dramatic disappointment, largely for
three reasons. In the first place, it happened that for
years a most unsisterly animosity had obtained between
Georgia and Carolina, a feeling based upon varied
economic and social circumstances and arising partly
from the simple fact of geographical propinquity. If
"Palmettodom" willed secession, that in itself tended
to make the Empire State cleave to the Union.

Second, it happened that Georgia was one of those
southern states whose territory extended well up into

the hill country of the Appalachians, and the people of this section of the state displayed the typical mountaineers' indifference to controversies concerning slavery. They were not only indifferent to the interests of slavery, but they were in addition devotedly attached to the Union. The secessionists' appeal, therefore, was bound to be ignored in this part of the state.

Third, and doubtless most important, was the fact that the secession appeal reached Georgia at a time when she was enjoying the peak of her new prosperity. Such a period was no time for revolution, unless it was clear that revolution was necessary. Georgians looked longingly for the slightest of signs that the North would offer some compromise—some earnest of future fair-dealing that would make secession unnecessary—and they found it in the Clay compromise. Once this compromise was offered, there was no serious danger that Georgia would secede.

What would have occurred if the state had been, like South Carolina, in a state of economic depression and in a correspondingly depressed state of mind, is another matter. So, too, is the question as to why Georgia did secede ten years later, when prosperity (at least so far as cotton prices were concerned) still obtained. The answer to this last may lie in the fact that in 1860 the election of a "black-Republican" president did imply in unmistakable terms an ultimate menace to southern institutions. The state would doubtless have seceded in 1850 if the Proviso, also a final threat, had passed at that time. The view here taken is not that prosperity inclined Georgia to surrender, but simply that prosperity did incline the state to compromise.

If this view of the matter seems to overemphasize the significance of economic factors, the facts that follow must speak for themselves. It seemed desirable to the writer that, in addition to the narration of the political developments involved in the secession and Union movements of 1844-1852, some examination should be made of the economic and social bases of the political phenomena concerned.

The decision of Georgia to hold to the Union in 1850 was one of the outstanding events of the national crisis of that year. This decision was indeed a cardinal factor in the salvation of the Union then, and perhaps later, in that it gave check to both the northern and the southern extremists. The significance of its influence is perhaps not yet generally realized. The state did much to check the extremists of the South because of its acceptance of the compromise. It did something to check the extremists of the North, although in a more indirect fashion. The warning given in the "Georgia Platform," that thus far could the North go and no farther, was heeded by northern conservatives, who in turn were able to restrain to some extent the activities of northern extremists. It is hoped that the influence exerted by the Georgia decision in both sections will appear as the narrative proceeds.

CHAPTER I

ECONOMIC FACTORS

For some years preceding the American Civil War it was customary to speak of Georgia as the "Keystone" or "Empire State of the South." Such phrases were, to be sure, chiefly popular with Georgians, but their use was by no means limited to native sons and seems to have implied a consciousness that the state held among its neighbors a position of unusual importance. When, therefore, a great political crisis arose in 1850, which involved the relationship of the southern states to the Union, it was quite natural that Georgia should play a leading part in determining the attitude of the lower South toward the Union. The political preëminence of the state was in large part the result of economic preëminence, and an understanding of the one involves some knowledge of the other. Indeed, all phases of the crisis of 1850 in Georgia, and of the influence which Georgia exerted upon the lower South, were intimately related to the economic and social conditions obtaining within the state during that period.

Georgia was the keystone of an arch formed by the Seaboard states to the north and the Gulf states to the west. The "Keystone State" reached from the seacoast on the east across a wide plain and piedmont area to the hill country of the Appalachians in the northwest. It was divided into several well defined sections, running generally parallel with the coast from northeast to southwest across the width of the state.

The first of these sections was that of the coast lands, including the "sea islands." Along the shore of the mainland stretched the "tide swamp lands," which also reached inland along the banks of the rivers in the tidewater area. Here, in the region of the sweeping "Marshes of Glynn," were the most valuable lands in the state in 1850.[1] At no great distance inland, however, the fertile swamp was succeeded by the most desolate belt in Georgia, the aptly named "Pine Barrens," where there was a poor, siliceous soil covered with rank brush and "scrub pine."

At about one third the distance from the shore to the mountains the Pine Barrens merged gradually into "Central Georgia." This, the most important area in the state in 1850, may be bounded on the south by the fall line, crossing the state from northeast to the southwest and marked by the cities that naturally developed upon the rivers along this line. Since the Pine Barrens did not actually reach to the fall line, however, the southern boundary of Central Georgia is here considered as running somewhat below that line and as extending downward to include the fertile lands along the Savannah River.[2] The southwest portion of the state, while similar in general character to Central Georgia, was developed at a later period and was sometimes spoken of distinctively as "Southwest Georgia." On the north, a series of granite ridges, crowned in DeKalb County by the famous "Stone Mountain," marked the limits of Central and

---

[1] J. D. B. DeBow, *Industrial Resources of the Southern and Western States*, I. 355; G. M. White, *Georgia Statistics*, pp. 37, 284. For pleasing pictures of the coastal lands about 1850, see Georgia B. Conrad, *Reminiscences of a Southern Woman*, pp. 1-10; E. J. Thomas, *Memoirs of a Southerner*, pp. 7-24.

[2] For all of these areas, the river systems, etc., see Bonner's map of 1849 and map No. 1, p. 10.

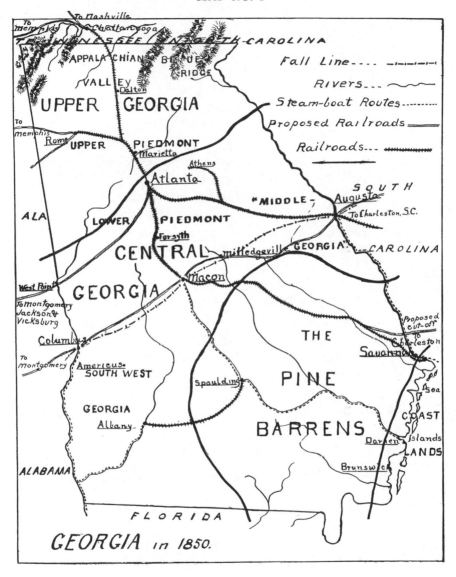

GEORGIA in 1850.

the beginning of "Upper Georgia." This area included, geologically speaking, the Upper Piedmont, the Blue Ridge, the Valley, and the main ridges of the Appalachians, which ran athwart the northwestern tip of the state.[3]

The soil of Central and Southwest Georgia was a fairly rich loam resting upon a clay foundation. The general fertility of these sections adapted them to the cultivation of cotton, and they came to form the Georgia "Black Belt." When exhausted by cotton cultivation and left fallow, however, the "scrub pine" eventually appeared, and the country assumed an appearance similar to that of the Pine Barrens. In Upper Georgia the soils of the valleys were fertile, but the cool climate of this region adapted it to the cultivation of fruits and grains rather than of the lowland staples. The hills afforded some mineral wealth and an abundance of potential water power.[4]

The settlement of the several Georgia sections had progressed slowly until about 1800, when only the coast lands and "Middle Georgia" along the Savannah river had been occupied. After that date the extinction of Indian titles and the adoption of a liberal land lottery system[5] enabled Carolina and Virginia settlers to push steadily across Central Georgia. The whole belt of Central Georgia had been occupied by 1830, but Southwest Georgia remained a sparsely settled country until

[3] For careful geographical descriptions of the Georgia sections see R. M. Harper, "Development of Agriculture in Upper Georgia," *Georgia Historical Quarterly*, VI. No. 1, pp. 6, 7; R. P. Brooks, *The Agrarian Revolution in Georgia*, pp. 69-80 (published as *University of Wisconsin Bulletin No. 639, History Series*, III. No. 3).

[4] DeBow, *op. cit.*, pp. 356, 362, 363; White, *op. cit.*, pp. 150, 151, 212, 439; A. Sherwood, *Gazeteer of Georgia* (fourth edition, 1860), p. 194.

[5] For the history and legal details of Georgia land administration see S. G. McLendon, *History of the Public Domain of Georgia*, pp. 122-129.

the forties. Meanwhile, some scattered settlements had been made in the Pine Barrens, and poor white "squatters" had drifted in from no one knew where,[6] to occupy the "piney woods." The soils of this region began to give out under cotton cultivation as early as 1820, save on the alluvial bottoms along the larger rivers. Here a few prosperous plantations were maintained as late as 1850.[7]

The late expulsion of the Indians from Upper Georgia left the Blue Ridge and Valley regions unsettled by whites until the later thirties, when the last of the tribesmen abandoned fields and cabins and trekked west across the Mississippi. Just before this occurred, gold had been discovered in the hills, and the first white settlers came in on the tide of a small "gold rush" that suggests the California epic of the next decade.[8] Squatters occupied old Cherokee cabins or built new ones, wherein they were still living in 1850. This settlement was supplemented in the forties by poor farmers, who moved up from Central Georgia, and by an immigration of mountaineers from the adjacent hill country of eastern Tennessee.[9] These elements blended into a rough and ready yoemanry possessing the usual virtues and defects of that class. Much of "Cherokee Georgia" was still in the frontier-farming stage of development in 1850.

If a "gold rush" brought settlers to Upper Georgia, then, by the same token, it was a "cotton rush"

[6] There was a tradition in Georgia that they were descendants of Oglethorpe's paupers, who had moved up the rivers from the coast. Some of these squatters may have migrated across the Savannah from similar pine barren districts in South Carolina.

[7] F. L. Olmsted, *The Cotton Kingdom*, II. 385.

[8] There are interesting pictures of the Georgia gold rush by G. Andrews, *Reminiscences of an Old Georgia Lawyer*, pp. 73, 187.

[9] Milledgeville *Federal Union*, October 24, 1847.

that had carried settlers across Central Georgia. The extension of cotton cultivation in this area led naturally to two other demands, in addition to the ever present desire for more land. There was, first, the demand for more labor to work the fields, and, second, the need for better transportation facilities wherewith to market their product. Both desiderata were destined to influence greatly the entire subsequent history of Georgia and of the Gulf states, which were experiencing a similar development in the same period.

There was never any doubt that the bulk of unskilled labor in Central Georgia would be supplied by Negro slaves. It was customary for incoming whites to bring their slaves with them, and this custom was the chief source of Negro immigration. Many were brought in, however, *via* the domestic slave trade, particularly after about 1830, and an uncertain number through the illicit foreign trade.[10] During the third and fourth decades, when the percentage of the net increase in population was greatest, both the absolute numbers and the ratio of increase were slightly smaller for the Negroes than for the whites. As the plantation areas of Central Georgia developed between 1840 and 1850, however, the demand for labor also grew, and the percentage of increase in the Negro population exceeded that of the whites in this decade. The state still possessed in 1850 a white majority of some one hundred and thirty-seven thousand, in a total population of about nine hundred thousand.[11]

[10] *Slavery and the Internal Slave Trade,* by the Executive Committee of the American Anti-Slavery Society, (London, 1841), pp. 12, 13, 20; W. H. Collins, *The Domestic Slave Trade,* pp. 42, 119, 120; W. E. B. Du Bois, *The Suppression of the African Slave Trade to the United States of America,* p. 183; A. A. Taylor, "The Movement of Negroes to the Gulf States," *Journal of Negro History,* III. No. 4, p. 368.

[11] The percentage increase of population, 1840-1850, for the Negroes, was about 35%; for the whites, about 28%. *Census of 1850.*

Since cotton could be best cultivated in Central and Coastal Georgia, it was in these sections that the Negro population became concentrated. They soon came to have a Negro majority in population, though this majority rarely exceeded seventy-five per cent. and was often less than sixty-five per cent. of the total. Hence the concentration of Negro population was rarely as great in the Georgia Black Belt as it was in those of South Carolina and Mississippi. Nevertheless, the Negro element was sufficiently large in the Georgia plantation areas to create a race problem of serious potentialities.[12]

The second demand stimulated by the spread of cotton culture was that for improved means of transportation. The chief problem in this connection was how to ship cotton from Central Georgia to the coast, these two sections being separated by the desolate pine belt. It was naturally most convenient at first to depend upon water transportation, and steamboats were introduced upon the Savannah about 1816 and upon the Ocmulgee and Chattahoochee about 1830. Mercantile towns naturally developed at the fall line on these rivers to handle this trade, the most important being Augusta on the Savannah, Macon on the Ocmulgee, and Columbus on the Chattahoochee.[13] Two of these towns shipped down the rivers to Georgia's one important port, Savannah, but some of their cotton was carried on to Charleston. The latter city was not so well connected by waterways with the interior coun-

[12] See Map No. 2, p. 14. For the development of the Black Belt counties; see R. P. Brooks, "A Local Study of the Race Problem," *Political Science Quarterly*, XXVI. 193-200. For the exact percentage of slave population in the several Georgia sections in 1850, which varied from 58.2 in the Lower Piedmont to 2.3 in the Blue Ridge, see R. M. Harper, "Development of Agriculture in Upper Georgia, 1850-1880," *Georgia Historical Quarterly*, VI. No. 1, p 14. The free Negro population was negligible.

[13] See map No. 1, p. 10.

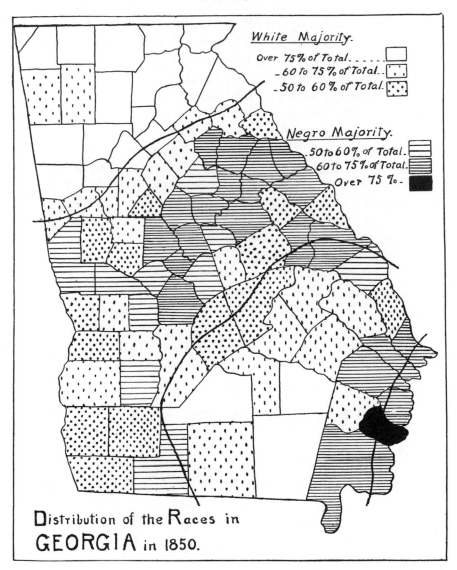

White Majority.

Over 75% of Total......
_60 to 75% of Total...
_50 to 60% of Total.

Negro Majority.

50 to 60% of Total
60 to 75% of Total.
Over 75%_

Distribution of the Races in
GEORGIA in 1850.

Reproduced, by permission, from map in A. C. Cole's *The Whig Party in the South.*

try as was Savannah. This mattered little in colonial days, but, when cotton culture spread to the Piedmont area of both South Carolina and Georgia,[14] it became imperative for Charleston to find some direct water connection with the new region. This was attained by securing control of the line of steamers running from Augusta to Savannah upon the river of that name and by extending the line on from Savannah to Charleston. In this way the Carolina port inaugurated a long and portentous rivalry with the port of Georgia for the control of the interior trade.[15]

The establishment of steamers upon the Ocmulgee and the Chattahoochee was practically concomitant with the early railroad movement. The demand for railroads was augmented in Georgia and the neighboring states by a growing realization that the South was falling behind the North in economic progress. It began to be apparent in the thirties that the South was becoming increasingly dependent upon the other section in finance, commerce, and industry. Some southern observers, notably the South Carolina extremists, were inclined to place the blame for this situation primarily upon northern legislation and sought, therefore, political remedies in nullification and secession. The bulk of well informed southerners of the thirties and forties, however, blamed the plight of their section upon economic conditions and sought, therefore, economic remedies. The chief specific remedies proposed in this period were, first, the increase of both the domestic and foreign trade of southern ports by the establishment of railroad connections between them and

[14] See Brooks, *Agrarian Revolution in Georgia*, pp. 83-85.
[15] See map No. 1, p. 10. For the story of water transportation in Georgia, see U. B. Phillips, *A History of Transportation in the Eastern Cotton Belt*, pp. 72, 73, 76-78, etc.; Mary Lane, "Macon, An Historical Retrospect," *Georgia Historical Quarterly*, V. No. 3, p. 27.

the Mississippi Valley; and, second, the development of manufacturing industries. Georgia took the lead in pushing each of these proposed moves in the interest of economic progress.[16]

Agitation for railroad development in Georgia began in Athens, Macon, and Savannah in the early thirties, and the first railroad charters were issued at that time. Plans were laid for roads to connect Upper and Central Georgia with Savannah and to develop in this connection "direct trade" between that port and Europe. No fewer than three "direct trade" conventions met in Augusta in 1837 and 1838, and a fourth at Charleston in 1839. This movement to ship direct to Europe—rather than *via* New York—proved fruitless at the time, but was revived again a decade later in connection with the increasing sectional antagonism of that period.[17] Meanwhile, the related railroad movement proved more productive of immediate results. The building of the roads was seriously delayed by the financial panic of 1837 and the subsequent depression of the early forties, but between 1840 and 1848 the "Georgia Central" was built from Savannah to Macon, the "Macon and Western" from Macon to Atlanta, and the "Georgia Railroad" from Augusta to Atlanta. Meanwhile, a road had long since been run across South Carolina from Charleston to Hamburg, the latter a village upon the Savannah river opposite

[16] The best brief and general statement of southern efforts towards economic development is in St. George L. Sioussat, "Co-operation for the Development of the Material Welfare of the South," in *The South in the Building of the Nation,* IV. 173. For more detailed expositions see Edward Ingle, *Southern Sidelights: A Picture of Social and Economic Life in the South a Generation Before the War,* chapter vii; R. R. Russel, *Economic Aspects of Southern Sectionalism, 1840-1861, passim,* published in *University of Illinois Studies in the Social Sciences,* XI. Nos 1 and 2.

[17] Sioussat, *op. cit.,* pp. 173-179; Ingle, *op. cit.,* pp. 123-126; Russel, *op. cit.,* pp. 17, 18, 29, 94.

Augusta. In this way Atlanta, in the Piedmont, was connected by two direct rail routes with the sea, the first running *via* Macon to Savannah, the second *via* Augusta to Charleston.[18]

At the same time the state of Georgia, urged on by state railroad meetings and by the great southern railroad convention held at Memphis in 1845, proceeded to build the "Western and Atlantic" north from Atlanta to Chattanooga, Tennessee. This point was reached in 1849, and from here it was hoped to make river and rail connections with the entire Mississippi Valley.[19] This accomplished, Atlanta would become the terminus for all goods shipped from the West to the southern seaboard, for once arrived at Atlanta, merchandise could be shipped thence to the sea *via* either Macon or Augusta. If the Erie Canal had made a great port on the northern seaboard, then the "Western and Atlantic" could create a similarly great port on the southern seaboard. Which of Atlanta's ports however, was to become the great "emporium"— Charleston or Savannah? In a word, the rivalry of these two ports for the Piedmont trade was now extended, as a result of the new rail connections with Chattanooga, into a potential rivalry for the trade of the entire West.

[18] For these railroad developments see Bonner's map of 1849 and map No. 1, p. 10. For the general history of the railroads see Phillips, *A History of Transportation in the Eastern Cotton Belt, passim;* for the details of financing and management see the annual reports of the roads, e.g., *Charter, Acts and Reports of the President, Engineer and Superintendent of the Georgia Railroad and Banking Company, passim.* For the complicated economic and political history of the South Carolina railroad running from Charleston to Hamburg, see T. D. Jervey, *The Slave Trade: Slavery and Color,* pp. 87-99.

[19] For the history of the "Western and Atlantic" see Phillips "An American State Owned Railroad," (The Western and Atlantic) *Yale Review,* XV. No. 3, pp. 260-272. For the connections planned between the "Western and Atlantic" and Nashville, Memphis, etc., see Map No. 1; and R. S. Cotterill, "Southern Railroads and Western Trade, 1840-1850," *Mississippi Valley Historical Review,* III. 428-432.

While the roads mentioned were being built, plans were also laid for running lines across the state from east to west. It was proposed to extend a road from Atlanta to West Point on the Chattahoochee, or to build a new line from Augusta to Columbus *via* Macon, such roads to be connected in time with lines to Montgomery and New Orleans. Columbus was particularly desirous of securing connection with Macon and Augusta, in the hope of becoming the chief trade center between Montgomery and Charleston. This meant, incidentally, that Columbus "boosters" looked forward to connections with Charleston rather than with Savannah in their own state. This fact may conceivably have had something to do with the pro-Carolina feeling so noticeable in Columbus in the late forties.[20]   As a result of all its building activity, Georgia possessed by 1850 over five hundred miles of railroads, a mileage which made it at least the fifth state in the Union in railroad development.[21]   The immediate economic advantages of these roads were obvious enough. Later experience showed, to be sure, that their advent was not an unmixed blessing,[22] but they gave Georgia at the time a great reputation for prosperity and progress and contributed to the business optimism of the Georgia people.

Most of the earlier railroads were joint banking and transportation enterprises, the banking privileges

[20] See the Columbus *Times* for January 4, February 1, March 28, May 2, 1848.

[21] There was a regular railroad "boom" in the state between *c*. 1846 and 1850; see the Savannah *Georgian,* for May 25, December 8, 16, 1847.

[22] The development of the roads tended in the long run to increase the quantity of cotton raised, to increase competition in this industry, and to fasten the one-crop system upon the South, with all its attendant evils. In Georgia the roads built up Atlanta at the expense of the ports. See Phillips, "Transportation in the Ante-Bellum South: An Economic Analysis," *Quarterly Journal of Economics,* May, 1905, pp. 450, 451. For the immediate effects of the roads upon Atlanta, see Augusta *Chronicle,* August 16, 1849.

having obvious advantages for corporations involved in heavy initial expenditures leading to small immediate returns. Lack of capital was a handicap to most early corporate enterprises in the state, which, being a relatively new one, was not possessed of such banking facilities as were enjoyed at Charleston. Banks established at Savannah and Augusta in 1810 having proved a success, however, a State Bank was founded at Savannah in 1828. This bank served as a place of deposit for state funds and issued paper currency. The Panic of 1837 and the mismanagement and legislative interference, which were common phenomena with many banks in the new states of this period, combined to wreck the State Bank in 1841. Its liabilities were met by a special bond issue to the amount of one million dollars. This state debt was increased in 1847 and 1851, when almost a million more was borrowed in order to finance the building of the state railroad.[23]

The bond issue of 1841 was made at a time of general business depression, when there was of course no surplus in the state funds. As a consequence, the bank's currency depreciated, and the state bonds were difficult to sell, even at "ruinous prices."[24] This situation was most embarrassing to the business interests of the state and led to strenuous efforts by the Whig party, which represented those interests, to restore the state's credit. These efforts, profiting from the general return of prosperity in the late forties, resulted in the payment of all back interest and some of the principal of the bonded debt by 1849. In that year the state treasurer, after paying all expenses and deposit-

[23] J. A. Flisch, "The State Finances of Georgia," *The South in the Building of the Nation*, V. 409; D. R. Dewey, "Banking in the South," *ibid.*, V. 467.

[24] Savannah *Georgian*, July 19, 1849.

ing seventy thousand in the debt sinking fund, still had a surplus of ten thousand dollars on hand. In the same year the amount of the state debt was less than one half that of South Carolina and only about one seventh of that of Alabama.[25] So encouraging was the outlook in the state's finances by this time—only five years after a period of serious depression—that the editor of the nation's chief commercial journal remarked that "No state in the Union has stronger claims upon the public faith than Georgia."[26]

The private banks of Augusta and Savannah shared in the return of financial prosperity in the late forties. With this prosperity came an increasing desire to compete with the older and stronger banks of Charleston for the business of their own state. Indeed, financial dependence upon Charleston was fast becoming offensive to local state pride. "It is absurd," observed the Milledgeville *Recorder,* "that we now have to borrow money from other states and send out of Georgia our interest. . . . Thus far Georgia has been only a great plantation for the benefit of the Charleston banks."[27] Thus some financial rivalry between interested parties in Georgia and South Carolina was added to the trade rivalry already noted. The Georgia protest against financial dependence upon Carolina, it may be noted in passing, was analogous to the general southern protest against financial dependence upon the North, and it led to an analogous dislike for the section in question.

One of the underlying reasons for the return of financial prosperity by 1849 was the return of agricultural prosperity at that time. Nearly a decade of de-

[25] *The American Almanac,* for 1850, p. 218.
[26] *Hunt's Merchants' Magazine,* XXI. 454.
[27] Quoted in *DeBow's Review,* VIII. 39 (January, 1850).

pression in cotton prices was then coming to a happy end.[28] Since southern methods in agriculture were generally of a wasteful character,[29] the period of depression had been particularly hard upon those sections of South Carolina and Georgia which had long been under cultivation. Georgia, however, was the better situated of the two states in this respect, since it still possessed, in 1850, large areas of practically new land in Southwest Georgia.[30] A strong movement for agricultural reform was also inaugurated in Georgia in the late forties by a remarkable agricultural monthly, the *Southern Cultivator,* which possessed the largest circulation of any periodical in the state.[31] Published at Augusta by the publishers of the *Chronicle,* this paper carried to planters throughout Georgia and the neighboring states an insistent demand for more scientific farming. As a result of this propaganda and that of the agricultural fairs,[32] some signs of improvement in farming methods were discernible by 1850.[33]

The chief factors in the return of high cotton prices by 1850 seem to have been short crops and an increasing European demand, consequent upon good

[28] This depression was variously ascribed to overproduction, and to the influence of the tariff in limiting British exports and consequently British purchasing power. See Russel, *Economic Aspects of Southern Sectionalism,* pp. 37-39.

[29] This was generally recognized at the time by progressive southern editors, see, *e.g.,* the editorial opinions quoted in the Augusta *Chronicle,* April 4, 11, 1849; Savannah *Georgian,* April 25, 1849, etc.

[30] See Augusta *Chronicle,* May 17, July 6, 1849.

[31] J. C. G. Kennedy, *Catalogue of Newspapers and Periodicals in the United States,* for 1850, in appendix to J. Livingston, *Law Register for 1852,* p. 291.

[32] For a description of one of the large Stone Mountain fairs see Augusta *Chronicle,* Sept. 15, 1849.

[33] Boston *Courier* (Savannah corr.), December 27, 1850. There was a concomitant demand for agricultural reform in South Carolina; see C. S. Boucher, *The Ante-Bellum Attitude of South Carolina Toward Manufacturing and Agriculture,* pp. 264-266, (published in *Washington University Studies,* III. Pt. II, *Humanistic Series,* No. 2).

harvests in England and the return to "normalcy" after the political disturbances of 1848.[34] As a result of all these factors, the price rose rapidly late in 1849, the average price of "middling upland" per pound at New York City going from 7.55 cents in 1849 to 12.34 in 1850.[35] By October 23, 1850, "middling fair" was selling at Savannah for 13.5, which, according to C. F. M'Cays' estimate, represented an advance of no less than eighty-five per cent. over the average price for the period of the five preceding years. The average price per pound of exported cotton of all grades rose from 6.4 in 1849 to 11.3 in 1850, and to 12.11 in 1851.[36]

The cumulative result of increasing cotton prices, of attempts at agricultural improvement, and of the prospect of still unexhausted soils in Southwest Georgia, was to render the Georgia planters a fairly prosperous and optimistic group by 1850. In addition to this, and what is perhaps of greater psychological import here, the planters expected a continuation of good times with increasing prosperity in the near future.

There was one other cause for optimism among the propertied classes of Georgia in the late forties; namely, the belief that manufacturing enterprises, then growing rapidly in the state, would soon become a source of great wealth to its citizens. The depression in cotton prices during the forties did more to foster

[34] Russel, *Economic Aspects of Southern Sectionalism*, pp. 33-35.

[35] F. J. Guetter and A. E. McKinley, *Statistical Tables Relating to the Economic Growth of the United States, Enlarged Edition*, p. 44 (Philadelphia, 1924); see also, Russel, *op. cit.*, p. 35; U. B. Phillips, *American Negro Slavery*, p. 370; R. B. Handy, "History and General Statistics of Cotton," *The Cotton Plant*, p. 42, published as *United States Department of Agriculture Bulletin No. 33*. (Washington, 1896), also in *House Documents, 54 Congress, 2 Session, No. 267*.

[36] *Hunt's Merchants' Magazine*, XXIII. 598 (December, 1850) gives M'Cay's estimates. For average prices of exported cotton see report of the U. S. Treasury Department for 1855, *Senate Documents, 34 Congress, Sessions 1 and 2*, V. No. 32, p. 116.

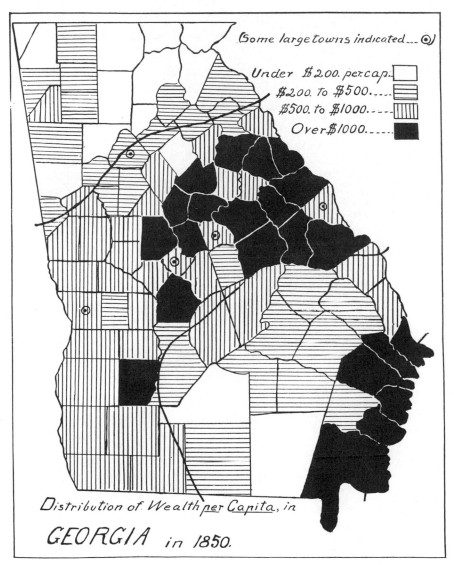

(Some large towns indicated ... ◉)

Under $200. per. cap.

$200. To $500.

$500. to $1000.

Over $1000.

Distribution of Wealth per Capita, in

GEORGIA in 1850.

Based upon the values of farm lands, farm equipment, farm stock, and slaves; estimating the average value of slaves at $500. Urban property values are not included.

industrial development in the eastern cotton belt than had the earlier protective tariffs. As returns on cotton investments fell, while dividends on industrial investments continued high in the North, it seemed reasonable that some southern capital should be diverted into the more promising industrial field. A systematic propaganda with this end in view was consequently carried on in both South Carolina and Georgia during the forties by progressive merchants and other men of property. While the most distinguished individual leader of the industrial movement was William Gregg, of South Carolina, there is some reason to believe that its advent in Georgia antedates the time of Gregg's activity and that it would have developed in Georgia along much the same lines had Gregg's influence never been exerted.[37]

The pro-industrial propaganda of the forties emphasized the promise of high dividends, the advantages of location adjacent to the source of raw materials, and the abundant supply of potential power and cheap labor[38] in the South. Did not all natural advantages in the field of cotton textile manufacturing, indeed, lie with the South rather than with the North?[39]

[37] Gregg's first essay appeared in 1844 and, as a matter of fact, called attention to the "rapid progress" already being made in Georgia manufacturing at that time; Russel, *Economic Aspects of Southern Sectionalism*, p. 41. Gregg was himself the nephew of a Georgia factory owner who had built one of the early mills in that state; Ingle. *Southern Sidelights*, p. 86.

[38] While there was always uncertainty as to the availability of slave labor for industries, the availability of "poor white" labor was well recognized in Georgia in 1850. See the Augusta *Chronicle*, April 27, May 27, June 1, 1849; *cf.* Broadus Mitchell, *The Rise of Cotton Mills in the South*, p. 25, published in *Johns Hopkins University Studies in History and Political Science*, XXXIX. No. 2. *Cf.*, also, Boucher, *Ante-Bellum Attitude of South Carolina Towards Manufacturing and Agriculture*, p. 249.

[39] The truth of this view, so well and so persistently expressed in the forties, is being demonstrated today, nearly a century later, in the steady transfer of cotton textile manufacturing from New England to the Piedmont of the Carolinas and Georgia.

Only the exclusive devotion of the South to cotton culture was preventing that section from achieving the industrial supremacy to which nature had predestined it.[40]

Such propaganda, however, had to labor against strong and persistent opposition. There was the traditional fear that manufacturing would lead to protective tariffs, the pet abomination of the South, and a general suspicion that it would in various ways upset the whole dominant plantation and slave-labor system.[41] There was, finally, the opposition to any change, which resulted from general social inertia, an inertia perhaps the stronger for the fact that many of the native whites of the state were in this period ignorant and illiterate.[42]

Apparently undaunted by the many difficulties to be met, the proponents of industrialism proclaimed their views throughout Georgia persistently and without fear.[43] The Whig papers of the larger towns, which, as will be noted later, usually possessed a larger circulation than did their Democratic rivals, were the

[40] For the appeal for manufacturing in Georgia see, e.g., the files of the Augusta Chronicle and the Savannah Republican for 1847-1850.

[41] For the traditional opposition to industrialism and tariffs, as well as the fear that the whole plantation and slave-labor system would be upset by the new order, see A. S. Jones, Speed the Plow: An Essay on the Tariff, By a Georgia Planter, pp. 16, 17. For tariff arguments pro and con in Georgia, consult the debate between the Augusta Constitutionalist and the Augusta Chronicle, as reported in the latter for May 16 and 18, 1849.

[42] About 20% of the poorer whites were entirely illiterate, there being no effective public school system in the state in 1850. See Map No. 4, p. 24, for the distribution of white illiteracy, which closely paralleled the distribution of wealth, as shown in Map No. 3, p. 22. For a general description of educational conditions in the state about 1850, see C. E. Jones, Education in Georgia, pp. 24-31, published as United States Bureau of Education Monographs No. 5 (1889). Cf. W. H. Kirkpatrick, "The Beginning of the Public School System in Georgia," Georgia Historical Quarterly, V. No. 3, p. 8. See also E. M. Coulter, "A Georgia Educational Movement During the Eighteen Hundred Fifties," ibid., IX, No. 1, 1-33.

[43] Cf. Channing, History of the United States, V. 76.

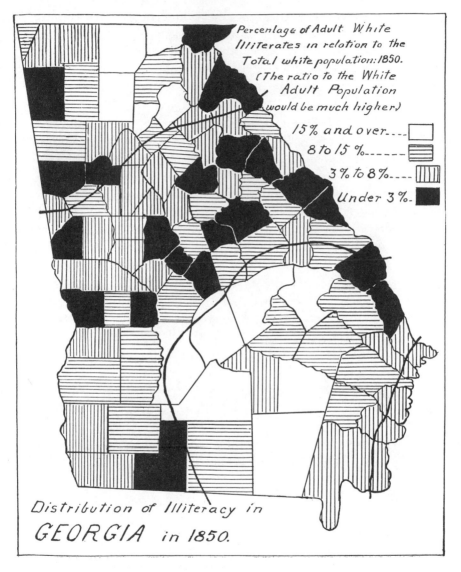

Percentage of Adult White
Illiterates in relation to the
Total white population: 1850.
(The ratio to the White
Adult Population
would be much higher)

15% and over____ ☐
8 to 15 %_____ ▤
3% to 8%____ ▥
Under 3%_ ■

Distribution of Illiteracy in
GEORGIA in 1850.

chief media employed in urging the new point of view. So persistent was the propaganda that it began to show definite and, in some ways, remarkable results during the fifth decade. In 1840 Georgia had possessed but a few insignificant cotton mills with a product of less value than that turned out in a number of the other southern states. During the next ten years, the relative increase in the value of cotton goods produced in Georgia was greater than that in any other state of the Union which had done an appreciable amount of manufacturing in 1840, and the value increase in absolute figures was greater in Georgia than in any of the states save Massachusetts and New Hampshire. Only two southern states remained in any way her serious competitors in 1850, Maryland and Virginia, and both of these were surpassed by Georgia in that year in the value of cotton textile products. Some seven northern states continued, to be sure, to greatly outrank the "Keystone" of the South in this respect, but the Georgia cotton products came very close in value to those of Maine and surpassed those of New Jersey. Woolen manufactures remained on a very small scale in the state, but made a relatively great advance in value from three hundred dollars in 1840 to over eighty-eight thousand dollars in 1850.[44]

[44] These statements are based upon official returns made to the Treasury Department in 1855, published in *House Executive Documents, 34 Congress, Session 1,* IV. Nos. 17 and 18, pp. 93-96. See also T. P. Kettrell, *Southern Wealth and Northern Profits,* p. 54. Some of the comparative figures on cotton manufactures are as follows:

State	Value Produced 1840	1850
Massachusetts	$16,553,423	$19,712,461
New York	3,640,237	3,591,989
Maine	970,397	2,596,356
Georgia	304,342	2,135,044
Maryland	1,150,580	2,120,504
New Jersey	2,086,104	1,109,524
South Carolina	359,000	748,338
Alabama	17,547	382,260

There were, in 1850, some forty cotton factories in Georgia, which ran more than sixty thousand spindles and used more than forty-five thousand bales of raw cotton per year. The number of textile employees, so far as can be estimated, was at least twenty-three hundred. There were mills in nearly all the chief Piedmont towns, but the main centers of manufacturing were Columbus and Augusta, whose situation at the fall line on navigable rivers gave them peculiar advantages. Most of the mills were small, but one in Columbus was housed in a six-story building and employed over two hundred people, while another in Augusta had four hundred employees.[45]

It is true that some depression in Georgia textile manufacturing ensued in the years immediately following 1850, though Georgia did not suffer so much in this respect as did some other states.[46] The very rise in cotton prices which so benefited the planters necessarily tended to embarrass the manufacturers. This, however, does not alter the fact to be remembered in connection with the political crisis of 1850; namely, that a small but influential group of Georgians believed at the time that great industrial prosperity lay just ahead for their state. "So we go," observed the Columbus *Times* at the end of that year of fateful political development, "Columbus will be a Georgia Lowell

[45] For an enthusiastic contemporary account of the relatively great progress of manufacturing in Georgia, see the *Scientific American*, as quoted in the Washington *Republic*, June 7, 1850; see also Richmond (Va.) *Whig*, April 30, 1850. There are, of course, many accounts in contemporary Georgia papers, *e.g.*, Augusta *Chronicle*, May 2, 1849. For numbers of operatives and other statistics see the *Census of 1850*; Kettrell, *op. cit.*, pp. 54, 55; and A. Sherwood, *Gazetteer* of Georgia (4th Edition, 1860) p. 193. For the general history of early manufacturing in Georgia, see *Ibid.*, p. 172, ff.; V. S. Clark, *History of Manufactures*, pp. 556, 557.

[46] *Hunt's Merchants' Magazine*, for May, 1852, gives comparative capital invested in Georgia manufactures in 1850 and 1852.

before long, and some of these days will beat her. Lowell never had, nor never can have, the advantages with which Columbus is endowed by nature for manufacturing purposes."[47] Thus it was that industrial enthusiasm was added to agricultural enthusiasm as a source of business optimism in Georgia.[48]

If the several economic interests in Georgia were prospering, or at least expected to prosper, as the end of the decade approached, how did the state's business classes view the economic situation as a whole? As one would expect, there was the same economic optimism in general as was associated with the several occupations in particular. All things seemed to work together for the good of those who loved Georgia, and the end of the decade promised to be as bright as the beginning had been gloomy. Cotton planting was, to be sure, still troublesome, and lands still persisted in wearing out, but improvements in prices and lands were in sight. Railroad building was booming, and manufactures, though still on a small scale, had increased at an unprecedented rate through the decade. Manufactures seemed to supplement planting and promised employment for the hitherto decadent classes of the population. Banking facilities and the state's credit were improving, and minor occupations were feeling the touch of general prosperity. Commercial and manufacturing towns were growing. Was not Georgia truly the Empire State of the South?

So, at least, felt her optimistic capitalist class. "Georgia," wrote an enthusiast in 1849, "makes more

---

[47] In Philadelphia *North American*, December 29, 1850. This "booster" prediction may yet be realised.

[48] There has been a tendency to overlook the significance of the early industrial revolution in Georgia, apparently because, in terms of absolute figures, the output of the South as a whole was very small in comparison with that of New England; see Kettrell, *op. cit., passim.*

cotton and corn—has more railroads—more manufactures—more shipping (save perhaps for New Orleans)—pays less taxes—has more schools—has more diversified mineral wealth—is nearly ready to furnish her own citizens and those of sister states with flour to eat, clothes to wear, iron to work—she has a smaller public debt—a finer climate or climates (as she has them by assortment)— . . . than most (may we not say, than any) of her sister states of the South."[49] True, she did not seem so prosperous when compared with the northern states. Some Georgians claimed, however, that the apparent economic superiority of even northern states was illusory. Perhaps the most dramatic expression of this claim was given by Alexander H. Stephens, who engaged an Ohio representative in debate in Congress in 1854 in an effort to prove that his state was more wealthy and prosperous than was Ohio.[50]

Georgia's economic leadership in the South was often conceded in her sister states. "Georgia will soon be a model state," remarked the Knoxville (Tennessee) *Register.*[51] Georgia has far outstripped any Southern state in railroad improvements," observed the Mobile (Alabama) *Register.*[52] The Mobile *Advertiser* agreed with this view.[53] The Raleigh (North Carolina) *Star,* in joining in this praise, recalled the state's earlier economic depression. "Ten years before she was as low in natural character and individual enterprise as ever was old Rip Van Winkle. Now,

---

[49] *De Bow's Review,* VII. 177.

[50] *More of Georgia and Ohio,* pp. 1-10. For the reply of the Ohio representative, L. D. Campbell, with its critical examination of Stephen's statistics, see Campbell's pamphlet, *Kansas and Nebraska,* pp. 4, 5.

[51] In Augusta *Chronicle,* May 16, 1850.

[52] In Washington *Republic,* January 11, 1850.

[53] Mobile (Ala.) *Advertiser,* November 28, 1850.

because of her press, factories and railroads, she is indisputably in advance of any other southern state in enterprise and success."[54]   A South Carolinian, writing from Charleston in 1849, remarked that "everyone who has traveled through Georgia this year seems to be struck by the energy, enterprise and go-ahead-itiveness of her people."[55]

Such opinions sometimes reached the North. James M. Crane, of Virginia, for instance, in speaking before the American Institute of New York, claimed that Georgia was "the New England of the South, with $55,000,000 invested in railroads and manufacturing." Immigrants were coming in, and it was advancing more rapidly than any of the southern states.[56] As a result of such addresses and of the trips of northern business men and travelers to Georgia, the northern papers began to comment on Georgia's leadership.[57]   Olmsted, "the Yankee Peripatetic," declared: "It is obvious to the traveler and notorious in the stock-market that there is more life, enterprise, skill and industry in Georgia than in any other of the Southern Commonwealths.   It is the Yankee-Land of the South."[58]

So much for opinion within Georgia and without upon the subject of her prosperity.   This brings us naturally to a consideration of the one development which seemed between 1847 and 1852 to threaten most seriously the whole scheme of that prosperity.   Every

[54] In Augusta *Chronicle*, June 13, 1849.

[55] *Ibid.*, September 20, 1849; see also Charleston *Courier*, November 18, 1850.

[56] *De Bow's Review*, VII. 177. (August, 1849).

[57] See, e.g., the Boston *Courier*, January 23, 1850; the Washington *Republic*, January 11, 1850; the Philadelphia *North American*, December 25, 1849.

[58] *Journey in the Seaboard Slave States*, p. 530.

factor but one in the dominant cotton planting system
seemed to be pleasing—land, prices, agricultural improvements—all these afforded a promising outlook.
Yet all the while that these had been improving in the
late forties, the other vital factor, that of labor, had
been threatened by a suddenly increasing menace—the
development of the antislavery movement in the North
and the political crisis which this precipitated in the
years mentioned. The antislavery attack upon the
Negro slave system loomed as a growing cloud upon
the political horizon and threatened, as the years
passed, to obscure the dawning light of economic optimism and prosperity. The antislavery attack raised
many delicate and difficult problems concerning Negro
slavery, upon which Georgians and other southerners
were undecided or, when decided, often divided in
opinion. As the political crisis of 1850 was most directly concerned with these problems involved in
slavery, and as the attitude of the Georgia people
towards that crisis depended in some measure upon
their attitude towards slavery, it is well here to review
the nature of these difficulties. Much needs only to be
stated to be recalled; a few facts require new emphasis
or illustration.

Practically all native Georgians regarded the
northern antislavery movement as an unprovoked attack upon southern institutions. It seemed to them
that the movement had become constantly more aggressive during the fourth and fifth decades of the century,
first in the effort to prevent the extension of slavery;
secondly, to undermine it where it already existed. In
opposing this attack, the proslavery men had acted
upon the defensive and had often been conciliatory,

but all to no avail.[59] The conduct of the antislavery Yankees seemed incomprehensible to many. While some granted that the abolitionists were well-intentioned but deluded men, most southerners saw in them merely an incomprehensible fanaticism.

This view was, of course, exactly the opposite of that held in the North by the antislavery men; namely, that the proslavery southerners had been a united and aggressive group, attempting to spread their institutions across the country and to control the Federal government in order to guarantee the success of this and other proslavery movements.[60]

Such views were unknown or ignored by the average Georgian. His interest was centered, if he were an intelligent citizen, upon the refutation of the abolitionists' attack upon slavery. This attack, it will be recalled, had three phases, slavery being condemned upon theological, moral, and economic grounds. The degree of time and effort expended upon these phases usually seems to have been in inverse proportion to their respective importance.

It was argued at some length that God's "Higher Law" forbade the holding of human beings as property. In reply, the southerners labored at equal or greater length, and with equal or greater conclusiveness, to show that scriptural authority approved the institution. This discussion, while of considerable in-

[59] *Letters from Georgia to Massachusetts*, pp. 1, 15-20. This pamphlet, the work of A. B. Longstreet, while not entirely fair to Massachusetts, is very suggestive for southern thought on slavery in 1850. It was largely ignored at the North. See Wade, *A. B. Longstreet*, pp. 286-287.

[60] For the persistence of this view of a united and aggressive Slavocracy, in modern scholarly work, see the first volume of Rhodes' *History of the United States*. For criticism of the same, see Boucher, "*In Re* That Aggressive Slavocracy," *Mississippi Valley Historical Review*, VIII. 1 and 2, pp. 13-16.

terest to a more or less theological age, did not often
touch upon practical points at issue.
Many of the moral charges made against slavery
met with flat denial in the South. There was, it was
held, no such breeding of slaves for sale as the abolitionists claimed was the custom. Georgians admitted,
to be sure, that slaves were "reared" in the border
states for sale in the lower South,[61] but this was not
necessarily the same thing as "breeding." It was generally admitted by abolitionists, moreover, that Georgia
itself was not even a "slave rearing" state.[62] If, on
the other hand, the abolitionist called attention to the
evils of miscegenation, the Georgians admitted the
charge, but retorted that the same evils existed to an
even greater extent at the North. Was not the ratio
of mulattoes to pure Negroes twenty times as great in
Ohio as in Georgia—to say nothing of prostitution?[63]
In like manner, it was customary, when the antislavery
critics decried the overworking of the slave, to call attention to the even more brutal treatment accorded the
"free" factory workers of Old and New England.[64]
So the argument proceeded, controversial and unscien-
tific declarations being answered by pronouncements
of a like nature.

It is interesting to recall that some southern
writers attempted to stay the debate by appealing to

[61] For description of a legislative debate based upon this point see
Savannah *Georgian*, November 13, 1849; Augusta *Chronicle*, September
12, 1849. *Cf. The Plantation* I. No. 2, p. 110.

[62] *Slavery and International Slave Trade*, by the Executive Committee
of the American Anti-Slavery Society, (1841) pp. 12, 13, 20. For an
exception to this rule see the Boston *Liberator*, August 9, 1850.

[63] *The Plantation*, II. No. 2, p. 384.

[64] Harper, *The Pro-Slavery Argument, passim.* For northern replies
to this argument, see, *e.g., Inquiry into the Condition and Prospects of
the African Race in the United States, By an American*, (Philadelphia,
1839) *passim;* Paine, *Six Years in a Georgia Prison*, p. 16; *Ohio State
Journal*, (Columbus), October 18, 1850, etc. *Cf.* Dodd, *The Cotton Kingdom*, p. 61.

the common business interests of northern manufacturers and southern planters. Not the least interesting of such appeals was that made by a few sociologists, who explained to the northerners that the abolitionists hated capitalists as well as planters and would attack the holdings of the one as well as of the other. Abolitionists or Socialists—they were all the same, declared Hundley.[65]

The economic indictment of slavery was, other things being equal, the one best calculated to command the planter's serious consideration. This indictment, drawn up originally by such southern writers as Dr. Thomas Cooper, was later taken over by such critics as Olmsted and Helper. The analysis of slavery as an expensive form of labor is a familiar one, and much of the economic backwardness of the South was explained by northern critics in terms of this analysis.[66] While some southerners replied to this by denying the assumption that the South was backward —and it is of interest here that Alexander H. Stephens cited the prosperity of Georgia to support such a denial —most southerners admitted the backwardness, but attributed it to factors other than slavery. The "Calhoun Democrats" in Georgia blamed it upon northern legislation, while the Whigs usually ascribed it to the plantation system and to the lack of manufacturing enterprise.

Nevertheless, there were some signs of wavering in the southern defence of the economic aspects of their institution. At almost the very time that Fitzhugh and others were urging the slave system as the best

[65] D. R. Hundley, *Social Relations in Our Southern States*, pp. 279-281. See also Fitzhugh, *Cannibals All*, pp. 54, 144, 356, 357.

[66] See Boston *Post* and Boston *Atlas* for April and May, 1849, *passim*. Cf. Phillips, *American Negro Slavery*, pp. 350, 394, 397, 399.

system of labor *per se,* influential papers in Georgia
seemed just a little uncertain about the institution.
Though still courageous, they were apparently whis-
tling in the dark. When the Boston *Atlas* and Boston
Post proceeded in 1849 to condemn slavery upon economic grounds, the Savannah *Georgian* and Augusta
Chronicle essayed to reply. The *Georgian* rejoiced
with apparent relief that the progress of manufactures
would now "demonstrate that slavery does not impede
progress," the implication being clearly that a demonstration had hitherto been wanting. It admitted, however, that slave labor was "not as cheap as what is
styled 'free labor' at the North."[67] The *Chronicle* rebuked this admission, declaring that the *Georgian*
confused the system of slave labor with the planting
system of agriculture. "If all our slaves were replaced
by European immigrants," it declared, "and the same
wasteful methods of planting were employed, conditions would be just as bad."[68]

A week later, however, further thunders from Boston led the *Chronicle* to make a statement as remarkable
for its insight as for its frankness. "Slaveholders must
demonstrate in a large way," it admitted, "and by visible results, that slave labor in Georgia is as profitable
to you and as useful to the world, as free labor is at
the North or can be at the South,—that it is not inimi-
cal to common schools, the improvement of the soil and
the progress of manufactures. . . . Our sectional

[67] Savannah *Georgian,* May 11, 1849.

[68] Augusta *Chronicle,* May 12, 1849. This distinction between slave-
labor and the plantation system was a significant one, since these two,
and a third factor, the race question, were often confused at the time,
and have been since. Indeed, the *Chronicle* itself seems, in the statement
quoted, to have overlooked the race factor. For a modern discussion of
the plantation system, as distinct from the slave-labor system, see
Phillips, "The Decadence of the Plantation System," *Annals of the
American Academy of Political and Social Science,* XXXV. 37-41.

movements are taken for weakness in this regard. *The whole matter will turn in the end on the pivot of dollars and cents.* We can only prove our view by attaining prosperity."[69]

It may be of some speculative interest here to raise the question as to what the attitude of such a paper would have been had the test it suggested failed in later years to bring a satisfactory result. In terms of its own analysis, this would have condemned slavery upon economic grounds. It is logical to suppose that the editors would then have favored some gradual modifications of the institution, in the economic interest of the planter class their paper represented. Whether so logical a course would have been followed, however, in view of all the conflicting circumstances involved, is difficult to say.

There had always been a divergence of opinion among Georgians as to the chances of eventual emancipation. Discussion of this question had been renewed in the middle thirties by the abolitionist propaganda of the time. At this time those who maintained the older philosophic objections to slavery were already becoming uncertain as to whether emancipation could ever be accomplished.[70] Some men of idealistic temper like Alexander H. Stephens maintained through the forties that slavery was a moral evil, but gradually lost faith that it would ever be abandoned.[71] Many Georgians, in conformity with the spirit of the age, had come by 1850 to hold that slavery was a good *per se,*

[69] Augusta *Chronicle,* May 17, 1849. Italics my own.

[70] *Remarks upon Slavery, Occasioned by Attempts to Circulate Improper Publications in the Southern States, by a Citizen of Georgia,* (Augusta, Ga., 1835), p. 30.

[71] Savannah *Georgian,* May 5, 1849.

which "would be of perpetual duration and must be preserved at all hazards."[72]

Nevertheless, there were observers both North and South who believed that the test proposed by the *Chronicle* would ultimately lead the South to emancipation. One northerner suggested that progress in machine inventions would make slave labor still more unprofitable, when slavery would "die amid the hosannas of both pro and anti-slavery men alike."[73] Another held that "throughout the world abolition has come naturally when increases in population and wealth increased the value of land and labor, thus making the price of slave labor high and unprofitable. The slave in the United States is now passing towards freedom by the natural road and any interference . . . will hinder this process."[74]

In the South it was believed by at least a few that the economic test had already convinced many that slavery should be abolished. Heydenfeldt, an Alabama citizen, stated in a long analysis of the slave problem addressed to the governor that "the South has the germ of a special and unknown anti-slavery party." This included not only the poor whites, "who regard the slave as a rival in production," but also "those who are wearied out with the struggle of unproductive labors . . . and those who desire more populous white com-

[72] Report of Chief Justice James H. Lumpkin to the Georgia legislature, concerning the Slave Code, December 1849, in the Boston *Liberator*, July 19, 1850, quoting the *United States Law Magazine* for January, 1850.
[73] T. Eubank, *Inorganic Forces Affecting Slavery* (N. Y., 1860), pp. 26, 27, 29.
[74] *Letter from a Philadelphian to a South Carolinian*, Washington *Republic*, June 17, 1850. For similar editorial opinion in the North, see the Cleveland *Plain Dealer*, December 25, 1850. A Georgian observed to Fanny Kemble, a decade before this, that there would be prompt abolition if slavery proved definitely unprofitable; Fanny Kemble, *Journal of a Residence on a Georgia Plantation in 1838-1839*, p. 77.

munities for the purposes of trade and education. This combination of opinion against slavery has prodigously increased within a few years, and is now increasing at a rapid pace. Numbers are every day added to those who long for the exodus of the slave."[75] This statement suggests exaggeration, but the fact that it was reprinted in a strongly proslavery Georgia paper, without denial, is of some interest. Such a view, even if allowance be made for exaggeration, taken in conjunction with the uncertain defense of slavery as an economic order in the Georgia papers, would seem suggestive. Some practical men, despite the prosperity of 1848-1850, were uncertain as to the economic desirability of slave labor. And those who insisted upon it were dogmatic in their conviction, offering little real economic evidence to support their view. This leads naturally to the question as to why intelligent southerners insisted upon the economic desirability of a labor system whose value, when denied, could not be well demonstrated.

The most obvious reason for the planter's refusal to view too critically the economics of slave labor was the irritation aroused by the other types of criticism. The reaction to scathing moral and theological attacks was a general justification that tended to defend all aspects of the institution. This psychological factor doubtless played its part, along with economic factors, in producing the general change in attitude towards slavery which characterized the development of southern thought between 1820 and 1850.[76] Southern pride

[75] Columbus *Times,* January 23, 1849. *Cf.* Ingle, *Southern Sidelights,* pp. 326, 327.
[76] For a statement of this change, see Dodd, *The Cotton Kingdom,* pp. 49-59, 61-69.

became involved in the defense of slavery, and the southerner of 1850 was apt to feel that the economic as well as the moral value of slavery must be defended at all costs.[77] Some Georgia observers were conscious of this psychological factor and believed that, had the abolitionists never spoken, voluntary emancipation would have proceeded apace in the South.[78] The second reason for the planter's failure to be critical of slave labor was the fear that such an attitude would encourage the northern demand for immediate emancipation and that this would raise the danger of large property loss. This, of course, was in northern eyes the chief reason for southern opposition to abolition.[79] It was, however, a business view and could have been overcome, other things being equal, by proof of economic advantages in gradual emancipation.

Other things, however, rarely were equal. The planter feared that free labor would be less efficient than slave labor and that this loss in efficiency might counterbalance other advantages in a free system. To be sure, northern men held that free labor was more efficient than slave, but here they often failed to realize the peculiar nature of southern labor. The slave was not only a slave, he was also a Negro, and most southerners were convinced that the Negro would not work as well a freedman as he did a slave.

It might have been urged in reply, and indeed was expected by a few antislavery men, that the place of the inefficient freedmen could be taken by white

[77] See, e.g., editorial of the Norfolk (Va.) *Argus*, in the Charleston *Mercury*, January 1, 1851.
[78] Jas. H. Lumpkin to Howell Cobb, January 21, 1848, *Toombs, Stephens and Cobb Correspondence*, p. 94.
[79] G. M. Weston, *Progress of Slavery*, p. 187.

laborers.[80] This seemed impossible to the planter, however, not only because of the difficulty of ridding the country of the Negroes,[81] but because he believed the Negroes alone were physiologically adapted to work in the rice and cotton fields.[82]

It is but a step from the statement of this racial factor affecting the labor system to the consideration of the general significance of race in the whole slavery controversy. It was this race problem which supplied the planter with a third motive for refusing to judge slavery simply upon economic grounds. Now it was axiomatic in the South that the Negroes were of an inferior race. This view needed no defense at home, but, in reply to abolitionist attacks, it was substantiated by quasi-scientific arguments concerning physiology, anthropology, and the like.[83] When it had been established that the Negro was inferior, it followed that he needed guidance and control, both for his own sake and for that of the whites associated with him in the community. Slavery supplied just what was needed as a system of control. It kept the Negroes working, kept them in their proper social position, and kept them contented.[84] Hence, when abolitionism attacked slavery,

[80] G. H. Hatcher to J. C. Calhoun, Jan. 5, 1848, Calhoun Papers, quoted by Boucher, "In Re That Aggressive Slavocracy," op. cit., p. 43.

[81] For Georgia opinion on the failure of the colonization movement, see T. R. R. Cobb, Law of Negro Slavery, XIV and XV, (1858).

[82] For the medical argument in favor of Negro slavery, see Dr. Cartwright's letter to Daniel Webster, De Bow's Review, III. 53-62. This contains an excellent résumé of the several reasons for opposing emancipation. See also Bryant Tyson, The Institution of Slavery in the Southern States, pp. 14, 15. For a clear modern statement, see Phillips, American Negro Slavery, pp. 400, 401.

[83] For a standard discussion of this sort, see J. H. Van Evrie, Negroes and Negro Slavery, Pt. I, passim.

[84] When there was some talk in Alabama in 1850 about danger of slave insurrection, the Savannah Republican, January 18, 1851, remarked that "no man really believes there is any dissatisfcation among the blacks." Cf. W. H. Russell, Pictures of Southern Life, p. 27; Mitchell, "Frederick Law Olmsted," Johns Hopkins Studies, XLII. No. 2, pp. 127-129.

it attacked three things simultaneously: a form of
property, a system of labor, and a scheme of social
control.

The fear that emancipation would disturb the
status quo in race relationships and bring on social
chaos was general and doubtless sincere in the cotton
states of 1850. Its sincerity is attested by its appearance in letters of a most private character as well as in
papers and speeches intended for public perusal. "The
abolitionists," wrote a Charlestonian to Governor Seabrook of South Carolina in 1850, "are every day raising up the pretentions of the blacks to equality with the
whites, and in the end, after we have conceded and
conceded, they will demand that too, and we will have
to quit the country . . . for lack of courage to maintain a right bequeathed by an illustrious ancestry."[85]
The need for slavery as a form of social control was
emphasized in all public manifestoes in the South
from this period to the Civil War.[86] That it was
emphasized may be explained by the assumption that
southerners found it a more effective argument than
the relatively selfish one concerning property loss.
But its sincerity and justice can hardly be questioned,
in view of the private expressions noted above and in
view also of subsequent events during the Reconstruction period.

[85] Thos. Lehre to Seabrook, September 6, 1850, Seabrook MSS.
[86] See, *e.g.*, *Address of the Hon. H. L. Benning, Commissioner from
Georgia to the Virginia State Convention*, Feb. 18, 1861. (Richmond
1861), pp. 22-26. For other expressions of this general view in public
addresses, see the Resolutions of the Second Session of the Nashville
Convention of 1850, (Washington *Republic*, Nov. 26, 1850); J. C. Calhoun's "Southern Address" of 1849; (*Address of the Southern Members
of Congress to their Constituents*, Washington, D. C.. 1849); and the
preamble to the Resolutions of the Georgia State Convention of 1850,
(*Proceedings of the Georgia State Convention*, Milledgeville, 1850).

The precedents to which southerners pointed to prove the reality of their race fears were, first, the supposedly degraded character of those Negroes who had been freed[87] and, second, the economic and social decadence which, they claimed, had been caused by emancipation in the French and British West Indies.[88] The southern literature concerning this West Indian story was large and suggestive, though it rarely made any allowance for environmental or other forces apart from the racial factors involved.

The general race problem seemed so vital a part of the slave problem that the phrase "the negro-politico question" began to be used in Georgia as synonomous with the "slavery problem."[89] Some southerners declared definitely that all other phases of the slave problem were of minor importance and that, were it not for it, emancipation would be gladly granted by many.[90] Perhaps the clearest claim that the race problem was the essence of the slavery question was not made by a southerner, however, but by a Philadelphia scholar writing just before the war. "There is too much talk," he declared, "of slavery in the abstract. Slavery implies both a master and a servant. Here the servant is a negro and the master a white man, and their racial characteristics determine their mutual relationships. *What is called the slave question ought to be called the*

[87] Savannah *Republican,* Jan. 6, 1848; *Free Negroism* (New York, n. d.). p. 6.
[88] B. Tyson, *The Institution of Slavery in the Southern States,* p. 37; *Free Negroism,* p. 7; J. Townsend, *The Present Peril of the Southern States* (Charleston, 1850), p. 10; *Slavery Indispensable Parallel to Civilization,* (Baltimore, 1855), p. 28; for British opinion on the islands, see *A Statement of Facts, illustrating the Administration of the Abolition Law and the Sufferings of the Negro Apprentices in the Island of Jamaica,* (London, 1837) *passim; The Case of the Free-Labor British Colonies,* etc. (London, 1852), *passim.*
[89] Boston *Courier* (Savannah Corr.), Dec. 27, 1850.
[90] Tyson, *op. cit.,* p. 37.

negro question. On the inherent, unalterable qualities of the negro hinges the whole question of slavery[91] . . . Slavery is an evil thing. But we have the negro and therefore must have the slave."[92]

It was incomprehensible to some that so many northerners could not see this aspect of the emancipation problem. "The economical effects of slavery have usually been argued from an amazingly unreasonable point of view," wrote a Virginian after the Civil War. "Our enemies persist in discussing it as an election to be made between a system of labor by free yeomen of the same race, and a system of labor of African slaves on the other; as though the South had any such choice in its power. If the social conditions in Virginia exhibited inferiority in its system of labor, the true cause of the evil was to be sought in the *presence* of the Africans among us, *not in their enslavement*."[93]

In an effort to impress the North with the seriousness of the race problem, southern writers reminded the northern people of the degree of their own race feeling. Indeed, many Georgians were convinced that northerners would not treat Negroes as well as they did, free or slave. Race riots in Cincinnati and Philadelphia, northern refusal of economic opportunities to Negroes, and opposition to free Negro immigration to

[91] The italics are my own. This view has been revived in late years with even greater force by writers on Negro history: "The slave question," says one of them, "was in a sense hardly more than an incident in the Negro Problem"; B. Brawley, *A Social History of the American Negro*, p. 116.

[92] S. G. Fisher, *Laws of Race as Connected with Slavery* (1859), pp. 8, 9. This is a remarkable essay, but seems to have attracted little or no contemporary attention. Its viewpoint was ignored by all postbellum northern writers on southern history, and its existence was generally overlooked by the southern. Cf. Stone, "Some Problems of Southern Economic History," *American Historical Review*, XIII. 790.

[93] R. L. Dabney, *Defense of Virginia* (N. Y., 1867), p. 296.

northern towns were cited to prove the point.[94] Abolitionist admissions that there was intense race prejudice
in New York State[95] were received with some pardon-
able satisfaction in Georgia, and the feeling naturally
developed that either these Yankees were hypocrites, or
they would appreciate the southern point of view on
the race situation.[96]

Southern warnings about racial troubles sometimes
did receive sympathetic attention in the North among
conservative circles. If abolitionism led to secession
and Civil War, it was admitted, that "would be terrible
and destroy southern prosperity. There would then be
no cotton supply for the North and this would be most
unfortunate."[97] Another northern writer, in discussing the South, admitted that "the grand objection in
the community to abolition (and it is probably nearly
universal) is the belief that the negroes, if freed, would
be a pest of society, . . . would prey upon the
whites and live uncontrolled. Many, no doubt, think
the lives and property of the whites would be at their
disposal . . . This is serious and demands deliberate attention."[98] Weston, an able and moderate critic
of slavery, recognized the claim that "the question of
slavery in the United States is embarrassed by a question of race and color." He implied, however, that the
claim was unfounded and suspected it was largely
propaganda to mask the simple fear of property loss.
"There is no reason," he wrote, "to suppose that even

[94] Savannah *News*, Feb. 8, 1850.
[95] New York *Tribune*, Dec. 16, 1850.
[96] Savannah *News*, September 7, 1850. This is the general view which
has recently been emphasized in the work of southern writers on the
race question. See A. H. Stone, *American Race Problem, passim.*
[97] Philadelphia *North American*, December 21, 1849; March 4, 1850.
[98] *Inquiry into the Condition and Prospects of the African Race
in the United States, by an American* (Phila., 1839), p. 130.

the liberation instantly and *en masse* of the slaves at the South would be attended with peril, whatever losses and inconveniences it might occasion. Negroes are not beasts, but men—not caged, but at large, easily governed, whether as free labor or as slaves." He insinuated that the moment the owners found slavery unprofitable, they would suddenly discover that Negroes were not at all socially dangerous and could be freed with safety. "Moreover," he declared, "as soon as the race is thrust upon its own resources, it will be unable to survive in the struggle for existence, will gradually disappear, and thereby automatically remove even the possibility of a race problem."[99]

Other northern observers denied the precedents cited in the southern argument concerning the effects of emancipation in the West Indies. Things were not so bad there as they had been painted, and what was bad was not necessarily due to the racial qualities of the Negroes.[100] At times the whole argument that the factor of race entered into the slavery question was categorically denied and denounced by the more bitter enemies of the slave apologists. "This southern claim of a social danger in emancipation," declared Senator Benton of Missouri, "is but a pure and simple invention of John C. Calhoun, not only without evidence but against evidence."[101] Finally, it is probable that the majority of northern men never quite appreciated the force of the southern view concerning race, largely

[99] Weston, *The Progress of Slavery*, pp. 243, 244. *Cf.* Van Evrie, *Negroes and Negro Slavery*, Pt. I, 309 ff.

[100] Philadelphia *North American* (corr.), Dec. 22, 1849. For a careful antislavery view of developments in the Indies, see the British *Anti-Slavery Advocate* for Feb., 1857, quoted in W. Chambers, *American Slavery and Color*, (London, 1857), pp. 125-136.

[101] T. H. Benton, *Thirty Years' View*, II. 735. *Cf. Jefferson Davis. A Memoir. by His Wife*, I. 456.

because they themselves were not in contact with the problem.[102]

The subject should not be dismissed until the last and perhaps the most peculiar phase of its discussion is noted. This is the fact that the writings of the most intense proslavery advocates were used by antislavery men to prove that the race problem was really not important. Writers like Fitzhugh, who had developed the logic of slavery apologetics to an apotheosis of the system, had logically concluded that slavery should be established in all countries, regardless of race or other factors. This, said some abolitionists, proves that what the southerners want is not race control, but slavery as a labor system *per se*. No doubt they have been forced to it by a realization that many of their slaves are now largely white in blood and that the old argument about "race control" will no longer justify holding such people in servitude.[103] Such criticism, of course, assumed for its own purposes that extremists like Fitzhugh represented average southern opinion.

The realization of the significance of the race problem in Georgia and other cotton states led to two divergent political attitudes towards the American Federal Union, and it is this influence of the problem upon political opinion that justifies its discussion in the introduction to a political narrative. In the first place, the fear of racial difficulties that might follow secession was one reason that led Georgians to desire to postpone hasty action against the Union so long as there was

[102] For an instance of ignorance of the meaning of the problem, see the New York *Evening Post*, Jan. 12, 1848. *Cf.* the Savannah *News*, Jan. 21, 1848.

[103] W. Chambers, *American Slavery and Color*, (London, 1857), pp. 1, 2.

hope that slavery could be preserved in the Union. Secession, it was thought, would give the abolitionists full control of the northern government. This would mean more encouragement to fugitive slaves, and this, in turn, would result in efforts in the border states to sell all their remaining Negroes to the cotton states. This region would then see hastened the day when a surplus Negro population would become an economic and social burden. Or, if secession led to civil war, this might in turn lead to servile war with all its consequences. Hence secession, instead of saving slavery, would destroy it.[104]

In addition to this, some Georgia planters felt that a strong Union government would be a guarantee of social safety to the planter when plantation life had become more highly developed in the Black Belt, and the rest of the poor whites had been forced to leave the region. "Does it not become us as an intelligent people," asked a Georgia planter, "to anticipate that period when so large a proportion of our population will have become slaves, and ask whether we will not want then the Federal Government to give us safety and security?"[105]

All of this relates, however, to the slavery question in general. The specific phase of the general problem which became most acute in the United States in the forties was the question of the extension of slavery. There had long been an economic question of slavery extension, involving the migration of masters and slaves from the old to the new slave-holding states. The whole process had several effects. It usually left the old states with wornout lands and at the same time

---

[104] Macon *Journal*, in the Natchez (Miss.) *Courier*, Oct. 29, 1850.
[105] Eli H. Baxter to the Committee, the Macon Union Celebration, Feb. 19, 1851, *Proceedings of the Macon Union Celebration*, pp. 8, 9.

brought them into competition with the more prosperous newer communities. It also increased the supply of cotton and the demand for slaves, which meant, other things being equal, a decrease in the price of cotton and an increase in that of slaves. This, though it might not have serious effects upon the newer and more prosperous states, tended still further to the economic embarrassment of the planters of the older states. As Georgia was one of this latter group, the immediate economic interests of her planters were apt to be opposed or at least indifferent to the acquisition of more slave territory.[106]

Slave extension, however, was attractive to some Georgians, as to other southerners, as a political expedient. Since abolitionism was growing simultaneously with nationalism in the North, the control of the Federal Government by antislavery men would probably mean forced abolition at the command of that government. Such control must therefore be avoided, and the only way to avoid it was to extend slavery and admit new slave states. Those who favored slave extension because it would give such political protection to the ultimate interests of slavery, did not hesitate to claim for it other and more immediate advantages. Dire consequences were predicted in case there was no outlet for the normal increase in the slave population of the older states. If all the slaves were held in the old states, where soils were exhausted, their natural increase would soon render their numbers superfluous.

[106] For an excellent contemporary analysis of this situation, see Weston, *op. cit.*, pp. 205-209, 217. This, to be sure, is *a priori* reasoning, but it offers a partial interpretation that well fits the facts of the average planter's indifference or opposition to slavery expansion. There is a mass of evidence concerning his indifference in Cole's *Whig Party* and in Boucher's *"In Re* That Aggressive Slavocracy," *Mississippi Valley Historical Review*, VIII. Nos. 1, 2.

Even if their value fell greatly as a result of this (and this was not always admitted), they would still become "not worth their board and keep." They would "eat the master out of house and home." This would, after years of economic depression, force the owners to fail completely or to emancipate.[107]   But this process involved the whole danger of the race problem, and possibly race war, which has already been discussed. "It is not unreasonable to believe that the time will come," observed a Georgia editor, "when the value of slave property will have become so slight that the owner will be more than willing to get rid of his slaves. But what a horrible freedom that will be to the African —proceeding from the worthlessness of his labor— which will mean suffering and degradation." This, in turn, would mean social turmoil and race danger for the whites.[108]

It is typical of the confusion of opinion that existed concerning slavery extension that, while some men thus demanded it to save the old states from having too many Negroes, others opposed it in order that too many Negroes should not leave the old states. "If the extentionists have their way," wrote a famous South Carolinian, "our state will lose all her negro labor, while her ague and congestive fever abide."[109]   In other words, old slave states like Georgia and South Carolina needed a large Negro population for labor, but must avoid one that was too large, lest it become an economic burden.   Just how an extension of territory proposed at any particular time would affect this

[107] Milledgeville *Federal Union*, January 15, 1850; Jackson (Miss.), *Flag of the Union*, February 14, 1851.

[108] Savannah *Georgian*, January 5, 1848.

[109] General James Hamilton to the Charleston *Mercury*, in the Washington *Republic*, December 2, 1850.

nice balance in Negro numbers was difficult to say; and this difficulty may partially explain that confusion of southern opinion that often existed when extension seemed imminent.

It should now be possible to correlate what has been said about prosperity in Georgia in 1850, about the threat to that condition imminent in the antislavery movement, about the attitude of Georgians toward the institution of slavery so attacked, and about the special question of slavery extension which involved all of these and led to the political crisis to be studied. In 1850 the antislavery forces of the North attempted to prevent all further slavery extension. They also attacked other phases of slavery, such as its existence in the District of Columbia. What should the attitude of Georgians be towards this movement and this crisis? Two divergent answers were given, one looking towards compromise with the North, the other towards separation from the North. Why was this divergence?

The answer may be given in the form of a relatively simple hypothesis, so far as the dominating planter classes were concerned. Their immediate economic interests, as suggested, were opposed to the extension of slave territory. There was no economic reason, then, for demanding secession from the Union simply because the North insisted that there should be no further slavery extension. There was, moreover, a special reason for avoiding such a crisis; namely, the desire of all propertied men to avoid danger of social turmoil. The Union had permitted the development of good business conditions; the same Union might be necessary to preserve such conditions. Planters who went no further than this in their analysis of the crisis of 1850 were, quite naturally, insistent that compromise be made with the North in order that the preservation of the Union might insure the preservation of peace and prosperity.

The moment, however, that a planter was convinced that the various northern attacks on slavery would lead gradually but inevitably to abolition, he foresaw not only the sudden ruin of prosperity, but all the other social dangers that have been described. If this were the case, the very Union that had seemed a protection now appeared to him as a league with destruction. Hence it must be abandoned at once. Thus the very planter who had previously been the most ardent champion of the Union, would now become its most intense enemy. In both cases his economic and social interests were the same; the difference was due simply to a difference of opinion as to how far these interests were in danger.

The two views that resulted from this situation were apparently most divergent. One planter argued earnestly for the Union and the other against it. Each was so sincerely desirous of defending the economic interests of slavery that he could scarcely believe the other sincere in the same desire. In reality, however, their views were not so divergent after all. The "Union man" was usually just one step behind the secessionist, and that step was simply a matter of evidence and conviction. Cite more convincing evidence to prove that the Union would lead to abolition, and, presto, he would become as violent a disunionist as the other fellow. The manifestoes of the Union party in Georgia in 1850 clearly recognized the truth of this and carefully served notice upon the North that any further evidence of a tendency towards emancipation

would make all Georgian secessionists.[110] The sudden
spectacular shift of such Georgia leaders as Toombs
and Stephens from a strong Union position to a
southern-rights position—and back again—may be
explained in part by these very circumstances.

Why, however, were a great majority of Georgians
of the planter and merchant classes satisfied in 1850
that the Union did not necessarily menace slavery?
Why was it so difficult to convince them that their ultimate interests were in danger? One rather obvious
answer may be given, which is at least worthy of serious consideration. A class that prospers does not wish
to court danger before it is thrust upon it. The prosperity of the Georgia planters was a bird in hand; the
vague hopes held out by secessionists were two—but
in a bush.

This opinion is not merely a present hypothesis, but
one which was held consciously at the time by observers
of Georgia. Such critics were convinced that, had business conditions been bad, the Georgia capitalist classes
would have been far more ready to see in the antislavery movement a cause for extreme measures. Economic ills and psychological depression would almost
certainly have been blamed, rightly or wrongly, upon
the Federal government. A Union that had brought
these things would have been no Union to preserve.
General James Hamilton, who was a rather keen critic
of economic factors in the drama of 1850, passed
through Central Georgia in the fall of that year, when
the political crisis over the secession movement was
supposed to be at its height. He found the state "in

[110] See, e.g., the "Georgia Platform" of 1850, which is but this one
step removed from a southern-rights document, H. V. Ames, *State
Documents on Federal Relations*, pp. 271, 272.

a condition of philosophic calm," since "thirteen cents a pound for cotton was a powerful contributor to make civil war and revolution exceedingly distasteful to her people."[111] In like manner, observers in South Carolina, who desired aid from Georgia in a secession movement, feared that the good times there would defeat their purpose. "Dis-union feeling in Georgia," declared the Columbia *South Carolinian,* "is neutralized by the high price of cotton." Her prosperity will make her unwilling to make any sacrifice for the cause of secession.[112] Governor Seabrook, a leader of the secession movement in South Carolina, declared privately to Quitman of Mississippi in 1850 that "prosperity makes the masses indifferent to the crisis."[113]

So, too, felt northern observers in Georgia. The Savannah correspondent of the Boston *Courier,* although taking the other side in the political controversy from that held by the Carolina papers, reached exactly the same conclusion as to the economic forces at work. "It is very fortunate for this Union," he observed, "that cotton is thirteen to fourteen cents a pound, instead of four to five. There is now a state of prosperity they do not care to disturb—but were it otherwise, all the depression in trade and prices would have been attributed to the burden of the Union and to the baneful effects of national legislation and northern agitation."[114] Such hypotheses, while they probably

[111] Letter to the Charleston *Mercury,* reprinted in the Washington *Republic,* December 2, 1850. Hamilton wrote from Texas, November 11, and must therefore have passed through Georgia not later than October, i.e., in the early part of the Georgia convention campaign of that fall.

[112] Columbia tri-weekly *South Carolinian,* June 21, 1849. The Mobile *Daily Advertiser* made the same analysis of the situation in Alabama, see *National Intelligencer,* Dec. 6, 1850.

[113] Seabrook to Quitman, July 15, 1850, Seabrook MSS.

[114] The Boston *Courier,* November 20, 1850; *Cf.* Richmond *Whig,* March 5, 1851.

exaggerated the potency of purely economic factors, can hardly be ignored in the light of all the circumstances which have been and will be considered.

There is perhaps no better way of emphasizing the potency of economic prosperity in preserving the pro-Union feeling in Georgia than to consider the contrast existing between that state and South Carolina. One of the outstanding phenomena in the political history of the period was the fact that the very planter class which was conservative in Georgia and the Gulf States was radical in South Carolina, for in the former it was pro-Union in feeling, while in the latter it led the secession movement. This relatively radical attitude of the Carolina planters had prevailed there since the early thirties, and it is suggestive that its development had been concomitant with the economic decadence of the state.

South Carolina, in the old colonial and early statehood days, had been a prosperous country, especially in the plantation area along the coast, and this had made possible the development in Charleston of an able and highly cultured planter society. This society dominated the economic, social, and political life of the state to an extent that was unique even in the cotton country. As the area of cotton cultivation extended westward, however, and the old lands of the state wore out, Carolina began to suffer all the typical ills inherent in the slave and plantation systems. The worst of the situation seemed to be the impossibility of finding any remedy. Agricultural improvement seemed hopeless, for it was easier to take up new lands to the west than to improve the old ones at home. "The soil's slow restoration cannot be made while Georgia and Alabama are to the west," admitted a Charleston paper in 1838.[115]

When this situation was apparently made more difficult for South Carolina by the tariff policy of northern manufacturers in the twenties, it was natural that the planters should have laid many of their difficulties at the door of Federal legislation. A distrust of the economic advantages of the Union became at this time a more or less permanent attitude in the state. An apparent victory upon the tariff issue in 1833 led to but a short-lived satisfaction in South Carolina, since the next two decades saw the rapid development in the North of the antislavery movement, which in a new and perhaps more dangerous manner threatened the state's economic system.

Meanwhile, the lower tariff schedule had not brought the state final relief from its difficulties. The Whig tariff of 1842 was one of the causes of its second serious political protest—the so-called "Bluffton Movement." South Carolina suffered even more than Georgia, during the cotton depression terminating about 1848, from lessened dividends and loss of both white and Negro population. In like manner, its recovery after 1848 was less certain than that in Georgia. The latter had an obvious advantage in its newer lands; better facilities for water and rail transportation; the presence of more northern capital and many energetic northern tradesmen, teachers and mechanics; and, finally, an advantage in that the inherent general disadvantages of the slave planting system had not as yet developed through so long a period as they had in the older state. As a result, there was by 1850 a distinct contrast in the economic philosophy of the capitalist

[115] Charleston *Courier*, March 16, 1838, in Jervey, *Life of Robert Y. Hayne*, p. 456.

classes in the two sister commonwealths. Although in Georgia the planters, merchants, and editors were inclined to be "boosters," across the river there was much pessimism. While Dr. Lee at Augusta was preaching optimism through the *Chronicle* and the *Southern Cultivator,* ex-Governor Hammond at Charleston was warning of approaching decay. In addressing the convention of the South Carolina Institute at that city in 1850, he reminded his hearers that returns on cotton investments in the state since 1842 had averaged but four and one-half per cent. "At such rates," he continued, "our state must soon become utterly impoverished and of consequence wholly degraded. Depopulation must take place rapidly. Our slaves will go first and that institution from which we have heretofore reaped the greatest benefits will be swept away. . . . This process is already apparent around us. Since about 1830 floating capital has continuously left the state, about $500,000 annually. . . . Owners have emigrated, taking an average of 8,300 slaves per annum, so that by 1840 South Carolina had 83,000 less slaves than the average population increase should have given her."[116]

At the same time that the capitalist class was thus emigrating or facing decreasing dividends, the condition of the mass of poor whites was most depressing. The yeomanry of South Carolina was a smaller group and less independent economically and politically than the same class in Georgia.

The need of doing something for this class and, what was more important, of doing something for capital, led to a demand for manufactures in Carolina, as it had in Georgia. This movement, though led by

[116] Quoted in *De Bow's Review,* VIII. 501 (June, 1850).

the able William Gregg, proved relatively less successful in the older state. In addition to the same forces
that impeded the movement across the river, there was
in Carolina a conservative influence that displayed
more old-fashioned opposition to "associated capital."
The almost complete disappearance of the Whig party
in the state, for the very reason that traditions there
were so opposed to the tariff and other views of that
party, severed that connection with a northern pro-
industrial party which was a factor in promoting a
tariff and industrial party in Georgia. In like manner
—it may have been because of the more intense anti-
northern feeling in Carolina or because of the more
aristocratic tone of government and society there—
fewer northern engineers, mechanics and tradesmen
went into the state than did into Georgia, the "Yankee-
land of the South." Hence by 1850, when the first depression in cotton manufacture set in, Carolina manufacturers, as well as planters, were rather depressed in
spirit.   William Gregg drew such a dark picture of
industrial prospects that year, in writing for *De Bow's
Review,* that the able editor thereof felt called upon to
deprecate his conclusions.[117]

Meanwhile, the development of trade at the port of
Charleston had been disappointing. River connection
with the interior was poor for transportation purposes
within the state, and the attempt to control the river
trade up the Savannah, in rivalry with the port of that
name, had long since failed. The attempt to compete
with Savannah for the Augusta trade by running the
Charleston and Hamburg Railroad to a point across
the river from the Georgia city had also partly failed,

---

[117] *De Bow's Review,* VIII. 134 (February, 1850) ; *Cf.* Boucher,
Ante-Bellum Attitude of South Carolina, pp. 256-261.

because of the refusal of Augusta to permit bridge connection there. This also was a factor in discouraging the great dream of attracting the bulk of the lower Mississippi Valley trade to Charleston.

Thus all interests, planting, manufacturing, and trade, seemed rather discouraging to the planter society of South Carolina in the late forties. In this state of mind, they were more inclined to see the worst in the possible consequences of the northern antislavery movement. The traditional distrust of the Union, the heritage of the thirties, increased this inclination. Or, to put the matter in another way, South Carolinians were less inclined to hide from themselves the ultimate menace of this movement to their institutions than were the Georgians, whose prosperity inclined them to conservatism and compromise. While a Union that had been associated with decadence, and which now threatened the very existence of Carolina's economic life, was no Union to preserve, there were some attractive possibilities in a Southern Confederacy. Free trade, the panacea for Carolina's ills, could be inaugurated. Then there was a hope that Charleston would become the great port of such a Confederacy as soon as the Augusta bridge was built and western connections made. But here again Charleston interests were threatened by competition with Savannah. This rivalry was a factor in determining the relationships between the two states in 1850 and in determining their respective attitudes toward the Union. These relationships, therefore, merit special consideration.

Cultured Charleston had long looked upon Georgia as a new and relatively crude western country. Georgians, in return, made fun of the "dandies" of effete

Charleston.[118] This feeling, typical of the eastern-western sectional consciousness of the time, was not in itself serious, but it prepared a psychological basis for the support of any real political or economic antagonisms that might later develop. When the Nullification crisis appeared in the thirties, such an antagonism arose. Most Georgians had economic or political reasons for standing by the central government in that controversy.[119] From that time on, many Georgians suspected Carolina as the home of reckless and self-seeking radicalism.

Meanwhile, the feeling towards the sister state had not been improved by the efforts of Charleston to replace Savannah in the control of Georgia's up-country trade. Savannah felt more strongly upon this matter, to be sure, than did other parts of the state less directly interested; indeed, towns like Columbus, which looked more for trade connections to Charleston than to Savannah, probably felt inclined to favor the former. Generally speaking, however, the sense of state pride was as strong in Georgia as in the sister state, and, for reasons noted above, the state pride of Georgia was particularly sensitive in all matters pertaining to Carolina. The obvious efforts to take Georgia trade from Georgia's port, therefore, aroused in many Georgians economic antagonisms to "Palmettodom." It has also been noted that there was some feeling of financial rivalry between the states.

Unfortunately for South Carolina's political aspirations, as it later developed, Charleston continued in

---

[118] Andrews, *Reminiscences,* pp. 44, 45; Longstreet's *Georgia Scenes* also contains suggestions of this.

[119] For a careful narration of the Nullification movement in Georgia see the article of that title by E. M. Coulter, in the *Georgia Historical Quarterly,* V. No. 1, pp. 3-39.

the forties the attempt to wrest the bulk of the upland trade from Savannah. The trade of the whole West seemed ultimately at stake, and Charleston sorely needed it to retrieve her fallen fortunes. Savannah began to complain in the late forties that at all the railroad conventions Charleston spoke loud and long concerning "the Charleston avenue to the west—via the Georgia railroads." Should not Georgia's port be the chief beneficiary of Georgia's state railroad that reached through the mountains to the West?[120] So reasoned "Old Yamacraw," but Charleston continued zealously in her attempts. Her merchants were active in Upper Georgia seeking trade connections, and the people there sometimes criticized Savannah for not being equally energetic. Nevertheless, they showed a sympathy for their own port and urged it on to greater activity. Savannah, of course, was not inactive in words. Her press carried on a running controversy with that of her rival as to the respective merits of their ports, their distance from the interior, their shipping facilities, and the like. This sometimes even degenerated into delightful quarrels over their respective health conditions, each claiming that disease was more general and more fatal with their rival than with themselves.[121]

[120] Boston *Courier*, January 1, 1850. See map number 1, p. 10. It should be noted in fairness to Charleston that her citizens contributed capital to the building of some of the Georgia roads and to those in Tennessee with which it was hoped the Western and Atlantic would connect. A recent writer declares that it was most unfortunate for Charleston to have depended on its connection with the Georgia road to Tennessee rather than upon a direct road to Cincinnati, which Hayne had desired to build. See T. D. Jervey, *The Slave Trade: Slavery and Color*, pp. 87-99.

[121] *De Bow's Review*, VII. 558, 559 (December, 1849); VIII. 243-245, (Mar., 1850). As a matter of fact the health conditions at Charleston seem to have been better than those at Savannah. See Ingle, *Southern Sidelights*, p. 129.

The final and most exasperating effort on Charleston's part to eliminate competition from Savannah came in 1847, just as the political crisis with the North was becoming serious. When the Georgia legislature met that fall, the merchants of Charleston petitioned that body for the incorporation of a railroad to be built from some point on the Georgia Central Railroad to Silver Bluff on the Savannah River. Such a line would have tapped the trade coming down from Atlanta and Macon to Savannah, a little above the latter city, and would have diverted it to the river, whence it could be carried *via* a Carolina road to Charleston. This proposal seemed the last word in arrogance. The Milledgeville *Federal Union,* usually friendly in its attitude, now felt that there would naturally "be some feeling on this throughout Georgia."[122] When the petition was considered in the House, it was made the subject of bitter criticism, the most intense attack, according to the Carolina papers, being made by a representative from Augusta. This gentleman, a Mr. Miller, thought the Charleston proposal so unreasonable that "he hoped to live long enough to see an impassable gulf or Chinese Wall between Georgia and South Carolina, that we may be forever separated from her arrogant medlers." The *Federal Union* questioned whether these words were actually used, but adminished Charlestonians to show fair play if they would avoid trouble.[123] The Charleston *Evening News* felt, however, that "the Georgia press is now engaged in the unworthy pursuit of provoking a feeling of state jealousy, if not the passion of revenge, for imaginary wrongs, in the people of Georgia towards the people of

[122] December 21, 1847.
[123] *Ibid.*

South Carolina. This nursing of state feud is unfortunate." It then added the comment of particular interest here, that, since the southern states were approaching a crisis over the slavery question, it was "especially necessary, now that the North is attacking us, that the two republics . . . be friendly."[124]

The *Evening News* might have said with greater truth that it was especially vital at this time to South Carolina that the relations of the two "republics" be friendly! Not only had the South Carolina leaders to contend with the general ill feeling towards South Carolina, but there was also the specific problem of the port trade. If South Carolina were to secede in 1850, and Charleston were to be cut off as a port by federal interference, while Georgia remained in the Union, could Savannah be trusted not to take advantage of such a situation? Would she not secure the whole trade at issue? This aroused some anxiety in Charleston, where it was suspected Savannah favored the Union partly for the express purpose of securing this trade. "If South Carolina secedes," wrote a famous Carolinian that year, "the Union will establish floating customs houses, and the mail will go direct from Wilmington [North Carolina] to Savannah. In the meantime the whole of our inland export trade will go to Savannah, and our kind neighbors, after all their bluster, will be reaping the full fruits of their patriotic moderation."[125] Other observers in South Carolina, such as Bishop Capers of the Methodist Church, expressed the same opinion. Indeed, the belief that this

---

[124] Charleston *Evening News*, December 14, 1847.

[125] Gen. Jas. Hamilton, to the Charleston *Mercury*, in the Washington *Republic*, December 2, 1850.

was the situation seems to have been held in widely-separated parts of the South.[126] It was indeed a fact that the economic advantages which would result for Georgia, if she remained in the Union while "Palmettodom" seceded, were at times calculated in the former state. The Marietta *Helicon* pointed out the very possibility that Hamilton and Capers had warned Carolina against and welcomed the thought that political developments might now throw all the Charleston trade to Macon and Savannah. The Savannah *News,* although a southern-rights paper, granted that "there is something in this idea."[127]

The economic inferiority of South Carolina and the rivalry with Georgia were matters of common comment in the newspapers of both the northern and southern states. Decadence in "Palmettodom" was usually ascribed to the aristocratic character of her society and politics, little allowance being made for the unavoidable difficulties of her position. Georgia was pointed to as "the land of promise," in contrast with Carolina, "the land of protest."[128] A New Orleans paper opined that "Georgia produces riches and South Carolina revolutions."[129] A Mobile journal believed that Carolina was jealous of Georgia and discouraged by her superiority.[130] Occasionally, even South Carolina editors were sufficiently candid and courageous to voice similar criticisms.[131]

[126] Jackson (Miss.) *Flag of the Union,* March 7, 1851; Richmond *Daily Whig,* December 17, 1850.

[127] Savannah *News,* November 10, 1850.

[128] Philadelphia *Public Ledger,* November 13, 1850; Boston *Liberator,* August 9, 1850; Washington *National Intelligencer,* January 4, 1851. The latter granted that economic forces were against South Carolina.

[129] Quoted in the Augusta *Chronicle,* September 3, 1849.

[130] Mobile *Daily Advertiser,* November 30, 1849.

[131] See Boucher, *Ante-Bellum Attitude of South Carolina,* p. 250.

Georgia papers, of course, emphasized such opinions. This was especially true of the Whig journals, which had no political associations across the river, but it was not entirely limited to them. "Carolina blamed all her troubles on the Union," remarked the Macon *Journal*, "but they are really due to her undemocratic institutions. While South Carolina has been blustering, Georgia has been toiling."[132] The Augusta *Chronicle* agreed and continued its scathing criticisms of the sister state with more or less regularity.[133] So it was that Georgia, the most progressive state of the lower South, was also the most hostile towards "Palmettodom." This was an attitude with which South Carolina would have to reckon when she essayed southern leadeship in 1850.

[132] Quoted in Jackson (Miss.) *Flag of the Union*, January 17, 1851.
[133] Augusta *Chronicle*, June 30, August 27, 1849.

CHAPTER II

SOCIAL GROUPS

In the course of his discussion of wealth and prosperity in Georgia, Olmsted declared that this wealth was confined to a small class. A large part of the population, he believed, lacked both capital and energy.[1] This observation suggests the importance of considering the several economic and social groups which entered into the state's population. If wealth was confined to the few, perhaps the political attitude it developed was also confined to the few, and, if so, what was the attitude of the many? Again, in considering the race problem as connected with slavery, it may be that different elements in the white population felt differently towards the Negro race. Here, too, if this were true, a difference in social viewpoint might lead to a different political attitude whenever the race problem was involved in political controversy. A brief discussion of the social classes or groups, as they existed in Georgia in the forties, is pertinent, therefore, by way of background to the political narrative.

The outstanding social type in Georgia and the other cotton states was, of course, the planter-aristocrat. This class has been sung in song and story, sometimes belittled, more often idealized. The first thing concerning it that needs to be noted here is the fact that it was a very small group. Just how many slaves and how much land a farmer must own before he became a "planter" was a rather uncertain matter,

[1] *Journey in the Seaboard Slave States*, p. 530. For the distribution of wealth in 1850, see Map No. 3, p. 22.

but only a small number of Georgians were commonly recognized as having attained this distinction. The census of 1850, for instance, listed about nineteen hundred planters in the state, as against some eighty-one thousand "farmers."[2] The great majority of slaveholders in Georgia owned a small number of slaves, more than one half of them owning less than five, and belonged therefore to the small farmer group.[3]

The planters, as the owners of lands and slaves, were obviously the chief propertied men of the period. As the evolution of the plantation system progressed, it tended to increasing concentration of such capital in their hands. The process had gone further in the black belts of South Carolina and Louisiana than it had in Georgia, but even in the latter state a super-planter type was already appearing by 1850. General H. H. Tarver of Twiggs county, for instance, was reputed that year to be the owner of one thousand slaves and fifty thousand acres of land, distributed among ten plantations in four counties, and yielding him a net annual income of about one hundred and ten thousand dollars.[4] The planter was ordinarily an able man, to begin with, or he would not have held his position in a relatively new country like Georgia. Unless of a crude *noveaux riche* type, he had usually had educational advantages, often in northern colleges, and opportunities of travel at home and abroad. This enabled him to give tone to the social circle he dominated, which, as the self-appointed statistician of Georgia remarked, "was no ordinary society."[5]

[2] Census of 1850.
[3] De Bow, *The Interest in Slavery of the Non-Slaveholder*, 1860 Tract Association, Tract No. 5 (Charleston, 1860), p. 3.
[4] Huntsville (Ala.) *Advocate*, January 29, 1851.
[5] White, *Georgia Statistics*, p. 284.

The possession of wealth and social prestige enabled the planters to dominate the political parties of the state as well as its business and social life. The more wealth and prestige was concentrated in their hands, the greater became the degree of this domination. In South Carolina it was almost complete. In Georgia, but a generation removed from frontier days, the farmer classes remained more independent and the democratic dogma more persistent than in the sister state. These had been real forces in the Democratic party of Georgia, as will be noted, but even that party was by 1850 coming under the leadership of the planter group. Its leaders in 1850, Howell Cobb, Lumpkin, Holsey, Towns, McDonald, Arnold, and the rest, were almost to a man planters or professional men associated with the planter class.[6] The Whig party, of course, openly advocated the interests of the same class, though it often expressed a politic reverence for the traditions of equalitarianism.

In his attitude towards both economic and political affairs, the planter was conservative, as befitted the man of property. He advocated "sound" financing, agricultural improvements, and, sometimes, the encouragement of railroads and industrial corporations. His attitude towards the slaves was apt to be more benevolent than that of the poorer whites.[7] He had a direct economic interest in their welfare, and there was

[6] When the Union party of 1850 insinuated that it contained all the "people of consequence," the editors of two of the most important Democratic journals, the Federal Union and the Savannah Georgian, proceeded to testify to their capitalistic interests.

[7] A remarkable instance of this benevolence occurred in Georgia at the height of the political crisis of 1850, when a Savannah planter contributed fifty dollars to purchase the freedom of a run-away slave held in New York City. Only a planter would have dared to so affront public opinion for the sake of a Negro. For his explanations see Savannah News, October 26, 1850.

no possibility of social jealousy between them, as there was between slave and poor white. He had less race prejudice, therefore, than did the average "cracker."[8] While ready to lead in the defense of his slave property in any crisis, he was inclined, as was pointed out above, to deprecate any excitement over the slavery question that seemed unnecessary to its defense. Hence, he was less responsive to appeals featuring intense race prejudice than was the poor white in the same neighborhood. For this reason also, the Black Belt, which the planter dominated, did not respond to race appeals as did the adjacent country of the Barrens. This attitude was often misunderstood in the North, where it was assumed that the "Oligarchs" must be the leaders of the "Aggressive Slavocracy";[9] and in the South, where the planters were sometimes accused of being so calm and conciliatory as to be untrue to their own interests.[10]

We have noted that the great majority of Georgia farmers had small holdings and owned few slaves. The eighty thousand or more members of this class were distributed through Central and Upper Georgia, holding small farms on the poorer lands of the Black Belt or good lands in the newer regions of Southwest and Cherokee Georgia. Most of the original settlers in Central and Upper Georgia had belonged to this class, and it was still the dominating one in Upper

[8] Jas. S. Hammond to Louis Tappan, September 1, 1850, Hammond MSS. Hammond made this point very specific to his northern correspondents.

[9] See e.g., Philadelphia *Public Ledger*, February 26, 1850.

[10] Augusta *Republic*, July 21, 1849; Augusta *Constitutionalist*, July 25, 1849; Savannah *Georgian*, July 31, 1849; Jefferson Davis expressed the opinion in 1850 that the accumulation of plantation capital in a man's hands was very apt to make him incapable of defending it; D. Rowland (ed.), *Jefferson Davis*, II. 76.

Georgia in this period. Here they lived in the simplicity of the frontier farmer, raising the hill country fruits and grains, doing their work with their own hands, and even making their own homespun clothes. They were thrifty and self-reliant, but at the same time crude,[11] provincial, and often illiterate.[12] A northern resident in the state found Upper Georgia a country generally similar to New England, but thought the people "were all of one hundred years behind the times in education and in all improvements." Even some wealthy men were illiterate.[13] Hundley, with his more sympathetic viewpoint, also found the yeomanry of the Cherokee country similar to the New England farmers, but thought the former better educated upon important political topics than were the Yankees. Although many of the Georgians could not read, they generally attended public discussions of political matters at courthouse gatherings and public barbecues and in this way achieved a lively interest in current topics. He found nothing in the North which corresponded to the public barbecue as a source for political education and for the development and expression of public opinion.[14]

It has also been observed that a majority of the Georgia farmers owned but a small number of slaves. De Bow calculated, upon the basis of the Census of 1850, that about one half of the population of the cotton states, exclusive of the cities, belonged to slaveholding families, but that of these about one half

[11] For description of the customs and amusements of the Cherokee country, see White, *Georgia Statistics,* p. 439; Longstreet, *Georgia Scenes,* pp. 113-117.
[12] See Map No. 4, p. 24, for the extent of illiteracy in the several sections of the state.
[13] Emily Burke, *Reminiscences of Georgia,* p. 21.
[14] Hundley, *Social Relations in Our Southern States,* p. 207.

owned less than five slaves.[15] In Central Georgia many small farmers owned from one to fifteen slaves, but in Upper Georgia the majority owned none at all. Where a few were owned, the masters worked by their side in the fields.[16] Here, therefore, where there was a very small Negro population, the slave was generally less restricted in his relations with the whites than was the case in the Black Belt.[17] The Negroes were not present in sufficient numbers in the hills to offer any threat of economic competition with the poor whites, nor did the latter have to fear any race problem in case of abolition. Hence it is probable that the poor mountaineer, while he had no love for Negroes, was indifferent to the race problem which was forced upon the poor whites on the borders of the Black Belt. This suggests the possibility that there was a less intense racial consciousness in the hill country than with the poor whites on the edge of the Black Belt. If this were true, it would imply less response to political appeals featuring the race problem than would have been accorded such appeals in or near the plantation districts. As a matter of fact, the "southern rights" appeal of 1850 did involve race appeal, and the strongest response came from the poor farmers on the edge of the Black Belt, while it was largely ignored by the poor farmers in the hill country.[18]

The small farmers of Central Georgia, however, were in a different position from those of Upper

[15] De Bow, *The Interest in Slavery of the Non-Slaveholder*, p. 3. For more specific estimates in the case of Georgia see R. P. Brooks, *The Agrarian Revolution in Georgia*, p. 85.

[16] See Alfred H. Stone, "Free Contract Labor in the Ante-Bellum South," *The South in the Building of the Nation*, V. 143.

[17] Burke, *op. cit.*, p. 21; Hundley, *op. cit.*, pp. 194, 195. This, of course, is the rule in race relationships. See Stone, *American Race Problem*, p. 13.

[18] See Map No. 7, p. 320.

Georgia. Many of the former owned a few slaves and hoped to own more, while those who did not probably hoped to do so in the future. This tended to identify the interests of the small slaveholder with those of the large, to the advantage of the latter. The poor farmer of the Black Belt also feared the racial consequences of emancipation, and this intensified his proslavery views. He was carefully reminded by proslavery writers that while the planter might use accumulated capital to escape a country turned over to free Negroes, the poor farmer would have to stay and face the freedmen.[19]

The attitude of the Cherokee farmers towards slavery is difficult to determine. It has already been suggested that they probably felt less intensely on the race question than the farmers in the lowlands, but what was their attitude towards the vested interests of the slaveholders? The corresponding class in Virginia, Tennessee, and the Carolinas, was usually opposed to these interests. One would expect, a priori, a similar attitude on the part of the mountain people of Georgia. Cherokee and Southwest Georgia, moreover, were relatively newly settled sections, and this meant that there had been less time for economic and social stratification than had been the case in other states. Farmers in such new country were apt to be more hopeful and ambitious and more independent of planter domination. Helper, in his protest against the slaveocracy, declared that "in few other states are the non-slaveholders so little under the dominance of the oligarchy as in Georgia."[20] This, under some circum-

---

[19] De Bow, op. cit., pp. 11, 12. For northern interpretation of the small farmers' attitude, see Philadelphia Public Ledger, November 26, 1850.

[20] Helper, Impending Crisis, Compendium, p. 111.

stances, might have meant more open protest against the vested interests than would have been expected from the subordinated poor farmers of the Carolinas. As a matter of fact, the evidence in the case is slight, usually indirect, and difficult to secure. It is slight because the poor farmers were not an articulate class.[21] It is indirect for the same reason. What is known about them is largely what the upper classes thought fit to print concerning them, and this depended upon political expediency.

There is some evidence that the up-country non-slaveholders' dislike for the vested interests of the planters was a real force in 1850. When the political crisis over slavery extension arose in the late forties, the Cherokee Georgians were apt to associate the planter class with the slavery-extension group— which of course was just the reverse of the truth[22]— and, therefore, opposed the extension movement to the extent of their latent dislike for that class. As this played into the hands of the planter leaders of both old parties, who led the compromising Union party, these leaders had no protest to make, even though the mountaineers talked heresy against the slaveocracy. The protest came from the Southern Rights party, which claimed most loudly to speak for planter interests and which the mountaineers therefore opposed.

Some southern-rights leaders believed the class feeling against the slave owners was the chief obstacle in the cotton states to the extensionist movement. Governor Mosely of Florida, writing from Tallahassee, whence he could presumably survey conditions in

---

[21] Small town newspapers of Upper Georgia, which may have reflected small farmer opinion, have usually been lost.

[22] Always excepting South Carolina

nearby Georgia, Alabama, and Florida, declared that
"the chief obstacle to unity against the Wilmot Proviso was the belief that it tended to promote the
prospective welfare of the poor or non-slaveholding
whites."[23]   In Georgia the protest of the nonslave-
holding whites against slavery extension varied from
statements of polite indifference to energetic objections
to fighting the slaveholders' battles.   The more conservative people of Upper Georgia, where the bulk of
the population belonged to the Democratic party,
wanted to know why they should join a movement to
protect the owners of Negroes, when they owned none
themselves.[24]

When the critical year of struggle between the
Southern-rights and Union parties was reached, Union
leaders did not hesitate to proclaim to Cherokee farmers that they had no interest in the slavery struggle;
that the extensionists were working for the selfish
interests of the planter class; and that if this led to a
conflict with the North, the small farmers, who had no
interest in the issue, "would have to fight the battles of
the lordly slaveholders."[25]   The extensionist group
protested vehemently about this heresy against the
peculiar institution, on the ground that by dividing
southerners it would "play right into the hands of the
abolitionists," the common enemy.   As a matter of fact,
as was observed, it played into the hands of the planters
themselves, who, opposed to slavery extension and to
anything threatening turmoil, were largely associated
with the non-extension Union party.   They gladly co-

[23] Mosely to Seabrook, May 18, 1849, Seabrook MSS.
[24] W. H. Hull to Howell Cobb, January 26, 1849, "Toombs, Stephens,
and Cobb Correspondence," *American Historical Association Annual Report, 1911*, II. 142.
[25] *Federal Union*, April 9, 1850.

operated with the mountaineers against the Southern-rights, extension-at-any-price party, and were not over critical of the motives which brought them this up-country support.

A certain number of Georgia whites, who were neither planters nor farmers, were the residents of the larger towns. Here a small group of merchants and professional men were associated with the planters in business and society and in their general interests and point of view.[26] Smaller merchants and professional men tended to share the economic and social status of the small farmers, and their views upon slavery were apt to be those of the class into which they hoped to rise. Some of the small merchants and professional men, however—particularly the "ginger-pop lawyers" —tended to favor secession. They read the local extremist papers and did not partake of the conservatism that comes with the possession of wealth.[27]

The attitude of Georgia mechanics towards slavery and political matters probably did not vary much from that of the small farmers in the same section of the state. Occasionally, however, they came into competition with slave labor, in which cases they were apt to become antagonistic to the institution.[28] Northern observers often claimed that this was the case.[29] There is little evidence showing any general antagonism, however, on the part of native mechanics against slavery, though they opposed opening their trades to

[26] Dr. Richard Arnold, a leading Democrat of Savannah, emphasized his statement that all Savannah people of "respectability," with the exception of only one family, were conservative Unionists in 1850; Arnold to Forney, December 18, 1850, Arnold MSS.

[27] See Philadelphia *Public Ledger*, November 26, 1850.

[28] For an interesting case of this kind in newspaper work, see the Savannah *Georgian*, September 14, 1850.

[29] Parsons, *Tour Among the Planters*, p. 17.

Negroes.[30]   As for the white laborers, many of them were not native Georgians.   Those who were natives were an unimportant and inarticulate class.

At the bottom of the social and economic scale among the whites were the "poor white trash" of the Pine Barrens area.   The term "cracker" was sometimes applied in Georgia to poor and middle-class farmers in almost any part of the state, though to the northern mind it probably connoted chiefly the poorer type.   Within the state, the latter were more distinctively referred to as the "Piney-Woods People," the "Sand Hillers," the "Clay Eaters," and like euphemistic terms.   This class merits especial attention, both because it had some political significance in a state where all men could vote and because it was itself the subject of much controversy involving the general question of slavery.   It should not be confused, as is sometimes done, with the better type of poor farmers in the hills.[31]

The typical "Piney-Woods People" lived upon small clearings in pine districts, or poor, worn-out soils upon which they planted a little corn, cotton or garden truck. A few pigs and chickens ran half wild about the place. From such sources they supplied their immediate wants in food, while the women spun the cotton into the cloth necessary for clothing.   For shelter they depended upon one-room shacks, which were of the crudest character within doors and without.   The men eked out their miserable existence by hunting and fishing and perhaps pilfering or illicit trading with the slaves of nearby plantations.   Occasionally they would ride into

[30] See Russel, *Economic Aspects of Southern Sectionalism*, pp. 53, 219.
[31] This confusion persists in recent writing.   See, *e.g.*, Russel, *Economic Aspects of Southern Sectionalism*, p. 51.

the nearest town in an ox-cart, if they owned one, to barter poultry or a single bale of cotton for a few necessary articles of trade. They were neither proprietors nor laborers, but rather squatters upon the soil that no one else would take. Lack of any free capital and lack of energy made it impossible for them to secure any better holdings.

They were an independent and taciturn people, but necessarily led a life that was most primitive in character. They were usually utterly ignorant and sometimes depraved.[32] Drunkenness was general and often extreme, as they indulged "in the vilest rot-gut rather than the honest apple-brandy of the yeomen." They were also apt to be weak and sickly as well as lazy. Indeed, from what is now known in medical science, it would seem that some of their proverbial "laziness" was due to chronic infection with hook-worm or other diseases which were endemic in the community.[33]

As a result of all these characteristics, the "poor white trash" were despised by slaves as well as by the more energetic and successful whites. The poor whites returned the dislike of the slaves with interest. Their very inferiority made them the more jealous of their one claim to distinction; that is, their white blood.

[32] For graphic representation of poverty and ignorance in the Pine Barrens, see Maps 3 and 4, pp. 22, 24.

[33] For contemporary descriptions of this class from the northern viewpoint, see, Weston, *The Progress of Slavery*, pp. 39-42; and *Poor Whites, passim;* Olmsted, *Journey in the Seaboard Slave States.* pp. 413, 415, 545, 507, 535-540; and *The Cotton Kingdom*, II. 385; Burke, *Reminiscences*, pp. 205-209. For the southern view, see De Bow, *Economic Resources of the Southern States*, II. 106; Governor Hammond's Address to the South Carolina Institute, in *De Bow's Review*, VIII. 519; Andrews, *Reminiscences*, p. 43; Hundley, *Social Relations in Our Southern States*, pp. 255-269; and the quotations from Augusta newspapers given by Phillips in *Plantation and Frontier Documents*, II. 167 *(Documentary History of American Industrial Society.)* For comment on the poor whites and hookworm disease see P. H. Buck, "Poor Whites of the Old South," *American Historical Review*, XXXI. 45, 46.

They were, therefore, the class which most disliked the Negro, which was probably most race-conscious, and which was most responsive to any political appeal featuring the race problem. This was especially true of those who lived on the edge of the plantation areas and who there came into contact with the Negroes. Conditions in this area were indeed ideal for arousing race feeling, as the Negroes were too near and numerous to permit of the indifference of the mountains, and at the same time not sufficiently numerous to permit of the tolerance of the planter-dominated Black Belt. Speaking of the poor whites across the river in South Carolina, James H. Hammond declared they "felt the distinction of race and color more sensibly than any other and if emancipation could take place would be the deadliest enemy of the free negro. The negroes, on the other hand, fear and hate the [poor] whites."[34]

In addition to being anti-Negro in feeling, the "Clay-Eater" was ignorant and hence especially responsive to appeals involving provincial prejudices. His dislike for the Yankee and the North could, of course, be stimulated with much greater ease than could any such feeling a planter might possess.[35] This responsiveness to race and sectional prejudice probably explains the fact noted that, in the test of 1850, the people on the edge of the Pine Barrens supported the southern-rights movement more generally than did those of any other section of the state.[36]

[34] Hammond to Louis Tappan, September 1, 1850, Hammond MSS. See also, for Georgia, the Savannah *Republican*, November 21, 1850, and Jan. 4, 1851; Fanny Kemble's *Journal*, p. 146; Oneida (N. Y.) *Herald* in the *Federal Union*, Oct. 30, 1849; Weston, *Progress of Slavery*, p. 40.

[35] This was the opinion of some critical northern observers. See the Oneida (N. Y.) *Herald*, in the *Federal Union*, Oct. 30, 1849; Weston, *The Progress of Slavery*, p. 40.

[36] See Map No. 7, p. 320.

It must be remembered, of course, that the poor white population of the Barrens was small in relation to that of the state as a whole. In 1850 it did not much exceed forty thousand out of a total white population of over five hundred thousand. Even this small estimate makes no allowance for the presence of a few planters and other superior individuals in the Pine Barrens area. Nevertheless, the class was large enough and obviously unfortunate enough to attract considerable attention from both northern and southern observers. The former believed that the class was the direct result of the slave system. It was held that the planters monopolized good lands, drove the poor whites to the worthless tracts, and then did not even permit them to escape from these to work as laborers. For labor was given a race stigma, and most of the demand for it was already supplied by the slaves. Thus there was no place for the poor whites in the dominant economic system of the cotton states. They were a class without any economic *raison d'etre* and, as such, predestined to become the parasites and pariahs of southern society. Could there be any more damning indictment of slavery than this, its effect upon the southern whites themselves? So ran the northern indictment.[37]

Georgia observers were quite ready to admit the degradation of this people, but felt the northern explanation was partial and partisan in character. Northerners blamed everything upon environmental

[37] J. E. Cairnes, *The Slave Power*, pp. 78, 79. This was also the thesis of Helper and many other northern and southern critics of the institution. *Cf.* Phillips, *American Negro Slavery*, p. 355. For an especially forceful expression, see Weston, *Progress of Slavery*, pp. 40-42. For a modern northern expression, which makes no allowance for other factors, see Hammond, *The Cotton Industry*, pp. 62, 63. Northern critics who blamed all upon slavery were blissfully indifferent to the fact that a similar "poor white" class existed in some northern states, *e.g.*, the "Pineys" of New Jersey.

influences and ignored some potent hereditary forces. The "Piney-Woods People," Georgians held, were largely the descendants of Oglethorpe's paupers and indentured servants, or of similar people from the Barrens of South Carolina. They had originally been an inferior people and had passed their failings on to their descendants. Only this hereditary inferiority could explain their failure to take better lands in the first place or to leave these lands, once they were exhausted, to take better ones on the easy terms offered early in the century.

It was even claimed by some extreme proslavery writers that this lowly position of the poor whites, due to hereditary influences, had been improved by the existence of slavery in their environment. The planter, it was claimed, was forced to treat all whites well in the presence of the Negroes, in order that the latter might not forget their position of racial inferiority. In this way the slave system dignified the white race as such, and this dignity was shared by the poorest whites as well as by the wealthy.[38]

The several classes which have now been noted were those distinguishable by social and economic criteria. There were three other groups in the state to be distinguished by their geographical origins, each of which possessed some political significance. These were the South Carolinians, the "Yankees," and the European immigrants.

South Carolinians had moved over into Georgia throughout the first half of the century. The economic

---

[38] For an elaborate argument to this effect, see B S. Green's preface to his translation of A. G. de Cassagnac, *History of the Working and Burgher Classes*. (Philadelphia, 1872). This preface is printed as a separate pamphlet, a copy of which is in possession of the Georgia Historical Society. *Cf.* Rowland, *Jefferson Davis*, II. 73, 74.

decadence of the former state, already referred to, had increased this tendency. They had been of all classes, planters with their slaves, poor whites from the Barrens, and merchants or professional men from the towns. They seem usually to have settled in Georgia in a region or town generally similar to that from which they came. Many of those living in Georgia in 1850 had been adults at the time of immigration, and therefore tended to maintain in Georgia the political attitude towards the slavery question and the Union which was peculiar to their old home. This was of some significance, for, as newspaper editors, lawyers, merchants and politicians, they helped to lead the southern-rights movement in Georgia towards the secessionist principles of South Carolina. It is impossible to estimate the numbers of this element in the state, but it was taken for granted at the time that there were "thousands of them."[39]

Meanwhile, an equally important immigration was reaching the state during the forties from the North. At that period, of course, the greater number of northerners emigrating to new country went west along their own parallels of latitude in search of land. A smaller number, however, saw in the cotton states, especially in Georgia, opportunities for merchants, tradespeople, and professional men. There were mechanics and engineers in the North, and they were needed for the new railroads and factories in Georgia. There were school teachers, both men and women in plenty, and these were needed for the new schools in Georgia. Finally, there were opportunities for trade which the shrewd and energetic Yankee thought he

[39] Savannah *Georgian,* September 17, 1849.

could exploit more effectively than could some of the natives. These were the opportunities that attracted most of the northerners, although a few purchased land, and others married heiresses to the same. Those who held land usually merged with the native planter class. But the bulk, coming for business or professional reasons, were apt to concentrate in the towns,[40] where this very fact in turn tended to preserve their northern characteristics and point of view. Some came as the representatives of business houses in the North. Others arrived with letters from such firms recommending their introduction to business opportunities or their employment as clerks. Some "came down as mere peddlers but later set up as storekeepers and merchants."[41] Hand in hand with these came the skilled mechanics. Even in the thirties, the Yankees had found opportunities in special occupations requiring training and skill. Olmsted notes the early appearance of New England fishermen off the coast, and by 1833 Maine lumbermen had found it profitable to work the pine districts.[42] Journeymen printers came down to work upon the presses in Savannah and perhaps elsewhere.[43] But the chief demand for northern mechanical skill arose in connection with the railroads and the new factories.

It was natural that few Georgians in the early forties had received any training as engineers, superintendents, or mechanics in railroad and cotton mill industries. Hence, during that decade, most of the

---

[40] Individual Yankees, however, established themselves even in the hill country. See C. Lanman, *Letters from the Alleghaney Mountains* (1849), p. 56.

[41] [A. B. Longstreet], *Letters from Georgia to Massachusetts*, pp. 20, 21.

[42] *Niles' Register*, XLVII. 55, September 27, 1834.

[43] Savannah *Georgian*, September 14, 1850.

Georgia factories employed superintendents and mechanics who had received their training back home in New England. In like manner, northerners were employed upon the railroads.[44] Occasionally northern capitalists came down to look after their investments in new factories, though this type was apt to desire to "get rich quick" and to retire—probably to the North.[45] At first a few factory operatives also arrived, but there was no need for them. Olmsted states that "New England factory girls were occasionally induced to come to the Georgia mills but soon left because of the degraded position of laborers."[46] The native poor whites could supply all the operatives desired.

Not a few Yankees came to the state to seek employment in educational work. The increasing prosperity towards the end of the fifth decade of the century led to efforts championed by churches and newspapers to reform the educational system.[47] It was a period of considerable interest in education, and opportunities for teaching in new schools increased. These opportunities were seized upon by northern teachers, who had received their training in states where the public school movement was already well under way. As was the case with the Yankee mechanics, they were attracted especially to the more progressive towns, where they were most in demand. Here New England schoolmasters or "schoolmarms" acted

[44] For contemporary notices of such employment, see the Milledgeville *Recorder*, February 25, 1850; Savannah *Republican*, March 25, and May 4, 1850; Augusta *Chronicle*, August 17, 1849; *Cf.* also, *De Bow's Review*, XI. 311; Hundley, *Social Relations in Our Southern States*, p. 118; Paine, *Six Years in a Georgia Prison*, p. 14; etc.

[45] *De Bow's Review*, VI. 293.

[46] *Journey in the Seaboard Slave States*, p. 536.

[47] The Georgia papers of the period, especially the Whig, are full of urgent appeals for educational reform. For the detailed educational history of the decade, see Jones, *Education in Georgia*, *passim*.

as tutors in the better families or taught in the "Female Colleges" and other schools of secondary grade.

How important an element were the Yankees in the Georgia towns, and what was their attitude towards the political problems of the period? Northern observers were inclined to claim all things for them. Parsons observed that "many if not most of the successful business and professional men in Georgia were from the North."[48] Olmsted went further and claimed that "the better class, which gives Georgia its reputation for prosperity is very largely composed and directed in enterprise by persons born in the free states. The number of these, proportionate to all the white population, is much greater than in any other Southern State."[49] Olmsted, of course, was thinking of industrial and mercantile prosperity rather than of the basic agricultural interests. Yet there is no question that industrial and trade prosperity was a most important factor in creating Georgia's excellent business reputation, and that the energy of northern men in these lines contributed largely to their success. There is southern as well as northern testimony to this effect. Hundley stated that the Yankees formed "no inconsiderable part of the southern middle classes," and he testified to their energy and ability.[50] The editor of one of the strongest southern-rights papers in Georgia granted that "most of the teachers who are able have come from the North."[51]

[48] *Tour among the Planters*, p. 26.
[49] *Journey in the Seaboard Slave States*, pp. 530, 536.
[50] Hundley, *op. cit.*, p. 104; "The older, steadier business men were Yankees" comments a Georgia observer; L. B. Wylie, *Memoirs of Judge Richard H. Clark*, p. 4.
[51] Milledgeville *Federal Union*, August 10, 1847.

Georgians, of course, would not have agreed with Olmsted's sweeping claim about the "better class" in the state, but the South Carolinians, who most disliked the Yankees, insisted that the chief business towns of Georgia were largely populated and controlled by them. In 1852, for instance, a Charleston gentleman traveling through the eastern part of the state found Augusta "nothing but a northern city on southern soil." Upon reaching Savannah, he found that here too "northern influence is very potent," though not quite so much so as in Augusta.[52] Georgians sometimes joined in this view. An up-country man even urged that trade be sent from there to Charleston rather than to Savannah, since the former town "was the only *Southern* city on the entire coast. Savannah and New Orleans are off-shoots from Yankeedom."[53] Columbus, the second chief manufacturing town, also had some Yankee residents, though there are no reports of such large numbers as in Savannah and Augusta. It is probably not without significance in this connection to recall that Columbus was never so inclined to compromise with the North during the slavery controversy as was Augusta. Northerners who lived in the latter city in the early fifties recall it as one where most of the stores and trades were handled by northern people. They rarely met native Georgians, save in the churches, where they came into formal contact with plantation people from the surrounding country.[54]

[52] *Incidents of a Journey from Abbeville, South Carolina, to Ocala Florida* (Edgefield, South Carolina, 1852), pp. 5, 11. A Georgia observer, looking back after fifty years, recalled no less than seventeen merchants of Savannah "and many others," who were Yankees. See L. B. Wylie, *Memoirs of Judge Richard H. Clark,* p. 4.

[53] Marietta (Ga.) *Cherokee Advocate,* in Savannah *Republican,* February 15, 1851.

[54] Mrs. R. H. (Julia) Woodward, letter to author, Guilford, Connecticut, September 10, 1923.

One activity of this group is of particular interest here; namely, the connection of northern men with the newspapers of Georgia. Three of the most important conservative Whig papers of the state, the Macon *Journal,* the Augusta *Chronicle,* and the Savannah *Republican,* had in 1850 editors of northern origin. Some minor papers, like the Macon *Citizen* and the Marietta *Helicon,* also had editors of this class. Men like Dr. Daniel Lee of the *Chronicle* and J. L. Locke of the *Republican* were especially influential. It may be of some significance that these journals were generally conservative during the political controversy with the North. On the other hand, several of the Democratic journals, notably the Milledgeville *Federal Union* and the Columbus *Times,* had editors of South Carolina origin, and it may be equally suggestive that these papers led in the southern-rights movement. So well placed in such positions, indeed, were the representatives of these two groups, that the Georgia press served as an arena in which Yankees and Carolinians did battle for their respective views. What was true of the press, moreover, was true in some measure of other urban institutions. The Georgia towns were the meeting ground of "Yankey-Land" and "Palmettodom."

The degree to which the presence of northern editors was of political significance would depend upon the degree to which northern men in Georgia preserved their original attitudes towards slavery and the Union. Georgians were divided in opinion on this point, some feeling that citizens from the North accepted entirely the local view on these subjects, and others suspecting that they always preserved "unsound" Yankee ideas. Hundley was of the opinion that the traders, having "set up in some permanent employment, then profess to be intensely pro-slavery," though they seldom own slaves unless acquired by marriage, preferring otherwise to hire. This is because "they cannot entirely overcome their anti-slavery prejudices, or else because they hope to return North."[55] There was probably some truth in this statement. On the other hand, it did not apply to that class of northerners who, coming to the state in their early youth, had had time to merge entirely their interests with those of their new home. Indeed, it was notorious that some of this type, like Judge Warner of Georgia and Governor Quitman of Mississippi, became, as proselytes often have done, veritable leaders of the extreme proslavery and prosouthern view.

The natives were more suspicious of the views of Yankee teachers, editors, and mechanics, than they were of the merchants. Mechanics were suspected because they had no such obvious business motives for defending slavery as had the last named class.[56] Indeed, this group was occasionally threatened with slave competition, as in the case of the printers already cited, and their environment was therefore not liable to render them more favorable to the institution. Some of these men certainly held abolitionist views through years of residence in Georgia towns and even confided as much to slave-holders who had become their trusted friends.[57] The same was true of some teachers, who naturally held to theoretical ideals more tenaciously than did the merchants, whose business was linked with that of the planters. This fact was recognized by Georgians, who sometimes felt that the presence of

[55] *Social Relations in Our Southern States*, p. 105.
[56] Olmsted, *Journey in the Seaboard Slave States*, pp. 511, 512.
[57] Paine, *Six Years in a Georgia Prison*, pp. 36-51.

even the able Yankee teachers was "unfortunate," since they were "not of our institutions and therefore cannot arouse the state to the cause of education."[58]

Distrust of northerners increased, of course, in proportion to the increase in southern-rights feeling concerning the slavery controversy. Those who took extreme southern views on this subject in the late forties became less friendly to the incoming Yankee traders in that period than had hitherto been the case.[59] In some cases, they even attempted to boycott the newcomers entirely.[60] At the height of the political controversy, all northern editors connected with Union party journals became the subjects of general distrust on the part of rival southern-rights papers. The *Federal Union* and Augusta *Constitutionalist* insisted that Lee should be forced to resign from the *Chronicle,* as a Yankee of antislavery and anti-state rights opinions. His publishers backed him in a formal statement, however, and his paper returned the compliment by pointing the finger of suspicion at the radical Carolinians associated with the southern-rights press. The Union party, as a general rule, rallied to the support of such members as were of northern origin, claiming for them complete allegiance to southern institutions and ideals.[61]

In like manner, of course, feeling against the North in general increased in proportion as the political storm grew. "Our southern friends often abuse and denounce the whole northern people as our enemies,"

---

[58] *Federal Union,* August 10, 1847.
[59] [A. B. Longstreet], *Letters from Georgia to Massachusetts,* p. 20.
[60] Savannah *News,* Nov. 11, 1850.
[61] See, *e.g.,* the letter of General Eli Warner to the Committee, February 14, 1851, *The Macon Union Celebration,* p. 15.

declared a Georgia planter in 1851.[62] This feeling in
Georgia, however, was confined largely to the small
group of extreme southern-rights men. There is
every indication that, save in times of intense excitement, the feeling in Georgia towns towards Yankees
was friendly, if not cordial. They were welcomed in
business, though not always in society.[63] The very
presence of so many able northern people in the cities
must have dispelled the more provincial forms of
prejudice, if these had existed in the beginning. The
correspondent of the Boston *Courier* in Savannah,
who had many suggestive observations to make, found
that there was "less sectional prejudice in Georgia
against the North than in any other truly southern
state."[64] Individual Yankees, as was noted, were even
able to argue abolitionist ideals with urban friends
without fear of denouncement.

Feeling was strong against abolitionsists, yet even
here moderation was sometimes practiced. In 1848,
for instance, a man and woman lecturing upon "mes-
merism" in Savannah were found talking to the Negroes, telling them that they worked too hard. The woman told the Negro women that "if she were in their
position, she would not bear another child," and the
like. It seemed a typical case of the abolitionist-on-
mission from the North and might have led to dire
consequences. They were simply ordered from the
county, however, no violence being offered. "Stern
measures" would be used only as a last resort.[65] In the

[62] *Ibid.*

[63] Letter of Mrs. Julia Woodward, September 10, 1923.

[64] Boston *Courier,* January 23, 1850. A decade later W. H. Russell, an
English observer, noted that hatred of the North was much greater in
South Carolina than in Georgia; W. H. Russell, *Pictures of Southern
Life, Social, Political and Military,* p. 11.

[65] Savannah *Georgian,* June 5, 1848.

country districts, of course, where ignorance was common, the probabilities of provincial prejudice against the Yankees was greater than it was in the towns.[66] The last group of whites that requires attention is the European immigrants. The total number of Europeans in Georgia was small, as compared with that in the northern states,[67] but they were concentrated to such an extent in the two mercantile towns of Savannah and Columbus as to have therein considerable political and economic importance.[68] The Germans, English, and Irish were all represented. Germans and Englishmen came for much the same motives as actuated the northerners,[69] while the Irish came to swell the numbers of the state's eleven thousand white "laborers." Some of the Irish worked in labor gangs in connection with the railroads and on the plantations as well as in the cities.[70]

The Europeans of the laboring class disliked the Negroes, or were at least jealous of them as possible competitors.[71] At the same time, they were usually devoted to the American government, having sought

[66] For testimony to this effect, see Paine, *op. cit.*, pp. 36-51.

[67] This, of course, was often ascribed by northerners to the immigrants' dislike for slavery. Southerners claimed it was due simply to the lack of industries. (*Hunt's Merchants' Magazine*, XXI. 498.) There is also the possibility that it was due to race feeling.

[68] One third of the white population of Savannah in 1850 was foreign born. This, of course, was a higher percentage than that of some northern ports. See Stone, "Some Problems in Southern Economic History," *American Historical Review*, XIII. 779-797.

[69] Thus an able German musician by the name of Brenner, who came to Augusta about 1849, began there the first manufacturing of pianos in the state. This attracted considerable attention. See Savannah *Republican*, Feb. 14, 1851.

[70] Phillips, *American Negro Slavery*, pp. 301, 302. The actual number of foreign born in the state in 1850 was given as 6452. Over one third of these were resident in Savannah; C. E. MacGill, "Immigration to the Southern States, 1783-1865," *The South in the Building of the Nation*, V. 600.

[71] Olmsted, *Journey in the Seaboard Slave States*, p. 512.

refuge under it from the depressing conditions obtaining in Ireland and Germany in the late forties. They were inclined, in 1850, therefore, to hold conservative views concerning the Union government and voted almost to a man with the Union party. In normal times the Irish belonged generally to the Democratic party and were associated in Savannah with the same phenomena of political turbulence as were connected with their countrymen in the northern ports. A "large portion" of the voters in Savannah were said to be Irishmen, and their allegiance to the Union party in 1850 was an important factor in carrying that city for the Union cause.[72]

Each of these social groups was to play its part in the political struggles of 1847-1852. The interests and attitudes of each group were in large measure determined by economic conditions, and these, in turn, determined the make-up and policies of the parties. Out of economic conditions, then, developed social groups, and out of social groups, political parties. The development of the parties from these underlying factors may now be considered.

[72] Columbus *Sentinel,* in the Natchez (Mississippi) *Courier,* December 6, 1850; Dr. R. D. Arnold to J. W. Forney, December 18, 1850, Arnold MSS. There was a similar situation and result in Columbus.

CHAPTER III

In the early days of the Federal Union a majority of Georgians were associated with the Republican party. This was the result of the frontier character of the greater part of the state. The power of Federalism was consequently slight, and the "Era of Good Feeling" was ushered in at an earlier period in Georgia than in most of the other states. As elsewhere, it was attended by the usual "bad feeling" between Republican factions, out of which grew the first definite division of the people into rival political parties.

It will be remembered that Middle Georgia was settled largely by Carolinians and Virginians, each of which groups preserved for some time its distinction from the other. This distinction was based upon the economic and cultural superiority of the Virginians, and it was sometimes heightened by their success in securing the better lands in the new country. Feelings of personal friendship, based upon social solidarity, prepared each of the groups for a projection of its differences into the political field. This projection did not depend for its realization upon the development of any distinct class consciousness or real economic issue, but merely upon personal rivalries, which would arouse one man's friends against another's.

The particular question which first brought out the latent antagonism seems to have been the political controversy precipitated by the Yazoo frauds connected with the state's western land claims. The bitter local fight against the fraud and speculation involved was led by the Virginia group, whose propertied interests rendered them conservative in financial matters, while the Carolinians were as a rule interested in defending the project.[1] Group lines were drawn more definitely as bitterness increased. Leaders appeared. Senator James Jackson, who led the attack upon the Yazoo cabal, was associated with two able politicians, George M. Troup and William H. Crawford, while the Carolinians were marshaled by that most redoubtable champion, "General" John Clark. A personal quarrel ensued in 1803 between Troup and Clark, which increased the bitterness between their partisans and well illustrates the rough and tumble personal character of the politics of the period.[2] By 1820 the two groups were fairly distinct throughout the state and had assumed as political appellations the names of these two champions. The "Troup Party" and the "Clark Party" struggled between that date and 1825 for the election of the legislature, the governor, hitherto, being chosen by that body. In 1825 the Clark group, displaying a relatively democratic viewpoint based upon the character of its supporters, placed the election of the governor in the hands of the people. The first election under this system showed clearly that the Troup party represented the planter interests of the coast and eastern Central Georgia, while the other represented those of the small farmers in the newer settlements in western Central Georgia and the Pine Barrens.[3]

[1] U. B. Phillips, "Georgia and State Rights," *American Historical Association, Annual Report,* 1901, II. 89-96, (hereinafter cited as *Georgia and State Rights*). J. E. D. Shipp, *Life and Times of Wm. H. Crawford* (Americus, Georgia, 1909), p. 46.

[2] John Clark, *Considerations on the Principles of William H. Crawford* (Augusta, 1819), pp. 1-6; Andrews, *Reminiscences,* p. 61.

[3] Phillips, *op. cit.,* pp. 89-96.

Two interesting exceptions to this rule appeared. In the Pine Barrens a tier of three counties, Laurens, Tattnall, and Montgomery, went for Troup, apparently because of the accident that this was Troup's home country,—a matter of some weight in personal politics.[4] On the other hand, a tier of counties running athwart Central Georgia remained consistent supporters of the Clark faction, even after they were completely merged in the Cotton Belt. These exceptional areas are of interest, because they persisted throughout the entire length of ante-bellum history and were quite noticeable in the 1850 period. There seems to have been no economic basis for this phenomenon,[5] which must therefore be attributed to personal origin, though leading to the formation of habits that persisted through periods of economic and political crisis.[6]

With the exception of these areas, the several sections of the state aligned themselves politically, from this time on, in groups that generally had economic and social bases. That lines were not always sharply drawn was due to three circumstances. The first was the fact that in the early days social distinctions between farmer and planter were not as marked as in the later period of concentrated plantation capital and resultant social stratification. The second was the circumstance that in the early period there were few issues other than the personal to heighten political distinctions. The third, of particular concern here, was the fact that the constitutional issue concerning the respective rights of the federal and state governments

---

[4] Phillips, *op cit.* pp. 104, 105.

[5] See White, *Georgia Statistics,* pp. 116, 117, 332, 333, 363, 422, 534, 535, etc.; Olmsted, *The Cotton Kingdom,* II. 386-391; Savannah, *Georgian,* September 13, 1849.

[6] See Maps Nos. 5, 6, and 7, pp. 109, 171, 320.

never entirely adapted itself to the political divisions based upon economic foundations. Whenever it arose, it tended to split the two parties and led to a regrouping of political forces. As a result of these several circumstances, the story of Georgia politics between 1830 and 1850 was often so void of real issues as to seem meaningless, and at other times was so confused as to defy analysis.

The first serious constitutional issue arose in the late twenties, in connection with the question of Indian lands in the state. The position taken by Governor Troup against the Federal government, in his effort to seize these lands, tended to identify his party with the state-rights view, while in opposition the Clark party defended the authority of the Union. Thus early, the one became the Troup-State-Rights party and the other the Clark-Union party.[7] In a search for a constitutional theory justifying the state's opposition to the Federal government, the former was inclined to hold that sovereignty was vested in the people of the states or in the states themselves, while the latter held that the rights of the state should be emphasized only within the limits of the supreme law of the Federal Constitution.[8]

Late in the twenties, the constitutional issue was intensified by the development of southern opposition to the new protective tariffs and by the dramatic opposition of South Carolina to that legislation. The tariff of 1828 led to serious protest in Georgia, as in other states, and the legislature declared it unconstitutional and suggested the calling of a "Southern Con-

[7] Miller, *Bench and Bar of Georgia*, I. 261. These names were not firmly fixed, however, until after 1833.

[8] Phillips, *op. cit.*, p. 123.

vention" to devise "a suitable mode of resistance."[9] The election of Jackson, a southern man trusted by both Georgia parties upon the tariff and the Indian questions, quieted agitation in Georgia from 1828 to 1832. In the latter year, the approach of the crisis between South Carolina and the Federal government again involved Georgia in the controversy. The question which now faced the people was not the question of the protective tariff, for to this there was general opposition, but the question of the constitutional remedy. Would Georgia support South Carolina in the nullification of the Federal statute?

Excitement became intense in the state, as Carolina nullified, and Jackson threatened. State-rights men demanded a state convention to determine upon necessary action; this demand was furthered by party caucuses, debated, and finally approved in the legislature. The action of the convention, however, was to be submitted to the people and to the legislature itself.[10] The public debate, which preceded and followed the choice of the delegates, brought out the forces at work in favor of both the Union and nullification positions. As these forces were analogous to those in operation in 1850, and as this analogy was consciously realized in the later period, it is well to note it here.[11]

The outstanding force favoring nullification was the leadership and influence of South Carolina. Her politicians were active in sending literature and speakers across the river as apostles of the nullification creed. Efforts were made to create a strong feeling

---

[9] H. V. Ames, State Documents on Federal Relations, pp. 153, 154.

[10] Miller, Bench and Bar, II. 322.

[11] For illustrations of contemporary comparisons of the two periods, see The Macon Union Celebration (February 22, 1851), pp. 12, 19, 25, 41, 44, etc.

of fraternity between the two states upon this common doctrine.[12] Some Georgians became convinced that the economic future as well as the sovereign rights of their state were threatened by the tyrannical and unconstitutional attempt to thrust a ruinous protective tariff upon them. Such men became willing disciples of the Charleston leaders. They condemned the tariff, warned of federal usurpation, and villified the Union men as "old federalists," "modern consolidationists," and "submissionists" to northern oppression.[13] On the other hand, they denied indignantly that they were "agitators," "traitors," or "disunionists." They loved the Union, but they loved Georgia more. In addition to urging the support of courageous Carolina, they advocated economic pressure against the North. If the Yankees would tax them through the tariff, then let Georgia tax the Yankees' goods when they were offered in the state for sale.[14]

If the tariff policy was persisted in, the nullifiers declared, Georgia might not only support the sister state but should herself nullify the tariff law. Had she not already nullified the decision of the federal court in the case of the Indian controversy? Nullification was, as Calhoun held, a purely constitutional remedy which would save rather than destroy the Union. As a program of action looking in this direction, the state convention should call or coöperate with a general southern convention to decide upon joint southern action.

[12] Augusta *Chronicle*, March 7, 1832; Macon *Georgia Messenger*, March 10, 1832, etc., quoted in E. M. Coulter, "The Nullification Movement in Georgia," *Georgia Historical Quarterly*, V. No. 1, p. 11.

[13] *Proceedings of the States' Rights Party Convention*, November 13, 1833, (Milledgeville, 1833), *passim*.

[14] David Christy, *Cotton is King*, p. 93 (Cincinnati, 1855). It is possible that Christy confuses this matter of dating the first demand for taxing northern goods.

On the other hand, even as early as 1833, the very fact that South Carolina led the state-rights movement was in itself calculated to defeat it. It has been pointed out in a previous chapter that there had long been feeling between Georgia and Carolina based upon economic and social rivalry. This had not been improved by the political rivalry between Crawford and Calhoun and by the latter's unfriendly attitude toward Georgia's Indian policy. Georgia's pride was, therefore, incensed at the attempt of South Carolina to "lead her by the nose" towards any political policy whatsoever. This feeling was so strong that it would have been wiser had the Carolinians concealed to some extent their missionary efforts on behalf of nullification. In addition to the dislike for "Palmettodom," there existed in the minds of most Georgians a sincere and traditional love for the "Union of the Fathers," which was a force of considerable potency in preventing the average man from finally committing himself to an anti-Union policy. Moreover, the average farmer was not conscious of direct injury from the tariff. As it happened, the political crisis came in a period of agricultural expansion in the western part of Georgia, and there were anticipations of prosperity that prevented great economic discontent and brought aversion for any disturbance that might possibly lead to civil war.[15] In addition to this, many looked to Jackson for sympathy in the Indian difficulties and were anxious, for this reason, not to break with the administration. In other words, the economic forces were against a radical state-rights stand in 1833.

[15] R. D. Arnold, *Oration Delivered to the Union and Southern Rights Association of Chatham County*, July 4, 1835, pp. 1-5.

Those who for all these reasons opposed nullification attacked its supporters as "traitors," "agitators," and "disunionists." The latter were accused of wishing to make the state into a "mere dependency of Palmettodom." The tariff was bad, declared the Union men, but it could be remedied within the Union and by constitutional means. Calhoun's theory of an indivisible sovereignty resting in the state was a mere "metaphysical entity" of his own creation. Sovereignty, as Madison had held, was divided between the state and the Federal governments, and nullification was not a power reserved to the state.[16] If nullification was not a constitutional remedy, any attempt to apply it was sheer revolution. Union men would, therefore, shun it until such a desperate time as might find them ready for revolution.[17] The Union men were not "submissionists," but as good southerners as any others in the community. Indeed, in their effort to save the state from the Carolina heresy, they were better southerners than their opponents. All good men and true were urged to lay aside old party lines and stand by the state and the nation.

As the debate preceding and following the nullification convention continued, it became increasingly apparent that the nullifiers had thundered out of all proportion to their numbers.[18] The radicals began to tone down as the contest proceeded. Dislike for South Carolina, love for the Union, economic prosperity and consequent fear of civil disturbance—all the forces

[16] *Ibid.*, Arnold would have been interested in the recent works of Laski and others denying the indivisibility of sovereignty.

[17] This was analogous to the position taken by Georgia conservatives in 1851, that "the right of secession" was a revolutionary, not a constitutional one.

[18] Miller, *Bench and Bar*, I. 40, II. 322; Coulter, *op. cit.*, p. 29; Phillips, *Georgia and State Rights*, pp. 130-132.

mentioned disinclined the masses in Georgia to radical political expedients. Then a compromise program was adopted at the national capital, which made certain the victory of the conservative forces in the home state.

The nullification controversy was analogous in many ways to the slavery controversy of 1850. It was more than a mere analogy, however. It was, to some extent, related to the later crisis as cause to effect. To begin with, it increased the political distrust of South Carolina and the fear that this state wished to dominate her neighbor. This feeling became so common that it even affected the attitude of the Georgia delegation in Congress towards that of South Carolina. "Georgia came," wrote General James Hamilton to Langdon Cheves nearly twenty years later, "to dislike us . . . more than the people of Massachusetts. When in Congress I was often grieved and sometimes amused by this jealousy."[19] This attitude was to be a potent force in Georgia when South Carolina once again essayed southern leadership.

In addition to this, the necessity for defending the Union acted as a stimulus to Union feeling in Georgia. Seventeen years later, when faced with a similar necessity, many old Union men recalled with pride their unswerving attachment to the Union in the days of 1833. The old battles were recalled, and the old tradition of standing by the Union was effectively invoked once more.[20] It is possible, to be sure, that with some Georgians the reverse of this became true; that is, that some ceased at this time to hold the same reverence for a Union, whose value, having been calculated once, might again be questioned. That this was not so true

[19] Charleston *Courier,* in the Savannah *Republican,* January 16, 1851.
[20] For such sentiments, see the letters in the *Macon Union Celebration,* pp. 12, 19, 25, etc.

as might logically have been the case was due to a peculiar political shift of many of the southern-rights men of 1833, which led them into the Union party during the next decade.

The effect of the constitutional controversy upon the political parties was, as has been suggested, to force new alignments and consequent political confusion. The issue did not fit itself perfectly to the old partisan patterns. It is true that the Troup party, with something of a state-rights tradition inherited from the Indian episode, tended more to favor nullification, while the Clark party tended to stand by the Union. This party saw in Jackson the especial champion of its small farmer interests and democratic principles and was particularly loath to break with him over other issues. They were, moreover, the class in Georgia which had least in common, socially or economically, with the planter-aristocrats leading the South Carolina movement. Nevertheless, a few old Clark men did become nullificationists and joined the State-Rights party. On the other hand, the more conservative Troup men, who opposed nullification, came to coöperate with the bulk of the old Clark party against that doctrine. The factors causing this last shift were, apart from general conservatism, the political quarrel which had been going on between Calhoun and the Troup leader, Crawford, during the twenties and the failure of Calhoun to support Troup's Indian policy.[21] The transitional stage in this realignment was well indicated by the use for some time of the appellations, "Troup-Union" and "Clark-Union" parties.[22]

[21] J. A. Turner, "William C. Dawson," in *The Plantation*, I. No. 1, p. 80, (1860).

[22] Phillips, *Georgia and State Rights*, p. 132.

So far as the majority of the Union party of the later thirties was made up of the old Clark men, it was quite natural that this party should have continued to be preëminently the party of the smaller farmers, concentrated in "Cherokee," western Central Georgia, and in parts of the Pine Barrens. To the extent that the bulk of the State-Rights party was composed of old Troup men, its strength was necessarily greatest in the plantation areas of Central and Coastal Georgia. These last two regions had at first been politically as well as socially distinct, for the coastal planters represented the oldest aristocracy in the state. The early sectionalism between the coast and the interior disappeared gradually, however, as wealth increased in Central Georgia and as transportation between the two areas across the Pine Barrens improved. Economic and social solidarity led to political solidarity.

The chief political phenomenon of the late thirties was the alignment of the Union and State-Rights parties with the existing national organizations. It was to be expected, *a priori,* that the Clark-Union party of small farmers would find itself in sympathy with the Jacksonian Democracy. Their economic status and democratic ideals naturally tended, other things being equal, to bring a union with the administration group. In other states, notably in North Carolina, special circumstances nullified this economic tendency, but in Georgia the force of local circumstances actually furthered it. The pioneers who settled Upper Georgia were, on the one hand, indebted to Jackson for his friendly attitude concerning the Indian matter and, on the other, were a rugged and self-reliant type, most suspicious of the South Carolina planter aristocracy and opposed to South Carolina leadership in Georgia political affairs. When the election of 1840 came, therefore, it found the Georgia Union men supporting the national Democrats, and the latter name began to be used in the state at about this time.

Meanwhile, the local State-Rights party had followed its Carolina leader, John C. Calhoun, into a political alliance with the National Republicans of the North. The alliance of southern anti-tariff and state-rights men with northern pro-tariff nationalists was as anomalous as anything in American party history and was based largely upon the expediency of common opposition to the Jackson administration. This "Whig" party was, of course, an essentially unstable combination, whose equilibrium could be maintained only so long as the two elements maintained an equal influence. When the nomination of Harrison in 1840 showed the National Republicans in control under Clay's leadership, Calhoun called upon the state-rights Carolinians to leave the organization. The more moderate nationalism of Van Buren having meanwhile succeeded the militant policy of Jackson in the Democracy, it was possible for the Calhoun men in South Carolina to return, prodigal-like, to their original political home. They were received there with rejoicing by the Democratic fathers, who bestowed upon them such political fatted calves as aroused some jealousy among the more faithful of the brethren. The return of the Calhoun-ites was hastened by the growth of antislavery feeling among the northern Whigs, as well as by the tariff and nationalistic policies of the latter. It was also aided at home by the gradual disappearance of the nullification issue and a consequent reunion of the

Union and nullification parties in Calhoun's own state.[23]

The question in Georgia was whether this movement back to the Democracy would carry with it most of the local Whigs. The situation was complicated when the presidential campaign of 1840 necessitated action one way or the other. Several circumstances had arisen which made it theoretically improbable that the bulk of the Georgia Whigs would leave the party. They were probably becoming more and more concerned with the practical advantages of their new political alliance. The Georgia leaders, unlike the more ambitious Calhoun, began to see a real place for themselves in the national organization. The fact that the outstanding Georgia Whig politician of the period, John McPherson Berrien, became the strong ally of the northern Whigs at the very time that Calhoun had to abandon them is probably illustrative of this opportunism. It was true, to be sure, that Clay was committing the Whig party to the tariff and to the nationalism of the old National Republicans. Interesting manufacturing possibilities, however, were opening up before the bourgeoisie of the Black Belt, to which group the majority of the Troup state-rights Whig party leaders belonged. They, therefore, began to be more favorable to moderate protective principles for the same reason that Calhoun himself had favored them some twenty years before; that is, because of the hope that they might share in their benefits. It was also true that the northern Whigs were beginning to display suspiciously antislavery tendencies, but the planter class, as has been observed, were usually not

[23] A. C. Cole, *The Whig Party in the South,* pp. 28-30, 44-49; E. M. Carroll, *Origins of the Whig Party,* chapter v. *passim.*

anxious to agitate this issue. As for the nationalism of the northern allies, this was probably not so objectionable in 1840 as it had been in 1835, since the nullification question had, meanwhile, apparently become a dead issue. All of these considerations would seem sufficient, *a priori,* to explain what actually did finally occur; that is, that the majority of the Georgia Whigs were able to continue the political alliance with the northern party, though it was an alliance which was always of an inherently unstable character.[24] So surely as a real issue like the slavery question should arise, so surely would this alliance be threatened with destruction.

Nevertheless, the return of Calhoun from the dry husks of Whiggery was not entirely without influence in Georgia. It was logically impossible for the more extreme men of the old State-Rights party to remain within the Whig camp after its control had passed into the hands of the Clay nationalists. It was also highly objectionable for the more extreme proslavery men to remain in alliance with a northern party already so tainted with antislavery associations. It was this last objection which was most emphasized by the malcontent Georgia Whigs, and this, the first appearance in Georgia internal politics of slavery as a major issue,

---

[24] For contemporary opinion in Georgia on this development, see Johnston and Browne, *Alexander H. Stephens,* p. 140; for a description of the national background see Cole, *op. cit.,* pp. 48-51. Phillips is of the opinion that the Whig leaders stayed with their party with the "half conceived idea" of dominating it for southern interests, *(op. cit.,* p. 148.) while Stephens, looking back after nearly thirty years, says that as a State-Rights man in 1840 he disliked both Harrison and Van Buren, but his objection to the northern principles of the former were outweighed by his objections to the financial principles of the latter. It is possible that some such a view was in the minds of many of the Georgia Whigs, rather than such a rational analysis as has been given above. Yet this would not necessarily invalidate that analysis.

was ominous of the coming storm.[25] A number of Whig leaders who held these views, Colquitt, H. M. Mc-Allister, Haralson, Cooper, Chappel, and others, bolted to the Democratic party after the nomination of Harrison and proceeded to appeal energetically to the mass of Whig voters to do likewise. The Whigs, they claimed, were moving under northern influence towards "consolidation" and "federalism." They were tainted with protectionism and antislavery principles and were therefore essentially "unsound" upon all the old principles of the true southern Whig party. The Democrats, now that Jackson was out, were more to be trusted than the changing Whigs.[26]

It is difficult to say how many state-rights Whigs bolted the party in answer to this appeal. Only a close study of the elections between about 1836 and 1842 would reveal this with even approximate accuracy, and this hardly falls within the plan of the present study. The victory of the Whig party in Georgia in the national election of 1840 would seem to indicate that its losses in the state had not been very extensive. This evidence is not conclusive, however, because of the fact that there was at the time a temporary swing of the Democratic farmers to the "Tippecanoe" ranks. Whig victories in the state elections in 1843 and 1845, however, do show that the number of state-rights Whigs who deserted in 1840 must have been small.

The lifting of the smoke of battle after the 1840 campaign, then, again revealed new alignments and

[25] Slavery, of course, had been a matter of controversy in the colonial period.

[26] H. M. McAllister, *Address to the Democratic-Republican Convention of Georgia*, Milledgeville, July 4, 1840. (Milledgeville, 1840); W. F. Colquitt, *Circular to the States Rights Party of Georgia*, (Milledgeville, 1840); J. A. Turner, *op. cit.*, pp. 72-77, gives an able résumé of this story, written in 1860.

new elements in the two parties. These remained substantially the same from this time until the political struggle of 1850 again transcended old party lines.

Within the Democratic party were now two fairly distinct, though temporarily harmonious, elements. The first was the old Clark-Union party group, distributed throughout Georgia, but concentrated as before in the Cherokee section and weakest in the coastal area. These men always had been and usually remained Democratic, pro-Union voters. In the Cherokee section, as has been previously observed, they had little concern in slave-holding interests and probably less intense racial consciousness than that obtaining in the Pine Barrens area. The second element was that of the one-time state-rights Whigs, led by Colquitt and McAllister, who always had been and usually remained consistent state-rights and proslavery voters. Subsequent events showed that this element was strongest along the lower Savannah on the South Carolina border, in the Democratic belt in Central Georgia, in certain towns where the Carolina influence was strong, (notably Columbus and Savannah), and in parts of the Pine Barrens.

The presence in the old Union party of these "Calhoun Democrats," as they came to be called, led to concessions on the part of that party to the state-rights views and leaders. Colquitt was sent to the Senate, McAllister and McDonald were both nominated for the governorship. The Calhounites' persistence in their principles created some friction, but also brought results. One Union Democrat complained afterwards that they "continued to maintain their state-rights principles on all occasions and at the expense of the feelings of the old Union element."[27] Some Union men were influenced by this propaganda, which was especially effective within the party so soon as sectional issues again became acute about 1848. As a result, there were notable conversions of old Union Democrat leaders, such as ex-Governor Wilson Lumpkin and Governor George W. Towns, to the particularist creed. That the bulk of the Democrats had not been converted to extreme "Calhounism" by 1850, is indicated by the elections of that year. Yet it is also true that the bulk of the party was more sensitive to questions of state-rights and sectional interest in general at this time than would have been the case fifteen years before. This is shown in the election of 1851, when only about one fifth of the party maintained its originally strong Union position. This change in party feeling may be ascribed both to the intensification of the issue that year and to the "boring from within" by Calhoun Democrats, a process which by that time had been going on for more than a decade.

The extent to which this "boring from within" had been carried by the Calhounites was not fully realized by the old Union Democrats until the crisis of 1850 made it obvious for the first time. Then there was much indignation in the old Clark camp, and regret was frequently expressed that the party had ever admitted the old state-rights Whig element to membership. "As a Clark man," wrote John B. Lamar at this time, "as a Union man in 1833, and ever since as a

[27] John H. Lumpkin, letter dated "Rome, April 27, 1851," in the Savannah *Republican*, May 5, 1851. He regrets that "his old uncle, Governor Lumpkin, and other old Union men have accepted the states' rights view."

Democrat I have been associated with this party. . . Its stern opposition to the dis-union of a former day commended it to the favor of the people of the state." But the disunionists of 1833, "having failed to accomplish their baneful purpose over the heads of the Union men, have resorted to the more subtle policy of winning our confidence, insinuating themselves among us . . . only to betray us. We believed and accepted them. Too bad! Now from within the Democratic party they shout their old Whig-Nullification cries of 1833."[28]

The Whigs, meanwhile, retained after 1840 the majority of the old State-Rights party of the plantation areas (as was shown by the elections of the next few years) save for the few extremists who had gone over to trouble the Democrats. This very loss, while not sufficient to affect seriously the voting strength of the party, did purge it of its radical leadership and thus facilitated its progress towards a conservative position upon constitutional and sectional issues. The fact that the Whig party of Georgia retained in 1840 a greater majority of the old state-rights element than the same party succeeded in holding in the neighboring states has led to the suggestion, to be sure, that the Georgia Whigs also retained a greater degree of the particularist feeling than did their brethren in the other states.[29] There seems to be little evidence substantiating this view and much that would uphold an opposing thesis. It is safe to say that the Georgia Whigs became as strongly attached to

[28] J. B. Lamar, February 27, 1851, to the Committee, *The Macon Union Celebration*, p. 25.
[29] R. R. Russel, *Economic Aspects of Southern Sectionalism, 1840-1861*, pp. 73, 75, 76.

Union principles as did their political brethren in other parts of the Lower South.[30]

There was, to be sure, a little group of Whigs in Georgia who sided with the Calhoun Democrats in 1850 in urging radical state action, but this group was so small as to be politically insignificant in the struggle of that year. It was only as an omen of what was to come that this element was of interest at that time. The agitation of the fifties had to intensify greatly the sectional controversy before the bulk of the Georgia Whigs could realize that they too must swing to the party that Calhoun and Colquitt had joined in 1840, and to which a few Whigs like Berrien and Smythe went over in 1850.

As the Whigs inclined more and more towards nationalism as a result of all the circumstances noted, and the Democrats inclined more and more towards particularism as a result of the influence of the Calhounites, it began to look as if each party had just reversed its stand of nullification days. By 1846 it was the Whig party that was talking "federalism" and "protection," while the Democratic party was more apt to declare the "sovereign rights" of Georgia. The old party names of "State-Rights" and "Union" had not merely lost meaning, they had become essentially

[30] Russel cites as evidence of what he considers the state-rights attitude of the Georgia Whigs the fact that they failed, while in control of the state convention of 1850, to deny formally the constitutionality of secession. As a matter of fact, the Georgia Whigs did right strenuously deny the constitutionality of secession only a few months after the state convention met, when the state campaign of 1851 first made the "right of secession" a paramount issue. See, e.g., Savannah *Republican,* May 25, 26 and 27; July 25, September 6, 1851. There could hardly have been a paper in the lower South more strenuously opposed to the state-rights dogma in 1850 than the Augusta *Chronicle,* one of the most influential of the Georgia Whig papers, whose editor declared that a state could no more secede from the Union than could a county from a state. Governor Towns estimated in 1850 that "19-20ths of the old state-rights group are submissionists," Towns to Seabrook, September 25, 1850, Seabrook MSS.

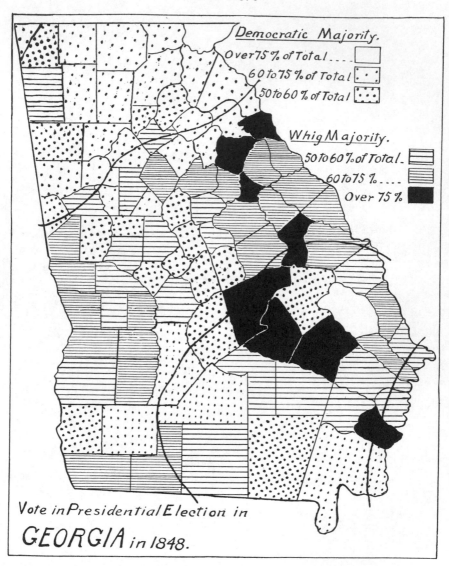

Vote in Presidential Election in
GEORGIA in 1848.

Reproduced, by permission, from map in U. B. Phillip's *Georgia and State Rights.*

false and misleading. Each party, of course, was quick to see the change which had come over the other and was loud in its condemnation of its opponent's inconsistency, the while it ignored its own. The reversal of attitudes involved was, indeed, a curious and remarkable one, and, coming as it did within the lifetime of one generation of leaders, it laid these gentlemen open constantly to the charge of inconsistency. Their past utterances, naturally embarrassing, were ever at the beck and call of their enemies, and the easiest defence was to return the compliment in kind. Charges and counter-charges were complicated by the fact that each party contained within itself a minority element that had maintained consistency; namely, the Union-Democrats and the small group of state-rights Whigs, and these minorities voiced from within the parties the same criticisms that the opposition hurled from without.[31]

Despite all these conflicting elements within the parties and the shifts which led to them, the economic basis of the two groups remained much the same in 1844 as it had been in 1834. The Democratic party, like the old Clark-Union party, had the support of the poorer whites. The Whig, like the old Troup party, was the planters' party and strongest in Coastal and Central Georgia in the plantation areas. In other words, the constitutional problem which has been described was not the determining issue in the formation or development of the parties, but a temporary question which realigned minorities rather than the bulk of the one party or the other. In any period of con-

[31] For examples of these confused charges of inconsistency see *e.g.*, Savannah *Georgian*, May 23, 1848; Savannah *Republican*, May 25, 1848; J. B. Lamar, February 27, 1851, to the Committee, *The Macon Union Celebration*, p. 25.

stitutional crisis, however, such a realignment of a
minority of one party with the other might be the determining factor in an outcome of both economic and
political significance. This was especially apt to be
true of a state like Georgia, in which the two parties
were of about equal strength in normal years.

That the bulk of the two parties were distributed
in the areas noted is clearly shown in the results of the
elections between 1844 and 1849;[32] that within these
areas they represented the classes stated is amply
demonstrated by contemporary recognition. It is true
that the Georgia papers were not as extreme in their
statements on this subject as were some in the Gulf
states, but it was sometimes asserted that the majority
of the planters were Whigs and the poorer farmers
usually Democrats. While the Montgomery *Alabama
Journal* declared that the Whigs owned seven eights
of the slaves in the South,[33] the Columbus (Georgia)
Times modestly observed that "the Whigs of Georgia,
it is believed, hold more slaves than the Democrats."
Again it remarked: "the Whigs of Georgia have the
property . . ."[34] The *Times* was a Democratic
journal and may have wished to minimize such statements, lest they be used to prove the Whigs "sound"
upon slavery interests; hence its "confession," as a
Whig journal termed it, was rather significant.[35] Yet
Whig statements were also modest in their estimates,
one declaring simply that they owned "as many
negroes" as the Democrats.[36]

[32] See maps in Cole, *The Whig Party in the South.*

[33] September 2, 1850.

[34] Columbus *Times,* July 13 and 27, 1849; see also the *Federal Union,*
October 30, 1849.

[35] Augusta *Chronicle,* July 20, 1849.

[36] Savannah *Republican,* June 23, 1849.

On the other hand, Whig journals in Georgia pointed with scorn to the fact that the poorest and most ignorant whites were the mainstay of the Democracy. The belief that economic improvement and education would make Whigs out of Democrats was one motive behind the Whig clamor for educational improvement. The Whigs cannot triumph, it was declared, until "education dispells the darkness from the sequestered regions, where common schools, churches, newspapers and postoffices are far between. In these is the home of unadulterated Democracy in Georgia."[37] A northern Whig editor held the same opinion, claiming that the greater number of Georgia Democrats were the "corn-crackers" and "the inhabitants of the uncultivated portions."[38] During the political struggle of 1850, the Whigs constantly insisted that the majority of the Democrats, who were associated with the southern-rights movement, were "people of no consequence."

In answer to this charge, the Democrats made a reply which should be noted. While being proud of their association with the good common people, they hastened to point out what has been stated in a previous chapter; namely, that there were many individual Democrats of wealth and influence. In their effort to show this, indeed, they succeeded in proving almost too much; that is, that most of their own leaders were wealthy men like the Whigs. They were usually planters, or professional men associated with planters.[39]

---

[37] Augusta *Chronicle*, July 21, 1849. For proof of the truth of this statement, *cf.* maps showing distribution of (1) illiteracy and (2) the parties, pp. 24 and 109.

[38] Oneida (N. Y.) *Herald*, in the *Federal Union*, October 30, 1849.

[39] The list includes such leaders as the Cobbs, Colquitt, McAllister, Towns, McDonald, Chappell, Judge Andrews, Judge Warner (of northern origin), W. C. Daniell, R. D. Arnold, the editors of the *Federal Union* and the Savannah *Georgian*, etc. Joseph E. Brown was an exception, he having come from the small farmer class.

Their presence in the Democratic party can be ascribed to political aspirations, to honest liberalism, and to the state-rights issue. This last had brought in the small group of planters led by McAllister and Colquitt, who belonged to the type of planter Democrats then dominant in South Carolina. Thus McAllister, the coastal rice planter, although a leader of the Democrats, actually represented the most exclusive social aristocracy in the state. Howell Cobb, on the other hand, represented a type of Democratic planter who merged political aspirations with an apparently genuine sympathy for the poorer farming classes.

The Democrats, of course, always claimed that they represented the good common people. In the early thirties the Clark party had shown in its political program a real desire to democratize the state's government. When, for instance, it secured control of the convention called in 1833 to amend the constitution, its members voted in that body for an amendment providing the "white basis," rather than the "federal ratio" basis, for representation in the state legislature. This was a move then in demand in the southern states by the poorer whites, who desired to take from the planter class its large representation based upon the slave population in the plantation areas. The Whigs opposed it on the specious ground that it was an attack upon slavery and one that would tempt the national government also to abandon the "federal ratio," to the detriment of all southern representation in Congress. Upon being submitted to a referendum, it was defeated, the Whigs claiming that "fully 10,000 Democrats" joined them in opposing the measure.[40] The

---

[40] Augusta *Chronicle*, April 12, 1849; for the "white basis" issue in the state constitutional conventions, see *Journal of a General Convention of the State of Georgia, 1833,* p. 22; *Journal of the Convention to Re-*

Clark party did, however, succeed in putting the election of the governor in the hands of the people and in establishing manhood suffrage for the whites.

In the forties, the Democrats continued to declare themselves the peoples' party, but there was little evidence of serious effort towards further political reform. The demand for the white basis of representation was not often raised in the latter part of the decade. A number of interesting and relatively radical changes were sometimes advocated by Democrats, but no serious effort was made to secure them. Some, for instance, desired the popular election of judges and of the national president. The Athens *Banner,* an energetic Democratic journal, even suggested the abolition of the state senate, on the ground that it was an undemocratic feature of the machinery of legislation.[41]

There was a continuous exchange of general charges between the two parties concerning their relatively democratic and conservative positions. An interesting illustration of this occurred in connection with the local reaction to the French Revolution of 1848. The association of Louis Blanc and the socialists with this movement led northern Whig papers to condemn it, the Newport (Rhode Island) *News,* for instance, declaring that Louis Phillipe had been overthrown for "slight and transient causes" by the "worst

duce and Equalize the Representation of the General Assembly of the State of Georgia, 1839, p. 44. While the convention of '33 passed the "white basis" resolution, 126 to 122, it was overwhelmingly defeated when brought up again in that of '39, by a vote of 192 to 83; *i.e.,* the Democracy had abandoned it by the end of the decade. For interesting comment on the struggle over this issue in the convention see J. Livingston, "Judge Nisbet of the Supreme Court of Georgia," *Biographical Sketches of Eminent American Lawyers,* Pt. IV, 548-558. The "white basis" demand emanated from Upper Georgia and the poorer white counties in other sections. This situation was analogous to that obtaining in Virginia and other southern states.

[41] Augusta *Chronicle,* July 21, 1849.

kind of radicalism—rank Dorrism."[42] The Georgia Whig press also found little to sympathize with in the revolution. The Democratic papers, however, eulogized it as a splendid republican achievement. The Savannah *Georgian* agreed with the Philadelphia *Pennsylvanian* that "Human rights and Whiggery— Dorrism and despotism—are extreme opposites as are the poles."[43] Democratic journals advocated the theoretical right of revolution, while the Whigs condemned this view, as making for dangerous radicalism.

One feels, however, that he is here dealing with a useful tradition rather than with an issue. The Democratic party of necessity cherished this tradition in appealing to its mass of small farmer supporters and often used it effectively against the Whigs. Yet its own leadership, as has been noted, had come largely into the hands of the well-to-do class, which had no intention in the late forties of any radical reforms. The Whigs simply had to avoid any affront to this tradition, lest it be used by the Democrats against them. Occasionally a particularly courageous Whig leader would openly challenge it. "The Terrible Toombs," usually more of a fighter than a philosopher, was strongly criticised during the bitter campaign of 1851 for his wealth and apparent aristocracy. The people of Elbert County, for instance, condemned his display of horses and servants as he campaigned the country. In reply, he admitted that he made more than five thousand dollars a year in that county alone.

---

[42] A reference to the "Dorr Rebellion" in Rhode Island for democratic political reforms. There is an obvious analogy between the way in which the Whig and Democratic papers reacted to this Revolution of 1848 and the manner in which Federalist and Republican ones had reacted to that of 1789-1800.

[43] *Georgian,* May 7, 1849.

"Who would say he had not earned it? He had a right to spend it as he chose. Perish such demagoguery— such senseless stuff!"[44] Toombs has also been credited with the remark, "We are the gentlemen," made in reference to the southern planter class.[45] Georgia planters, however, were usually careful not to display in political circles such notions of aristocracy as they might possess.

Indeed, the Whig planters never abandoned the claim that they themselves were the heirs of the democratic tradition. This had been a useful claim in the "log cabin" campaign of 1840 in Georgia and elsewhere. They even accused the Democrats of the taint of aristocracy whenever the latter were careless enough to lay themselves open to such a charge. Democrats were accustomed, for instance, to claim that the worst aristocracy in the state was that of the rice planters of the old conservative seaboard. Yet, in 1845, they ran McAllister, one of these same planters and a Calhoun Democrat, for the governorship. The Whig papers immediately attacked him as an aristocrat and implied that their political enemies were dominated by high snobbery. One of them referred to McAllister as "an aristocrat who has no sympathy with the people. He belongs to that class in Savannah known as 'Swelled Heads' who think the up-country people no better than brutes. . . . Why it will kill him to be so far back in the woods as Milledgeville. He will never stand the up-country crackers and the lack of his favorite brands of wine." There was a degree of truth in this statement, and it well illustrates the embarrassment under which the Democrats sometimes labored as

[44] Quoted by Stoval, *Robert Toombs*, p. 90.
[45] See Gamaliel Bradford, *Confederate Portraits*, p. 196.

a result of admitting the Calhoun planters to the party in 1840.[46]

This social criticism may have been one factor in McAllister's defeat by Crawford in this campaign. When the next election came, in 1847, however, the Whigs nominated Clinch, another rice planter, and the Democrats, in opposing him, simply duplicated the Whig attack upon McAllister.[47] In other words, the politicians of both parties saw in the Democratic dogma little more than a popular shibboleth, to which it was useful to render lip service upon appropriate occasions.

This, at least, is the conclusion that one would gain from the party press. In Georgia, as elsewhere, the papers of the day were an important influence in political life. The period between 1830 and 1850 saw the first full blossomings of so-called "personal journalism," when, in a state like Georgia, the papers were small affairs, whose owners, editors, and publishers were often one and the same person. In a few of the larger towns, however, such as Augusta and Savannah, the editorial staffs were in 1850 differentiated from the owners. This was true, for instance, of the Savannah *Georgian* and *Republican* and of the Augusta *Chronicle*.

Each town of any size had two journals in 1850, one Democratic and the other Whig, and in both Savannah and Columbus there were in 1850 two Democratic papers,[48] although these towns each numbered under ten thousand population. In Augusta there were

---

[46] In Savannah *Georgian*, July 7, 1847.

[47] *Federal Union*, July 27, and August 10, 1847.

[48] The Savannah *News* and *Georgian;* the Columbus *Times* and *Sentinel.* The *News* was "independent" but it tended towards Democratic views.

two Whig papers, the *Chronicle* and the *Republic,* and also two in Macon, the *Journal* and the *Citizen*. Under these circumstances, circulations were usually not large in the towns and were especially small in the Pine Barrens and Upper Georgia, where illiteracy was common and the "newspaper habit" had never been generally formed. Most of the papers were weeklies, though those in Augusta ran daily, tri-weekly and weekly editions; the Columbus *Times,* a tri-weekly as well as a weekly edition; and the Savannah papers, only daily editions. Daily and tri-weekly editions had a very much smaller circulation than the weekly. Thus the daily Augusta *Constitutionalist* had a circulation of about four hundred, the tri-weekly, of two hundred and fifty, and the weekly, of three thousand. The only daily in the state whose patrons exceeded one thousand in number in 1850 was the Savannah *News,* founded only in that year, but blessed with a rapid growth because it represented a new business venture —the cheap newspaper.

The Whig and Democratic weeklies were not evenly balanced in their circulation, that of the Whigs in the larger towns usually being slightly the greater, as would be expected. Among them, the weekly Augusta *Chronicle* had in 1850 by far the largest circulation of any paper in the state, about fifty-four hundred, save that of its own agricultural monthly, which reached about eight thousand subscribers. The Augusta *Republic,* the other Whig paper, was taken by three thousand subscribers, which means that the Whig papers of that city reached almost three times as many readers as did the Democratic. In Macon, likewise in the heart of the cotton belt, the Whig readers of the *Journal* and the *Citizen* were more than twice the number of the

Democratic readers of the *Telegraph*. In Columbus, the Whig *Enquirer* had a larger circulation than either of its Democratic rivals, and only in Milledgeville did the Democratic *Federal Union* lead the Whig *Southern Recorder* by a narrow margin, three thousand to twenty-eight hundred. In Athens and Rome the party papers were evenly balanced in circulation, although the Democrats had the larger following in this northwest section. The papers in the smaller towns reached five hundred subscribers or less. There was a smaller number of papers in proportion to total white population in Georgia than was the case in the South as a whole (there were not more than about thirty political papers in the state in 1850), but this meant in some cases a larger circulation per paper. The total circulation of all the papers carrying political news in the state in 1850 probably reached about twenty to twenty-five thousand subscribers out of a total white population of some five hundred thousand. These facts suggest that scarcely half of the literate white men read the newspapers, and that at least a slight majority of these received the Whig version.[49]   In the northwest, the Democratic majority received its political education as much through the barbecue and the court house gathering as it did through the press. The fact that a majority of the illiterate males were Democrats probably accounts for the smaller circulation of the Democratic journals.

[49] The facts here stated are based upon J. C. G. Kennedy, *Catalogue of the newspapers and periodicals published in the United States.* etc., included as an appendix to J. Livingston, *Law Register* for 1850 (New York, 1852). Kennedy is not entirely reliable, but can be checked to some extent by current press data. See also Ingle, *op. cit.*, p. 155. George White listed thirty-one political papers in Georgia in 1851, Augusta *Chronicle*, June 19, 1852.

Personal journalism in Georgia, as elsewhere, indulged in lurid rhetoric and flowing phrase. The rival papers in each town kept up a running controversy that in serious times assumed a very bitter tone. This was true of even the best papers. The editors of the Augusta *Constitutionalist,* for instance, publicly demanded in 1850 that those of the *Chronicle* be forced to resign, while a number of Democratic papers in the same year insisted that the Whig Macon *Citizen* be suppressed and the owner run out of the state. The *Georgian* was of the gentle opinion that the entire Whig press was "absolutely corrupt" and "wholly and purely a political thing."[50] Not to be outdone by such Democratic slanders, the Whig editor of the *Recorder* denounced what he was pleased to term the "rampant malignity and overleaping licentiousness" of his local rival.[51] The very freedom of language indulged in by opposing editors, however, was in a sense a measure of the general liberty enjoyed by the press. A Georgia editor of 1812 had lost his presses and had been tarred and feathered for opposing the war of that year,[52] but no Whig editor was in any danger of such treatment for opposing the Mexican War. The editor of the Macon *Citizen* was, however, threatened with mob violence and his paper temporarily suspended in 1850 for assuming what was termed an antislavery attitude.[53]

[50] *Georgian,* April 14, 1848.
[51] *Federal Union,* April 27, 1847.
[52] *Ibid.*
[53] *Georgian,* August 24; *Chronicle,* August 30; Boston *Liberator,* September 20, 1850. The *Chronicle* was also threatened, but the *Federal Union* (April 27, 1847) assured it that there was now a greater freedom of the press than there had been a generation earlier, and that it was therefore in no danger.

The Georgia press is, of course, important as an indication of what public sentiment was in the state, but it needs to be used with considerable caution in this connection. The personal character of newspaper management meant that editorials expressed primarily the opinions of editors and party leaders rather than those of the general public. It was true that in normal times public opinion would follow that of these same party leaders and would thus coincide with the views expressed by the press. In times of crisis, however, it was quite possible for politicians and editors to attempt to lead the masses in a direction they were loath to follow. There was more mental inertia among readers than among editors, and the latter were, therefore, apt to be far out in front of the crowd in a period of mental transition. In such times, excited editor-owners were quite capable of seeing public opinion through their own eyes and of making the most extravagant claims that the people were with them— only to have subsequent events completely disprove their statements. In the fall of 1850, for instance, a few papers with a small circulation, like the Columbus *Sentinel,* made the most bitter attacks upon the Union. It does not at all follow from such evidence that these attacks represented a sentiment prevalent in the state, or even in Columbus. As a matter of fact, other evidence shows that they represented no such thing.

The best checks upon the press as a measure of public opinion would seem to be the circulation figures of the particular papers being considered and the results of subsequent elections. Circulation figures would also seem to be significant as a criterion of the influence exerted by the press upon public sentiment. It is at least fair to assume that the weekly *Chronicle,*

with a circulation of over five thousand, exerted a
greater influence than any of the Democratic journals,
whose circulation never exceeded about three thousand
in this period. So, too, the *Chronicle* may have been
more influential than the daily Savannah *Republican,*
(whose circulation was less than one thousand), for the
Augusta paper had a daily edition which reached ap-
proximately five hundred subscribers in addition to its
large weekly one.[54]

The chief influence exerted upon public political
thinking, other than that of the press, was that of the
discussions held at "county caucuses," district conventions, public barbecues, courthouse gatherings and
other political meetings. The influence of such meetings must often have been more potent than that of the
press, since they were more dramatic and exciting and
must have appealed powerfully to a people who found
in partisan politics a natural diversion from monoton-
ous routine. "Small lawyers and still smaller politicians" thrived upon them, and there were few districts in Georgia where, in times of excitement, there
were not several opportunities annually to attend such
gatherings. Their peculiar importance in illiterate districts has already been noted, and indeed the great rôle
they played in Georgia politics generally can be attributed in part to the semi-frontier conditions obtaining in
parts of the state.[55] It has been observed, of course,
that the whole South "suffered from too much campaigning," which always involved such meetings,[56]

[54] Livingston, *op. cit.* It is to be remembered in this connection that
the Whig papers with the largest circulation also reached the most
influential elements.

[55] "Stump speaking," it is claimed, had in the old days of "grocery
treats" been considered somewhat "common," but was coming into vogue
by 1847 for even the most prominent politicians. See Andrews, *Remin-
inscences,* p. 22.

[56] Ingle, *Southern Sidelights,* pp. 39, 41, 42.

and this is no doubt true.   Yet it would have been a cruel mentor who would have taken their politics from these people.

The even balance of the parties in Georgia made campaigning there an even more exciting diversion than in some of the other southern states.   Elections were always closely contested and slight defections, based, as was said, upon the appearance of superfluous candidates or of some subtle constitutional issue, might determine the final result.   This fact, combined with the temper of the voters, made the Georgia elections unusually hot affairs.   Arnold describes the way in which the Irish lined up with their shillalahs at the Savannah polls in order to encourage all "good" voters; namely, Democrats—and Arnold was himself a Democrat!   Feeling became unusually tense during the critical struggle of 1849-51.   A Carolinian passing through the state in the latter year observed that "We in South Carolina talk about political excitement but we do not know until we come here what excitement is."[57]

Any discussion of public opinion in the state is incomplete without some reference to the party leaders. These leaders, it has already been observed, had excellent opportunities for moulding public opinion; first, through their influence over a press which zealously printed their speeches and other sayings, and, second, through the political meetings which were the order of the day.   The population which concerned most politicians was relatively small, and leaders who traveled widely through the counties could make a personal appeal to most of their constituents.   This was of considerable potency with a people who had not entirely

[57] Incidents of a Journey from Abbeville to Ocola (1851), p. 11.

outlived an age when politics had been almost purely personal and who relished politics as a sport necessarily involving intense loyalties if it was to be completely enjoyed.   In a word, conditions seemed rather ideal for the political domination of the state by a few outstanding personalities.   It is doubtless a fair assumption that under such circumstances leaders were bound to arise; hence, in Georgia, Troup, Clark, and Crawford appeared in the twenties, and Cobb, Toombs, and Stephens flourished in the forties.

The influence of these leaders was so great that there is, indeed, some danger of exagerating it, some temptation to assume that they directed all things in Georgia politics.   Much the same caution needs to be observed in estimating their influence upon public opinion as is necessary in judging the influence of the press. In times of crisis and transition, the individual leader was apt to change opinions more rapidly than could the relatively inert masses, not only because he was giving more time and effort to the study of the new political phenomena involved in the crises, but also because, if he was an office-holder, he was apt to be subjected to greater political stimulation and excitement than was the man back on the farm.   In such times, the politician, like the editor, might move so rapidly in his advance to new viewpoints that he ceased to keep in touch with, to guide, or to represent the masses.   It then became simply a question as to whether they would eventually catch up with him, or whether he would have to go back to them, if he was to maintain influence and office.   Examples of both types of action are to be observed in the Georgia politics of the transition period about to be considered.

Party leaders, while influencing the viewpoints of constituents, did not control the machinery of their party organizations in Georgia to the extent that political "bosses" have in many states during the post-bellum period. Senators and representatives, to be sure, directed the distribution of federal patronage in the state,[58] and the governor naturally had some influence over the state patronage. The governors themselves, however, were usually men of ability and of some political independence rather than the tools of bosses behind the scenes. Crawford was a leader of his party, and McDonald was not only a leader, but was capable of carrying through measures condemned by a majority of his political associates. The state legislature was not dominated, as a rule, by the senators sent to Washington; and these latter sometimes displayed, on the other hand, a remarkable independence of the assembly at Milledgeville. Berrien's successful controversy with the latter, and his denial of "senatorial responsibility," is an obvious illustration of such independence.[59]   Cobb's influence in "Cherokee" and the Upper-Piedmont and that of the "Two Inseparables" in the Black Belt approximated most closely that of the modern boss, but by no means fully equalled it.

The state, indeed, was still too young and its people consequently too much attached to the individualism of the frontier to permit of much machine control of the political organizations. Party methods and organization were imperfect in the forties. As late as 1848, for instance, there was still considerable opposition in Georgia to the nomination of presidential candidates

[58] There is considerable evidence of this in the *Toombs, Stephens, and Cobb Correspondence* (as cited above, p. 72, n. 24), *passim*.

[59] *Remarks of R. D. Arnold on the Georgia Legislature's Resolutions Against Senator Berrien, passim.*

by national party conventions. Nominations for state offices were, to be sure, made by local and state party conventions; but, as will be noted, the control exercised by these meetings over nominations was never a complete one.

The nomination of candidates for the state House of Representatives was made by county meetings open to party members—by "county caucuses," as these gatherings came to be called. The same method was used for the nomination and election of delegates to senatorial district conventions, wherein nominations for state senators were made, two counties usually being combined to form such a district. State conventions of each party were held annually, at which candidates for governor were nominated and resolutions on policy were adopted. Yet within the counties individuals continued to "come out" for office on their own initiative, much to the distress of the party leaders, as this often meant that two or more candidates of the same party ran for the same office. Elections sometimes hinged upon the extent to which each party could dissuade such overzealous members from nominating themselves. When, for instance, the Democrats won the control of the legislature in 1847, their journal at the capital thankfully observed that "there was an unusually small number of supernumerary candidates this year."[60] This tendency towards irregular candidacy was unusually common in Georgia; "Father" Ritchie, of the Washington *Union,* observed it with considerable astonishment.[61]

[60] *Federal Union,* June 15, 1847; see also issue for August 27, 1847. For the details of nominating methods see the Columbus *Enquirer,* July 15, 1851.

[61] *Federal Union,* September 28, 1847.

CHAPTER IV

STORM CLOUDS, 1844-1848

The chief national issue in state politics during the thirties had been that relating to the United States Bank. During the forties this ceased to be an issue,[1] the renewal of tariff agitation pushing that problem into the forefront of political controversy.[2] Before the excitement over the tariff and National Bank questions had died down in Georgia, a new problem had arisen which was destined to eclipse both of these in importance; namely, the renewal of the desire for the extension of slave territory in the west. When Texas first requested annexation during the late thirties, there was no opposition from either party in Georgia, nor was there, on the other hand, any organized demand for its admission to the Union. It was assumed that it should be annexed in the course of the general westward movement. Tyler's revival of the matter in 1844 found both Whigs and Democrats in favor of annexation. The presidential campaign of

---

[1] The Whigs continued a sort of academic defence of the Bank through the forties. Problems relating to banks and other corporations within the state also divided the parties during that decade, the Whigs claiming to be the best friends of incorporated business. The Georgia Democrats, however, had come under conservative leadership to such an extent as to prevent their offering any serious opposition to banks or other corporations. Indeed Democratic papers sometimes encouraged the formation ·of manufacturing companies, though they opposed granting them the special privileges desired by the Whigs. See, *e.g.,* the Milledgeville *Federal Union*, November 30, 1847, January 4, 1848.

[2] The state election of 1841 was won by the Democrats upon the tariff issue, and the victorious party attempted unsuccessfully to prevent the Whig Senator, Berrien, from supporting Whig tariffs in Congress. See J. A. Turner, "William C. Dawson," *The Plantation*, I. No. 1, 82; *Remarks of R. D. Arnold on the Georgia Legislature's Resolutions Against Senator Berrien* (Savannah, 1843), p. 3.

that year brought out clearly the opposition in the North to any further extension of slave territory and, as a result, aroused new desire for the same in the South.[3] This was at first expressed in Georgia by both parties, the Democrats supporting Polk, who was openly for annexation, and the Whigs, in their state convention of July, 1844, adopting Alexander Stephens' resolutions favoring future annexation.[4]

Meanwhile, the agitation for annexation was producing more serious feeling across the river in South Carolina than it was in Georgia. It is to be remembered that the middle forties was the period of greatest cumulative economic depression in the South and that South Carolina had suffered more than had the newer states of the lower South. This economic depression quite naturally expressed itself, as has been noted in a previous chapter, in a corresponding depression of mind. Under these circumstances, leaders were apt to seek an explanation of their difficulties in the machinations of northern political enemies rather than in weaknesses inherent in the local economic system. When, therefore, northern antislavery men attempted in 1844 to prevent the annexation of Texas, and, to add insult to injury, other northerners attempted to prevent any revision of the Whig tariff of 1842, it was natural that certain Carolina leaders should see in these efforts an explanation of their own difficulties. Early in 1844, for this reason, they inaugurated a militant campaign for Texan annexation and tariff reform, and by June of that year they began for

[3] For evidence against the view that the annexation of Texas was originally demanded by the "Slavocracy" see C. S. Boucher, "*In Re That Aggressive Slavocracy*," *Mississippi Valley Historical Review*, VIII. 23-25.

[4] M. L. Avary, (Ed.), *Recollections of A. H. Stephens*, p. 17.

the first time openly to advocate secession as the only
remedy in case these demands were not granted. South
Carolina, they held, should not preserve a union which
offered her nought but exploitation and insult. This
"Bluffton Movement," as it came to be called, was led
by such capable spokesmen as R. B. Rhett and was
supported by such powerful papers as the ever zealous
Mercury. It met with opposition, however, from the
equally zealous *Courier*[5] and from the powerful Calhoun, and eventually it failed to receive the support of
a majority, even in the Palmetto State.[6] Its leaders,
it may be said in passing, then bided their time until
the opposition to the extension of slavery in the newly
acquired Southwest precipitated a sectional struggle
which lent their secessionist appeal a new potency
throughout the South. Calhoun then joined them and
led this more serious effort, which developed into the
secession movement of 1850.

The Bluffton Movement, so far as it aimed at immediate secession, exerted little influence in Georgia,
where it was condemned by the Whigs and by many
of the Democrats.[7] Calhoun's influence with the state-
rights element in the Georgia Democracy was such
that even this group did not generally support it. It
doubtless found individual sympathizers among this
latter group, and these individuals were to be heard
from when Calhoun took over and restimulated the

---

[5] See, *e.g.*, the Charleston *Courier*, June 29, 1844.

[6] For general descriptions of the movement see C. S. Boucher, "The
Annexation of Texas and the Bluffton Movement in South Carolina,"
Mississippi Valley Historical Review, VI. 9, ff.; N. W. Stephenson,
Texas and the Mexican War, pp. 168-176.

[7] Milledgeville *Federal Union*, July 30, 1844; Columbus *Enquirer*. July
31, 1844. The Savannah *Republican* immediately indicted South Carolina
as "the center of all the heresies that disturb the nation," and declared
that she wished to be "the center and focus of the new Southern Republic"; *Republican*, June 18, 1844.

movement in 1847. The chief influence of the Bluffton movement itself was probably to increase the
prejudice already felt in Georgia towards South Carolina as a center of political radicalism and disturbance.

As the summer of 1844 progressed, however, it
became apparent that the general agitation in favor of
the annexation of Texas, of which the Bluffton movement was the most extreme expression, would affect
the presidential campaign in Georgia. While the
Whigs had expressed formal approval of annexation
in their July state convention, in response to what
seemed the general public sentiment of the state, some
of their leaders soon realized that this stand would
involve them in difficulties with the strong antislavery
element in the northern wing of their party. They
therefore refrained, in the fall of 1844, from emphasizing the issue. For this same reason, Clay, the Whig
presidential candidate, maintained a somewhat ambiguous position upon the annexation question. Con-
versely, the Democrats in Georgia, who felt that they
had less to fear from their northern antislavery
brethren, emphasized the battle-cry of "southern
rights" in Texas. Polk, their national candidate, had
openly espoused annexation. In the course of the
campaign, a few of the more extreme Democrats, echo-
ing the Bluffton agitation, demanded that Texas must
be had with or without the Union. This effort to
exploit sectional loyalty led the Whigs to raise the appeal to national loyalty, each party standing ready
then, as later, to make whichever appeal seemed
expedient. The Democrats, the Whigs declared, were
secretly harboring disunion sentiments.[8] This accusa-
tion, however, did not save the day for the Whigs.

[8] Savannah *Republican,* July 16, 1844.

Clay's ambiguity on the annexation question and his lack of personal appeal in the small farmer sections lost him the state in November, and Polk carried Georgia, as he did all the other states of the lower South.

When Congress convened in the winter of 1844-1845, the southern Whigs found themselves approaching a choice between continuing to favor annexation, as the apparent desire of the southern people, or opposing it in order to avoid an issue bound to alienate their northern allies.[9] When, therefore, the annexation question was brought up by the victorious Democrats, it found the Georgia Whig members torn by conflicting emotions and divided in consequence. Berrien, in the Senate, had believed for years that any attempt on the part of the South to keep pace with the North in territorial expansion was hopeless. He saw in the Texas movement, therefore, a matter which could avail the South nothing and which might arouse a storm over slavery that would divide his party. He boldly opposed annexation in any form, arguing at length against it upon technical constitutional grounds.[10] Colquitt, his colleague, expressed the typical enthusiasm of the Democrats for annexation and found it difficult to believe in the sincerity of Berrien's technical objections.[11] In the House, the Democrats, Cobb and Haralson, declared the recent election showed that all Georgians favored annexation.[12] Stephens admitted they all favored the principle, but expressed

[9] Toombs to Stephens, February 16, 1845, *Toombs, Stephens, and Cobb Correspondence*, p. 64. See also J. W. Burney to Howell Cobb, January 31, 1845, *ibid.*, p. 62; Junius Hillyer to Cobb, February 15, 1845, *ibid.*, p. 63.
[10] *Congressional Globe*, 28 Congress, 2 Session, pp. 343, 344.
[11] *Ibid.*, pp. 347 ff.
[12] *Ibid.*, pp. 176-180.

the typical Whig dislike for Tyler in declaring that most of them opposed the President's particular plan of annexation. He warned the House, moreover, that a serious struggle over slavery was apt to be precipitated. Yet he supported annexation by joint resolution and was followed in this by Clinch and the other Georgia Whigs.[13] Thus Berrien led the way toward Whig opposition to anything threatening a renewal of the slavery controversy, while Stephens and Clinch expressed the general opinion of both parties in Georgia that Texas should be added to the Union.

When the War with Mexico followed annexation, the dilemma in which the southern Whigs found themselves became more acute. The war was almost certain to mean further expansion and this, in turn, a serious sectional quarrel over the status of slavery in all new territory acquired. Such a quarrel would probably divide the Whig party along sectional lines. On the other hand, any opposition to the war would be condemned by the Democrats as unpatriotic—a charge that any party would ordinarily wish to avoid.

News reached Washington in May, 1846, of Zachary Taylor's fight on the Rio Grande, and war was declared with almost no opposition in Congress. A momentary patriotic impulse seemed to sweep southern Whigs as well as Democrats into the war movement. The Georgia press well demonstrated this feeling during the weeks which followed the declaration of war. Within a month, however, there was a definite reaction in the local Whig press, and editorials attacking the war began to appear.[14] Even the fear of opposing a successful war was not so great as the fear of what

[13] *Ibid.*, pp. 190-194.
[14] John B. Lamar to Howell Cobb, June 24, 1846, *Toombs, Stephens, and Cobb Correspondence*, p. 82.

would happen to the Whig party, and perhaps to the Union, if further territory were acquired. Stephens and Berrien led the opposition to the war. The Democrats, of course, made the most of this opportunity to call the Whigs disloyal, thus returning the compliment paid them in the election of 1844. Whig attacks upon the war and the administration were termed "virulent and loathsome."[15]

Meantime an interesting incident occurred at Washington which might have warned the Whigs that their worst fears were to be realized. On August 6 David Wilmot, of Pennsylvania, introduced, as an amendment to a war appropriation bill, his famous Proviso forbidding the extension of slavery into any lands secured from Mexico.[16] In so doing he is supposed to have expressed the chagrin of some northern Democrats over the refusal of southern Democrats to support them in securing all of the Oregon country from England,[17] but this Proviso was enthusiastically backed by the northern antislavery Whigs. On the other hand, all the southern Whigs, including the Georgians, voted against the proviso in August, 1846. From this time on there was never any serious division of opinion within Georgia regarding the Wilmot Proviso. It was a measure which practically all Georgians must oppose. The explanation of this attitude is simple enough. The Proviso represented an open attack upon what seemed to southerners their com-

---

[15] *Ibid.*

[16] *Congressional Globe,* 29 Congress, 1 Session, p. 1217.

[17] This phase of the matter was realized by the Georgia Democrats, see J. H. Lumpkin to Howell Cobb, Nov. 13, 1846; *Toombs, Stephens, and Cobb Correspondence,* p. 86. *Cf.* C. E. Persinger, "The 'Bargain of 1844,' as The Origin of the Wilmot Proviso," *American Historical Association, Annual Report,* 1911, I. 189-195. This does not mean that Wilmot was personally motivated by such chagrin. See C. B. Going, *David Wilmot: Free Soiler,* pp. 117-141.

mon rights in the territories. It was, therefore, not only an insult to southern pride, but an earnest of further and final attacks upon slavery, which would surely follow were this one successful. Whig slaveholders were certain to oppose an ultimate threat to their institutions as energetically as would the small-farmer Democrats.[18] If there was a small class in the hill country which viewed all this as "a lordly slaveholder's battle" in which it had no interest, this class was not articulate nor able to influence greatly the general opposition to the hated measure. This did not mean, however, that the Whig slaveholders would court the issue. Both their economic and political interests demanded that it be evaded.

The introduction of the Proviso attracted little immediate attention in either South Carolina[19] or Georgia. The adjournment of the Senate prevented final action upon the measure, and the congressmen who returned home in the fall apparently did not bring it to the notice of their constituents. Indeed, there was in Georgia in the fall of 1846 a curious lull before the coming storm. John H. Lumpkin's letter analyzing the political situation at the time did not mention the Proviso.[20] The same was true of Howell Cobb's other political correspondents, who apparently had never heard of the measure; and even the Democratic press was silent. The Democratic tariff of that year, the Mexican War, the local elections—these monopo-

---

[18] Washington *National Intelligencer*, October 21, 1847. See Cole, *Whig Party*, p. 123. The fact that Waddy Thompson, late minister to Mexico, had already announced in October, '47, the worthlessness of the new territories for slave interests, did not alter these essential considerations to any great extent.

[19] Phillip Hamer, *The Secession Movement in South Carolina*, pp. 1, 2.

[20] *Toombs, Stephens, and Cobb Correspondence*, pp. 86, 87. Lumpkin was Cobb's chief political lieutenant in Upper Georgia.

lized attention.[21] Abolitionists were occasionally be-
rated, but some felt that there was little cause for alarm
even in this quarter. "Abolitionist Efforts at Boston
are Below Par," ironically announced a Democratic
journal.[22] So far as the introduction of the Proviso
was known, it was evidently considered a temporary
flare-up of no serious consequence.

The situation changed as soon as Congress convened early in the winter. Polk recommended a war
appropriation bill, and, on January 3, 1847, King, of
New York, introduced such a bill, including a prohibition of slavery in all territorial acquisitions which
might be secured.[23] This met with almost immediate
public approval in the North, resolutions favoring it
passing in the Pennsylvania legislature, January 22,
and in that of Ohio, February 8, 1847.[24] During the
course of the winter, most of the other northern states
took similar action.

This display of northern feeling alarmed the southern delegations in Congress and the press of the southern states. Members of the two parties, however,
reacted differently. The Whig congressmen were
greatly alarmed, realizing at once that the dangers
which threatened their party and the Union were now
imminent. Two days after King introduced his measure Alexander H. Stephens declared in a letter:

A storm is brewing over the slavery question. The North
is going to stick the Wilmot Amendment to every appropriation
and then all the South will vote against such a measure. Finally

[21] For typical topics of the day see the Savannah *Georgian,* August
20, 1846.
[22] *Ibid.,* November 26, 1846.
[23] *Congressional Globe,* 29 Congress, 2 Session, p. 424.
[24] H. V. Ames, *State Documents,* pp. 243, 244.

a tremendous struggle will take place and perhaps Polk, in starting one war, will find a dozen on his hands. I fear the worst.[25]

Toombs, his colleague, openly warned the House a few days later that it was raising an issue which might destroy the Union. Thus early in the debate, he told northern members that the South would "stay in the Union on a ground of perfect equality, or not stay at all!"[26]

Having issued their warning, the next step for the Georgia Whigs was to find some method of avoiding the issue. Stephens, like Toombs, spoke of the danger of southern resistance to the Proviso and "invoked gentlemen not to put this principle to the test."[27] Stephen's plan for escaping the danger was soon revealed. On January 22, he introduced resolutions declaring that the United States had no intention of acquiring territory as a result of the war.[28] While some of his fellow Whigs discouraged this move, lest it seem unpatriotic,[29] most northern and southern Whigs could agree upon the policy and gave it their votes in the House. It served to unify for the time the two wings of the party.

Berrien followed a similar course in the Senate. On February 2, he introduced resolutions of the same character as those of Stephens[30] and, speaking a few days later, appealed to the Senate to "exclude from the national councils this direful question."[31] The

[25] Quoted in Johnston and Browne, *Alexander Stephens*, p. 218.
[26] *Congressional Globe*, 29 Congress, 2 session, p. 140.
[27] *Ibid.*, p. 401.
[28] *Ibid.*, p. 310.
[29] Johnston and Browne, *op. cit.*, pp. 210, 211.
[30] *Congressional Globe*, 29 Congress, 2 session, p. 222.
[31] *Ibid.*, p. 330.

Georgia Whigs were clearly leading their section of the party in the policy of evasion.[32]

The Georgia Democrats, meanwhile, were ready to face the issue for the same reason that they had courted it during the fall campaign of 1844. They feared less a break with their northern wing than did their opponents and saw an opportunity to uphold "southern rights" at the expense of the Whig evasionists. Cobb, in the House, contented himself with a condemnation of the Proviso, a demand that southern territory be acquired, and an offer to extend the Missouri Compromise line to the Pacific in order to compromise on the territory secured.[33]   Colquitt, as a Calhoun Democrat, went further, in that he condemned both northern members and his Whig colleagues. The Whig resolutions were "but a little display of party tactics" to hold their party together. He "deeply regreted" the position of his colleagues "in opposing the acquisition of territory for fear of agitating the question of slavery." He protested, "as a Georgian," that the people of the South had no such fear of protecting their rights, which they would continue to do at all hazards.[34]

[32] The opposition of the Whigs in general, and of Berrien in particular, to the Mexican War has been severely criticised by Justin Smith, *The War With Mexico*, II. 268-293. Berrien is condemned as inconsistent, and as one who was willing to sacrifice not only California, but even national self-respect, in order to preserve Whig solidarity. He was ready, declared Smith (II. 288) to place the American nation in the light of one "combining the villain, the ruffian, the simpleton and the comedian." A more severe indictment of the Georgia senator could hardly have been penned by a contemporary opponent. Yet Berrien may have sincerely believed that it was *patriotic*, in the long run, to prevent territorial expansion and the sectional struggle bound to follow this. He may also have been sincere in the belief that the War was an unjust one, in which case his condemnation of the American government would have been at least a partially justifiable one.

[33] *Congressional Globe*, 29 Congress, 2 session, p. 362.

[34] *Ibid.*, p. 439.

On February 19, John C. Calhoun introduced in the Senate his famous "Southern Platform" resolutions, declaring federal prohibition of slavery in a territory or incoming state unconstitutional.[35] Calhoun, after holding back the more radical politicians of his own state in 1844 and 1845, had now become convinced by the Proviso agitation that there was no longer any question of its ultimate threat to slavery. He became at once an aggressive leader, who desired to force a final decision upon the Proviso and wished to see the South united upon that issue. The "Southern Platform" was intended as a statement of principles upon which the whole South could unite.[36]

The appropriation bill, with the Proviso attached, passed the House, but was defeated some days afterwards in the Senate, which sent the bill back to the House. That body then receded from its position and accepted the unamended bill, abandoning the Proviso. Congress then adjourned, postponing the whole issue and leaving it to the states. Would the southern states rally to the "Platform" as the northern had to the Proviso?

The response showed the extent to which feeling had already been aroused by the congressional debates. On March 8, 1847, the Virginia legislature passed a series of resolutions supporting Calhoun's position and threatening resistance to the Proviso to the last extremity.[37] The Governor of Mississippi, in his reply to the Virginia resolutions, declared that the South would resist even to secession and civil war. In Alabama, appeals were made to the voters to unite against

[35] Crallé, (Ed.), *Works of J. C. Calhoun,* IV. 339-349.
[36] H. V. Ames, "John C. Calhoun in the Secession Movement of 1850," *University of Pennsylvania Public Lectures,* 1917-1918, pp. 106, 107.
[37] Ames, *State Documents,* pp. 244-247.

the hated measure.[38]   Calhoun, on his return to South
Carolina, was the subject of ovations and public resolutions upholding his "Platform."[39]   In December of
the following fall, the Alabama legislature formally
approved the Virginia resolutions, and in February,
1848, Texas did the same.

In Georgia the opening of Congress had found the
party journals quarreling over their respective attitudes towards the Mexican War.   The Whigs condemned the evils of Polk's administration and opposed
openly, or by implication, its war policy.   The Democrats proclaimed the Whigs' disloyalty and promised
them the fate of the Federalists of 1815.[40]   The news
of the renewed Proviso debate was received with regret, even by the Democratic press, on the ground that
internal dissensions were unfortunate in war time.[41]
As the debate in Washington proceeded, the party
papers tended to reflect the attitude taken there by the
state's representatives.   Whig papers blamed the crisis
upon the Democratic war policy and supported the
efforts of Stephens and Berrien to prevent the acquisition of Mexican territory.[42]   The Democratic journals
supported Colquitt and condemned the Whig tactics
against territorial expansion as shameful and "unworthy of Georgians."[43]   All the papers opposed the
Proviso, and early in the spring it was declared that
the votes cast in the national House upon that measure

[38] Niles' Register, LXXII. 178, 179.

[39] Hamer, The Secession Movement in South Carolina, p. 4.

[40] Milledgeville Southern Recorder, in the Milledgeville Federal
Union, January 26, 1847.

[41] Federal Union, January 26, 1847.

[42] Augusta Chronicle, February 19; Savannah Republican, March 2,
1847.

[43] Federal Union, February 16; Savannah Georgian, February 19,
1847.

"should arouse every southern man to a sense of the danger."[44] It was the opinion of even the Democratic papers, however, that the issue was one which could be compromised, and the extension of the Missouri Compromise line to the Pacific was suggested as the proper means to this end.

There was no body in session in Georgia during the spring which could take official notice of the Calhoun "Platform" or the Virginia Resolutions. Late in June was the time for the two parties to hold their customary annual state conventions. Before these met, however, there were interesting developments across the Savannah river. When Calhoun returned to Charleston he made a public address, March 9, 1847, in which he emphasized his conviction that the Proviso issue must be met promptly by unified southern opposition. A final decision in the sectional struggle must be obtained, and any postponement of this decision would be most dangerous for the South.[45] During the months that followed, there matured in his mind the plan for a southern convention as the best means for securing the sectional unity he deemed essential.[46] The next step was to urge this plan upon his friends in Georgia and the Gulf States in the hope that they could organize therein a public sentiment favorable to it. His letters to be noted below indicated a belief that the time was already ripe for a "Southern Movement" in Georgia, an illusion that displayed considerable ignorance of the real conditions in that state. Yet his opinions were to exercise some influence, a fact already

[44] *Federal Union,* March 2, 1847.
[45] Hamer, *op. cit.,* pp. 3, 4.
[46] This plan for a "Southern Convention," of course, had been suggested at various times before, *e.g.,* during the Bluffton movement; see Savannah *Republican,* July 8, 1844.

apparent when the Georgia party conventions met early in the summer.

The Democratic convention assembled at Milledgeville[47] on June 28 to consider the nomination of a candidate for the governorship, to discuss the possible nominees for the presidential election in 1848, and to consider the Proviso. G. W. Towns, then member of the House of Representatives, secured the nomination for the governorship in opposition to H. V. Johnson. There was some debate upon presidential nominees, and resolutions urging the war hero, Zachary Taylor, were introduced. The Whigs were known to be considering Taylor, and it was suggested that the Democrats should forestall them. A group led by Cobb opposed him vigorously, since he was hardly a Democrat, and his views were unknown. It was finally decided to leave the matter to the party's national convention in the ensuing year.[48]

As soon as the Proviso and the sectional controversy were brought into the debate, ominous differences of opinion appeared. Cobb and the more militant Union Democrats displayed a desire to avoid taking any stand that might embarrass relationships with the northern Democrats. He introduced resolutions declaring "confidence in our brethren of the Northern democracy." As some of these "brethren" had voted for the Proviso, this met with a spirited protest from the state-rights Democrats. This element, whose history has been discussed in a previous chapter, had returned to the Democratic party with Calhoun in 1840 and had always maintained a strong state-rights and pro-southern attitude. Hence it was inclined at once to

[47] Then capital of the state.

[48] For Democratic opinions of Taylor's availability, see the *Federal Union*, April 27, 1847.

sympathize with Calhoun's position in 1847. Cobb's resolutions were withdrawn for the sake of preserving party harmony, but they forecast the division of the party which was certain to come if the sectional controversy continued.

Edward J. Black, a state-rights Democrat, then spoke in favor of the Virginia Resolutions, advocated Calhoun's move for southern party unity, and praised that leader as the one destined to save his section. This brought immediate opposition from the majority, already suspicious of Calhoun's intentions. Gardner, editor of the Augusta *Constitutionalist,* recalled old antagonisms when he warned the Calhounites that "a defense of Calhoun is not the high-road to success in the Democracy of Georgia."[49]

The sentiment against the Proviso, however, was strong, and all could agree on resolutions generally similar to those of Virginia. No Proviso legislation, it was declared, "could be recognized as binding"—a statement that suggested the old idea of nullification. The party pledged itself to vote for no presidential candidate in 1848 who did not "unequivocally declare his opposition to the Principles and Provisions of the Wilmot Proviso." It was said that slavery had a right to enter all the territories, but the party was ready to accept the Missouri Compromise line as a compromise of fact rather than of principle.[50] Other resolu-

[49] Edward J. Black to J. C. Calhoun, Jacksonboro, Ga., n.d.; (evidently written in the fall of '47), Calhoun Papers. (A collection of unpublished letters, supplementing the *Calhoun Correspondence,* which has been edited for publication by the American Historical Association. The present writer is indebted to Professor C. S. Boucher, one of the editors, for the use of the letters herein cited.)

[50] Boucher, *"In Re* That Aggressive Slavocracy," *op. cit.,* pp. 44, 45, observes that the acceptance of the Missouri Compromise line sometimes embarrassed southerners as "a complete admission" of the power of Congress over slavery in the territories. This admission was usually specifically denied in Georgia, as in the resolutions noted above.

tions adopted related to the support of Polk and the War and to the usual attacks upon a United States Bank and a protective tariff.[51] The convention adjourned without airing in public the first divergences over the sectional problem.

Meanwhile, the Whig convention met at Milledgeville on July 1. The Calhounites intended to appeal to Whigs as well as to Democrats to drop their old party affiliations for the sake of sectional unity. It should be remembered that Calhoun had some grounds for expecting Whig support, in that the Whigs had been allied with him in their opposition to Polk and the War. Toombs had given him direct encouragement in this expectation. As late as April 30, he had written to Calhoun: "Our policy towards the whole Mexican question it is now evident will be in your hands. . . . The people of the South are now anxiously waiting to see which direction you will give it."[52] The Carolinian had also been encouraged by the fact that resolutions supporting his "Platform" had been adopted in one or two local Whig conventions in Georgia which preceded the state convention.[53] In his reply to one of these, he took the opportunity to make a public appeal to the Whigs of the state, which received wide attention in both the North and the South at the time.

"I am happy," he declared, "that my resolutions have met with the approval of your meeting. . . . I hail it as an omen that the Whigs of Georgia are prepared to do their duty in reference to the vital question involved. . . . I hope it is the precursor to the

---

[51] *Niles' Register*, LXII. 293 (July 10, 1847) ; Savannah *Georgian*, July 1, 1847; Holsey to Cobb, Dec. 31, 1847, *Toombs, Stephens, and Cobb Correspondence*, p. 93.

[52] Toombs to Calhoun, April 30, 1847, Calhoun Papers.

[53] Samuel A. Wales to Calhoun, Eatonton, Georgia, June 17, 1847, Calhoun Papers.

union of all parties with us to repel an unprovoked assault upon us—one that involves our safety and that of the Union. We have the constitution clearly with us. . . . We must not be deceived. The time has come when the question must be met. It can no longer be avoided, *nor, if it could, is it desirable.* The longer it is postponed the more dangerous will become the feelings between the sections. With union among ourselves there is nothing to fear, but without it everything. The question is far above the party questions of the day. He who is not with us is against us."[54]

Three days after this appeal was written, the Whig party convention met at Milledgeville. It was at once apparent that the Whigs who would support Calhoun were in such a minority as to be submerged in the great body of typically conservative members. Any of the latter who had, with Toombs, been "waiting anxiously to see what direction" Calhoun would give to "the whole Mexican question," evidently did not desire to follow the direction he had chosen. This led too obviously to a split with northern party allies and to the precipitation of a crisis in sectional relations. The conservatives were in such complete control of the gathering that the only evidence given of sympathy with Calhoun was the passage of a resolution thanking him for his opposition to the Mexican War.

The Wilmot Proviso was condemned as "unjust and unconstitutional," but no threats of resistance were made. The convention then proceeded to the nomination of candidates for governor and for the presidency. Duncan L. Clinch, a coastal planter, de-

---

[54] *Niles' Register,* LXII. 323, 389 (Aug. 21, 1847). It was reprinted in both northern and southern journals with appropriate comments. The Boston *Atlas, e.g.,* threatened that a solid South would be met by a solid North.

feated William C. Dawson for the first honor. Resolutions followed favoring Zachary Taylor as the next
presidential nominee. There was less opposition to
this proposal than there had been in the Democratic
conventions, presumably because the Whigs stood in
greater need of filching some glory from a war which
they had opposed. Governor Crawford's administration was highly praised, especially for its financial
record. So far as all other issues, local or national,
were concerned, the resolutions merely observed with
modest brevity that "Whig principles are too well
known to need repetition."[55]

The declarations of the party conventions made it
plain that the Proviso issue would be injected into the
state campaign. The Democrats took the initiative,
since their position still enabled them to emphasize the
sectional appeal. Towns largely devoted his letter
accepting the Democratic nomination to an attack upon
the Proviso, which he termed "a strange amalgama-
tion of religious fanaticism and political knavery." The
South must resist it, with nothing to concede or to
compromise.[56] In his speeches which followed and in
the Democratic press, it was emphasized that the party
had in its platform not only condemned the Proviso, but
had promised final resistance thereto. It had pledged
itself to back no presidential nominee who was not
clearly opposed to the measure and had nominated for
governor one whose principles were also clearly known.
The Democrats were not backward in proclaiming
themselves, therefore, the party of "southern rights."

[55] Savannah *Republican*, July 2, 1847; *Georgian.* July 2, 1847; *Niles'
Register*, LXII. 389 (August 21, 1847). Crawford, one of the state's
Whig leaders, had been governor since 1843, *i.e.,* during the period of
financial recovery described in chapter I.

[56] *Federal Union*, July 27, 1847.

On the other hand, the failure of the Whigs to dupli-
cate the Democratic resolutions was fiercely attacked.
They could not be trusted to defend the rights of their
own section.[57]

The fact that Clinch issued no statement of principles weakened his position upon the chief issue. The
Whigs had condemned the Proviso, and there was no
doubt that in this they expressed the views of their
constitutents. Yet they were necessarily more anxious
to evade the issue than were their opponents. When
urged to support only a clearly anti-Proviso presidential nominee, they replied by pointing to "Old
Zach," their choice, as one of whom no questions need
be asked. Indeed, the Whigs preferred to avoid national issues altogether and to emphasize matters of
state interest, such as the creditable financial record
of the Crawford administration. The Milledgeville
Southern Recorder openly held that, as this was a state
election, matters of national concern should not be
dragged in to confuse the contest.[58] The Augusta
Chronicle, however, ever the boldest of the Whig
papers, continued to discuss national issues, denounc-
ing Polk and the War, and Towns as a supporter of
both. The Democrats were held responsible for the
whole difficult Proviso problem, which they had thrust
upon the country, despite Whig warnings, because of
their war policy.[59]

Both parties apparently maintained internal harmony in the face of the common political enemy
through the summer and fall. It has been noted, however, that the sectional issue was already disturbing

[57] *Federal Union,* July 27; *Georgian,* August 11; Columbus *Times,*
August 17, 1847.
[58] In the *Federal Union,* August 3, 1847.
[59] Augusta *Chronicle,* August 8, 10, 1847.

this apparent good feeling. Calhoun's efforts to organize a southern movement in the state continued. The response among the Whigs was so slight as to make it almost negligible. The small Calhoun element in the party had been submerged, though not eliminated, in the June convention. Appeals to the masses of the Democrats were also unsuccessful. Efforts were at first made to swing even the old Union element into the new movement. Isaac Holmes, South Carolina congressman, wrote to Howell Cobb urging the necessity for southern unity and for the abandonment of the old parties.[60] The net result of such appeals to Union Democrats, as will be noted below, was simply to increase their latent antagonism and suspicion of the South Carolina movement. The response of the state-rights element, which had existed in the party since 1840, was certain to be more friendly. To the leaders of this group Calhoun supplied inspiration, and received in return confidential reports upon the prospects facing his movement within Georgia.

His most regular and in some ways most interesting correspondent was Wilson Lumpkin, ex-governor and one-time Union Democratic leader, who had been converted to the state-rights position. Lumpkin agreed entirely with Calhoun in his analysis of the national situation and on the need for southern unity against northern aggression. At times, he seemed to be urging Calhoun on rather than merely receiving his suggestions. But in his comments on the political situation in Georgia he warned him constantly that the time was not yet ripe for the formation of a southern party. "With but very few exceptions," he wrote in

⁶⁰ Holmes to Cobb, August 21, 1847, *Toombs, Stephens, and Cobb Correspondence*, p. 88.

August, 1847, "the people of Georgia are wholly un-
prepared to yield up their old party attachments. . . .
The press tries to lull their sense of danger." It
would require further developments and agitation "to
produce a conviction of the utter corruption of both
the great parties."[61] On November 18, in response to
further urgings from the Carolinian, Lumpkin replied: "I concur with you that concert of action is the
first object to be obtained, and I can see no way of
effecting this but by a convention of the states interested." But this plan for a southern convention, which
his friends desired, could not now be proclaimed in
Georgia. It would only stir up antagonisms and opposition within the Democratic party. Calhoun was
warned that he overestimated the chances for its success in the state. Perhaps, however, some developments in the legislature about to convene or in the
coming session of Congress would supply the stimulus
necessary to arouse the state to a sense of its danger.[62]

Similar warnings reached Charleston from other
Democrats in Georgia. One of them, however, had
some practical suggestions to offer. Edward J. Black
came from Scriven County, which, lying just across
the Savannah, had a large element of South Carolinians in its population. He declared to Calhoun in the
fall:

I am writing you on the proposition you make of *retaliation.*
But how is it to be effected? I confess the attitude of the
Democratic party within this state, as I found them in the con-
vention of June last, was anything but satisfactory to me. I

[61] Wilson Lumpkin to Calhoun, August 27, 1847, Calhoun Papers;
see *ibid,* for similar letters dated March 11 and December 20, 1847.
Wilson Lumpkin was an uncle of John H. Lumpkin, Cobb's lieutenant.

[62] Wilson Lumpkin to Calhoun, November 18, 1847, "The Correspondence of John C. Calhoun" (J. F. Jameson, Ed.), *American Historical Association, Annual Report,* 1899, II. 1138.

found the great mass of the party inclining strongly to their old ways of temporizing with principles and postponing necessary and ultimately inevitable issues. . . . We have succeeded in electing Mr. Lawton,[63] native of South Carolina and a Democrat, from this senatorial district. He professes to be your friend. [Lawton was ready to introduce resolutions in the state senate favoring "retaliation." Such prospective resolutions would stand a better chance there than ones demanding immediate or preëmptory action.] If you think so and can find time to draft a set of resolutions for me, with a succinct preamble setting forth the states that have assailed us, and the nature, manner and time of the assault, I will keep the original strictly to myself and send a copy by Lawton to our friends at Milledgeville. . . . If you can send me anything let me have it shortly. . . . I would draw them up myself, but know I cannot do as you can.[64]

It is possible that Calhoun did send something to Black and Lawton, as the latter was one of the first to introduce resolutions upon the slavery question when the legislature convened late in November. Two years later, when the legislature of 1849 met, he was again one of the leaders in introducing a series which were later passed by that body and became nationally known as the "Georgia Resolutions."

The letters from Black and Wilson Lumpkin show clearly why the Calhoun Democrats in Georgia failed to come out in the open during the fall of 1847. Such appeals for southern unity as were made were unofficial and were made upon individual responsibility. The most interesting of these was contained in a remarkable pamphlet entitled *Letters from Georgia to Massachusetts and to the Southern States.* The anonymous author, in reality A. B. Longstreet, ostensibly desired to show the Old Bay State the error of

[63] W. J. Lawton, of Scriven.
[64] Edward J. Black to Calhoun, Jacksonboro, Georgia, n.d. (*c.* Nov. 1847), Calhoun Papers.

its ways, but was actually appealing to the southern people. He began by giving a vivid résumé of the comparative history of the two states with regard to slavery, as seen from the Georgia point of view. His indictment of Massachusetts was scathing and impressive. He then proceeded to explain why Georgia could not emancipate and predicted with remarkable accuracy the course of the civil war which would ensue if the abolitionist attack upon slavery was continued.[65] Having thus appealed to Massachusetts at length in his first letters, he confessed to his southern audience in the later ones that he had achieved nothing but "trouble for his pains." Let this be a warning to the South! The section was about to be overwhelmed by northern aggression, yet remained apathetic in the face of the attack. People agreed that the Proviso was an evil thing, but turned from its consideration to the more interesting question, "What's the price of cotton?" For the sake of party harmony and office, southern Democrats would suffer all things from northern Democrats, and southern Whigs from northern Whigs. These dangerous and degrading party alliances must be abandoned if the South was to be saved—if the Union was to be saved![66]

Such an appeal, while anonymous and unofficial, gave a detailed exposition of the views of the Calhoun Democrats. It plainly hinted at the possibility of secession and therefore was apt to arouse the very suspicions and opposition among the Union Democrats that Calhoun's correspondents had warned him must be avoided.

[65] *Voice from the South: Comprising Letters from Georgia to Massachusettes. and to the Southern States*, (Baltimore, 1847), pp. 9-53.
[66] *Ibid., Georgia to the Southern States*, p. 3 .

Calhoun's course on the War, which had attracted the sympathy of Georgia Whigs, had correspondingly repelled Georgia Democrats. This was especially true of the Union Democratic element in the northwestern part of the state, for here Calhoun had been opposed and suspected since nullification days.[67] The Democratic press also condemned his attitude. When, in the spring of 1847, he took the lead in southern opposition to the Proviso, some of the papers which had opposed him on the war began to support him on the Proviso.[68] However, as the summer proceeded, and it became apparent that he was planning radical resistance to the Proviso and was actually courting the issue in a counter-offensive against the North, the Democratic journals again opposed him. The *Federal Union* deprecated the idea of a "Southern Movement,"[69] although it admitted that relationships were becoming strained with the northern Democrats.[70] The Savannah *Georgian,* whose traditional attitude was anti-Carolina, naturally condemned Calhoun.[71] Gardner, of the Augusta *Constitutionalist,* proclaimed in July that the support of Calhoun would not be popular in the Georgia Democracy.[72] Indeed, Samuel J. Ray, of the Macon *Telegraph,* seemed to be the only Democratic editor of consequence who was ready to support him when the southern movement was first announced in 1847.[73]

The Union Democrats quite naturally felt, therefore, that they had the bulk of the party with them in

[67] W. H. Hull to Cobb, May 22, 1846, *Toombs, Stephens, and Cobb Correspondence,* p. 79.
[68] *Federal Union,* February 23, 1847.
[69] October 26, 1847.
[70] August 17, 1847.
[71] *Georgian,* February 5, May 3, November 21, 1847.
[72] E. J. Black to Calhoun, n.d. (*c.* November, 1847), Calhoun Papers.
[73] *Ibid.*

their opposition to the southern movement.   Holsey, of the Athens *Banner,* Cobb's organ, was scornful of the Calhounites.   He wrote to Cobb of their "absolute monomania."[74]   He showed a shrewd understanding of the popular psychology, moreover, in explaining why it would be wise for the leaders of the party to maintain a strong Union position.   No party, he declared, could succeed in Georgia which threatened the Union.   The love of the Union was too thoroughly implanted in the minds of the masses of both parties.   Should we do anything "to weaken the bonds of the Union our own shaft would recoil upon us."[75]   This was accurate prophecy of what was to follow.

When the election for members of the legislature was held early in October, the Whigs secured a slight majority in that body; but in November the Democrats succeeded in electing Towns governor by a majority of thirteen hundred.[76] This was their first victory in a gubernatorial election since McDonald's last election in 1841. The vote for Towns in 1847 was twenty-five hundred greater than had been that for the Democratic candidate, McAllister, two years before. The Democrats themselves were inclined to credit this gain largely to Whig efforts to evade the slavery extension issue—especially to their anti-annexationist policy during the last congressional session and to their evasion of the Proviso and "Platform" problems during the campaign.[77] The small Whig majority in the legislature (four members in the House and one in the Senate)

[74] Holsey to Cobb, December 31, 1847, *Toombs, Stephens, and Cobb Correspondence,* p. 91.
[75] *Ibid.*
[76] The vote was as follows: Towns, 43,220, Clinch, 41,931.   See the *Federal Union,* November 9, 1847, for the returns.
[77] Savannah *Georgian,* October 8, 1847.

was ascribed to a superfluous number of Democratic candidates in the counties and senatorial districts.[78] The majority was so slight, however, that the presence of a few members of uncertain attitude practically balanced the parties.[79]

The legislature convened as usual late in November and plunged immediately into the several phases of the slavery problem then before the country. The Senate opened with a four day discussion of the Mexican War and the Proviso. The opposition to the latter was impressively unanimous. It happened that resolutions from Connecticut and New Hampshire supporting the Proviso were among the first business presented, and there was a general feeling that the reply from Georgia should make clear to the North just how the state felt on this critical matter. Several resolutions for this purpose passed without opposition. Those of Harden, a Democrat, declared that Georgia "viewed with solemn apprehension the approach of a crisis menacing the annihilation of the Union. If the Union is broken we will place the moral responsibility upon the North where it belongs."[80] This statement of the defensive position of the state was followed by an appreciation of such northern congressmen as seemed to be coöperating with those from the South in an effort to avert the crisis, public thanks being extended to those who had voted against the Proviso.[81]

Lest the northern people, however, persist in the attempt to exclude slavery from the territories, under a false impression of the attitude of the southern people, a solemn warning was issued upon this matter.

[78] *Federal Union,* November 9, 1847.
[79] Macon *Telegraph* in the *Georgian,* October 12, 1847.
[80] Savannah *Georgian,* December 4, 1847.
[81] *Ibid.,* December 14, 1847.

The important standing committee on the state of the republic was instructed to bring in "such a report upon the Proviso as is a just exhibit of the feelings of the people of Georgia." The committee prepared an interesting preamble to their resolutions in response to this instruction. "The people of Georgia," it declared, "have for a series of years been divided and disturbed by other questions, [than slavery] so much perhaps as to induce the *false hope* that upon this vital question there may now prevail discord and discension. This is not true. Georgia has but one mind—is as one man—all political parties are ready to plant themselves upon the same platform and join heart and hand in the assertion and maintenance of their constitutional rights in the territories."[82]

This preamble was adopted by the unanimous vote of both Whigs and Democrats. There is no doubting its sincerity or the solemn character of its warning to the North. The statement that southern men were often divided in this period is true, but for Georgia it meant not a division upon the Proviso itself, but only a difference of opinion as to whether this issue should be cultivated or avoided.

The divergence between the parties on the question of evading the Proviso had already been made clear in the party conventions early in the summer and now promptly reappeared in the legislature. The developments in the Senate illustrate this divergence. The Democrats introduced resolutions which supported the Mexican War at the same time that they opposed the Proviso. Other resolutions, however, offered the Missouri line as a compromise *of fact* on the question of territorial expansion. The Whigs defeated the

[82] Savannah *Republican,* May 23, 1848.

latter with the assistance of Union Democrats, as
their aim was to avoid the whole issue by denying any
accession of territory.[83] They were simply following
the tactics determined upon by Berrien and Stephens
and other southern Whig leaders in the last session of
Congress. They denounced the effort to combine opposition to the Proviso (an opposition which all shared)
with approval of the war (an approval which was not
shared by the Whigs at all). "The Whigs took high
ground against the war," declared a Democratic member, "and denounced it as infamous. They also went
against any further acquisition of territory."[84] The
resolutions introduced by Calhoun's friend, W. J.
Lawton, were not even permitted to be printed, on the
ground that they did not represent majority opinion.[85]

Nevertheless, the resolutions finally adopted concerning the war were so framed as not to antagonize
the Democrats too greatly. They did not condemn the
Mexican War in particular, but held that war was
repugnant *per se* and should always be avoided when
possible. The present war should be terminated speed-
ily and in a liberal spirit, without the dismemberment
of Mexico. Polk was censured for casting aspersions
upon those who opposed his war policy. These resolutions passed the Senate by a vote of twenty-three to
twenty-one—a strictly party vote.[86] They offer a final
refutation of the charge that the Georgia slavocracy
desired practical extension of slave territory.[87] Simi-

[83] L. G. Glenn to H. Cobb, December 1, 1847. *Toombs, Stephens and
Cobb Correspondence,* p. 89.

[84] *Ibid.*

[85] Savannah *Georgian,* December 8, 1847.

[86] *Federal Union,* December 7, 1847.

[87] This mistaken charge, made directly or by implication, persists
even in scholarly works. See, *e.g.,* W. E. Dodd, *Expansion and Conflict,*
p. 174.

lar resolutions were accepted in the House in the same manner.

After December, the legislature abandoned the territorial topic to Congress and proceeded with the discussion of state affairs. The scene of the sectional drama shifted, therefore, to the national capital. The Georgia delegation, which returned to Washington in December, 1847, was evenly divided between the parties; there being four Democrats—Howell Cobb, John H. Lumpkin, Iverson, and Haralson; and four Whigs —Stephens, Toombs, Jones, and Thomas B. King.[88] Colquitt and Berrien remained in the Senate. Colquitt resigned in January, however, and went to Florida, whereupon Governor Towns appointed Herschal V. Johnson in his place. Colquitt and Towns were both state-rights Democrats, and it was natural that Johnson, also of that group, should be given the appointment.

When Congress convened in December, 1847, the most pressing topic of national interest was the continuation of the Mexican War. The Whigs renewed their opposition, and Stephens took the lead in supporting resolutions introduced in the House declaring the war to have been begun "unjustly and unconstitutionally" by the President.[89] A slight Whig majority made it possible to pass these resolutions, and to this condemnation of the War the Georgia leader ascribed the subsequent efforts of the administration to arrange peace with Mexico.[90] Early in February, Trist negotiated the treaty which was later ratified and which provided for that very extension of territory which

[88] *Congressional Globe,* 30 Congress, 1 sess., pp. 1, 2. Iverson replaced Towns, who had resigned to become governor.
[89] *Ibid.,* p. 343.
[90] Avary, *Recollections of A. H. Stephens,* p. 21.

the Georgia Whigs had so steadily opposed. The question of the extension of slavery into these new territories had now to be faced by Whigs and Democrats alike. The situation was complicated by the necessity for the organization of a territorial government in the Oregon country.

It must be remembered that even the actual acquisition of the new territories in the Southwest did not make the question of slavery extension an entirely practical one. It had been realized by many southern as well as northern men ever since the return of Minister Waddy Thompson from Mexico that the new country was practically unfit for slavery.[91] The Georgia political leaders were inclined to admit this directly, or by implication, though some southern politicians would not do so.[92] Toombs and most of the Whigs were inclined to oppose the Proviso on the grounds mentioned above; that is, that it was not only an insult to southern pride, but an earnest of what was to follow. If it was a "mere abstraction," why were northern men so anxious to adopt it?

A portion of the Democrats in Georgia, as elsewhere in the South, had desired the annexation of much larger areas in Mexico, into which slavery might be extended in actual practice.[93] Hopes for a similar extension into Cuba were shortly to be aroused. It was feared that the "abstract" application of the Proviso to New Mexico and California would be a precedent for its "practical" application to other portions of Mexico or Cuba. Because of these fears, H. V. Johnson declared he would vote against the "application of

[91] *National Intelligencer*, October 21, 1847; see Cole, *The Whig Party*, p. 122.
[92] See Phillips, *Robert Toombs*, p. 55.
[93] See, *e.g.*, the Columbus *Times*, February 15, 1848.

the Proviso to the moon."[94]   The more radical Democrats were to be joined in this position by Berrien and the more radical Whigs.[95]

Early in January, Senator Douglas, of Illinois, introduced a bill providing territorial government for Oregon, to which Hale, of New Hampshire, moved an amendment prohibiting the introduction of slavery therein. This at once raised the abstract issue of the Proviso and so precipitated a tense debate in the Senate. In the course of this debate, Calhoun, in line with his policy of forcing the issue and conducting a counter-offensive against the antislavery forces, claimed that the Constitution "followed the flag" into all the territories and consequently guaranteed the protection of slavery therein. Johnson, of Georgia, supported him in this contention, as might have been expected, as did most of the Georgia congressmen save Stephens. Both Berrien and Johnson voted against Hale's amendment,[96] which was defeated. Davis, of Mississippi, then moved an amendment guaranteeing slavery in Oregon while under the territorial government.

Here the issue was complicated by the receipt of a message from Polk urging the territorial organization of the vast regions of California and New Mexico. In an effort to solve the whole problem, the question of all the territories was finally referred, July 18, to a special committee of which Clayton, of Delaware, was made chairman. On July 20 this committee reported the bill generally known as the "Clayton Compromise."[97] This bill provided territorial government for the three

[94] Speech of August 10, *Congressional Globe, loc. cit.*, p. 1061.
[95] Berrien's views are noted below in connection with his "Address" of 1849.
[96] *Congressional Globe, loc. cit.*, p. 1061.
[97] *Ibid.*, p. 956.

territories, prohibited slavery in Oregon, and left the question of slavery in the other two to the Federal courts. Should the courts agree with Calhoun's thesis that slavery was protected by the Constitution in all the "land," then it must be protected in conquered California and New Mexico; but should it decide that the Constitution did not necessarily apply to the territories, or that the question of slavery was one relating to private rather than public law, then the old Mexican law prohibiting the institution must be maintained despite the conquest.

This plan to refer the whole matter to the courts was viewed by most southern men as a real compromise. The mass of the Georgia Democrats had clearly displayed in 1847 a desire for compromise, and while they had suggested the Missouri line or "popular sovereignty" as a means to this end, they could be expected to support the Clayton plan or any other that seemed feasible. It was natural, therefore, that their representatives in Congress should have supported it. The more extreme Calhoun Democrats in Georgia were opposed to compromise, to be sure, but none of this type were in Congress. Johnson in the Senate and Iverson and Haralson in the House, despite their Calhoun leanings, supported the Clayton plan.

The Georgia Whigs had evaded the issue in 1847, now they must meet it. As was to be expected, they displayed an immediate desire to compromise, an attitude similar to that of the Democrats. Berrien led the way in the Senate by working zealously for Clayton's plan. Toombs and King followed him in the House. Then it was that Stephens did the unexpected and apparently risked his career by joining with northern members to defeat the proposed solution. His explanation was simple. Like his colleagues, he desired the preservation of southern rights in the territories, but he feared a Supreme Court decision would hold that the Mexican law against slavery still obtained there. He himself was convinced that this was the case, and he intended to save the South this humiliation even though it brought him universal condemnation.[98]

Meanwhile, the House had prepared its own Oregon Bill, which prohibited slavery in that territory. In the Senate the bill was amended to provide for the extension of the Missouri line to the Pacific. This Berrien and Johnson supported, the plan appearing to them as a compromise in substitution for that of Clayton. Upon its return to the House, the Senate amendment was rejected by the northern majority, but every member of the Georgia delegation voted to uphold it.[99] Upon its return to the Senate, on August 12, Berrien and Johnson opposed any retreat by that body from its position,[100] but on the last day of the session the House bill was accepted. Polk signed it under protest. The "Proviso" was thus applied to Oregon.

The adjournment of Congress left the status of California and New Mexico still a matter of uncertainty. Upon this question the struggle in Congress was certain to be bitter, and there were reasons why this crisis should be evaded or at least postponed by both parties. It happened that 1848 was a presidential year. A crisis would divide parties along sectional lines and would risk the control of the next administration. Hence the Proviso problem must be shelved

[98] Ibid., p. 1055; Johnston and Browne, *Life of Alexander H. Stephens*, pp. 229, 230; Stephens to the editor of the *Federal Union*. printed in that paper September 12, 1848; and in the *Toombs, Stephens, and Cobb Correspondence*, pp. 117-124.

[99] *Congressional Globe, loc. cit.*, p. 1062.

[100] *Ibid.*, p. 1078.

again, and the territories must wait at least another half year for organization.

The problem of nominations for the presidency had now been in the air for some time. Within the Whig ranks there were two serious possibilities, Clay and Taylor. From the viewpoint of many southern Whigs, the former was disqualified by his nationalism and uncertain attitude towards slavery, as well as by his ominous record of defeat.[101] Crawford, Toombs, and Stephens had early opposed his nomination on these grounds.[102] Taylor, on the other hand, was not only a popular hero, but a southern planter, who could be trusted to protect the South against the Proviso. Stephens used his influence at home to secure Taylor's nomination by the Georgia Whig convention in June, 1847, which committed the state party to Taylor.[103] He was also a leader in promoting Taylor's cause at Washington at the close of the year.[104] The Georgia Whig press was uncertain in the summer of 1847 which of the two candidates to support. The Milledgeville *Recorder* came out late in May as the first journal clearly to support Taylor, which it continued to do consistently throughout the campaign.[105] Some of the party organs attempted to compromise by urging Clay for president and Taylor for vice-president.[106] Until the Democratic state convention met at the end of June, 1847, the Whig press was afraid the Democrats might "kidnap" Old Zach for their nomination, since they claimed him as their "own child."[107] After this con-

---

[101] Savannah *Republican*. March 10, 1848.
[102] Cole, *op. cit.*, pp. 127, 128.
[103] Johnston & Browne, *op. cit.*, p. 224.
[104] Avary, *Recollections of Alexander H. Stephens*, p. 21.
[105] *Federal Union*, June 1, 1847.
[106] *Ibid.*, May 18, 1847.
[107] Savannah *Republican*, May 23; *Federal Union*, May 25, 1847.

vention had adjourned without naming Taylor, there was little discussion of candidates among the Whigs until the caucus met at Millegdeville in December and recommended that a party convention meet in June, 1848, simply to choose a Taylor electoral ticket.

Opposition developed in January, 1848, to the nominations of Taylor by the June convention and by the late Whig caucus, on the ground that such nominations followed antiquated methods of party procedure. The Savannah *Republican* began to favor the recognition of the party national convention and to urge that a Georgia delegation be chosen thereto.[108] The "consolidationist" principles of the Augusta *Chronicle* at the same time inclined that paper to a similar view. Only the *Recorder,* among the important journals, held out for ignoring the convention.[109]

The press of the period was sensitive to the opinions of party leaders, and it was probably their pressure that swung the Whig papers into line for Taylor during the winter of 1848. The one notable Whig leader who held out for Clay was Senator Berrien. He was supported in Augusta by the *Republic,* a paper founded, perhaps for that purpose, at the beginning of the year. The editor was James M. Smythe, a former associate editor of the *Chronicle,* of "independent" inclinations.[110] Berrien and Smythe led the small band of Whigs who refused to join the rush for Taylor. Berrien himself had long been a friend of Clay and had been associated with that leader in advocating such Whig principles as the protective tariff, the Bank, and nationalism. These principles were now apparently to be ignored in the effort to run a man who

[108] Savannah *Republican,* February 6, 1848.
[109] Savannah *Georgian,* February 8, 1848.
[110] *Ibid.,* January 15, 1848.

had little to recommend him save southern origin and military renown. The opposition of the Clay Whigs in the South may perhaps be viewed as the protest of those few conservatives who "viewed with alarm" the substitution of personalities for traditional Whig issues in the coming campaign. It was Berrien's contention that open loyalty to the traditional party principles would improve the prospects for a successful campaign.[111]

As the spring approached, the press campaign for recognition of the national Whig convention succeeded, and this made it incumbent upon the dominant Taylor group to defend their favorite, now no longer guaranteed the state's support simply because of the earlier nominations. The state convention was to meet early in June to send delegates to the national convention in Philadelphia. There followed a campaign for Taylor against the almost isolated opposition of the Augusta *Republic*.

However, the contest was hopeless for the Clay minority in the state. The party convention met at Milledgeville early in May and was dominated by the Taylor majority. Smythe spoke in favor of Clay and offered resolutions declaring the party's attitude towards the tariff, the currency, and the war. These resolutions were not accepted, but the majority sought to soothe the Clay men by adopting the pretty declaration that Clay was deserving of "the undying confidence of the Whigs of Georgia." None of the majority opposed this lip-service to an abandoned chieftain —and none believed it. The delegates chosen to go to Philadelphia were understood to be Taylor men, though

[111] Berrien to J. S. Pendleton, September 6, 1848, Berrien MSS.; Berrien to A. F. Owen; quoted in Miller, *Bench and Bar,* I. 78. See Carroll, *Origins of the Whig Party,* chapter v.

they were not formally bound to any candidate. They could vote for anyone "whose views on the Proviso and Southern Rights accord with our own."[112] The Whig national convention nominated Taylor without serious opposition and, as was expected, adopted no real platform. Fifteen antislavery northern delegates bolted because of what they claimed was southern domination of the meeting. These men merged with antislavery Democrats and the abolitionists of the "Liberty Party" to form the "Free Soil Party" of the North, which nominated Van Buren for the presidency. In Georgia, the nomination of "Old Zach" was received with great acclaim by all Whigs save the small Clay element. Some of the latter, like Berrien, acquiesced in the result and urged all to do likewise.[113] The Whig leaders claimed during the campaign, however, that most of the Clay men refused all support to the party candidate.[114]

Meanwhile, the Democrats were threatened with a somewhat similar schism. To be sure, the Democrats had no two outstanding rivals to decide between. In Georgia the party convention of 1847 pledged them to no candidate, but required simply that the nominee be an anti-Proviso man. The moderate Democrats were ready to accept a northern leader of such principles, though they preferred a southerner.[115] In the late spring of 1848, however, it became apparent that the feeling among the Calhoun Democrats against the North was rising, which meant trouble within a party committed to a compromise policy.

[112] *Federal Union,* May 16, 1848.

[113] Berrien to Pendleton, September 6, 1848; Berrien MSS.

[114] Toombs to Crittenden, September 27, 1848; *Toombs, Stephens, and Cobb Correspendonce,* p. 128.

[115] W. C. Daniell to Cobb, June 20; T. R. R. Cobb to Howell Cobb, May 31, 1848, *Toombs, Stephens, and Cobb Correspondence,* pp. 106, 109.

This was entirely natural. Another session of Congress, with its attendant debates on the slavery issue, had enabled the southern movement to make further progress in the minds of state-rights Democrats. The last Congress had seen not only the controversies over the Oregon Bill and the Clayton Compromise, but had also witnessed the introduction of another Proviso measure[116] and of a bill to abolish slavery in the District of Columbia.[117] Even conservative Whigs, like Toombs,[118] and Stephens,[119] and Democrats, like John B. Lamar,[120] began this year to fear that compromise might fail in the face of so persistent a northern attack, in which case they felt that the Union could not be preserved. It was in the spring and summer of 1848 that the possibility of a dissolution of the Union was first openly discussed in Georgia.

If conservatives began to have their doubts, it is not strange that the temper of the state-rights Democrats was rising. The outward and visible sign of this spirit early in 1848 was the diversion of the Augusta *Constitutionalist* to the support of the heretofore isolated Macon *Telegraph* in upholding the "southern movement." These two papers began to demand the nomination of a southern candidate at the coming national Democratic convention. The stand of the *Telegraph* in particular coincided with that of Calhoun and so threatened trouble for the moderate majority of the party. It pointed out that there were new and dangerous tendencies in the northern Democracy and went on to say:

[116] *Congressional Globe,* 30 Congress, 1 Session, p. 391.
[117] *Ibid.,* p. 872.
[118] Stoval, *Robert Toombs,* p. 61.
[119] For Stephens' fears see Johnston & Browne, *op. cit.,* p. 231.
[120] Lamar to Cobb, July 12, 1848, *Toombs, Stephens, and Cobb Correspondence,* p. 116.

We should demand in the Baltimore Convention, that all men be repudiated unless they support the rights of the South. The admission of Wilmot Proviso delegates should be the signal for the delegates of the Southern states to withdraw. Time-serving politicians may counsel the South to slurr over this great issue, lest the harmony of the party be broken, but we tell our delegates from Georgia that unless the Herkimer delegates are kicked out of the convention, the people of the South will not feel bound by its action. . . . We tell our delegates to Beware! In maintaining our rightful power in the Confeder-acy . . . we will sacrifice if need be, our old Party ties, old Party favorites, and the older and dearer favorite, the very Union itself![121]

The Democratic press generally refrained from attacking such sentiments for fear of alienating the more radical journals on the eve of the convention. There were a few exceptions. Holsey's Athens *Banner,* the most pro-Union Democratic paper, did become involved in controversy with the *Constitutionalist.* Again, when the *Telegraph* deplored the Savannah *Georgian's* persistent attacks upon Calhoun, the latter journal retorted that the *Telegraph* had denounced Cass and was guilty of "an overweening devotion to Calhoun."[122]

The moderation of the majority of the Democratic journals, in refraining from attack upon the Calhoun papers, bore fruit in the state convention and the campaign.[123] McAllister and Judge Cone, state-rights men, led the delegation that was sent to the Baltimore convention. There they shocked the moderates at home by voting for Yancey's southern-rights resolutions, but later returned the liberalism of the moderates by supporting Cass, of Michigan, after the second

[121] Macon *Telegraph,* in the Savannah *Republican,* May 25, 1848.
[122] Savannah *Georgian,* June 30, 1848.
[123] H. L. Jackson to Cobb, June 21, 1848; James Jackson to Cobb, July 9, 1848, *Toombs, Stephens, and Cobb Correspondence,* pp. 110, 116.

ballot.[124]   Cass was nominated, and a stand on the slavery question avoided.

Both of the radical papers upheld Cass in the campaign that followed.[125]   Despite rising feeling on the sectional issue, the exigencies of the presidential campaign thus temporarily averted an open split in the Democratic party.   Yancey's effort, upon his return to Alabama, to repudiate the Baltimore nominations was condemned by all the party journals in Georgia.[126]

This conservatism left individual southern-rights Democrats, who thought the situation too critical to be subordinated to party, uncertain and discouraged.   A few abandoned their old newspapers in disgust.[127] Some may have considered voting for Taylor, as a southern candidate, but there was no open movement in this direction, and no real Calhoun Democrat would have been likely to do so.   Some of them, like Wilson Lumpkin, continued to write Calhoun for advice and encouragement.   The old Georgia leader was almost in despair at the apathy of his people.   "United," he declared, "the South could conquer a peace.   But it is so un-united.   Tens of thousands . . . are all against us. Look at our little *pigmy* Stephens from Georgia. . . . Like Van Buren, they can only hope for the distinction of infamy, but they prefer that to obscurity. . . . What shall we do?"[128]   Senator H. V. Johnson beseeched Calhoun to send them "strong letters," for "it is believed that will be of much service to us in

[124] Washington *Daily Union*, May 27; Savannah *Georgian*, June 6, 1848.
[125] H. L. Jackson to Cobb, June 21, 1848, *op. cit.*, p. 116.
[126] *Federal Union*, June 19; Columbus *Times*, June 19; *Georgian*, June 3, 1848.
[127] Columbus *Times*, February 15, 1848.
[128] W. Lumpkin to Calhoun, August 25, 1848, Calhoun Papers.   For a similar letter from a Whig see B. F. Porter to Calhoun, July 17, 1848, *Ibid.*

Georgia, that it will go far to unite our people upon the principles upon which the rights of the South ought to be maintained."[129]

Harmony being temporarily preserved among the Democrats, and most of the Whigs holding together for Taylor, the order of the day now became the attack upon the opposing party. Despite all the din and fury of the presidential campaign, the tactics followed by each party were in reality simple and obvious. Each strove to prove that the other was not to be trusted to defend the South against northern antislavery aggression. The other group was leagued with abolitionists and, for the sake of party and office, would betray the home land. Each claimed its own northern allies were friends to southern interests and that it alone could, therefore, save the section. In this way, the ominous Proviso problem dominated the campaign, though it had not as yet seriously divided the parties.

The Whigs, of course, eulogized Taylor as the great hero of the war. After some lip-service to the principle of keeping the Proviso issue out of the campaign,[130] the Whigs hastened to occupy the vantage point of "southern rights." Taylor, the southern planter, was the only candidate the South could trust. He was not a "northern man with southern principles," but "one of ourselves." Little was said of Fillmore, of New York, the vice-presidential nominee, other than that "he is well known for his efficient public services." The Democrats, on the other hand, had nominated Cass, a northerner of uncertain attitude towards slavery. They were leagued with him and with Wilmot and other northern abolitionists and, therefore,

[129] H. V. Johnson to Calhoun, August 25, 1848, Calhoun Papers.
[130] Savannah *Republican*, May 25, 1848.

could not take true southern ground.[131] Whig readers were aroused by such startling headlines as the following:

THE SOUTH BETRAYED

or

THE IDENTITY BETWEEN THE FRIENDS OF GEN. CASS, THE FREE SOILERS AND ABOLITIONISTS, EXPOSED AND PROVED BY DOCUMENTS OF UNQUESTIONABLE AUTHORITY.[132]

The Milledgeville *Recorder* even claimed that Cass had voted for the Wilmot Proviso. This the Democratic press flatly contradicted and challenged the enemy to prove.[133]

To all such accusations the Democrats replied in kind. In 1847 they had refrained from attacking Taylor; indeed, they had defended him, even after the Whig state convention had nominated him.[134] The more conservative party organs, like the *Georgian*, withheld attack until the fall of 1848, when Toombs wrote that they still "refrained from opposing Taylor in any way."[135] This statement, however, was not entirely true. Individual Democrats questioned the General's opinions on slavery in 1847, and others questioned his eligibility early in 1848. The Columbus *Times*, for instance, opened the year with a poetic rhapsody beginning:

[131] Savannah *Republican*, May 15, 21, 23, June 12, 1848; Augusta *Chronicle*, April 7, June 12, 1848.

[132] Macon *Journal*, in the *Republican*, October 14, 1848.

[133] *Federal Union*, June 20, 1848.

[134] When a Democrat questioned Taylor's "soundness" in the summer of 1847 the Democratic *Constitutionalist* defended him. See T. W. Thomas to Cobb, July 7, 1848, *Toombs, Stephens, and Cobb Correspondence*, p. 115.

[135] Toombs to Crittenden, September 27, 1848, *Toombs, Stephens, and Cobb Correspondence*, p. 128.

Ungrateful Taylor! by the voice of Polk
Thou wast from naught into existence spoke!
More of King's English thou had'st slain by far
Than Indians in the Seminole War.
Turn now and study what to thee is new—
The Constitution and the statutes too.

It concluded with the thrilling peroration:

Thy lofty deeds the nation still shall praise,
And wish thee better, longer, happier days,
O'er thy past errors it will still lament
But never, never, make thee President![136]

Early in the summer, suspicion of Taylor's "soundness" on the slavery issue began to be expressed,[137]
although the more conservative Democratic press hesitated till fall to declare this definitely.   By that time,
the open claim of northern Whig papers that Taylor
would accept the Proviso, if it passed in Congress,
gave the Democrats opportunity for direct attack.
Taylor's silence was now interpreted as a mask for
antislavery opinions, and the South was warned that
in voting for him as a true southron it was about to
be "betrayed."[138]

Each party appealed to the malcontents in the
other and emphasized dissentions among the enemy.
The Whig papers agreed enthusiastically with the Calhoun Democrats' indictment of northern Democrats.[139]
On the other hand, it has already been noted that the
Democrats encouraged the Clay Whigs.   In addition
to this, they made the most of the apparent split between Stephens and Berrien upon the Clayton Compromise.   The debate on this compromise was carried

[136] Columbus *Times,* January 2, 1848.
[137] *Federal Union,* May 30, 1848.
[138] Savannah *Georgian,* September 27, October 2, 1848.
[139] Milledgeville *Recorder* in the Columbus *Times,* January 1, 1848;
Savannah *Republican,* May 25, 1848.

on during the summer in Congress and was certain to echo in the state campaign. The dissension between the two Whig leaders at Washington tended to emphasize the divergence of Berrien and his Clay Whigs from the rest of the state party. Berrien was supported, as usual, by the Augusta *Republic* and mildly by the Savannah *Republican,* while the other Whig journals followed the *Chronicle* in defending Stephens.[140] Some Whigs wrote Stephens anonymous letters opposing him, and Berrien, while upon a flying trip to Atlanta, was assured that many Whigs in that section were with him. The Elder Statesman was convinced that only sympathy for Stephens' illness prevented further attacks upon him, though he suspected that Stephens would mistake this sympathy for political support.[141] The Democratic journals promptly agreed with Berrien, and their attack upon Stephens was the most bitter move of the campaign.[142] Senator Johnson carried it into Stephens' own district, where the latter was a candidate for reëlection to the national House, and even appealed to Calhoun for direct support in annihilating the Whig leader upon the issue of the Clayton Compromise.[143]

Congressional elections were to be held in Georgia early in October, a month before the presidential election. Georgia was divided at the time into eight districts.[144] The results in most of these could be predicted with fair certainty, as they corresponded roughly with the geographical sections whose re-

[140] Augusta *Republic,* August 25, in the Savannah *Georgian,* August 31, 1848; Augusta *Chronicle,* July 31, August 25, 1848.
[141] Berrien to Major Harris, October 2, 1848; Berrien MSS.
[142] *Federal Union,* August 1 and 29; Savannah *Georgian,* August 2, 25, and 31, 1848.
[143] H. V. Johnson to Calhoun, August 25, 1848, Calhoun Papers.
[144] See Map No. 6, p. 171.

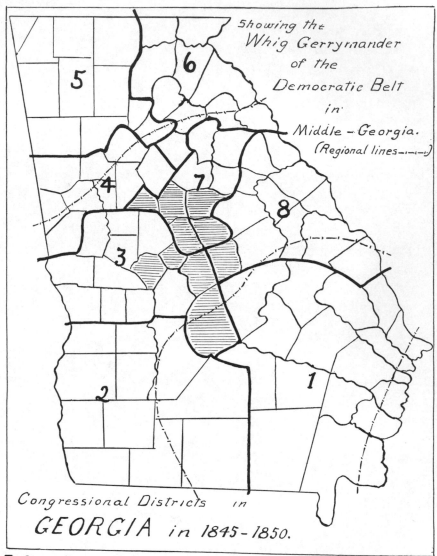

Showing the
Whig Gerrymander
of the
Democratic Belt
in
Middle – Georgia.
(Regional lines—·—·—·)

5

6

4

7

8

3

1

2

Congressional Districts in
GEORGIA in 1845 - 1850.

The Shaded Counties voted Democratic in 1848 and in several consecutive earlier Elections.

spective economic interests determined political alignments. The fifth and sixth districts in Upper Georgia were practically certain to go Democratic for
Cobb and Hackett, the latter replacing John H. Lumpkin, who had been appointed judge of the superior
court for the Cherokee circuit. The first district,
which included the coast and Pine Barrens areas—
sometimes referred to together as "Lower Georgia"—
would probably go for the Whig, Thomas B. King.
The plantation region there was always Whig, as
were the counties of Tattnall and Laurens in the pines
area. The only uncertain factor was the city of Savannah in Chatham. The third district in Central
Georgia was expected to go Whig by a small majority.
The presence therein of the exceptional Democratic
counties of Twiggs and Pike and the city of Macon
in Bibb promised a closer vote than in the seventh and
eighth districts of Central Georgia. These two were
dominated respectively by Stephens and Toombs, who
were almost certain to carry them by large majorities.
The second district, in Southwest Georgia, was the
most uncertain in the state. Here the population had
been until the forties largely made up of small farmers,
but it was now receiving planters as they moved down
to the new lands.

The certainty that the slavery issue would be the
chief one before the next Congress gave added importance to the congressional election; but it was also
certain that the national presidential vote would be
close, and this gave zest to the more dramatic presidential struggle. The feeling among the rank and file
of both parties, however, failed, as often before, to
keep up with that of politicians and editors. There

were reports that the people were apathetic.[145] We
are in the midst of a bitter fight among editors and
candidates," wrote Toombs, "but there is . . . little
excitement among the people. . . ."[146] This tendency
of politicians to overstate feeling and viewpoints
should always be recalled in estimating public opinion
in the state. There was no questioning the zeal of the
"editors and candidates."

The feeling in both parties was not improved by a
vicious personal attack upon Stephens, which almost
cost him his life. In the course of the controversy over
his vote against the Clayton Compromise, Stephens
had been bitterly condemned by both Senator Johnson
and Judge F. H. Cone, the latter a leading Democratic
delegate to the recent Baltimore convention. Stephens, whose personal courage was as pronounced as was
his physical weakness, challenged Johnson to a duel,
and met with a dignified refusal. Johnson was credited with the remark that he had "a soul to save and a
family to support, and Stephens has neither." Cone
engaged in a number of verbal tilts with Stephens
which led to misunderstandings of a serious character.
The two happened to meet upon a railway platform in
Atlanta on September 3, where, after a brief alterca-
tion, Stephens struck Cone with his cane, and the latter
attacked him with a knife with apparent intent to kill.
Only good luck, some by-standers, and the skill of
Doctor Eve, a physician of the Georgia Medical College, saved Stephens' life. The attack seemed peculiarly brutal for the reason that Cone weighed over
two hundred, and Stephens but ninety pounds.

[145] W. H. Hull to Cobb, July 22, 1848, *Toombs, Stephens, and Cobb*
Correspondence.
[146] Toombs to Crittenden, September 27, 1848, *ibid.*, p. 127.

The Whig press immediately claimed that the attack was deliberate and political in character.[147] Stephens was to be "put out of the way," at least for the rest of the campaign.[148] Democratic journals regretted the tragedy, but implied that Stephens shared the responsibility for it.[149] They feared that the martyrdom of the Whig leader would lose Democratic votes in both Georgia and nearby states and claimed that the Whigs were deliberately attempting to make political capital of the incident.[150] Cone was indicted, pleaded guilty, and was fined eight hundred dollars.[151] He was later entirely reconciled with Stephens and in 1860 was honorably known in the state as the "Nestor of the Ocmulgee bar."[152]

As the October congressional elections approached, the Whigs expressed confidence, and the Democrats some anxiety. Both realized that the vote would be close. The Whigs were more confident of the Taylor vote for November than they were of the congressional results, yet Toombs claimed that five and perhaps six of the eight men to be chosen would be Whigs. The actual results of the elections fell short of Toomb's claims, but they were nevertheless encouraging to his party. The total Democratic vote in the state in the congressional election was about forty thousand, in excess of the total Whig vote by only two hundred and sixty. This was another excellent indi-

[147] Macon *Journal,* September 5; Savannah *Republican,* September 5 and 6; *Chronicle,* September 5, 1848.

[148] Johnston and Browne, *Alexander H. Stephens,* p. 233.

[149] *Federal Union,* September 19, 1848; *Georgian,* September 26, 1848.

[150] *Federal Union,* September 19, 26, 1848; G. S. Houston to Cobb, September 23, 1848, *Toombs, Stephens, and Cobb Correspondence,* p. 126.

[151] *Constitutionalist,* September 24; Savannah *Georgian,* September 26, 1848.

[152] *The Plantation,* I. 82.

cation of the nice balance of power that existed between the parties in the state. The October election was more significant in this connection than the presidential election in November, in which the personal popularity of Taylor prevented typical results. As a result of the almost evenly divided vote, four districts elected Whig and four Democratic candidates. Any slight Democratic excess in the total vote failed to affect this equal division, perhaps because the districts had been arranged by the Whigs with a view to just such contingencies.[153]

An analysis of the vote by districts shows, first, that the vote was generally lighter in both parties in October 1848, than it had been in the state election of the preceding year. The outstanding phenomena were small Democratic gains in Lower Georgia and losses in the fifth and sixth districts of Upper Georgia. In Lower Georgia, there were slight Democratic losses in the interior counties of the Pine Barrens—Appling, Tattnal, and Bulloch—but gains in those on the outer areas of that region and the coastal counties. In Upper Georgia, there was a decided falling off in the Democratic vote as well as a decrease in that of the Whigs.[154]

These results cannot be explained by the fact that the vote for governor was sometimes larger than that for representatives. There was in Upper Georgia a lack of interest in the congressional situation, which surprised and humiliated the Democratic leaders.[155]

[153] For the Whig gerrymander of the Democratic belt across Central Georgia, see Map No. 6, p. 171, showing the congressional districts in 1848.

[154] This analysis is based on the county returns in the Savannah Georgian and Republican for October 13, 1848.

[155] Iverson to Cobb, October 17, 1848; G. S. Houston to Cobb, October 23, 1848, Toombs, Stephens, and Cobb Correspondence, pp. 129, 130.

Apparently the impending struggle in Congress over the slavery question was not of such interest to the poor farmers of the hills as to bring out their votes. On the other hand, an increased interest was manifested on the coast and in the outer counties of the Barrens, where the Calhoun faction was relatively strong.

Frantic efforts by the leaders to bring out the full Democratic vote in Upper Georgia for the November presidential election were fairly successful, but led to curious results. Thousands deserted Cass and voted for Taylor.[156] This was not necessarily due to any feeling against Cass upon the sectional issue. They loved not Cass less, but Taylor more. The up-country people were sturdy, but ignorant and, therefore, just the type to whom the personal appeal of a military hero was strong. This was as true in 1848 as it had been in 1840. The logical superiority of the Democratic arguments against Taylor probably did not reach a people who could not read the papers.

There was some defection in other parts of the state, presumably for similar reasons. In Lower Georgia, for instance, there was defection in the relatively illiterate, interior counties, though the Democratic vote in Savannah and the coast counties held its own as compared with the congressional election.[157] This was probably due, first, to the more critical attitude of a literate population; second, to the usual appeal to the foreign vote. "Irishmen," proclaimed the *Georgian,* "remember that the Whigs abuse General Cass because he does not love the British."[158]

[156] J. F. Cooper to Cobb, November 11, 1848, *Toombs, Stephens, and Cobb Correspondence,* p. 137.

[157] Savannah *Georgian,* September 13, 1849.

[158] *Ibid.,* November 7, 1848.

One feature of the Democratic defection should be especially noted. All the leaders were loyal to the party candidate. In a day when newspapers so generally followed political leaders, it was natural that all the papers were also loyal. The people, however, pursued in some cases a course quite independent of politicians and editors. "Is it not extraordinary," wrote a friend to Cobb, "that so large a ring of the Democratic party has deserted without a solitary leader? The rank and file have rebelled by regiments. . . ."[159] But this had occurred in 1840 and would occur again in 1850, and the tendency to vote independently in important elections may be termed a characteristic of the Georgia Democracy in this period. For this reason, as has been noted, the estimates of politicians and editors were not always reliable guides to the state of public opinion.

Democratic defection was great enough to give Taylor a majority of twenty-eight hundred votes in the state, which was about double that given Governor Towns in 1847 and exceeded that of Polk in 1844 by about eight hundred. The loss of a few Clay Whig votes probably prevented the Taylor majority from being slightly greater than it was.

Meanwhile, Taylor had been supported by the Whigs of other southern states and by the northern Whigs, who viewed him as one likely to oppose slavery extension. He received altogether a popular majority of one hundred and forty thousand votes. His victory in the electoral college was made certain by Whig success in New York, where Democratic losses to the Free Soil Party seriously handicapped the former party.

[159] J. F. Cooper to Howell Cobb, November 11, 1848; *Toombs, Stephens, and Cobb Correspondence*, p. 137.

The congressional elections throughout the country resulted in a Whig majority of ten in the House, which now also contained thirteen Free Soil members.[160]

[160] Rhodes, *History of the United States,* I. 97.

CHAPTER V

The effect of the election of 1848 on the position of the parties in the South, as related to the slavery question, was marked and immediate. The Georgia Whigs, whose emphasis upon Taylor's southern origin had rather accentuated the sectional appeal, now had to avoid this appeal, lest it embarrass their incoming administration. That administration would need the support of both the northern and southern wings of the party, and there was need for coöperation with northern allies. So far as southern interests were concerned, Taylor himself was a guarantee of their protection; hence there was no cause for alarm or agitation. The logical consequence of victory, therefore, was conservatism, a policy which harmonized perfectly with Whig economic interests and traditions.

The Democrats, on the other hand, were now to be in opposition and would have no scruples about embarrassing the new government. Cass having been defeated, there was no longer the same necessity for southern men to defend northern leaders. It was to the interest of Georgia Democrats to show that the Taylor régime could not be trusted to protect the rights of the South. Nor was there any lack of sincere belief that the northern Whigs were bent upon attacking the South and that southern Whigs, in attempting to maintain their alliance with them, must needs be traitors to their section. The logical consequence of Democratic defeat, therefore, was more militant sectionalism, a policy less objectionable to Democratic interests and traditions than to those of the Whigs.

In Georgia the results of the vote were scarcely known before this realignment on national issues became apparent. Forsyth exaggerated the new conservatism among the enemy, but did not mistake its general trend, when he wrote (November 10): *"The Whigs in our streets are even now preparing excuses for General Taylor, in the event that he 'holds his hand' when 'the Proviso' is presented to him. The party will uphold him in it."*[1] Shortly after this was written, Toombs appeared in Columbus and, in speaking on the Proviso, urged calmness and moderation. He emphasized the fact that the South had no real practical interest in the southwestern country. Such statements were easily misconstrued by Democrats to mean that the Georgia Whigs would now accept the Proviso.[2]

Meanwhile, the Democrats began to view with an alarm which was doubtless sincere, as well as politically expedient, the coming struggle in the new Congress over the territorial problem. This struggle had now been twice postponed, and feeling in both sections (at least among politicians) rose with each postponement and the consequent opportunity for further agitation. The *Georgian* explained the whole situation to its readers. There was real danger of the passage of the Proviso now and uncertainty as to Taylor's action in such a case. The position of the South was, therefore, a most dangerous one:

"Arrayed against her is [sic] not only the Northern Proviso men but the unenlightened moral opinion of the world." The

[1] John Forsyth (of the Columbus *Times*) to Cobb, November 10, 1848; *Toombs, Stephens, and Cobb Correspondence,* p. 136.

[2] Columbus *Times* in the New Orleans *Bee,* December 16, 1848.

South might temporarily secure peace by accepting the Proviso, without immediate injury to Georgia or the other slave-holding states, but the difficulty of the race situation would make such a policy suicidal. Slave numbers would increase rapidly therein until the slave labor system would become so burdensome as to demand emancipation. And what then? Experience proved that the two races could not live together in a state of social equality. The result of emancipation would, therefore, be the ruin of both races. Would Taylor avoid all these dangers by defeating the Proviso? "Will he save the South from facing the alternative of the rights of the Union and the rights of the South? No common hand can direct through the storms that impend. God save the Republic!"[3]

The Democratic journals of Augusta, Macon, Milledgeville, and Columbus were even more agitated than was the *Georgian*. The *Constitutionalist* and *Telegraph* had only restrained temporarily their sympathy for Calhoun's southern movement during the recent campaign and now returned to their advocacy of his policy. More ominous was the drift of the *Times* and the *Federal Union* in the same direction. The latter, which had condemned "Yanceyism" in the fall, now openly approved resolutions of the South Carolina legislature, which declared the time for discussion of the Proviso passed and called for southern unity in resisting it "at every hazard."[4] Whig editors, in reply, asserted their confidence in Taylor and denied that any crisis was at hand.

As a matter of fact, affairs were approaching a crisis in Congress, and there were indications that popular feeling was rising in some sections. Antislavery agitation was increasing in the North, and proslavery feeling was apparently growing in the South. The fall campaign had given a decided impetus to the southern movement in South Carolina.

[3] Savannah *Georgian*, November 13, 1848.
[4] *Federal Union*, December 19, 1848.

In November, Governor Johnson's message to the legislature of that state urged southern political unity and the call of a southern convention as the best means to this end. Calhoun "happened in" while the legislature was considering this message and influenced the resolutions which that body passed supporting the Governor's views.[5] Thus fortified by the support of the legislature, Calhoun proceeded to Washington with the determination to organize in Congress that unity among southern delegates he had long desired. The impending struggle there was bound to react favorably in southern states other than his own. The time seemed to him ripe at last for the open formation of a southern party and for the final decision which such a party would demand.

He did not have long to wait for an occasion justifying his first move. President Polk, a moderate southern Democrat, urged in his December message that Congress adopt some compromise on the territorial issue. The antislavery majority in the House ignored this recommendation and proceeded with a militant effort to adopt the Proviso. On December 13, 1848, the House instructed its territorial committee to bring in bills providing territorial organization of California and New Mexico excluding slavery.[6] In addition, resolutions were introduced forbidding slavery in the District of Columbia.[7] On December 21 the resolution of Giddings, of Ohio, was passed instructing the committee on the District to report a bill prohibiting the slave trade therein.[8] This move created

[5] Hamer, *The Secession Movement in South Carolina*, pp. 28-29.
[6] *Congressional Globe*, 30 Congress, 2 Session, p. 39.
[7] *Ibid.*, pp. 38, 55.
[8] *Ibid.*, p. 84; J. R. Giddings, *History of the Rebellion* (1864), p. 276.

intense indignation among southern members and led immediately to a call for the meeting of a southern caucus. The call was generally ascribed to Calhoun, though this was denied in Georgia, when the conservative Democrats used his name to discredit the meeting.[9]

The caucus was attended by some eighty members of both parties. Most of the Whigs went with the sole intention of thwarting any unified or radical action which Calhoun and his friends might suggest. This was also the motive of the conservative Democrats, among whom Cobb was the outstanding leader. The latter's association with the Union Democrats in Georgia and the conservative northern leaders of the party strongly disinclined him to a "Southern Movement." He and his colleague, Lumpkin, conferred with the President before going to the caucus, and Polk naturally encouraged them in their intention to oppose Calhoun.[10]

The caucus first met in the Senate chamber on December 23. All the Georgia members were present and took a prominent part in its proceedings. Indeed, it soon appeared that the three Georgians, Toombs, Stephens, and Cobb, were the leaders of the conservatives of both parties in opposing Calhoun's program. The Carolinian introduced a strong "Southern Address" which the Georgia triumvirate boldly but unsuccessfully denounced, this paper being adopted in a final session of the caucus on January 22. Only two Whigs were in favor of Calhoun's address, but the Democrats voted almost solidly for it. Cobb and

---

[9] H. V. Johnson to Calhoun, June 28, 1849, Calhoun Papers.
[10] Quaife, M. M. (Ed.), *The Diary of James K. Polk*, IV. 280, 281.

Lumpkin were followed by but two other Democrats in voting against it.

Toombs, Stephens and Cobb were severely criticized for their opposition, Iverson of Georgia joining Calhoun in the attack on the triumvirate. Berrien attempted to pour oil upon troubled waters by 'submitting a proposed appeal to the nation, which he hoped would be acceptable to both the conservatives and the extremists and which, of course, was acceptable to neither. Cobb then issued in self-defence an "Address" of his own, which explained the position of the conservative Democrats.[11]

There issued from the caucus, therefore, three separate addresses, those of Calhoun, Cobb, and Berrien, though only the first was formally adopted. Outside of Georgia, of course, it was Calhoun's address which was of primary importance. This contained an able restatement of his general sectional philosophy. After reviewing the history of the antislavery movement, it decared that the inevitable consequence thereof was abolition. The South must, therefore, defend herself at all hazards. The specific remedy, however, was left to the southern people. Postponement of the inevitable decision would but strengthen the North and weaken the South against a final reckoning.[12] The argument was perfect and, in the light of later events, undoubtedly prophetic.

[11] For general accounts of the southern caucus see Cole, *The Whig Party in the South*, pp. 140, 141; Phillips, *Robert Toombs*, p. 62; for the activities of Georgia members see Savannah *Georgian*, January 1, February 1; Charleston *Mercury*, February 2, 1849; Baltimore *Sun*, December 27, 1848; Toombs to Crittenden, January 22, 1849, *Toombs, Stephens, and Cobb Correspondence*, p. 141, *etc.*

[12] Calhoun, *Works*, VI. 290-313.

The address written by Cobb followed lines already laid down by him during the previous fall.[13] It was a Democratic protest against the formation of a southern party. Calhoun, in his effort to attract southern Whigs to his movement, had, it declared, attacked northern Democrats equally with northern Whigs. This was unfair to the former, who had in their ranks many more friends of the South than had the other party. For this very reason, the national Democracy could be trusted to protect the South, while, by the same token, national Whiggery could not. The southern Whigs, moreover, could not be expected to join a southern party which would oppose an administration they had just helped to put into office. Hence the southern party could not possibly accomplish its purpose, and, even if it could, its formation would endanger rather than preserve the country. The Democracy alone could save both the South and the Union.[14]

Berrien's address was a carefully worded appeal to the American people to compromise the slavery problem before it was too late. There was no phase of it which could not be settled if the two sections would but be fair to one another. The District problem could be adjusted, and the precedent of 1820 showed that the same was true of the territorial question. If the South was contending for an abstraction in the Southwest, the "Provisoists" were also pursuing a phantom. There was a real possibility of the future expansion of slavery in the tropics, however, and this

[13] Cobb to a Committee of Citizens in Charleston, S. C., November (4?), 1848, *Toombs, Stephens, and Cobb Correspondence*, pp. 134, 135.
[14] *To Our Constituents, By Messrs. H. Cobb, L. Boyd, B. L. Clark and John H. Lumpkin*, (Washington, D. C., 1849). Also printed in *Niles' Register*, LXXV. 231, 232; Savannah *Georgian*, March 14, 1849; reprinted in the Cobb Papers, *Georgia Historical Quarterly*, V. No. 2, 39-52.

territorial problem must therefore be definitely settled.
A real compromise which was fair to the South could
be accepted by all and might be reached under the
coming administration.   It was not to be achieved by
any one party.[15]

Such was the substance of the three addresses
which issued from the southern caucus.   Meanwhile,
the regular sessions of Congress continued, and with
them the further agitation of the slavery issue.   No
solution of the territorial problem had been found,
however, when Congress adjourned for the inaugura-
tion of Taylor early in March.   Congress had failed
to find any formula acceptable to the entire nation,
just as the caucus had failed to find any acceptable to
the entire South.

Once again the scene of the sectional drama shifted
from Washington to the states.   What would be the
effects of the last session's agitation, and especially of
the southern caucus, upon public sentiment "back
home"?   The response in South Carolina to the early
developments in Congress had been the passage by the
state legislature of resolutions declaring readiness to
coöperate with other southern states in resistance
to the Proviso at any cost.   Excitement there was so
intense that one faction led by R. B. Rhett was ready
for immediate and independent action, though the
majority were "coöperationists" and awaited the action of the sister states.[16]   Virginia was the first which
apparently responded to this appeal, for on January 20

---

[15] "Address to the People of the United States, by John McPherson
Berrien," in the Savannah *Republican*, February 5, 1849.   This address
has received little or no attention, in comparison with the other two, but
it has significance in connection with Berrien's subsequent position in
Georgia.

[16] Hamer, *Secession Movement in South Carolina*, p. 27.

its legislature reaffirmed its own resolutions of 1847, promising resistance to the Proviso, and added new ones requesting the governor to convene the legislature in case either the Proviso or laws abolishing slavery or the slave trade in the District were passed by Congress.[17]

Between February and April, 1849, resolutions were passed in the legislatures of Missouri and Alabama upholding Calhoun's address; in Tennessee declarations calling for united southern resistance were adopted. The most significant action, however, was taken in Mississippi. The congressional delegation of that state, unlike that of Georgia, had been united in support of the "Southern Address." This suggested that Mississippi was to rank next to South Carolina in the demand for a unified South. Events in the spring seemed to substantiate this suggestion, for a call was issued by prominent citizens of Jackson for a non-partisan convention to meet in that city on May 7, 1849, to consider northern aggressions and the proper remedy for the same. The convention met as scheduled and, after passing resolutions of a general character concerning slavery and the rights of the South, itself issued a call for a state convention to meet early the next October, to be composed of an equal number of Whigs and Democrats. This body, representing all the people of both parties, was to be authorized to express the state's attitude towards the slavery controversy. The harmonious coöperation of the two parties in issuing the call was the first indication outside of South Carolina of the progress of a real southern movement.[18]

[17] *Congressional Globe,* 30 Congress, 2 session, p. 441.
[18] Cleo Hearon, *Mississippi and the Compromise of 1580,* pp. 46-50.

While the southern states were passing resolutions, the northern states were even more active in this respect. Their legislatures proceeded through the winter and spring, almost without exception, to declare the right of Congress to exclude slavery from the territories and the desirability of so doing.

Meanwhile, what of Georgia? The addresses issued from the southern caucus reached the state at the end of January. As two of them were the work of Georgians, and the third that of the great leader across the river, they were bound to arouse unusual interest. Discussion of them had barely begun when word came of the resolutions of Virginia, and then, as the year progressed, of those of other states. These events of the winter of 1849 introduced two new elements into the situation in the "Empire State." The first was an echo of the demand in Congress for a more stringent fugitive slave law. This may be viewed as a phase of the growing militancy characteristic of the general position of the southern Democrats. The second was the secret conversion of a few able and extreme southern-rights Democrats to a belief in the advisability of immediate secession. The most obvious effect of the winter's agitation, however, was simply to emphasize tendencies already noticeable after the presidential election in the fall of 1848.

The Democrats of Upper Georgia tended, as would have been expected, to support Cobb's opposition to Calhoun and approved his "Minority Address."[19] Holsey, of the Banner, did become somewhat alarmed by

[19] T. W. Thomas to Cobb, February 16, 1849, Toombs, Stephens, and Cobb Correspondence, p. 152; W. H. Hull to Cobb, January 26, 1849, ibid., p. 142; Augusta Chronicle, March 28, April 4, 1849.

adverse criticisms he had heard,[20] but the reports he
sent Cobb did not seem to worry that leader. The latter continued at Washington to coöperate with the
conservative northern Democrats and to maintain his
stand against Calhoun. "God grant that we may be
able to floor the old reprobate," he wrote his wife, "and
thereby preserve the honor of the South and secure
the permanency of the Union. If it would please our
Heavenly Father to take Calhoun and Benton *home* I
should look upon it as a national blessing."[21] On his
return to the state early in the summer he wrote Buchanan, who had begun to fear the Georgian might lose
his district in the contest with the Calhounites, that his
stand was entirely approved by his constituents.[22]

The effect of the winter's excitement upon the
Democrats of Central Georgia was another matter. To
this section returned Senator H. V. Johnson and Representatives Iverson and Haralson, signers of the
"Southern Address." They were full of fight and
desirous of backing the appeal for a sectional movement, though it is probable that they still hoped such a
movement would redound to the advantage of the
Democracy. Calhoun's address and the new Virginia
resolutions received immediate support from the
Democratic editors of the Black Belt even before the
congressmen returned. It has already been noted that
the election of 1848 had persuaded many of the Democratic editors to support the southern movement, and
the winter's developments so furthered this tendency

[20] Holsey to Cobb, February 13, 24, 1849; *Toombs, Stephens, and Cobb Correspondence,* pp. 149, 154.

[21] Cobb to his wife, February 8, 1849, "Cobb Papers," *Georgia Historical Quarterly,* V. No. 2, p. 38.

[22] Cobb to Buchanan, June 17, 1849, *Toombs, Stephens, and Cobb Correspondence,* p. 164.

as to convert all of them outside of Upper Georgia to the radical creed. Opinions became more decided and aggressive, most of Calhoun's ideas being incorporated in the Georgia editorials.[23] The possibility of secession was more openly discussed than in the preceding year, and a running controversy developed with certain northern papers as to the probable consequences of this "last resort."[24] A politic silence was maintained, however, with regard to Cobb's "Minority Address" in an obvious effort to avoid further friction between the Cobb and Calhoun factions in the state party.[25]

A few extreme leaders in Central Georgia became converted by the spring of 1849 to a belief in the inevitable necessity of secession—as it was put in those days, they came to believe in "secession *per se.*" Prohaps the most remarkable leader of this group was Henry L. Benning, a lawyer of Columbus and then but thirty-five years of age.[26] He wrote Cobb frankly of his new convictions, which were remarkable in more respects than one. Secession, he felt, was a necessary but by no means a complete solution of the problem facing the South. The new Southern Confederacy, he declared, should be a "consolidated" republic, in order "to put slavery *under the control of those most interested in it.*"[27] Such a secessionist was, indeed, like the extreme Whigs, a "very Federalist" in his constitutional

---

[23] See, *e.g., Federal Union,* April 3, 1849.

[24] See, *e.g.,* Philadelphia *North American,* January 3, 1849; *cf.* Columbus (Ga.) *Times,* January 16, 1849.

[25] *Federal Union,* January 30, 1849.

[26] See, for his biography, the article by his daughter in *Men of Mark in Georgia,* III. 259; A. R. Lawton, *Judicial Controversies on Federal Appellate Jurisdiction,* Presidential Address, the 38th Annual Meeting of the Georgia Bar Association, (Tybee, Ga., 1921), pp. 21, 22.

[27] Benning to Cobb, July 1, 1849, *Toombs, Stephens, and Cobb Correspondence,* p. 171.

principles, and differed from them only with regard to the expediency of having a national or sectional union. Planter interests demanded a "consolidated" government in either case. For such a secessionist as Benning, therefore, the state-rights plea was but a political expedient—one useful in destroying the old Union, but to be abondoned in creating the new.[28]

Benning, however, could not speak for the mass of the people of Central Georgia, although he did write Cobb that he had personally met but one Democrat about Columbus who supported Cobb's position.[29] Other leaders of the Calhounites had resorted during the winter and spring of 1849 to the usual expedient of "getting up" popular meetings, both to stimulate and to express public feeling. Some half dozen ostensibly non-partisan meetings were held, which the Democrats claimed were large and enthusiastic, and which the Whig press declared were attended only by Democrats and by very few of them. Indeed the Whig press was quite specific, publishing lists of meetings and estimated attendance which do not seem to have been definitely denied by the Democratic papers.[30] Whig editors in Central Georgia echoed the Democrats of Upper Georgia in the statement that the

[28] He has been described, indeed, as "an ardent States Rights man," and so he was, so far as relations with the actually existing Union were concerned. As a member of the Georgia Supreme Court during the fifties, his opinions voiced the most extreme views of that school. See Lawton, *op. cit.*, p. 21. *Cf.* F. L. Owsley, *State Rights in the Confederacy*, pp. 1-3.

[29] Benning to Cobb, July 1, 1849, *Toombs, Stephens, and Cobb Correspondence*, p. 171. *Cf.* H. D. Foster, "Webster's Seventh of March Speech and the Secession Movement, 1850," *American Historical Review*, XXVII. 250.

[30] For enthusiastic Democratic accounts of public meetings, see *Federal Union*, January 23; Columbus *Times*, February 6; Charleston *Mercury*, March 23, 1849. For Whig figures and criticisms see the *Chronicle*, March 27, May 14; *Republican* May 28, 1849.

southern movement appealed only to editors and politicians, and that, despite all the fuss the latter were
creating, the masses were unmoved.[31]   There was indeed little evidence in the few public meetings held
early in 1849 to indicate popular excitement.

In a word, the Democratic editors and politicians
were now engaged in the difficult task of arousing an
inert public opinion, prior to the actual commission of
any overt act by the North.   Calhoun's address may
have, as Holsey put it, "prepared men's minds for
trouble," but it can hardly be said to have aroused the
people of Central Georgia in 1849.   What a persistent
press campaign might do by the end of the year remained to be seen.

The reaction of the Whigs to congressional developments in the winter of 1849 is somewhat easier to
follow than is that of the Democrats, for the reason
that less division obtained among them, and that what
division did exist did not follow the sectional lines that
tended to divide the Democrats.   The Whigs, like the
Democrats, had to face divergent action on the part
of their representatives in the southern caucus.   There
was the embarrassing contrast between the efforts of
Toombs and Stephens to break up the caucus and the
desire of Berrien to have it publish some sort of an
"Address."   The Whigs avoided taking sides in this
divergence of opinion.   The attitude of Toombs and
Stephens was generally praised, but in Savannah
there was also some moderate editorial approval of
Berrien's address.   Calhoun's address was termed
"provocative," while that of the Georgia Whig senator was "firm yet conciliatory."[32]   The Augusta

[31] W. H. Hull to Cobb, January 26, 1849, *Toombs, Stephens, and Cobb Correspondence*, p. 142; *Republican*, May 28; *Chronicle*, May 14, 1849.
[32] Savannah *Republican*, February 15, 1849.

Republic was of the same opinion. The more conservative Whig journals, led by the *Chronicle,* were generally silent on Berrien's position.

The Whig attitude toward Cobb's Address was uncertain. Democratic minority factions should be encouraged, of course, and Cobb's views agreed with those of the Whigs in opposition to the southern movement. On the other hand, his address had featured a denunciation of the northern Whigs and the consequent condemnation of that party as "unsound." This was not to be welcomed by the Whigs so long as they still clung to Taylor and the national organization. Hence there was some criticism of the "Minority Address" on these grounds.[33]

The Georgia Whig journals admitted that the northern legislatures had passed many resolutions of an insulting character, but these were but "words," and wise men would wait for deeds before stirring up trouble. After all, observed the *Chronicle,* the Whigs were the largest slave holders, and if they were not alarmed for the safety of the institution in which they had the greatest interest, why should others be so? It was, indeed, most kind of the Democrats to insist upon "protecting" the Whigs' economic interests, but would it not be in better taste to await an invitation?[34]

As was to be expected, the Whig leaders who opposed the southern movement featured its South Carolina leadership and appealed to the traditional Georgia feeling against the neighboring state. Their newspapers had long been ironical and bitter at the

[33] Augusta *Chronicle,* June 22, 1849.

[34] Augusta *Chronicle,* April 25, 1849. This point did sometimes confuse the Democrats, who had usually not clearly analyzed Whig motives for conservatism. See, *e.g.,* W. H. Hull to Cobb, January 26, 1849, *Toombs, Stephens, and Cobb Correspondence,* p. 148.

mention of Calhoun's name. First they ridiculed his domination of the sister state. "Mr. Calhoun took snuff yesterday, about 2 P. M.," observed the *Republican,* "whereupon 129 members of the South Carolina legislature *sneezed.*"[35] Then they condemned the whole South Carolina movement under his leadership and the effort to lead Georgia in its wake. Was it not absurd that Georgia should allow Carolina to "interfere" in her own affairs? These "mighty warriors of Palmettodom" were but trouble-makers, and the "fuss in Carolina" should be ignored. The Georgia Whigs understood the real objectives of the Carolina movement long before they were openly proclaimed by the Calhounites. South Carolina, it was declared, did not desire any compromise with the North, but, under cover of the southern movement, was heading directly for secession. The majority of Georgia Democrats were not secessionists *per se,* said the Whigs, and did not realize that this was the real purpose of their friends across the river. They would discover this in time, however, and refuse to be pulled along by radical Palmettodom. "We wish it particularly understood," said the *Republican,* "that Georgia will not become an appendage of this political comet—which is ever ready to dash into the midst of our glorious constellation of stars and destroy the harmony of their orbits. We are not yet tired of the Union, and we mean to stand by it."[36]

On the other hand, the small group of former Clay Whigs displayed a tendency to accept the southern-rights views held by a growing number of Democrats. It seems curious that this small faction, which

[35] Savannah *Republican,* November 8, 1848.
[36] *Ibid.,* November 19, 1848, January 1, 1849.

had in 1848 stood for conservatism, and opposed the sectional appeal emphasized by the southern Whigs in Taylor's campaign, should now have become the more radical wing of the party. The change is well illustrated in the person of Berrien, who stood by Clay and the old Whig principles in 1848, but who in the winter following desired action in the southern caucus and began to display some sympathy for the southern movement. It must be remembered, however, that one potent political force making for the conservatism of the majority of the Whigs; namely, their loyalty to and influence in the Taylor Administration, did not operate at all upon the Clay minority. These were aggrieved independents, who expected no favors from Taylor and who did not trust him to protect the South against the Proviso. Under such circumstances it was natural that they were soon to break with the majority. In this they represented the second secession of a body of Georgia Whigs from the main party on the ground that it could not be trusted to protect southern interests —the first having been the famous secession of the "State Rights Whigs" in 1840. The Clay faction naturally rallied around Berrien's address as the formal expression of their principles. Unlike the Union Democrats, however, the Berrien Whigs were very few in number and were not concentrated in any one particular section. Sectionalism in Georgia affected the Democracy much more vitally than it did Whiggery. It is true that the strongest groups of the minority Whigs seemed to be in Savannah and Augusta, and in those cities resided the popular leaders of the faction. These little local bodies, however, can scarcely be said to have formed sectional groupings within the state.

Each party attempted to drive a wedge between the two factions in the other, just as they had during the preceding year. In the spring of 1849 this effort was largely concerned with demanding of the enemy press which of its spokesmen in the southern caucus it upheld. The Savannah *Republican* insisted that it had attempted unsuccessfully for a month to discover whether its local opponent preferred the address of Calhoun or that of Cobb. The *Georgian* thereupon made the retort courteous that it had tried unsuccessfully "ever since 1848" to learn the *Republican's* preference between Stephens and Berrien.[37] The Whigs wished to know why Democrats condemned Stephens in the caucus, but not Cobb; while the Democrats inquired why Whigs heaped such abuse on Calhoun, but were so considerate of Berrien.[38]

While these discussions were in progress, a new and startling element was introduced into the national situation by the discovery of gold in California and the consequent rush of population thither. During the winter and spring developments in that territory attracted considerable attention in Georgia. Early indications that the population of California would be of a character opposed to slavery were rather welcomed by the Georgia Whigs, but regretted by the Democrats. The former rejoiced at the prospect that California would soon become a state with a constitution excluding slavery, for the state-rights Democrats certainly could not oppose the right of a state to decide this question for itself. Thus statehood in California would accomplish just what the Whig leaders had long desired, *i.e.*, the evasion of the difficult constitutional issue concern-

[37] Savannah *Georgian,* April 12, 1849.
[38] Augusta *Chronicle,* April 11, 1849.

ing the territories.[39]   For such sentiments, however, the Democrats rebuked them, on the ground that a free constitution in California would be but the Proviso in legal disguise.[40]

Thus appeared the first sign that the advocates of state-rights would abandon a strict adherence to their cardinal doctrine in the case of California, denying it the usual prerogative of a state to determine for or against slavery.   This was to be done on the ground that the unusual character of its population of "forty-niners" prevented it from being a truly American state. A somewhat similar reason had already been urged for abandoning the "popular sovereignty" compromise plan for New Mexico, on the ground that here the population was too largely Mexican to become truly American.[41]

Meanwhile, perhaps something could be done by southern-rights men to prevent California from being over-run by free-state adventurers.   One way to avert this fate was to encourage the settlement of southern men with their slaves in the territory.   Here, of course, all the forces of nature were against the South, for there was no demand for slaves in the new country. Would Georgians sacrifice their economic and other interests for the sake of political expediency in this matter?   At least one optimist, Robert R. Howard, thought they would.   Early in April he issued a call for five hundred Georgians to accompany him to the new Eldorado.   The object of the expedition was, in addition to finding gold, "to enjoy their rights in com-

[39] Augusta *Chronicle*, January 14, 1849.

[40] Columbia *South Carolinian*, January 16, 1849.

[41] Holsey to Cobb, February 13, 1849, *Toombs, Stephens, and Cobb Correspondence*, pp. 149, 150.

mon with other citizens in a territory."[42] For this purpose, presumably, each of the five hundred was to come armed and to bring with him from one to four male slaves. The company, which was to have a quasi-military organization, would assemble at Milledgeville on May 1, 1849.

The more extreme Democratic papers applauded this call enthusiastically. The conservative ones advised against the movement, however, on the ground that Georgia needed her men at home, though they admired "the Southern spirit of the call."[43] The matter attracted some attention in the North among the antislavery papers, where it was spoken of as an "armed immigration to California" which "looks rather vapory."[44] The Columbus *Times* replied that it hoped it would actually take place and that thousands of others from all over the South would go with them.[45] The expedition does not seem, however, finally to have materialized. A few Georgians went to California as individuals, with their slaves, and in some cases returned with them years later.[46]

The first test of party policy and the party factions in 1849 came with the meeting of the Whig and Democratic state conventions early in July. Trouble was threatening in the Democratic convention between the Cobb and Calhoun factions, the latter being suspected of a desire to have the party officially approve the "Southern Address" and the southern movement. It was essential to preserve party unity, however, 'if the

[42] Columbus *Times*, April 3, 1849.
[43] Savannah *Georgian*, April 13, 1849.
[44] New York *Tribune*, May 1, 1849.
[45] May 8, 1849. This attitude suggests that which was later taken with regard to Kansas.
[46] C. A. Dunway, "Slavery in California After 1848," *American Historical Association, Annual Report*, 1905, II. 245.

state election for governor and the legislature was to be won in the coming fall. Governor Towns therefore exerted himself to prevent too open an attack upon Cobb.[47] When the state Democratic meeting was held at Milledgeville, July 11, 1849, the Calhounites did attempt to adopt the "Southern Address," but Cobb threatened them not only with a bolt of his Cherokee delegates but also with the "uncompromising hostility" of Polk's administration.[48] The delegates thereupon compromised for the sake of harmony, adopting the relatively innocuous resolutions of Virginia in the place of the "Southern Address," and nominating Towns for governor.[49]

The convention had no sooner adjourned than a chorus of derision arose in the Whig press. The Calhoun Democrats, it was pointed out, had condemned as traitors to the South all who would not approve Calhoun's pronunicamento, yet now they had not so much as mentioned that famous paper in their official resolutions. Evidently, remarked the wily Whigs, the Cobb faction controlled the Democracy, and as Cobb represented the "submissionist" wing, the people of Georgia might know what to expect from the Democratic party as the protector of southern rights.[50]

In this way the Whigs attempted to ridicule the Democratic claim to sectional preference; that is, they

[47] G. W. Towns to J. H. Lumpkin, quoted in Lumpkin to Cobb, June 13, 1849, *Toombs, Stephens, and Cobb Correspondence*, p. 163.

[48] Milledgeville *Southern Recorder*, in the *Chronicle*, August 2, 1849.

[49] The only expression of "rising feeling" in the Democratic convention was the adoption of a resolution against "squatter sovereignty" in the territories, a doctrine which the party had approved in 1847 and 1848. This was probably motivated by a fear that the doctrine would play into the hands of the Free Soilers. See the *Georgian*, July 13, November 13, 1849; H. V. Johnson to Calhoun, July 20, 1849, *Calhoun Correspondence* (as cited above, p. 147, n. 62), p. 1197.

[50] Columbus *Enquirer*, in the *Chronicle*, August 11, 1849.

continued to play the game that both parties maintained throughout the entire crisis of 1850—the game of party advantage and expediency. The Democrats replied as best they could, but many of the Calhounites felt the force of Whig jibes and wished themselves well rid of the incubus of Cobb conservatism.[51]

The Whig state convention met at Milledgeville on June 25. It was, the Whigs claimed, "the largest and most harmonious ever held in Georgia." The resolutions adopted reasserted opposition to the Proviso as violating all the compromises, asserted the necessity for final opposition in case it should pass, but expressed continued confidence in Taylor's administration. The platform was, generally speaking, a recapitulation of the resolutions adopted by the Whig majority in the last state senate, that of 1847-1848. Judge Edward Y. Hill was nominated for the governorship "with unaminity."[52]

The Whig platform was criticized by the Democrats on much the same ground that they themselves had been attacked. The Whig resolutions, said the followers of Towns, were strong enough when passed by the state senate in December of 1847, but were too weak for 1849. They spoke of resistance, but called for no definite action. The Whigs made much of Democratic divisions, continued the Democrats, but it was obvious that Whig leaders like Stephens and Berrien had been forced to remain away from the party's state convention in an effort to hide their differences. The Whigs would, no doubt, have liked to keep silence on the slavery issue altogether, but "agitation on the

[51] Columbus *Muscogee Democrat,* in the *Chronicle,* July 21, 1849.
[52] Savannah *Republican,* June 28, 30; Augusta *Chronicle,* June 28; Columbus *Enquirer,* July 3, 1849.

Proviso has reached such an extent" that "no convention dares adjourn at the present time maintaining silence upon it."[53]

Throughout the campaign, each party strove—as it had in 1848—first, to show itself "sound" and the enemy "unsound" on southern-rights, and, second, to prevent the development of faction in its own ranks and to encourage it in those of the other. The Whig attack on the Democratic convention had been directed towards all these ends and had been relatively effective. It was more than neutralized, however, by pointed Democratic attacks upon Taylor's "soundness,"[54]—now a matter of secret suspicion even among the Whig leaders—by renewed denunciations of Fillmore, and by a systematic effort to divide the Whig factions.

This last move was well planned and effective. On August 18 a "committee of citizens" addressed to the gubernatorial candidates the following questions, to which they requested the favor of public replies: (1) "Is the Wilmot Proviso constitutional?" (2) "Did you approve the Clayton Compromise?" (3) "What should the South do if the Wilmot Proviso passes?" Towns replied promptly to these queries. He answered the first in the negative, the second in the affirmative, and for the third repeated his statement that there should be "resistance at every hazard." Hill failed to reply, which brought upon him a torrent of Democratic denunciation. The Marietta *Helicon* claimed in his defense that the questions never reached him, but this the Democrats denied.[55]

[53] Savannah *Georgian*, June 30, July 13, 1849.
[54] Columbus *Times*, May 8, June 5, 1849.
[55] *Federal Union*, September 25, 1849.

The object of the questions was obviously to emphasize old Whig differences on the Clayton Compromise and to accentuate new ones then developing with reference to the constitutionality of the Proviso and the best mode of resistance thereto. The bulk of the Whig party probably agreed with the Savannah *Republican* that the Proviso was unconstitutional,[56] inasmuch as they agreed with Calhoun and Berrien that the constitution "followed the flag" into the territories and prevented congressional interference with slavery therein. The tendency of the Augusta *Chronicle* to support Stephens' denial of this thesis, in connection with the Clayton Compromise, had already indicated the presence of a conservative group of Whigs who differed from the others in constitutional theory. Lee, of the *Chronicle*, insisted that Calhoun had come to accept "an erroneous theory of the National Government." According to Lee, Calhoun claimed that sovereignty was indivisible and resided in the state government. Lee, however, held to the good old Madisonian view, that sovereignty was divisible and that a large share of it had been allotted to the Federal government.[57] In the course of his remarks to this effect, he came to the consideration not only of the constitutionality of the Proviso, but of "the right of secession" now being uncritically assumed by some of the Democratic editors. He was thus led to a denial of any legal right of secession, a denial so strong as to be remarkable in a journal having one of the largest circulations in the lower South in this period. "A city might just as

[56] The Augusta *Republic* "informed" the Georgia people in June that the Whigs were opposed to the Proviso, and thereby insulted the rest of the party, which resented the implication that there ever had been any doubt about it; Savannah *Republican*, July 2, 1849.

[57] Augusta *Chronicle*, July 20, 1849.

well proclaim its independence of state authority, as a state of the Union," he declared. "The strength of our national government has never been fully tested, but anyone who supposes it will break easily knows not of the character of the American people."[58]

This view implied, of course, that if there were any "right" of secession it must be simply the moral "right of revolution." But here again the editor was too conservative to grant much. He was disinclined to recognize even such a moral privilege and became involved in a second controversy with the *Constitutionalist* over the "right of revolution." The latter, with other Democratic journals, gloried in this right as a Jeffersonian tradition and on that ground had welcomed the revolutionary movements of 1848 in Europe. The *Chronicle* looked askance upon this view and assured its prosperous readers that "the right of revolution must be qualified to avoid anarchy." The Democratic journals, led by the Washington *Union,* were "hotbeds of Red Republicanism" and of "rank Dorism." Conservatives were reminded that "nearly 100,000 European democratic voters land every year, who are used to revolution!" Those who listened to Democratic demagogues should ask themselves whether they were really yet ready "to abandon the system of Washington, Jefferson and Madison, for the more democratic one of Rollin, Louis Blanc and Lamartine."[59]

Such views, said the *Constitutionalist,* displayed the characteristic Whig tendency to deny the people

[58] *Ibid.* This, of course, was the same view which such a Union leader as Richard Arnold had urged in 1833. For the modern revival of the theory of divisible sovereignty, which emphasizes division in terms of "functions" rather than in terms of "territorial contiguity," see, *e.g.,* H. J. Laski, *Authority in the Modern State,* pp. 74, 75; also the same author's *The Problem of Sovereignty,* p. 271.

[59] Augusta *Chronicle,* July 23, 1849.

the right to choose their own form of government. They amounted to a denial of the principles of Jefferson's immortal Declaration. Lee, entirely unabashed by this thunder, replied that those Jeffersonian principles would justify the very thing most dangerous to southern institutions; namely, servile insurrection. They were therefore incendiary conceptions, which should be suppressed in southern society.[60]

This was certainly "preaching federalism of the purest water," and the opportunity it afforded Democratic editors for criticism was relished by those gentlemen. They had now succeeded in enticing conservative Whigs into an attack on the abstract principles most dear to the heart of the Georgia people— the traditions of state sovereignty and democracy. A very torrent of denunciation descended upon the *Chronicle* from the Democratic papers of Augusta, Milledgeville, Columbia, and Charleston. These could now place the conservative Whigs in an unpopular position concerning abstract constitutional issues, and they intended to exploit this advantage to the utmost. This was especially true of the *Chronicle's* denial of the "right of secession" and its disapproval of the "right of revolution." The most effective Democratic use of the first of these questions was to be made in the next state campaign, that of 1851, but the beginnings of the issue are to be observed in 1849.

The most fortunate result of the constitutional controversy, from the Democratic point of view, was the bitter attack made by the radical Whigs upon their conservative brethren. Smythe, of the *Republic,* who represented what little remained of the old state-rights traditions of the original Whig party of 1833, was par-

[60] *Ibid.,* August 30, 1849.

ticularly incensed at the utter repudiation of these traditions by the neighboring party journal. "Where,"
he demanded, "is the great States Rights Party of
Georgia? With a change of names they have changed
their principles? . . . The doctrines of the *Chronicle* on a Consolidated Union would put us at the
mercy of the anti-slavery Northern majority."[61] Lee's
"open Consolidationism" was indeed too much for the
rank and file of the Whig party.[62] Lee's publishers
continued to back him, however, and the party leaders
could not afford to offend the powerful *Chronicle* during a critical campaign. It is small wonder that Judge
Hill, facing the running constitutional controversy between the two factions of his party in Augusta, hesitated to answer the leading questions sent to him by
the Democrats.

The latter were having their own troubles, meanwhile, in a desperate attempt to keep the Cobb and
Calhoun factions together until after the election.
The *Federal Union* persisted in criticisms of the "non-
signers" of the Southern Address, while the Athens
Banner continued its condemnation of Calhoun and all
his works. Flournoy, of the *Federal Union,* warned
Holsey that the Carolinian had good friends in Georgia and that the Athens editor must remember that
"his clique is not the whole party."[63] If that clique
continued to stir up trouble in the Democracy, the
organ at the capital threatened to retaliate by refusing
"to support any anti-Calhoun men for place." In

---

[61] Augusta *Republic,* July 21, in the Savannah *Georgian,* July 31, 1849.
[62] Alexander Stephens made an unsuccessful attempt to remove Lee
tactfully to Washington, by securing him a federal appointment. See
Stephens to G. W. Crawford, March 2, 1849, *Toombs, Stephens, and
Cobb Correspondence,* p. 155.
[63] Federal *Union,* August 28, 1849.

Athens some subscribers wrote the *Banner* to discontinue their subscriptions because of its anti-Calhoun policy.[64] The *Banner* replied that it would retaliate upon the "Calhoun Journals," which would see that it could "give as good as they send. These Calhoun men are not the Southern men *par excellence.*" Holsey dismissed Flournoy, who had particularly irritated him, as "a contemptable trickster—a disgrace to the Democratic party."[65] It was becoming increasingly apparent that the factions in each party could not long maintain even the pretense of harmony or the coöperation that went with it. Party loyalty would soon break under the increasing strain of the sectional issue. It had cracked in many places before the campaign ended, but managed to hold together until the election was past.

The usual local issues were injected into the state campaign, although they were obviously overshadowed by the one great problem. The Whigs discovered that Towns had been extravagant in administering the state penitentiary. He had pardoned a dangerous criminal! The Democrats found that Hill, like Berrien, had been too prominently connected with railroad interests and "special privilege." Both parties, after assuring their supporters of their earnest efforts to keep such matters below the surface, were forced by conscience to point to the shocking personal habits of the opposing candidate. In their respective efforts, for instance, to prove that the opposition leader was more given to drink than was their own hero, the capacities of each were portrayed in an interesting and impressive manner.

[64] Athens *Banner,* in the Savannah *Republican,* August 23, 1849.
[65] *Banner,* in the *Chronicle,* September 25, 1849.

Calhoun and the Carolina leaders observed with rising hopes the trend of events in Georgia and the Gulf states through the fall of 1849. While the Jackson convention in Mississippi would be the most important single event in the southern movement, the outcome of the campaign in Georgia was also of vital interest. The hope of South Carolina was pinned upon the southern-rights Democrats of her sister state, whose leaders and journals gave the impression that they would coöperate in a "real Southern Movement" in 1850. It was essential to this end that the majority of the Georgia legislature and the governor be southern-rights men. Calhoun maintained his personal touch with a half dozen or more of his friends in Georgia, his most systematic and valuable correspondents being, as before, Wilson Lumpkin and Senator Johnson. The latter reported in the summer that there was "great excitement in the party in this state upon the slavery question," but that, "notwithstanding demonstrations, I seriously feel that the people of the South are not properly awake to the danger—not thoroughly nerved to resistance." Yet he agreed with Calhoun that "now is the time for resistance." Lumpkin's estimate of Georgia public opinion late in July, 1849, was even more pessimistic than that of Johnson. He wrote:

I have to a great extent lost confidence in the virtue and intelligence of our Southern people. Upon the slavery question South Carolina is the only state in the Union prepared to do her full duty. . . . With a single exception in Georgia,[66] the Whig Press shrink from speaking out in a manly tone, and the Democratic press is not entirely free from former association with Van Buren and Benton. We have an office-seeking faction in Georgia who feel but little of the true spirit of *Southern Patriotism*. . . . Corruption has gotten too

[66] The Augusta *Republic*.

deep a hold upon the politicians and press of our country for us to indulge the hope that we can unite the South in self-defense, even upon this vital slavery question. And nothing short of the union . . . can save us from degradation, and from horrors which the strongest language can but faintly depict. You and I may struggle on through our few remaining days. But in our last hour I fear we will not be consoled with the prospects which await posterity in this section of our Union. It may soon be recorded that "the slave states *were.*"[67]

This letter is interesting for several reasons. It agreed with the private opinions of most of the extreme Calhoun men in Georgia that the people of that state, even the Democrats, were not prepared for extreme measures.[68] Second, it expressed clearly the despair of far-sighted southern nationalists over the blindness of their people to the dangers lurking in old loyalties to party and to Union. Third, it illustrates the private and sincere expression of the fear of social chaos following abolition. Finally, it offered a prophetic picture of the pathetic circumstances attending Calhoun's death within the next year, in the midst of a crisis in which he could see but little hope for his beloved Southland.

As the two parties neared the October elections, both made final appeals upon the slavery issue. The majority Democrats, with lessening regard for Cherokee sensibilities, proclaimed to the people that the great question of the election was of submission or resistance to the antislavery movement, and that the Democracy stood for resistance "to the last extremity." Town's letters and speeches proved him the "resistance candidate." Hill's silence and evasiveness

[67] Wilson Lumpkin to Calhoun, August 27, 1849, the Calhoun Papers. See also R. I. Moon to Calhoun, August 26, 1849, Calhoun Papers.

[68] The significance of this private pessimism of the Georgia Calhounites, and the contrast it offers to the optimism of their public proclamations, will be commented upon in the next chapter.

proved him the "Submissionist candidate."[69] The Whigs, for their part, claimed just as vehemently to be the only genuine southern party.

Special efforts were made by the party machines to prevent voting for irregular candidates for the legislature and to bring out a full vote. The Democratic executive committee, a body appointed by the July convention, sent out secret circulars at the last moment to the watchers at the county polls, with instructions for getting out every possible vote.[70] In the last six weeks of the campaign, the Democratic editors expressed increasing confidence of victory, and the Whigs admitted the danger of defeat.[71] The growing suspicion of Taylor's attitude toward the Proviso; the definite southern-rights stand taken by Towns, in contrast with Hill's evasiveness; and the extreme conservatism of the *Chronicle* wing of the Whig party—all tended to strengthen the Democratic claim to sectional preference. Signs of wavering in party loyalty appeared here and there, even among the Taylor Whigs.[72]

The election was held on October 1. In the returns from the first forty counties reported, Towns showed a gain of about one thousand votes over his own record for 1847. The final results gave him the election with a majority of 3192, the vote standing: Towns, 46,514; Hill, 43,322. The vote in 1847 had been Towns, 43,220; Clinch, 41,931. This meant that the Whig

[69] Savannah *Georgian,* September 13, 1849; *Federal Union,* September 11, 18, 1849.

[70] Augusta *Chronicle,* September 25, 1849.

[71] Macon *Telegraph,* August 14; the Macon *Journal,* August 14; in the *Chronicle,* August 25, 1849.

[72] Washington (Georgia) *Gazette,* in the *Chronicle,* July 21, 1849; T. W. Thomas to Cobb, August 19, 1849, *Toombs, Stephens, and Cobb Correspondence,* p. 174.

vote of 1849 was greater than that of 1847 by 1391, while the Democratic was greater by 3294.[73] In other words, there had been a slight but definite relative gain of about nineteen hundred votes in the Democratic poll for governor in 1849, as compared with that of 1847. In like manner, it became apparent that there had been a small but definite Democratic gain in the legislature—sufficient to change the control of that body. The Democrats secured twenty-six seats in the Senate, the Whigs twenty-two, while in the House the former won sixty-seven seats, and the latter sixty-three. The successful Democratic candidates represented all three factions in their party, and their small gains were not peculiar to any section of the state.[74]

Little was said by the Whig press in explanation of the October defeat. The Democratic organs in Central and Lower Georgia immediately hailed it as a victory for southern-rights over Whig "submissionism" and pointed to concomitant Democratic victories in most of the other southern states as indications of a similar victory throughout the South.[75] The most elaborate expression of this view was that given by the southern-rights Whigs, who had steadily warned their conservative brethren of impending defeat, and who now felt no hesitancy in coming forward to the old tune, "I told you so!" The election was lost by

[73] *Georgian*, October 4; *Chronicle*, November 21; Philadelphia *North American*, November 23, 1849.

[74] Savannah *Republican*, October 10, 1849; *Journals of the Georgia House* and *Journals of the Senate*, for 1849-'50, pp. 1, 2; *Members of the Legislature*, (printed list showing party affiliations, for the Legislature of 1850, in possession of U. B. Phillips); Iverson to Cobb, October 6; J. H. Lumpkin to Cobb, October 19, 1849, *Toombs, Stephens, and Cobb Correspondence*, pp. 175, 176.

[75] Savannah *Georgian*, October 4, 1849; *Times*, October 9; *Federal Union*, October 9, October 16, 1849.

the Whigs, said Smythe, primarily because they had continued to support Taylor, while the southern people were losing confidence in him.[76]

This interpretation of the election implied a growing confidence in the Democracy as the southern-rights party. Extreme Calhoun Democrats, however, in their exasperation at the moderation displayed during the compaign towards the Union Democrats, sometimes denied this, and offered what was probably the most critical analysis of the campaign. Both parties, they held, failed to take a real stand on slavery for fear of factional splits, hence there had been popular indifference to the election, and its results could not be of great significance.[77]

The evidence in the case of Georgia does indicate only an average interest in the election, the slight increase in the votes of both parties over 1847 being only such as could have been produced by the normal increase in population. There is no evidence, moreover, of any intense popular agitation outside the parties, save for the statements of Calhounites, who were themselves undoubtedly excited. On the other hand, the small but definite relative gain in the Democratic vote can only be ascribed to some growth of sectional feeling, since the slavery issue was the only important one raised during the campaign. The Democrats undoubtedly were most successful in urging the sectional appeal. Some potential Whig votes were probably given to Towns by the Clay Whigs, though the exact number, which must have been small, cannot be determined. The latter were, in all probability,

[76] *Republic,* in the *Federal Union,* October 16, 1849.
[77] J. R. Mathews to Calhoun, October 7, 1849, Calhoun Papers.

responsible for their party's defeat. If so, the Whig organization was the first to suffer in Georgia because of the sectional struggle. The Democrats, however, were to have their turn within a year.

The effect of the election victory upon the majority of the Democrats, so far as can be judged from the press, was to increase their emphasis upon southern-rights and to make for greater sympathy for the extreme demand of southern political unity. In a word, the Democratic editors, having espoused a general sectional appeal as a result of the election of 1848, were now ready to go further and definitely adopt the southern movement as a result of the election of 1849. Several forces were responsible for this change in attitude. In the first place, the events of the past year had doubtless persuaded some that sectional unity was now essential, and editors who were watching the northern press were apt to be peculiarly susceptible to such persuasion. In the second place, those Democrats who, as Calhounites, had held their peace during the campaign for the sake of party harmony, were less likely to keep silent now that a Democratic state administration was safely in office. Finally, it was probable that the southern movement, ostensibly a nonpartisan one, might be turned to partisan advantage in Georgia. Some gain had apparently accrued to the party as a result of urging the sectional appeal in the recent election. More popular excitement would undoubtedly develop as a result of the coming struggles in the legislature and in Congress. If the Whigs maintained their conservatism, the Democrats could appeal to the people for support as the only true southern party. In fact the elections were no sooner over than the Democrats did appeal to all Whigs to rally with them for southern unity.[78]

The course of events in sister states through the fall gave added impetus to the support of the southern movement in Georgia. Since the spring agitation in South Carolina, which had led to the appointment of a Central Committee of Vigilance and Safety, there had been a general silence in that state upon the sectional issue. The general agreement upon national topics there made further agitation unnecessary, pending developments in the other states.[79]   Calhoun, however, continuing his leadership of the whole southern movement, had been duly informed of the coming convention in Jackson, Mississippi, and his advice was requested as to the course to be followed there. He urged again his belief, expressed in private correspondence as early as 1847, that the only way to save the Union was to unite the South by means of a southern convention. It seemed reasonable to suppose that two years of excitement had now prepared the people to respond to this appeal. Senator Foote, of Mississippi, was assured by both Whig and Democratic leaders in his state that the October convention would act upon Calhoun's advice, and the latter was notified to this effect.[80]

The prospects for the southern movement outside of South Carolina seemed most favorable, then, in Mississippi. The Jackson Convention met just at the time the state election was being held in Georgia, and the Carolinians had two interesting events to follow at the same time. The Mississippi convention was

[78] Columbus *Times,* October 23, 1849.

[79] Hamer, *The Secession Movement in South Carolina,* pp. 45, 46.

[80] Foote to Calhoun, September 25, 1849, *Calhoun Correspondence,* p. 1204.

representative of both parties and all sections of the state. "Among those present" was General Daniel Wallace, envoy extraordinary from South Carolina. As the secret emissary of Seabrook, the General had to exercise great caution in approaching the members, lest he arouse the latent hostility to South Carolina which existed in Mississippi and other southern states as well as in Georgia.[81] Wallace did succeed in holding private conversations with leading Mississippians of both parties, who convinced him that their state was ready to coöperate with his own, and these impressions he sent back in detail to Seabrook. He had also to report, however, his own surprise at the extent of anti-Carolina feeling.[82]

The policy of keeping Wallace and all he represented in the background made possible the harmonious procedure of the Jackson convention. Resolutions were adopted which even the Calhounites considered "up to the mark." These, besides making the usual demands for resistance to the Proviso, to the prohibition of the domestic slave trade, and to the abolition of slavery in the District of Columbia, issued the long-sought formal call for a southern convention. The slave-holding states were urged to send delegates to a meeting to be held at Nashville on the first Monday in June, 1850, "with a view and the hope of arresting the course of aggression," and, if necessary, "to devise and adopt some mode of resistance" to the same.[83]

[81] It is doubtful, however, whether the anti-Carolina feeling was as strong in Mississippi or Alabama as it was in Georgia, where the geographical contacts had led to trade rivalries, and the other usual frictions resulting from proximity, which did not obtain in the Gulf states. It is difficult to believe that a Georgia convention, with Whigs and Union Democrats present, would ever have admitted a South Carolina representative under any circumstances in 1849 or 1850.
[82] Wallace to Seabrook, October 20, 1849, Seabrook MSS.
[83] Hearon, *Mississippi and the Compromise of 1850*, pp. 63-68; Ames, *State Documents*, pp. 253-258.

This call was hailed with hope in South Carolina, which had so long awaited just such encouragement from her western sisters. How would the others receive it? Calhoun watched this question closely and urged his correspondents throughout the South to respond to the Jackson call.[84] Meanwhile, Carolina could lead in this response. When the legislature convened late in November, Governor Seabrook urged that provision be made for representation at Nashville. The coming convention, he declared, was intended to save the Union; but if this proved impossible, it was to provide for the independence of the slaveholding states. With this contingency in view, he urged preparation for military defense. The legislature largely ignored this last request, but it did name delegates-at-large to Nashville, provided for the local election of other delegates, and authorized the governor to call it in special session in case Congress passed the Proviso or kindred measures.[85]

In the course of the next few months, provision for representation at Nashville was also made in Virginia, Alabama, Mississippi, Florida, Texas, Arkansas, and Tennessee. In the first three of these states, provision was also made for the calling, under certain circumstances, of special state conventions.[86] The long heralded southern movement was really beginning to "move"!

The proceedings of the Jackson convention reached Georgia at the same time that the state election results were being made known. Southern-rights Democrats, flushed with a victory ascribed to their own principles,

[84] There was a series of letters to this effect. See the *Calhoun Correspondence*, pp. 762, 769, 773, 775, 778, 1195, etc.

[85] Hamer, *The Secession Movement in South Carolina*, pp. 43-45.

[86] Ames, "Calhoun and the Secession Movement of 1850," p. 121.

naturally welcomed the expression of similar principles in Mississippi, and urged that the coming legislature in Georgia accept the call to Nashville. Said
the *Federal Union:*

> The position of the South has been weakened by a lack of
> harmony. But Mississippi had designated the path which will
> lead to union in counsel and harmony in action. . . . All
> who love the South *better than themselves* are beginning to see
> that, if her rights are maintained, she has none to look to but
> herself. Before the Legislature of Georgia adjourns we hope
> to see our gallant state standing among her sisters of the South
> on the same platform now occupied by Mississippi. A united
> front at this time will probably dispel the clouds that threaten,
> and save the Union, but vaccilation and dissention now means
> further Northern aggression, which will continue until the
> South will finally be forced to destroy the Union. Now is the
> time to act—to act cooly—calmly—resolutely—firmly.[87]

A few of Calhoun's friends in the state wrote him
in like manner that it was time to plan "seriously and
calmly" for a southern party in Georgia.[88] J. H.
Howard, one of the Columbus extremists, wrote that,
had he been elected to the legislature, he would have
worked for resolutions "pointing to some *definite*
action and sent them to all the states." Would Calhoun please advise "in *confidence*" as to the right
course of a southern member of Congress at the coming session,[89] and also as to "what preventive remedy" the state's legislature should adopt the meanwhile?[90] Calhoun's guidance was thus sought by
the extremists for the Georgia legislature of 1849-
1850, as for that of 1847-1848; yet, even in the latter
body the origin of his advice had to be kept a close

---

[87] *Federal Union,* November 20; see also the Columbus *Times,* November 20; the *Georgian,* November 18, 1849.

[88] J. R. Mathews to Calhoun, October 7, 1849, Calhoun Papers.

[89] This may have been intended for Alfred Iverson, of Columbus,
Representative from the Second Georgia District.

[90] Howard to Calhoun, October 8, 1849, Calhoun Papers.

secret. It seems quite possible, considering all the circumstances, that suggestions were sent by the Carolinian to his followers at Milledgeville in answer to such requests (even as he sent suggestions to his Mississippi supporters) and that the Georgia extremists hoped to secure action based upon his plan. The Whigs, to be sure, could be expected to oppose any such action, and so too could the Union Democrats, but much was hoped from the Democratic majority. Something could certainly be accomplished if Congress precipitated the renewed and more bitter sectional struggle, which now seemed well nigh inevitable.

CHAPTER VI

The Georgia Legislature convened in the little town of Milledgeville on November 5, 1849, a month before the Congress met in Washington. The state body awaited no cue from the latter as to the course it should take upon the slavery question, although it was bound to be influenced by the debates at Washington, just as Congress in turn was influenced by developments in the states. There were twenty-six Democrats and twenty-two Whigs in the state Senate, while in the House there were sixty-six Democrats and sixty-three Whigs. The Democratic lead was so slight that had the Whigs held together on any vital national question they could have defeated the other party with the assistance of the Union Democrats from Cherokee. A small number of the latter group, who split from the rest of their party on such issues, can be identified by their votes in both houses.[1] As the Whig members themselves proved to be about evenly divided upon national questions, however, no such defeat of the Democrats was possible.

Having convened on November 5, the Assembly met on the next day to receive the Governor's message. The greater part of this document dealt with the usual economic and social topics of the time, and his views on these matters revealed the moderate character of Democratic principles in this period. There

[1] *Georgia House Journal*, 1849-1850, p. 487, ff.

was little trace of the economic and social radicalism of previous decades.[2]

With regard to the pressing question of slavery, Towns first recommended that better laws be passed to protect the slaves from cruelty or misusage. While this house-cleaning was in progress at home, the state should take a strong stand against the antislavery movement. It will be remembered that Towns was a southern-rights Democrat and that he had been elected the preceding October after openly declaring for final resistance to further northern "aggressions." He claimed, therefore, that he had a mandate from the people to take action against such attacks, and, as a southern-rights man, he was anxious to use his position as governor to further the southern movement. His message proclaimed that, with the meeting in the immediate future of the new Congress and the development of the statehood movements in California and New Mexico, the sectional crisis was at hand. Further attempts to pass the Proviso, in open or disguised form, were to be anticipated, and "further aggression was not to be endured." In proof that he desired action as well as words, Towns now urged, as had the Governor of Mississippi, that he be authorized "to convoke a convention to take into consideration the measures proper for . . . safety and preservation, in the event of the passage of the Wilmot Proviso, or other kindred measures, by the Congress of the United States."[3]

[2] Most of the Governor's views on economic matters were praised by even the most conservative Whig papers, which again illustrates the extent to which the state Democratic party had come under the control of conservative leaders by 1850. See, *e.g.*, the *Chronicle*, November 8, 1849.

[3] *Georgia House Journal*, 1849-50, pp. 37-50; *Debates and Proceedings of the Georgia Convention*, 1850, Appendix; Letter Books of the Georgia Governor, 1850.

This message clearly placed Towns in the front rank of those southern-rights leaders who were demanding action as well as words. It received wide attention in the North, where it was regarded as a serious move,[4] and was enthusiastically praised by the Democratic press of Georgia and South Carolina. In the latter state, it was received as the most hopeful sign that the "coöperationists" had yet seen in the sister state, and the *South Carolinian* was encouraged to remark that it "had always trusted in Georgia."[5] The Georgia Whig press did not welcome the suggestion of a state convention, however, and the aggressive *Chronicle* took occasion to raise again the cry against "disunion." Towns' appeal for a special convention, it opined, was "a confession that the Democratic state government is weak," and thus has to "call in a New Power which is to do *a thing* which even Governor Towns has not presumed to intimate ought to be done."[6]

The Governor's message was at once referred in both houses to the standing committees on "the state of the Republic," after which action most of the time between November 6 and 12 was consumed by routine business. There was considerable excitement in the air, however, both because of the mutual exchange of views between members and because the news coming in on national affairs was disquieting. The southern-rights men were particularly incensed by the news from California. Here a proposed state constitution excluding slavery had been adopted a few weeks before. The opinion expressed by Hopkins Holsey early in the year now became general among this group; namely,

[4] See, *e.g.*, the Philadelphia *Public Ledger*, December 19, 1849.
[5] Columbia Tri-Weekly *South Carolinian*, November 10, 1849.
[6] *Chronicle*, November 8, 1849.

that the mixed population there had no right to form a state. It was held, moreover, that President Taylor's part in backing the statehood movement proved it an effort to "apply the Proviso in disguise" to a state so outrageously large that it would "swallow the whole West."[7] To cap the insult, it was now learned that a Georgia Whig Representative, Thomas B. King, had "deserted" his post in a critical Congress to become the President's agent in carrying out this unhallowed design. King was reported to be urging his own election as a senator from the proposed new free state.

On November 12 a series of resolutions on the national situation was reported to the Georgia House,[8] and on November 15 a similar series was presented to the Senate.[9] These resolutions, drawn up in response to the Governor's message, were of a more radical character than any yet presented to those bodies. They contained the usual declarations upholding slavery and asserting the unconstitutionality of the Proviso. Those of the House contained in addition an eighth resolution providing for the calling of a state convention in certain contingencies, and also a ninth, which conveyed a veiled threat of secession. This threat was contained in the statement that "nothing short of persistence in the present system of encroachment upon our rights by the non-slaveholding states can induce us to contemplate the possibility of a dissolution" of the Union.[10] For the first time the possibility of secession was thus given formal expression in Georgia, and the general reception accorded

[7] *Georgian*, November 26, 1849. There had been talk of including in California even the area now occupied by Nevada.

[8] *Georgia House Journal*, 1849-50, p. 49.

[9] *Georgia Senate Journal*, 1849-50, p. 63.

[10] *House Journal*, p. 49.

this and the other resolutions at once indicated that for the first time the Georgia assembly was in the control of a majority composed of southern-rights members.

The cumulative effect of the agitation of the preceding year and of contemporary events at Washington and throughout the nation was beginning to tell even upon the Whig members. As a matter of fact, the resolutions introduced in the House were written by the Whig Gartrell. They were intended, the Savannah *Republican* explained, "to set the Whigs right before the public on slavery,"—thereby admitting by implication that there had been some doubt on this point during the fall campaign.[11] It was the swing of about half of the Whigs in the House and about one third of those in the Senate to the southern-rights position that placed the control of the Assembly from now on in the hands of the leaders of that persuasion. The number of Union Democrats who sided with the conservative Whigs was too small to overcome this combination.

Late in November a conference of the Democratic leaders of both houses resulted in the appointment of a special joint committee on the state of the republic, to which were referred all bills or resolutions relating to the slavery controversy. This committee was dominated by Gartrell and the militant Calhounite, W. J. Lawton, of Scriven, and these two became the radical leaders of the Assembly during the weeks that followed.

On December 19 the joint committee reported again a series of resolutions generally similar to those which Gartrell had originally submitted to the House.[12]

[11] *Republican*, November 13, 1849.
[12] See *House Journal*, pp. 72, 100, 315; *Senate Journal*, pp. 309-312.

Lawton had added meanwhile a long preamble and an additional resolution,[13] which were acted upon separately and so may be considered as distinct measures.

The preamble reviewed the whole story of "Northern encroachments" and declared that abolition, "the last dishonor that can be reserved for us," was now at hand. Only a final stand, it declared, could save the South from this dishonor. In a word, the preamble was a restatement of Calhoun's "Southern Platform." It is interesting to recall that it was to Lawton that Calhoun had been requested to send resolutions in 1847, and that Lawton had shortly thereafter introduced radical resolutions in the House of that year, only to have them treated with scant courtesy by the Whig majority. He had bided his time, however, had been reëlected from Scriven in 1849 and was now again urging radical action—this time upon a House quite willing to give ear to Calhoun's philosophy.

Lawton's preamble was followed by a new resolution, which urged the formal adoption of the southern party movement.[14] The preamble and this solidarity resolution were now adopted by the House, despite opposition by a minority composed of members of both parties.[15] A resolution was adopted at the same time for printing and distributing five thousand copies throughout the state. This measure meant in reality nothing less than a state subsidy for southern-rights propaganda. Fortunately for the conservatives, all of Lawton's proposals met with defeat in the Senate, where strong opposition developed to the formal adoption of a southern party.[16]

[13] *Federal Union*, February 12, 1850.
[14] *House Journal*, p. 314.
[15] *Ibid.*, p. 315.
[16] *Senate Journal*, pp. 285, 286.

The joint committee had submitted to both houses, in addition to the solidarity resolution now defeated in the Senate, a series of ten resolutions similar to those originally introduced in the House of Representatives by Gartrell. We have already noted that most of these resolutions were of a general character, but that the eighth provided for the calling of a state convention as the Governor had suggested, and that the ninth threatened secession. The original eighth resolution indicated three events which would justify the calling of a convention; namely, the passage of the Proviso, the abolition of slavery in the District of Columbia, or the continued refusal of northern states to deliver up fugitive slaves. When Gartrell had written, at the beginning of November, these seemed the chief threats to be warned against. Since that time, the news concerning California had added a fourth. Hence the joint committee added a phrase destined to become the chief subject of controversy within the legislature and later the cause of the actual meeting of the state convention. This was a curt statement naming as an additional contingency calling for a convention, "the admission of California in its present pretended organization."[17]

At about the same time that the joint committee was reporting the ten resolutions and Lawton was attempting to add his preamble to them, separate bills were introduced in both houses calling for the state convention in case the same events named in the eighth resolution occurred. Furthermore, Jenkins, Whig leader of Augusta, introduced resolutions approving the Mississippi call for a southern convention and providing a system for selecting state delegates to it.

[17] *House Journal,* p. 485.

Final consideration of all of these measures, however,
had to be postponed until after the Christmas recess;
when the legislature reconvened in mid-January, the
ten resolutions again received primary consideration.

The first seven, of a general character, were accepted without serious protest on January 26, but
opposition at once developed against the eighth resolution, which now read as follows:

> That in the event of the passage of the Wilmot Proviso by
> Congress, the abolition of slavery in the District of Columbia,
> the admission of California as a state in its present pretended
> organization, or the continued refusal of the non-slave holding
> states to deliver up fugitive slaves as provided in the constitu-
> tion, it will become the immediate and imperative duty of the
> people in this state to meet in convention to take into consid-
> eration the mode and measure of redress.

When this was read again in the House on January 24, two plans of opposition at once developed. Jenkins, spokesman for the conservative Whigs, moved
that consideration of the entire resolution be postponed
until after the meeting of the proposed southern convention. The obvious motive here was to delay plans
for decisive state action until there had been time for
a general compromise of the whole sectional struggle.
On the same day, W. T. Wofford, for the Union Democrats, moved to amend the phrase, "the passage of the
Wilmot Proviso by Congress," by inserting after the
word "Proviso" the phrase "over territory south of
36° 30', known as the Missouri Compromise Line."[18]

Jenkins' motion for delay was lost by a large majority, but Wofford's amendment received serious consideration. This is of interest, because it shows that
at least a few conservative Union Democrats were
still standing by the original party platform of 1847

[18] *House Journal,* pp. 485, 486.

and 1848, which had offered the Missouri line as a compromise scheme. This offer the southern-rights Democrats had officially held to as late as the election of the preceding October in order to placate the conservative faction; but they had abandoned it in spirit since the early summer of 1849, when their temper became less conciliatory and when it became increasingly apparent that the North would not accept the Missouri line anyway. Now safely in power, the southern-rights element need no longer suppress its opposition to the Missouri Compromise scheme. The conservative Whigs, however, were still anxious to secure a compromise and could be counted on to back Wofford's motion more generally than they would the motion of their own leader.

Wofford's proposed amendment was, therefore, supported in debate by Jenkins and by J. A. Nesbit, of Macon, another conservative Whig leader. This combination of moderate Whig and Democratic elements in the eighth-resolution debate was the first clear evidence of the coming realignment of party forces in the state, a realignment that became the basis for the subsequent Union party; although there is no evidence that such a party was consciously planned until about a fortnight after this debate occurred. In like manner the attack of Lawton upon Wofford's amendment was joined by the radical Whig, Gartrell, and this alignment was suggestive of the elements which were later formally merged into the Southern Rights party.

The debate lasted through January 24, 25, and 26. It was the most important one of the session and derives additional interest from the fact that it was concomitant with similarly stirring discussions in the national Congress at Washington. Jenkins and Nesbit claimed that the principle of the Missouri line would unite the South and at the same time could be accepted by the conservative North, thus forming the basis of a compromise that would save the Union. Lawton replied that it was inconsistent with the other resolutions denying the right of Congress to interfere with slavery in the territories. He proceeded to read the resolutions of the Georgia Whig Senate of 1847 to prove that that party had then opposed the Missouri line. Wofford countered by recalling that Lawton's party, on the other hand, had then favored the line. It was no more inconsistent with a denial of congressional power over the territories in 1850, Wofford declared, than it was in 1847, when all the Democrats had officially accepted it. Gartrell here came to the assistance of his Democratic ally by making the pertinent point that when the Missouri Compromise had been offered to the North in 1847, it was hoped it would be accepted. Now subsequent events, particularly the defeat of the Missouri line amendment to the Oregon territorial bill, had demonstrated conclusively that the North would not accept that compromise. It was foolish to offer the North a concession that would only lead to the humiliation of a refusal.

Jenkins answered that it was even more foolish to call a state convention for reasons which were indefensible. He pointed out that the admission of California as a free state was entirely constitutional and that a desire to protect slavery should not lead them into the weak position of denying it. This would be particularly unfortunate, because no act of theirs could ever carry slavery into so unsuitable a country anyway. Jones, of Paulding, denied this last point, claiming that gold mines could be best worked with slaves and that California was, therefore, well adapted to the institution. He concluded with the usual Democratic protest against allowing a migratory population there to form a state that "swallowed the whole west." Ramsey, of Harris, further stirred up the "Ultra" members by proclaiming excitedly that slavery should be everywhere "untrameled" and that he would "see it carried to California at the point of the bayonette if necessary."[19]

On January 26, the vote was finally taken in the House on the Missouri line amendment to the eighth resolution, eighty-one members voting against and forty-two in favor of the measure. Twenty-seven Whigs combined with southern-rights Democrats in defeating it, while six Union Democrats joined the conservative Whigs in supporting it. An equal number of Union Democrats from Cherokee failed to back the amendment, perhaps because they had been convinced by Gartrell that it was useless to offer the Missouri principle to the North.[20]

At this stage of the proceedings, southern-rights feeling was further agitated by an incident that well illustrates the character of some of the forces influencing the acts of the Assembly. A special message was received from Governor Towns transmitting resolutions on slavery lately received from the Connecticut Assembly. These resolutions demanded the passage of the Proviso, the privilege of jury trial for fugitives claimed as slaves in the North, and concluded with the announcement that "no threats of disunion" would deter Connecticut from supporting these measures.[21]

[19] For these debates, see the chief Georgia papers for January 29 and 30, 1850. The summary here given is based upon the accounts in the *Federal Union* and the *Chronicle*.

[20] *House Journal*, p. 487.

[21] For these resolutions in full see Ames, *State Documents*, pp. 261, 262.

The challenge in such statements was unmistakeable, and Governor Towns was prompt to make the most of it. His message made bold to say:

The absurd and insolent pretensions so generally set up and advanced by the North are boldly set forth and insultingly re-affirmed in these Resolutions. Believing that now is the time for Georgia to act in a manner worthy of herself, I can but repeat the opinion, expressed in my first message to the Legislature on this subject; that your property, your honor, and the Union itself will be lost forever if the South fails to assert its rights and adopt measures to carry them out.[22]

The response of both houses was the passage of resolutions to return "under a blank cover" these and any other resolutions on the subject that might subsequently be received from Connecticut. If Towns hoped, however, that his message would so arouse sectional ardor in the assembly as to discourage further opposition to the eighth resolution and the state convention bill, he was doomed to disappointment.

The amendment to the eighth resolution now having been defeated in the House, the resolution was there adopted by a vote of ninety-two to twenty-eight. The ninth resolution, implying the possibility of secession, was then accepted without opposition, Linton Stephens, of all the House, alone voting against it.[23] The "Georgia Resolutions" thus safely passed the House.[24]

The state convention bill was now in order in that body. The first clause in this bill was similar in wording to the eighth resolution, just passed, in that it named the contingencies upon which the convention should be called by the Governor. This fact gave the

[22] *House Journal*, pp. 488, 489.
[23] *House Journal*, pp. 509, 510.
[24] For their final form see *Acts of Georgia*, 1849-50, pp. 409, 410; Ames, *State Documents*, pp. 259-261.

conservatives an opportunity to repeat the opposition just made to the resolution. As soon as this first clause was considered, an effort was made to amend it by adding the Missouri line to the phrases concerning California and the Proviso. J. W. Anderson, of Savannah, the Democratic speaker, lost patience and ruled the amendment out of order. The majority were fair, however, and would not sustain his ruling. The amendment was then lost, sixty-seven to forty-six, and the convention bill passed, ninety-two to twenty-eight. Numbers of Whigs and Union Democrats, who supported the proposed amendment, finally voted for the bill to show that the state was behind the measure.[25] All of the twelve who finally opposed it were ultra-conservative Whig followers of Jenkins and Linton Stephens.

The conservative Whigs decided that here was the time to record formally their opposition to the California clause and to appeal to the people of the state on this issue. Accordingly, the Whigs were asked to sign a protest to be entered on the House Journal. The twenty-five odd members who were voting with the southern-rights Democrats would have nothing of it, and a few of the Whigs who had supported the amendments failed to sign the protest. Twenty-nine conservative Whigs and one union Democrat finally affixed their names.[26] The statement made by the signers made clear the issue involved and the reasons for their stand. They insisted that it was unjustifiable to oppose California's right to admission and "solemnly protested" against calling a state convention for this reason, as this was "a measure whose inevitable tendency leads to a dissolution of this 'most perfect

[25] *House Journal*, pp. 510, 520; *Federal Union*, January 29, 1850.
[26] *House Journal*, p. 547.

Union.' "   The bill, it was declared, was particularly unfortunate at a time of crisis, which demanded calmness and moderation rather than precipitate action.[27]

Despite this protest, the convention bill was soon made law by passage in the Senate[28] and by the approval of the Governor. As finally worded, it declared that, should any of the contingencies named in the eighth resolution occur, "it should be the duty of the Governor to order, within 60 days, an election in every county to a State Convention, to convene at the capitol within 20 days after the election." A fund of thirty thousand dollars was to be appropriated for the expenses of the convention. A clause requiring members to take an oath of loyalty to the state was struck out just before the passage of the bill.[29]

The House had now passed the ten resolutions and the convention bill. During January it had also proceeded with the consideration of the third measure of primary importance to the southern movement; namely, the resolutions pertaining to a southern convention. These resolutions were originally written by Charles J. Jenkins, of Augusta, and declared that "We cordially concurr with Mississippi in the measure of calling a Southern Convention." They provided that the Georgia delegates thereto should be chosen by an electoral convention called for that purpose. Jenkins, the Whig leader in the House, proposed this resolution in order to make it plain that the Whigs were true to the South and would not oppose the Nashville meeting. At the same time, the scheme he proposed for choosing the Georgia delegates was such as to make it doubtful whether the state would actually be repre-

[27] *Ibid.*
[28] *Senate Journal,* p. 493.
[29] *House Journal,* pp. 513-517.

sented. Should a compromise be accepted in the national Congress prior to the meeting of a state electoral convention, it was quite possible that this latter body would be disinclined to send any delegates to Nashville at all. It seems likely that some such hope was in the minds of the Whigs in the legislature when Jenkins' plan was introduced.[30]

Although the Senate accepted Jenkins' plan, opposition developed among the House Democrats to the idea of an electoral convention. Amendments were, therefore, adopted in both Houses providing for the election of the state's representatives by the several congressional districts. The voters were accustomed to the machinery of electing representatives to the national Congress from these districts, and this same machinery was now to be utilized for the unusual purpose of electing representatives to a sectional congress.[31]

It was provided, however, that the governor should appoint the alternates in case any vacancies occurred after the election, such appointments to be made from the party among whose representatives the vacancy had occurred.[32] This provision, because of circumstances that later developed, did give Towns a considerable influence upon the personnel of the state's delegation. Since Towns was a strong Calhounite, his appointments were not likely to be of a strictly nonpartisan character. All things considered, then, the plan of selecting delegates to Nashville represented a

[30] Explanation of Jenkins' plan as given by his Augusta colleague, A. J. Miller, *Chronicle*, April 12, 1850.

[31] For the plan of election, see *House Journal*, pp. 350, 422, 494, 656; *Senate Journal*, pp. 494, 495.

[32] *Senate Journal*, p. 648.

tactical victory for the southern-rights majority in the legislature.[33]

By February 5 the Nashville convention bill, the ten resolutions, and the state convention bill had all been accepted by the Senate as well as by the House.[34] The program of the southern-rights group, however, was not entirely completed with the passage of the three main measures. Several minor ones were debated in February, which are chiefly interesting as expressions of a generally excited state of mind upon all matters pertaining to slavery and to the North. Bills were introduced by the radicals, for instance, to prevent northern men from collecting debts in Georgia,[35] and to levy a sales tax upon northern goods.[36] A resolution was also introduced calling upon the Georgia Congressmen to leave Washington immediately in case the Proviso passed. Only the most extreme members, however, would support these retaliatory measures, and they failed to pass.

A number of interesting bills were introduced concerning Negroes and slavery. Perhaps the most important was that which provided for a repeal of the law against the interstate slave trade. Southern-rights men held that it was not only difficult but undesirable to enforce the law. Jones, of Paulding, claimed that more slaves were needed as plantations expanded and that free admission of them to Georgia would "increase · . . the raising of such property in the sections of the Union best adapted to its culture." McDougal, of Muscogee, reminded his hearers

---

[33] For a summary of the methods of election adopted in the other southern states, see D. T. Herndon, "The Nashville Convention," *Alabama Historical Society Publications*, V. 213-216.

[34] *Senate Journal*, pp. 493, 509.

[35] Philadelphia *Public Ledger*, February 6, 1850.

[36] Philadelphia *North American*, December 7, 1849.

that an increase in the slave population would mean an increase, under the "federal ratio," of the state's congressional representation. Kennan, a conservative Whig, denied that the repeal of the law would add to the Negro population and declared it would only increase the Negro transients, who would be sent on to the Southwest; meanwhile, the slaves would be drained out of the border states and leave them practically northern states. Other Whigs added that an unlimited slave trade would disgrace the state with the "unmoral exhibition of slave markets" and would also embarrass it by the presence of the vicious Negroes, who were always the first to be sold.[37] The bill passed both houses, however, prior to the Christmas recess.

On November 11, two days after the bill to repeal the anti-slave-trade law was introduced, it was followed by another to deport all free Negroes in the state to Liberia at the state's expense. This proposal may have been suggested to the extremists by a similar measure then pending in the South Carolina legislature. Southern-rights extremists insisted that free Negroes were a dangerous racial element, that they were a vicious lot and given to making trouble with the slaves. This view was supported by an interesting petition from an association of mechanics in Augusta, which was doubtless motivated by a dislike for free-Negro economic competition. These attacks, however, elicited praise of the freedmen class by members who insisted that the free Negroes were not at all a vicious group and that they had rights as "Quasicitizens, with the status of infants," which should not be denied to them. The bill was finally defeated in the

[37] The account of this debate is based on that given in the *Chronicle*, November 15, 1849.

House, sixty-nine to forty-five. A bill to sell outside the state all free Negroes remaining in it on February 1, 1851, was likewise defeated.[38]

In addition to the various measures mentioned, the legislature considered and passed an unusually large number of routine bills and resolutions. Upon some of these the two parties divided in the traditional manner, as when the Senate Democrats passed a resolution upholding the tariff of 1846 by the strict party vote of twenty-three to twenty.[39] As the session progressed, however, and the measures pertaining to slavery were considered, the tendency toward the party realignments noted above became more apparent. The long threatened split upon the sectional issue was soon to take place between the Union and southern-rights factions in each party. It will be remembered that the southern-rights members had urged resolutions proclaiming the abandonment of the old parties and had constantly urged conservative members to join with them in common opposition to the North. They had even introduced a bill in the House "to repeal the present Whig and Democratic parties and in lieu thereof to establish a Southern Independent Republican Party."[40] Physicians may indeed heal themselves, but politicians can hardly be expected to "repeal" parties. Instead of joining the southern-rights group, the conservative Whigs and Union Democrats began to consider a mutual alliance in a new "Union Party."

The occasion of its formation was, curiously enough, an incident that in normal times would have but strengthened traditional party lines. It happened

[38] Boston *Liberator*, January 11; Savannah *Republican*, February 4, 1850.

[39] Vote of November 15, 1849, *Senate Journal*, p. 63.

[40] For comment thereon, see the Boston *Liberator*, January 11, 1850.

that, as soon as the southern-rights group had passed
the state convention bill, the Democratic majority proceeded with a long desired measure; namely, the re-
arrangement of both the state senatorial and the congressional districts so as to improve the chances of
Democratic nominees in these divisions. The Democrats claimed that their intention was to correct the
injustice of the Whig gerrymander of 1843,[41] but they
admitted that their chief purpose was to put the
powerful Toombs and Stephens into one district, or
into "moderate Whig districts," where they could not
roll up the majorities of thirteen to seventeen hundred
votes that now enabled them "to ignore the wishes of
the majority of the Georgia people."[42] The Whigs opposed the scheme bitterly, and their friends, the Cherokee Democrats, whose own congressional districts were
not involved in the controversy, showed some inclination to side with them. Personal encounters occurred
on the floor of the House between Democrats of the
two groups,[43] and the Whigs finally carried things to
extremes by absenting themselves from the House in
a body, thereby preventing a quorum and all action for
four successive days.[44] Only Jenkins, of Augusta, remained in his seat for a part of this time.[45] Hastily
summoned Democratic absentees finally restored a
quorum, whereupon the Whigs returned, and the gerrymander bill was passed, though it was later defeated
in the Senate.

[41] Map No. 6, p. 171. This gerrymander had worried even the national leaders of the party. See Polk to Buchanan, October 3, 1844,
Moore (ed.), *The Works of James Buchanan*, VI. 72.
[42] There was usually a slight majority of Democratic votes in the
state.
[43] *Chronicle*, February 20, 1850.
[44] *House Journal*, pp. 437, 458, 480, 843, 855.
[45] C. C. Jones, *Life of Ex-Governor C. J. Jenkins*, p. 12, says that
Jenkins never missed attendance. The Journals show, however, that
he was absent at times in this period.

It was during this struggle, and while the Whigs were spending the days in Milledgeville without attending sessions, that the first conscious plans were made for the organization of a Union party in Georgia. This was the logical step to take under the circumstances. The gerrymander struggle supplied the bitterness and the bolt from the House the leisure conducive to its final execution. Union Democrats, as well as Whigs, were named at the time as leaders of the proposed organization. It was rumored, for instance, that Wofford was to be the new party's candidate for governor in 1851. Others spoke of bringing Cobb back from Washington for this honor.[46]

The move to form a Union party was certain, by the mere process of elimination, to result in the formation of a Southern-rights party. In fact, the attempt to form such a party and to make it all-inclusive had been going on all winter. When the legislature adjourned, February 23, the members returned to their homes to organize their constituents on the new issues and along the new party lines.

These constituents had been watching the acts of the legislature through the winter, but their attention had also been focused, probably even to a greater degree, upon the developments in Congress. It is now well to recall the chief features of the dramatic Congressional session of 1849-1850, with especial reference to the leading part taken therein by the Georgia delegation.

The Georgia representatives and senators arrived promptly in Washington for the opening of the thirty-

[46] This account of the origin of the Union Party is based on that given in the *Federal Union*, March 4, 1851. This paper was unfriendly, but its editor was on the spot, and his story is consistent with the other facts known. The formal organization of the Union Party, planned from this time on, was not completed until the following December.

first Congress. The state's delegation was about equally divided between the parties; the Whigs being led as usual by Toombs, Stephens and Berrien, the Democrats by Cobb and H. A. Haralson.[47] Three members of the Georgia delegation were destined to play major rôles in the coming sectional drama.

The situation in Congress was disquieting. In the Senate the two major parties were well balanced, but in the House, where the Democrats had a slightly larger group than the Whigs, the balance of power was held by thirteen radical Free-Soilers. The alarm with which the Georgia Whig members viewed this situation was suddenly intensified, soon after their arrival, by the discovery that their growing distrust of Taylor was well founded. The President had indeed gone over to the enemy.[48] Toombs and Stephens immediately interviewed the President and were given frankly to understand that he would sign the Proviso if it reached him.[49]

Here was a truly alarming situation. The very leader whom Toombs and Stephens had regarded as a guarantor of southern rights would no longer defend them. It seemed to the Georgians that, if the bulk of the Whig party could also not be trusted, true southerners must fall back on the final defence offered

[47] The Georgia delegation included Senators Berrien and W. C. Dawson, the latter a Whig who had replaced H. V. Johnson, after the latter had filled out the unexpired portion of Colquitt's term. In the House were the Whigs, Toombs, Stephens, and A. F. Owen; T. B. King, the fourth Whig, resigned in order to represent the President in California. In the House also were the Union Democrats, Cobb and T. C. Hackett (the latter succeeded J. H. Lumpkin) and the southern-rights Democrats, Haralson and M. J. Wellborn.

[48] There were two versions as to why this had occurred. See, for the southern accounts, Coleman, *Crittenden,* I. 364, 366; Phillips, *Robert Toombs,* pp. 65. 66; for the northern account, Thurlow Weed, *Autobiography,* pp. 590, 591; Giddings, *History of the Rebellion,* p. 308.

[49] Toombs to Crittenden, April 23, 1850, Crittenden MSS.

by a unified southern party. They put the test at once
to the Whigs, assembled in caucus on December 1.
Their effort to pledge the party against the Proviso
failed, even with the southern members, most of the
latter still desiring to evade the issue. Toombs,
Stephens, Owen and three others thereupon withdrew
from the caucus and, for the time being, from the
party.[50] The Georgia Whig congressmen, after taking an active part against the southern movement in
the state campaign during the fall, had apparently
joined that very movement immediately upon reaching
Washington.

The House and Senate met for organization on
December 3. The former was immediately involved
in a bitter struggle over the election of a Speaker, each
party being desirous of controlling the appointment of
committees dealing with matters relating to the sectional controversy. In the course of this struggle
Toombs, supported by Stephens and Owen, became the
very leader of the "Fire-eaters" in the House, who demanded that no member unfriendly to the South should
secure the coveted position. He boldly demanded
compromise or disunion and startled the House with
perhaps the greatest display of oratorical fireworks
which that body had ever beheld.[51] After protracted
parliamentary procedure, however, the Democrats
finally secured the election, placing another Georgian,
Howell Cobb, in the chair. Cobb, true to his rôle as a
conservative, had remained calm, the while his Whig
colleagues became excited, and used his influence to

[50] *Ibid.*
[51] *Congressional Globe,* 31 Congress, 1 Session, pp. 27, 28; Phillips,
Robert Toombs, pp. 68-72. Toombs' efforts were "magnificent" or
"boisterous," as one wished to view them. *Cf.* Phillips, *Toombs,* p. 72,
and Giddings, *History of the Rebellion,* pp. 307, 308.

harmonize his party at the very time that Toombs and Stephens seemed about to disrupt theirs.[52]

Meanwhile, the Senate was being deluged with bills, resolutions, and debates relating to all phases of the slavery controversy. The friends of Taylor's administration were urging his general plan, which was simply to close the whole controversy over the territories by the prompt admission of California and New Mexico into the Union.[53] The southern-rights men would oppose this as a "Proviso in disguise," since California had adopted a free-state constitution, but the President hoped the southern Whigs would support the plan in order to end the struggle and quiet the country.

The conservative Whigs back in the Georgia legislature were indeed, as has been noted, actually favoring the admission of California at that very moment, on the terms that the President proposed; and the Georgia Whig editors desired it for the same reasons as those which motivated the President. The attitude of southern senators at Washington, however, was another matter; and it soon became apparent that many of them, including Berrien and Dawson, would not accept the President's formula. Its very simplicity now rendered it unacceptable. The excitement of the early debates tended now to make the southern Whigs ask more than the President offered. It was becoming increasingly obvious that, if the Union was to be saved, the entire slavery controversy must be settled.

---

[52] *Congressional Globe,* 31 Congress, 1 Session, p. 67; Cobb to his wife, December 22, 1849, *Toombs, Stephens, and Cobb Correspondence,* p. 180.

[53] For the defence of Taylor's plan, see J. S. Pike, *First Blows of the Civil War,* (New York, 1879), pp. 22, 53, 55, 64; also the daily issues of the Washington *Republic, e.g.,* that of April 24, 1850.

California's admission must be made contingent upon some general solution of the whole problem.

This attitude led Clay to introduce in the Senate, on January 28, 1850, his famous "Compromise" or "Omnibus" bill, which provided for the admission of California as a free state, the organization of territorial governments (without mention of slavery) in Deseret (Utah) and New Mexico, the compensation of Texas for lands surrendered to the latter, and the passage of a more stringent fugitive slave law. Most of the Whigs and conservative Democrats came eventually to support this formula, although Berrien of Georgia, as a southern-rights Whig, opposed it on the ground that it did not offer enough to the South. He called the attention of the Senate to the pending resolution in the Georgia legislature relating to the admission of California and warned his colleagues that his state would soon "take a tone much higher" in defence of southern rights.[54]

Proposals similar to those introduced by Clay were in due time made in the House and received there the support of the same conservative elements in both parties that upheld them in the Senate. Cobb and Hackett, of Georgia, naturally welcomed the proposal of a general solution, although Haralson and Wellborn opposed it. Toombs, despite his fierce oratory, and Stephens, despite his pessimism concerning the outcome of the whole issue,[55] displayed a willingness to

[54] Philadelphia *North American*, February 13, 1850.

[55] Stephens' attitude in December and January was, in some ways, more extreme than that of Toombs. He despaired of the preservation of the Union, and decided that secession was inevitable, sooner or later. Nevertheless, he refused to hasten the issue after the manner of Calhoun, Rhett, Benning, *et. al.* He gave as his reason for not doing so the fear that the radicals in Georgia, *e.g.,* while capable of starting a revolution,.

accept the compromise plan. As late as the middle of February, Stephens organized in the House a series of filibusters which prevented the separate admission of California as a free-state, but he was already prepared to vote for its admission, provided this was coupled with other schemes of compromise he favored. For this reason, he condemned the California resolution then pending in the Georgia legislature, since that resolution made no allowance for any general compromise to which the admission of California might be attached.[56]

The prospects for compromise improved as the winter drew to a close. Progress on Clay's plan was slow because of administrative opposition and the necessity for considering other proposed plans of compromise, plans such as that offered by Bell, of Tennessee, which focused attention on Texas rather than California. But early in March a series of great speeches in the Senate culminated in Calhoun's final appeal for northern justice and southern solidarity and in Webster's great appeal for the Union. Webster's "Seventh of March Speech" seemed to assure southern "moderadoes" of the support of northern conservatives and was therefore the most encouraging sign of compromise which had yet been displayed.[57] The death of Calhoun, coming a few days

were not capable of building up a good government. See A. H. Stephens to Linton Stephens, January 15, February 10, 1850, in Johnston and Browne, *Alexander H. Stephens*, pp. 244, 245, 247; see also p. 265. *Cf.* Pendleton, *Alexander H. Stephens*, pp. 95-99.

[56] A. H. Stephens to Linton Stephens, February 20, 1850, Johnston and Browne, *op. cit.*, p. 250; A. H. Stephens, *War Between the States*, II. 201-205, 232.

[57] See H. D. Foster, "Webster's Seventh of March Speech, and the Secession Movement, 1850," *American Historical Review*, XXVII. 255-264. For Bell's compromise plan and comment thereon by the Georgia Congressmen, see Sioussat, "Tennessee, the Compromise of 1850, and the Nashville Convention," *Mississippi Valley Historical Review*, II. 324-327.

later, softened to some extent the asperities of personal feeling which had been so aroused in the course of the debates. As the spring progressed the hopes of the conservatives continued to rise.

It remained to be seen what effect the congressional debates, and concomitant developments in the legislatures of the southern states, would have upon the country at large. In the North the press displayed increasing apprehension of a real secession movement,[58] though as late as February 4 one northern observer complacently remarked that "Disunion, as a remedy now for any governmental evil, has never entered the minds of one half-dozen sane persons in the United States."[59] The tactics of "the Terrible Toombs" particularly alarmed the northern conservatives, and brought down upon his head and that of Stephens the most bitter condemnation.[60] As a result of just such alarm as the Georgians inspired, the northern moderates became aroused to the danger of the situation and expressed themselves in a number of great "Union Meetings," which did much to reassure the conservatives of the South. Curiously enough, the chief northern editor who did not condemn Toombs was the extreme abolitionist, Garrison, who welcomed the Georgian's warnings as indications that bloodshed and civil war would soon begin at the capitol.[61]

[58] New York *Herald,* January 21; Washington *Daily Union,* January 23; Philadelphia *Bulletin,* February 1, etc.

[59] Philadelphia *Public Ledger,* February 4, 1850; see also Philadelphia *North American,* December 5, 1849; Columbus *Ohio Statesman,* March 1, 1850.

[60] Cleveland *Plain Dealer,* March 27; Columbus *Ohio State Journal,* July 20, 1850; Philadelphia *North American,* December 15, 1849. The Boston *Courier* termed Toombs and Stephens "swaggering Boabdils—mere bluffers," and observed kindly that the "gasconading of such empty headed brawlers is equalled only by their poltroonery when danger is at hand." *(Courier,* January 2, 1850). *Cf.* Benjamin Brawley, *A Social History of the American Negro,* p. 128.

[61] Boston *Liberator,* December 11, 21, 1849, March 29, 1850.

The southern Whig press, outside of Georgia, tended to condemn the Georgia Whigs for deserting their party, though such criticism was not so severe as that voiced in the North.[62] Only in Georgia did the Whigs tend to support Toombs and Stephens;[63] but here, as elsewhere in the South, the southern-rights Democrats rallied to them as new converts to the Cause.[64]

Press opinion in the North was unfavorable to the Georgia legislature for the same reasons that it was unfavorable to the Georgia congressmen. The radical bills and resolutions debated by the legislature were regarded by some of the northern Democratic journals as so many serious warnings to the North. The resolution calling upon Georgia congressmen to leave Washington in case the Proviso passed was viewed by the New York *Herald* as an indication of what all southern congressmen would do in such an emergency.[65] Northern Whig papers, however, considered the legislature violent and unrepresentative of the mass of the Georgia people. It was accused of planning secession in case California was admitted.[66] The retaliatory bill providing for the taxation of northern goods was ridiculed with some bitterness. This measure had included, when introduced, not only a tax of fifty per cent. on all such goods sold in Georgia, but also provisions that no Georgia taxpayer should spend more than fifteen days in the North in any one

[62] Washington (N. C.) *Whig,* December 12, 1849, in Washington (D. C.) *Republican,* January 11, 1850; Mobile *Daily Advertiser,* January 1, 1850; New Orleans *Bulletin,* in Augusta *Chronicle,* December 25, 1849, etc.

[63] Columbus *Enquirer,* December 12; Augusta *Chronicle,* December 8, 11, 20, 1849, etc.

[64] *Georgian,* December 20; *Federal Union,* December 18, 1849.

[65] New York *Herald, January* 9, 1850.

[66] Boston *Courier,* January 2, 1850; Philadelphia *North American,* February 21, 1850.

year[67] and that Georgia lawyers must not defend free-state men in the state courts.[68] It was, therefore, a general "non-intercourse" bill. The comment of the Boston *Courier* was not such as to improve feeling in Georgia. This bill, it declared:

was a remedy that would carry away the patient. How Georgians will enjoy paying more than any one else for manufactured goods. Then, too, it will help Georgia credit so much in the North! As for not spending more than 15 days in the North, what Georgian would want to go so many miles away from mosquitoes and yellow fever, when there is so much taxation and hard labor at home? Yea, let Georgia pass her law, build a Chinese Wall and discover which end of the Union it will hurt the most![69]

Within Georgia the Democratic press, save for one or two papers in Upper Georgia, such as the Athens *Banner,* generally supported the southern-rights majority in the legislature. California, it was agreed must not be admitted, and all good southerners should join the Democrats in this struggle.[70] The attitude of the Georgia Whig press towards the legislature, on the other hand, generally reflected that of the conservative Whig members of that body. The first seven of the ten resolutions were approved, but there was immediate and indignant disapproval of the California clauses in the eighth resolution and in the state convention bill.

The attitude of the Whig press underwent an interesting evolution during the course of the winter. As late as the beginning of December, the conservative *Chronicle,* it will be recalled, had claimed that no crisis was at hand and that excitement was dangerous and

[67] Probably an expression of Democratic resentment against the custom of wealthy Whigs, of spending the summer in the North.
[68] Boston *Courier,* December 28, 1849.
[69] *Ibid.*
[70] *Federal Union,* November 27; *Georgian,* December 27, 1849.

uncalled for. By the end of the month, however, events in Congress seem to have convinced even this journal that the House might be determined to pass the Proviso. This was the signal for a potential unity against the measure that was impressive. When even the *Chronicle* admitted that the country might be "on the eve of a great political convulsion and funds may be necessary to protect our honor and our interests,"[71] it was certain that all Georgia, save perhaps some mountain districts in Cherokee, was ready for final resistance to the Proviso. At the same time that the Whig papers took decided ground for final resistance to the Proviso, they displayed a consistent desire for any possible adjustment that was not dishonorable to the South. Because of this general attitude, the Whig editors seized with avidity upon any sign that the sectional struggle could be adjusted. They continued not only to approve Taylor's statehood plan but to believe that he would veto the Proviso if it reached him.[72] Reports began to reach Georgia as early as the first week in February that Congress would probably pass a compromise measure. The *Chronicle* was able by that time to observe quite cheerfully that "the essential differences between the North and the South are so slight in view of ultimate consequences . . . that time and the natural course of events are rapidly settling the whole question."[73] In all these opinions, the optimistic conservatism of the Georgia Whig editors was in marked contrast to the pessimistic excitement displayed at Washington by the Georgia Whig congressmen.

[71] *Chronicle*, December 28, 1849.
[72] *News*, January 22, 1850.
[73] *Chronicle*, February 9, 1850.

The reaction of the Whig papers to Clay's "Compromise," and to Webster's conciliatory "Seventh of March Speech," was prompt and enthusiastic. Dr. Daniel Lee, editor of the *Chronicle*, left Augusta for Washington in mid-January to report directly upon congressional developments, and his wire praising Clay's Omnibus scheme was the first news thereon to reach Georgia.[74] When Webster's speech was reported, the *Chronicle* could not find words to express its "high gratification." The Proviso was now certainly dead. Calhoun's speech urging a dual executive scheme to protect the South, on the other hand, was immediately condemned as "impracticable."[75] "Great Union Meetings" in New York and Philadelphia also offered assurance of the desire of northern conservatives for compromise, and such assurance was perhaps more potent than the speech of any one man, even though that man was Webster.[76]

The southern-rights papers, as would be expected, praised Calhoun's last great speech and continued to deny that he was a disunionist. Calhoun, the *Federal Union* observed, loved the Union, but "saw further into the future" than did the southern conservatives, a verdict with which posterity would probably agree.[77] Webster's speech also received some moderate praise, but the Clay Omnibus plan was immediately and emphatically condemned. It "yielded nothing to the South" and was therefore "insulting" and "no com-

[74] *Chronicle,* January 30; *Republican,* February 1, 1850.

[75] *Chronicle,* March 9, 12; Columbus *Enquirer,* March 12; *Republican,* March 9, 1850.

[76] Cobb later expressed the opinion that the northern "Union Meetings" were the most potent factor in giving the Georgia conservatives the necessary assurances early in the controversy; see Washington *Union,* December 19, 1850.

[77] *Federal Union,* March 19, 1850.

promise."[78]   The opinions of the New York *Sun* and London *Times*, to the effect that the final destruction of slavery was inherent in the plan, were quoted with approval.   If the South accepted a "Compromise" in which she made all the concessions, it would be but another step to the "final concession."[79]   The northern "Union Meetings" were hailed as encouraging signs, indicative of southern wrongs and southern earnestness, but they were no excuse for accepting the humiliating Omnibus plan.   Indeed, these very meetings offered evidence of the effectiveness of the strong southern protest, which must not be abandoned as soon as it began to prove of value.   If even the Yankees were beginning to appreciate southern claims, then "palsied be the tongue within her borders that would stifle her complaints."[80]   The knowledge that Toombs and Stephens would probably accept the Omnibus, first suggested in Toombs' letter of March 11 to Governor Towns, was therefore a shock and a disappointment to the southern-rights journals.   The Augusta *Constitutionalist* immediately condemned Toombs as a hypocrite, who was "blowing hot and by claiming that it was poorly attended.[86]

In its confidence, expressed early in February, that the difficulties between the North and the South could be adjusted nicely within the Union, the *Chronicle* had depended upon "an abiding faith in the common sense of the Georgia people."   This was another way of expressing a belief in the conservatism and union-loving qualities of these people.   After all, it

[78] *Federal Union*, February 5; *Georgian*, February 5, 1850.

[79] *News*, February 8, 1850.

[80] *Federal Union*, March 5, 1850.

[81] *Constitutionalist*, in the *Federal Union*, March 26, 1850.   For Toombs' letter, which was in reply to Towns' transmission of the Legislature's resolutions, see the *National Intelligencer*, March 26, 1850.

was not what editors and politicians thought, but what the masses thought, which would finally determine whether Georgia would accept an adjustment or whether she would take extreme measures. It is essential, then, to consider the real state of public opinion in the state during the winter of 1850. The phenomena to be considered are the county meetings, the estimates made by contemporary editors and other observers, one special election held in Georgia late in February, and, most important of all, the Nashville convention elections.

Late in December, several county meetings, some Whig and some non-partisan, were held, chiefly in the coastal counties of Glynn and McIntosh. These were called in order to support the stand taken by Toombs and Stephens in Congress and to demand final resistance to the Proviso should it pass. The *Chronicle* opposed such meetings, but the *Republican* praised them as a sign that both parties were united for ultimate resistance to that measure.[82]

After the December excitement in Congress had passed, the press dispatches being less alarming for the moment, there seem to have been few or no county meetings in January. The people were either indifferent or were waiting to see what Congress and the legislature would do. Early in February, after the eighth resolution had passed in the latter body and Clay's compromise had been introduced at Washington, efforts were made to get up southern-rights meetings in Bibb and Monroe Counties in Central Georgia. These were intended to praise the ten resolutions and to condemn the "Compromise." The *Chronicle* claimed that both of the attempted meetings were failures. The evidence that the Monroe meet-

[82] *Republican,* January 17, 1850.

ing proved a fiasco is indeed clear; it was so admitted, even by the radical papers. The Forsyth *Bee*[83] gave the following account of the situation in the heart of Central Georgia in February:

> With shame and mortification we have to record the humiliating fact that the Southern meeting advertised to come off yesterday turned out to be an entire failure. No interest was manifested by any one. When we take into consideration the vast interests at stake . . . we are overwhelmed with astonishment at the apathy and indifference manifested by the good citizens of Monroe. . . . Is it because they are wanting in patriotism?—we hope not. Is it because they are recreant to their own interests? But talk will do no good. We have tried it and are heartily sick of it. 'Ephraim is joined to his idols.'[84]

This popular indifference to southern-rights appeals in Monroe must have characterized the men of both parties, for Monroe had only a very slight majority of Whig voters[85] and was surrounded on three sides by the tier of Democratic counties that ran athwart Central Georgia.

Early in March interest in public meetings was transferred to Upper Georgia. On March 5 a general non-partisan meeting of conservatives was held at Cassville, Cass County, which adopted resolutions condemning the Nashville convention and the proposed state convention. These resolutions asserted the right of California to admission and expressed a "strong attachment" to the Union. "We pledge ourselves," they continued, "to support the President in using all constitutional means in his power to protect it from

[83] An independent journal of southern-rights sympathies.

[84] Forsythe *Bee*, February 6, in *National Intelligencer*, February 23, 1850.

[85] In the gubernatorial election of 1847 (the last one in Georgia largely unaffected by national issues) Monroe gave 670 Democratic and 688 Whig votes; *Georgian*, October 13, 1848.

violence for any cause now known to us." This meeting attracted wide attention in the North, where the
Whig papers viewed it as a sign of Georgia conservatism. Some Democratic editors decried it, however,
by claiming that it was poorly attended.[86]

Further evidence of strong Union feeling among
both parties in Upper Georgia was afforded early in
March by a pronunciamento from the grand jury of
the superior court in Gwinnet County, in the Cherokee
Circuit, which expressed an "abhorrence" of the idea
of disunion and exhorted all "not to give up the ship
of state."[87] A correspondent of Cobb in Upper Georgia wrote him March 10 that the whole slavery controversy had been "perhaps less anxiously watched" in
that section of the state than elsewhere.[88] The Marietta *Helicon* listed counties which it was already
sure were certain to oppose disunion.[89]

To cap the climax, reports began to come down
state that political leaders in the hill counties were telling the people there that, as non-slaveholders, they
had no interest in the general slavery controversy.
Such speakers declared that if the southern-rights men
brought on a conflict with the North, "they (the Up-
Country men) would have to fight the battles of the
lordly slave owners." A certain Judge Wright was
particularly active along this line in meetings at Dahlonega and in Cumming. "These reports," declared
the *Federal Union* in some alarm, "have been coming
in for some time."[90]

[86] Resolutions printed in the Washington *Republic,* March 14; see
also *National Intelligencer,* March 15; Washington *Union,* March 24,
Philadelphia *Public Ledger,* March 15, 1850.

[87] *Chronicle,* April 5.

[88] G. D. Phillips to Cobb, Habersham County, March 10, 1850,
Toombs, Stephens, and Cobb Correspondence, p. 185.

[89] Marietta *Helicon,* in Mobile *Daily Advertiser,* April 22, 1850.

[90] *Federal Union,* April 9, 1850.

Such evidence convinced the Union Democratic and Whig press in Georgia that Cherokee was strongly opposed to the southern movement in February and March, 1850, just as it had been during the two preceding years. The reported failure of the radical meetings in Monroe and Bibb led to similar conclusions with regard to Central Georgia. The *Republican* had declared in the preceding November that the people were tired and sick of the slavery controversy,[91] and the *Chronicle* repeated this with emphasis even in February 1850.[92] The Athens *Banner* (Union Democrat) agreed with the *Chronicle* that "it is an undeniable fact that the people of Georgia will not support the demagogery of the last Legislature."[93] In like manner, Whig papers outside the state were of the opinion that the Georgia congressmen did not represent the masses of their constituents. "In Georgia," observed the *Advertiser* in April, "a conservative spirit is manifesting itself *in spite of Toombs and Company.*"[94]

On the other hand, there was some evidence during the winter of 1849-50 that the idea of secession, secretly supported for years by extremists, was beginning to be discussed more openly than ever before. The Griffin *Whig* was "pained to hear the subject discussed in the newspapers and in social circles with so much earnestness and in such seeming indifference to its continuance." Nevertheless, it considered this the work of some of the "old nullifyers" who had joined the Democrats in 1840 and had been admitted to leadership.

[91] *Republican,* November 2, 1849.
[92] *Chronicle,* February 3, 1850.
[93] *Ibid.,* March 23; see also *National Intelligencer,* March 25, 1850.
[94] Mobile *Advertiser,* April 21, 1850, italics my own. See, for similar opinions, the Philadelphia *Public Ledger,* January 24, February 26; Baltimore *American,* January 17, 1850.

It was not a spontaneous or popular movement, this journal claimed, even among the Democrats.[95]

Few, if any, estimates of popular opinion in the state were made by southern-rights editors during the winter. Those who did claim that Georgia was "ready to peril everything" or "seek desperate remedies," usually based their opinion on developments in the legislature.[96] The South Carolina papers expressed a belief that Georgia "was moving," but this also was based upon the doings of the legislature. A few individuals expressed qualified opinions that secessionist views were becoming popular. Benning, the secessionist, wrote Cobb that Union sentiment in the South in general was "very unreliable."[97]   G. D. Phillips, of Habersham County, also wrote Cobb on March 10 that he personally was "for equality or disunion" and that he was sure that this was the "predominant feeling in Georgia."[98]   The significance of this statement depends, however, upon what he meant by "equality," which, so far as can be judged from the text of his letter, implied simply a demand for compromise.

A special election was held late in February in the first congressional district to choose a successor to T. Butler King, the Whig representative, who had resigned to undertake his California mission. The result of the election reversed that of 1848, the district now

---

[95] Griffin *Whig*, in *National Intelligencer*, March 23, 24, 1850. The Washington *Union* said that these extracts from the southern papers given in the *Intelligencer* "garbled" the news, and "that for one extract it gives from the hesitating Southern press we might present a hundred of the boldest character." (February 19, 1850). It did not present them, however.

[96] Federal *Union*, February 12; *Cf.* Philadelphia *Public Ledger*, February 4, 1850.

[97] Benning to Cobb, March 29, 1850, "Cobb Papers," *Georgia Historical Quarterly*, V. No. 3, p. 39.

[98] Phillips to Cobb, *Toombs, Stephens, and Cobb Correspondence*, p. 185.

giving a small majority to James W. Jackson, the Democratic candidate, over Fleming, the Whig.[99] This may have indicated, in view of the issues in Congress at the time and subsequent developments in Lower Georgia, some growth in radical southern-rights feeling in this district.

Taking into consideration all the evidence that has been suggested, it would seem probable that the desire for an adjustment of the national issue was stronger, in the minds of the masses of Georgia people, during the critical winter of 1850 than was the desire for secession or other extreme measures. Despite the worry occasioned among Whig leaders by the defection of the Clay Whigs in 1848 and 1849, there is no reason to believe that any large group of Whigs wavered in the desire for conciliation in 1850, if this could be had without the Proviso and therefore with honor.[100] Nor were there signs of wide-spread secessionist spirit in Central Georgia, even among the masses of the Democrats. The evidence concerning opinion in Central Georgia prior to March is, to be sure, largely of a negative character, save for the failures of southern-rights meetings noted. That is to say, there being no positive evidence of wide-spread "extremism" among the people of Central Georgia (such as had already been displayed, for instance, by public meetings "in many parts of South Carolina"),[101] it is probable that

---

[99] Washington *Republic,* March 4, 1850.

[100] The two to four thousand followers of Smythe and the Augusta *Republic* had largely lost their identity as Whigs after going with the Democrats in October, 1849. Cole reaches this opinion for the mass of the southern-rights Whigs in general; *Whig Party in the South,* p. 162.

[101] C. S. Boucher, "The Secession and Co-Operation Movements in South Carolina, 1848-1852," *Washington University Studies, Humanistic Series,* V. No. 2, pp. 78, 79. *Cf.* also the evidences of how popular excitement *did* express itself in Georgia in 1860, as given in Phillips, *Georgia and State Rights,* p. 196.

there was no such widespread extremism in existence. In Lower Georgia alone was there a suggestion of increasing excitement, and this suggestion is not a very conclusive one. In Upper Georgia, on the other hand, there was evidence that the masses of the Democrats as well as the Whigs continued their traditional opposition to extremism.

This blended conservatism and indifference of the Georgia masses to the secession movement was due, in large part, to the growing promise of the compromise movement at Washington and to those influences within the state which made its people so desirous of accepting compromise. A more complete statement of the nature of public opinion in the state must be postponed, however, until the positive evidence of the Nashville convention elections is considered.

The Whig papers had attempted to discourage the Nashville convention movement, or else had maintained a discreet silence upon it, since the preceding November. The *Chronicle* continued to question whether it would ever meet. When February came, the Whig editors combined opposition to the southern convention with opposition to the state convention, and the suggestion was soon made that the only way to redeem either affair was to infuse a conservative element into their respective membership.[102]

In the meantime, five of the seven chief Democratic papers in the state had enthusiastically welcomed the call to the southern convention and continued to advocate it vehemently through the winter. They denied that it was intended to plan immediate secession, but they began to declare openly that unless it forced

---

[102] Columbus *Enquirer*, April 2; *Chronicle*, November 17, 1849, February 9, April 17, 1850.

real and immediate concessions from the North it would mean secession by the South.[103]

The Athens *Banner,* of course, did not back the convention, but it was replaced by the erstwhile Whig organ, the Augusta *Republic,* which had become one of the most militant of the southern-rights organs. Smythe, its editor, supported the Nashville convention, announcing in the best oratorical style of the day: "We hope for the best, but if driven to choose between the Union and dishonor we will look to the streaks upon the eastern sky of the South, which promise her the refulgent sun of independence."[104]

The independent Savannah *News,* which had favored a southern convention during the winter, admitted in March that such a meeting might not be needed. It believed, however, that "the movement has now gone so far that honor requires it be carried out. Even if a Compromise is reached the Nashville Convention will be useful to ratify."[105] This was the only important southern-rights paper in the state which may be said to have changed its attitude because of the compromise movements in Washington.

While all the radical papers mentioned favored both the southern and the state conventions as essential parts of the one general southern movement, one paper, the Columbus *Times,* favored the latter to the exclusion of the former. This journal mildly opposed the calling of a general southern convention to redress southern wrongs. It explained that "We had rather risk the decision of our own state . . . than to be mixed up with others."[106] This opposition or indiff-

[103] *Federal Union,* March 5; Columbus *Sentinel,* in *National Intelligencer,* March 19, April 11; *Georgian,* March 5, 1850.
[104] Augusta *Republic,* in *National Intelligencer,* March 11, 1850.
[105] Savannah *News,* March 12, 1850.
[106] Columbus *Times,* in *National Intelligencer,* February 17, 1850.

erence to the Nashville movement in favor of the state convention, however, was unique among the chief southern-rights papers.

The legislature had provided, in planning elections to Nashville, that preliminary meetings were to be held in each county early in March to choose delegates to congressional district conventions. These, in turn, were to nominate one or more candidates from each party. Then, on April 3, the voters in each county would vote for two of these nominees to represent their district at Nashville, one from each party. Meanwhile, the legislature was to choose two delegates-at-large. As the time for the preliminary March meetings approached, the southern-rights papers appealed to the people to make certain that the counties send representatives to the district meetings.

When the time came, very few county meetings were held. The Savannah *Republican* claimed that not more than a dozen were held and that not more than one thousand voters out of some ninety-five thousand participated. In most counties, so few men appeared that no delegates were sent to the district conventions.[107] The Athens *Banner* gave a realistic account of an attempt to "get up" a town meeting. "At 3 P. M. on Saturday last," it said, "was the hour and the day appointed for a meeting of the Democratic party of this city at the Town hall . . . for the purpose of sending delegates to a district convention . . . There seemed to be not the least interest manifested. On arriving at the Town Hall we found some half dozen present, and in about fifteen minutes a few more entered, making a total of sixteen. The town bell was rung by the marshall, but all in vain. The People Would Not Come and those present broke up without

[107] *Republican*, March 23, 1850.

action."[108]   Such was the character of some of the few preliminary meetings held. Nevertheless, the district meetings were held towards the end of the month and nominees named for each of the eight districts. Needless to say, these district conventions were not representative affairs.

The real test of popular sentiment towards the Nashville Convention was to be made on April 3, when the people voted for the nominees. A final appeal was made by the southern-rights papers for a large vote. "All Georgians," urged the Macon *Telegraph*, "should rally around the citadel of the South" by casting their votes for the candidates.[109]

The result of the April election was startling, even to those who had partially anticipated it. After all the months of preparation, after all the struggles in the legislature, and after all the fan fares of southern-rights trumpets to announce its coming, the southern convention election simply did not arrive! It was a complete and dismal failure for the plain reason that the great masses of both parties ignored it. A conservative estimate, based upon the press figures for the different counties, would place the total number of votes cast in the state at about two thousand five hundred out of a total voting population of about ninety-five thousand. Many counties held no election whatever.[110] In some cases the voters proceeded on their own initiative to vote such strange yet significant tickets as "No Convention," or "No Disunion." The vote in Columbus, for instance, was listed as follows:

[108] Athens *Banner*, in *National Intelligencer*, March 28, 1850.
[109] Macon *Telegraph*, in *National Intelligencer*, April 11, 1850. *Banner*, there were 7 which had not even opened the polls; see *National*
[110] Of the first 25 counties listed in the returns published by the Athens *Intelligencer*, April 17, 1850.

For candidates 113
"No Convention" 98
"No Disunion" 78

The normal vote of Muscogee County, wherein Columbus was located, was about one thousand nine hundred.[111]

A noticeable feature of the returns was the fact that the insignificance of the vote cast was due almost, if not quite, as much to Democratic as to Whig indifference.[112] The vote in Coastal Georgia, both in Chatham (Savannah) and other counties, was proportionately higher than in the other sections, and these were Whig counties.

The Whig and Union Democratic press was filled for the next week with ironical accounts and comments upon the indifference displayed towards the convention. The election was a "farce," a "flash in the pan," an "abortion"—and such other phrases as came to the heads of triumphant and metaphorically-

---

[111] A few county votes may be noted, which are illustrative of results in the several sections of the state; for complete figures see *National Intelligencer*, April 17, 1850. It may be noted that the vote in Coastal Georgia was proportionately higher than in the other sections.

	Votes Cast	Normal Vote	Usual Majority Party
Upper Georgia			
Floyd	53	1,300	Dem.
Lumpkin	27	1,500	Dem.
Paulding	no polls		Dem.
Central Georgia			
Jasper	89	1,000	Dem.
Hancock	42	800	Whig
Pike	29	500	Whig
Troup	14	1,500	Whig
Oglethorpe	no polls		Whig
Coastal Georgia			
Chatham (Savannah)	439	1,400	Whig
McIntosh	43	165	Whig
Pine Barrens			
Emanuel	no polls		Dem.
Effingham	18	260	Whig

[112] *Cf.* Cole, *Whig Party in the South*, p. 170.

minded editors. The southern-rights press was goaded with ironical comment and inquiry. "The mountain labored and brought forth a mouse," observed the Griffin *Whig*. "The whole affair fell still-born," commented the Washington *Gazette*. "We were told by people abroad," said the Cassville *Standard*, "that there has been more excitement in this county (Cass) than in any other part of the state. Yet 2,000 of our 2,300 voters staid at home and let the golden calf of the new-light have its tinsel rubbed off! Oh, naughty people!"[113] The *Chronicle* demanded that the Charleston *Mercury*, which had declared "Georgia is moving," should "now inform its readers which way she has moved." The Nashville convention, all agreed, was now a dead affair in Georgia, and it was doubtful if the state would be represented therein.[114]

The reaction of the southern-rights press was varied. Several papers frankly recognized that the people had defeated the whole convention movement and that the vote indicated indifference or opposition to the southern movement. "We could weep over the divisions in the South if it would do any good," exclaimed the Augusta *Republic* in considering the failures of the preliminary meetings.[115] The Savannah *News*, silent for some weeks after the elections, finally admitted that the elections were "humiliating" and marvelled at the "strange apathy of the Georgia people." It came to feel that the southern convention should never be held if it was to be unrepresentative.[116]

[113] *Chronicle*, April 11, 1850.

[114] For these and other quotations from the Georgia press, see the *National Intelligencer*, March 29, April 4, 7, 11, 13 and 18; the Washington *Republic*, April 15, and 16, 1850. The Washington *Union* again claimed that the *Intelligencer* was "garbeling" the Georgia press, but cited no evidence. (*Union*, April 7.)

[115] Augusta *Republic*, in *National Intelligencer*, March 29, 1850.

[116] *News*, May 20, June 13, 1850.

In like manner, the *Constitutionalist* frankly admitted that "the meager vote given for delegates . . . is a virtual defeat of the Southern Convention movement in Georgia. So far as this state is concerned, we look upon it as dead and buried."[117] On the other hand, the Charleston *Mercury* denied that the election had much significance,[118] and the *Georgian* retorted hotly to enemy taunts, appealing to its co-workers to carry on for the Cause.[119]

The fact that the southern-rights press had failed to represent and had been entirely out of touch with popular opinion was very obvious. The explanation of the results made by these editors is interesting. Some said, for example the *News*, that the results were due to the inexplicable and incredible "apathy" of the people. The *Federal Union*, however, admitted on the morning of the election that the vote would be light because of the following factors: (1) the continued faith of some Whigs in President Taylor and hope for his favor; (2) the mistaken fear in both parties that the convention was a secessionist move; and (3) a belief that an adjustment could be reached in Congress. A week after the election, it made the added discovery that (4) the lack of opposition between the candidates deprived the election of interest and therefore lessened the number of votes cast.[120]

The only other factor suggested by journals of this group at the time of the election was that stated by the Montgomery (Alabama) *Atlas*, which blamed the defeat in Georgia upon "the indifference of the ignorant mass, who are illiterate or take no papers. Many did not know there was to be a Nashville Conven-

[117] *Constitutionalist*, in *National Intelligencer*, April 18.
[118] Charleston *Mercury*, April 13, 1850.
[119] *Georgian*, April 13, 1850.
[120] *Federal Union*, April 2, 9, 1850.

tion."[121] There was probably some truth in the belief that many Democrats who did not take the papers were, for this reason, out of touch with the pro-convention propaganda and consequently indifferent to it. A farmer in Forsyth County, for instance, who wrote that people there did not "take the papers," remarked that they "could not see that Congress had yet *done* anything against them, and until it did they would behave themselves." "We hope," he concluded ironically, "that our city editors, who know everything about 'Southern Rights,' and all that, will inform us what the correct doctrine is."[122]

The conservative press interpreted the popular indifference to the election as being due primarily to "a general conviction that the irritating questions will be settled satisfactorily at the present session of Congress." As a secondary cause, they mentioned the belief that in any case the Nashville meeting would be too unrepresentative of the South to function successfully as a southern convention.

It is an interesting fact that none of the chief papers, not even the southern-rights journals, suggested until some time after the election that the people might have ignored Nashville because their interest had been drawn exclusively to the state convention project.[123] This silence, combined with the fact that, prior to the election, the southern-rights papers associated the state and the Nashville conventions together as two great phases of the same southern movement, would seem to indicate that the repudiation of the Nashville convention was, at least to a large extent, a repudiation of the southern movement in general. It

[121] Montgomery (Ala.) *Atlas,* in *Chronicle,* April 23.
[122] *Chronicle,* April 7, 1850.
[123] The Columbus *Times* may have been an exception to this. No files of this paper for 1850 have been examined by the author.

is significant that the *Federal Union* itself blamed the result of the April elections in part upon the popular impression, which it said existed in both parties, that the Nashville convention *might* lead to disunion. The implication concerning the popular opinion of disunion is obvious enough.

The evidence of the March and April elections, then, would seem to corroborate other evidence already considered in support of the conclusion that a majority of both parties in Georgia either desired compromise, or else were indifferent to the whole controversy, during the winter and spring of 1850. There is evidence, moreover, that during this period the masses of those interested were confident that the compromise they desired could actually be attained.[124]

The indifference or opposition to the secession movement was displayed, it is to be remembered, despite the inflammatory speeches of the Georgia congressmen, despite the radical measures of the legislature, and despite the excited appeal of the southern-rights editors. The unrepresentative character of the legislature is to be explained in part by the fact that it was chosen during the fall of 1849, when the passage of the Proviso in the coming Congress seemed imminent and when feeling in the state was consequently becoming warmer. Under these circumstances, an unusually large number of southern-rights men secured election to office in the legislature. This body, having worked itself up to a white heat in December, stayed hot all winter, the while the people cooled off with the progress of the compromise movement at Washington.

---

[124] *Cf.* H. D. Foster, "Webster's Seventh of March Speech and the Secession Movement, 1850," *American Historical Review*, XVII. 250, 251, (January, 1922). The view is here taken that there was imminent danger of secession in Georgia throughout the year 1850, until the fall campaign for the Union stemmed the secession tide.

Members of the legislature were by the very nature of their position, moreover, more apt to be agitated by each new development in the sectional controversy than were the people back on the farms. So, too, were the southern-rights editors, who followed each new phase of that controversy with intense interest and who were inclined to express the opinions of politicians thereupon, rather than those of the masses.[125]

It is small wonder that these editors "saw further," as they put it, than did many of their own readers— small wonder that such men pushed so far out in front of the southern-rights parade that they ceased to lead those who were supposed to be following them. This whole situation was to become more obvious as the year progressed, and as the secessionists made their final appeal to Georgia to "lead off."

[125] This tendency of the editors to express the views of politicians rather than of the people, was realized and regretted by some of the abler papers of the time; see, *e.g.*, the citicisms of the press in the Savannah *Georgian*, January 29; Charleston *Mercury*, January 26, 1848.

CHAPTER VII

THE CLEARING, 1850

As a result of the insignificant vote cast in the April election, the Whigs questioned whether any delegation should be sent from Georgia to Nashville, and most of their delegates proceeded to resign or failed at the last moment to go. There was little or no inclination among the Georgia Whigs, as there was among their brethren in Mississippi and Alabama,[1] to attend simply in order to prevent mischief. Some of the Georgia Democratic delegates also declined to attend. When notice of resignation was given in time, Governor Towns exercised his power, granted by legislative provision, to appoint a successor from the party to which the delegate belonged.[2]

The difficulties of securing a delegation is illustrated by the case of the first district. Here W. J. Lawton was suggested as a Democratic delegate, but declined the honor. Old Governor Troup, whose name the Georgia Whigs had once used as their party appellation, was then elected for this place, his letters to the press having identified him with the extremist element. At the last moment, however, he was prevented from going to Nashville by illness in his family. J. H. Cooper, who had been chosen as his Whig colleague, also finally refused to attend. The first district

---

[1] Cole, *Whig Party in the South*, p. 171.
[2] Of the eight Whigs originally elected only one, M. P. Crawford, of the second district, actually attended. The other seven resigned or failed to appear. Two of the Whig substitutes appointed by Towns did attend. In three districts, the sixth, seventh, and eighth, the Democratic as well as the Whig delegates declined to go and had to be replaced by Towns' appointees.

(Lower Georgia) was, therefore, entirely unrepresented.[3]

Prior to the election of the district delegates, the legislature had chosen as delegates-at-large the southern-rights Democrats McDonald and McAllister, typical Georgia "fire-eaters." McAllister declined the honor and was replaced by ex-Senator Colquitt. The Georgia delegation that actually attended at Nashville, then, consisted finally of eight southern-rights Democrats and three Whigs, and was led by the able secessionists, H. L. Benning and Charles J. McDonald. It was, therefore, largely unrepresentative of the mass of the Georgia people who had nominally chosen the members.[4]

Between the time of the April elections and the date set for the meeting of the southern convention at Nashville there was something of a lull in the general controversy in Georgia. There was, indeed, nothing to be done save to await the Nashville meeting and to follow the debates still proceeding in Congress.

[3] E. J. Harden, *Life of George M. Troup* (1859), pp. 528, 529; *National Intelligencer*, March 19, 21, April 11; Augusta *Chronicle*, June 13, 1850.

[4] The delegation was as follows:
     Ex-Senator Walter T. Colquitt, (Democrat)
     Ex-Governor Charles J. McDonald, (Democrat)
          Delegates at Large.
     M. P. Crawford, (Whig)
     James W. Ramsey, (Whig)
     Robert Bledsoe, (Whig)
     H. L. Benning, (Democrat)
     Obediah C. Gibson, (Democrat)
     Judge Obediah Warner, (Democrat)
     Simpson Fouche, (Democrat)
     John G. McWhertor, (Democrat)
     Andrew H. Dawson, (Democrat)
          District Delegates.
List as given in *Resolutions, Address and Proceedings of the Southern Convention*, Report of the Committee on Credentials, p. 25. *Cf.* D. T. Herndon, "The Nashville Convention," *Alabama Historical Society Publications*, V. 214; Augusta *Chronicle*, June 19; Washington *Union*, April 14, 1850.

Through May and June, the struggle in Congress over the specific items in Clay's Omnibus plan continued to be acute and at times stormy, though the general prospects for a final adjustment had been fairly good since March. Toombs and Stephens continued to warn the North that the South was in earnest when it demanded that a compromise must be made. In this effort to keep the North to the mark, Toombs was doubtless successful, but he went, at times, so far as to renew the impression that he was a true "fire-eater." It is small wonder that some of his more spirited addresses, such as his famous "Hamilcar speech,"[5] renewed among the Georgia extremists the hope that Toombs was one of them in opposition to the compromise. The Whig press, however, decried their assertions to this effect,[6] and some confusion continued to exist as to his real attitude. Northern antislavery editors, of course, renewed their dislike of Toombs for the same reason that the secessionists had renewed their hope in him. This was especially true after a false report had been circulated claiming that Toombs and Stephens had so threatened President Taylor, because of his attitude toward the "Galphin Scandal,"[7] as to hasten his unexpected death on July 9, 1850.[8] His death, exclaimed the Boston *Liberator,* has been partly induced by "the bullying of such desperate men

[5] See *Congressional Globe,* 31 Congress, First Session, p. 1216.

[6] *Chronicle,* July 6, 1850.

[7] The "Galphin Scandal" related to pre-Revolutionary land claims in Georgia and chiefly concerned Crawford, of Georgia, then in Taylor's cabinet, who was accused of using his position to secure personal profit. For a short account, see Rhodes, *History of the United States,* I. 203, 204.

[8] Rhodes, *op. cit.,* I. 176, credited this malicious story. Its fallaciousness is analyzed in Cole, *Whig Party,* p. 168, note 102; and in Phillips, *Toombs,* pp. 84, 85.

as Toombs of Alabama (?) and Stephens of Georgia."[9]

The death of Taylor, of course, removed the growing tension between the administration and the majority of the Whigs, while the moderation of Fillmore, his successor, brought the influence of the new administration to the compromise cause. The Omnibus plan was now almost certain of adoption, even though it was to be taken entirely apart in the process.[10] Since February the majority of the Georgia delegation at Washington had favored its passage. Owen, the third Whig representative, had followed his two colleagues in this, and Hackett, the second Union Democrat, followed Cobb. Wellborn, a third Democrat, also came during the summer to accept the adjustment.[11] Haralson alone, of the original delegation, maintained his opposition, but he was joined in this attitude by Joseph W. Jackson, the Democrat who had succeeded King as a result of the special February election in the first district.[12]

Dawson continued in the Senate his consistent course of moderation and his approval of Clay's plan. The position of Berrien, on the other hand, was a peculiar one. Clay had appealed to him personally, as an old Whig supporter, to accept the Omnibus, on

[9] *Liberator*, August 2, 1850; see also the Columbus *Ohio State Journal*, July 19, 1850. Some northern papers, however, praised Toombs; the New York *Sun*, e.g., considered Toombs as the ablest man "by far" from the South, an opinion which was seconded by the Richmond *Times*, quoted in the *Chronicle*, March 9, 1850.

[10] Hodgson is of the opinion that, had Taylor lived, the southern Whig party would have been broken up by the issue between the administration and the Clay supporters. This "would have precipitated in 1850 the revolution which the death of General Taylor postponed until 1860." J. Hodgson, *The Cradle of the Confederacy, or the Times of Troup, Quitman and Yancey* (1876), p. 276.

[11] For Wellborn's attitude, see his letter of September 16, published in the *Chronicle*, September 27, 1850.

[12] For Jackson's attitude, see Savannah *News*, July 31, 1850.

the ground that it would bring the country thirty years of peace.[13] Yet Berrien could not bring himself to accept Clay's plan. How far his alienation from the younger and more vigorous leaders of the Georgia party and how far his declining influence since the schism of 1849 were factors in his dissatisfaction, it is difficult to say. He was beset by letters from Whig friends at home who favored the Omnibus, but excused them on the ground that they were not present in Congress to witness the "deadly hostility of the North against slavery." This, he explained to a friend in Milledgeville, "makes my blood boil." He talked freely with Clay about his objections and made the interesting statement that Clay agreed personally with some of his views, but admitted that he could not openly say so, lest he "jeopardize" the chances of his bill.[14]

Yet Berrien was not a secessionist. When friends told him he must accept Clay's scheme or risk disunion and civil war, he replied:

I have no such fear,—I know the attachment of our people to the Union. If united we have ample means of resistance within the constitution. Withdraw southern votes for "protected" northern commerce and industry, and slavery will not be further interfered with.[15]

In other words, Berrien desired to reject the compromise and at the same time to attempt to apply economic pressure against the North as a means of defense which would be safer and saner than secession. This was a half-way stand between Union and

[13] Jefferson Davis, A Memoir by His Wife, (1890), I. 447.

[14] Berrien to Major Harris, July 19, 1850, Berrien MSS.

[15] Ibid. The recipient evidently pondered this letter seriously, as across the back in another hand are written the phrases: "The insufficiency of the Compromise measures", "Hostility of the North", "How to resist them in the Union?"

secession principles which was bound to place him and any Georgians who followed him in an uncertain and rather unsatisfactory position.[16]

On June 3, while the situation at Washington was still rather tense, the long heralded southern conventions contained groups of Whigs who lent a moderate Tennessee, which had a delegation of more than one hundred, all but a few delegates came from the six states of Georgia, Alabama, Mississippi, South Carolina, Florida, and Virginia. Most of the members were Democrats, but the Mississippi and Alabama delegations contained groups of Whigs who lent a moderate character to the personnel from those states. The delegations from South Carolina and Georgia were the most radical, being dominated by the secessionists, Hammond, Rhett, Barnwell, Benning, Colquitt, and McDonald.[17] This group directed the efforts to make the convention take extreme ground, though some of them already realized that the meeting was not a representative one and would probably exercise little influence.[18] Judge Sharkey, of Mississippi, was chosen president and McDonald, of Georgia, vice-president of the convention.

June 3 was taken up by President Sharkey's moderate address and the next day by the examination of

[16] He voted for the bills referring to Utah and New Mexico and to the Texas boundary, but against the California and District bills. In rejecting the California bill he warned the Senate that it would result in a call of the state convention in Georgia and that this might mean extreme action. The Baltimore *Sun* could not understand his position at all; see the *Chronicle,* July 15, October 6; Montgomery *Daily Alabama Journal,* August 9, 1850.

[17] D. T. Herndon, "The Nashville Convention," *Alabama Historical Society Publications,* V. 216-218; St. George L. Sioussat, "Tennessee, The Compromise of 1850, and the Nashville Convention," *Mississippi Valley Historical Review,* II. 332-336.

[18] Elizabeth Merritt, "James H. Hammond," *Johns Hopkins University Studies in History and Political Science,* Series XLI. No. 4, p. 95; hereafter referred to as Merritt, *James H. Hammond.*

credentials and the appointment of a general committee to which all resolutions introduced were referred. Benning and McDonald were made members of this body. The sessions of June 5 to June 8 were occupied with the introduction of numerous resolutions and by speeches concerning the same.

The Georgia delegation was quite active. On June 5, A. H. Dawson introduced resolutions endorsing a plan for a southern-rights press at Washington;[19] on the same day Benning introduced a veritable "platform" in the shape of twenty-three resolutions. These resolutions proclaimed the rights of slavery in the Union, demanded that nothing less than the Missouri line could be accepted by the South as a compromise of the territorial problem, urged southern party unity as essential to the protection of southern-rights in the Union, proclaimed the right to leave the Union, and insisted that a continued refusal by the North to enforce the fugitive slave law should be met by retaliatory non-intercourse measures.[20]

Benning's resolution declaring the Missouri line a *sine qua non* for compromise was interesting, as it offered the first evidence that the Georgia secessionists were about to adopt new tactics. The Missouri Compromise principle had been advocated by the southern-rights Democrats of Georgia in 1847 and had then been abandoned and refused by them in the Georgia legislature of 1849-50, only to be reasserted in the summer of 1850. This reassertion of the principle by the secessionists in June was, paradoxically enough, probably motivated by the same reason which had led the legislature to refuse it in January; namely, be-

[19] *Resolutions, Address and Journal of the Proceedings of the Southern Convention*, p. 33.
[20] *Ibid.*, pp. 35-39.

cause it was known the North would no longer accept the Missouri Compromise. Leaders like Benning and Hammond had long hoped, though they did not admit it openly, even at Nashville, that no adjustment could be reached.[21] They were therefore not averse to urging the South to demand a compromise which they were convinced would not be granted.

On July 7, Fouche of Georgia introduced interesting resolutions tacitly condemning the pending compromise schemes in Congress. These declared that "compromises" made by a weaker party with a "stronger" were in reality concessions made for the sake of repose, and that such concessions made at periodical intervals were bound eventually to concede everything. A last resolution asserted the right of a people to alter or abolish an oppressive government.[22]

These resolutions are of interest here in expressing the temper of the Georgia delegation, but they were not actually used as a basis for the resolutions finally adopted by the convention. The latter were founded upon proposals introduced by Judge Campbell of Alabama, and the address which accompanied them was said to have been the work of Rhett.[23] Twenty-eight resolutions in all were adopted, relating chiefly to a statement of the rights of slavery and the duties of Congress in this connection. The most important were

[21] For Benning's early attitude, see his letter to Cobb, July 1, 1849, *Toombs, Stephens, and Cobb Correspondence,* p. 171. On Hammond see Merritt, *James H. Hammond,* pp. 97, 98. For a contemporary analysis of the inconsistency of Benning's resolution with the attitude of the Georgia legislature, see the Washington *Union,* August 13, 1850.

[22] *Resolutions, Address and Journal of the Proceedings of the Southern Convention,* p. 50. For convenient telegraphic summaries of the proceedings see the Washington *Union,* June 6, 7, 8, 11, 12, 13, 14, 15, 1850.

[23] Sioussat, "Tennessee, The Compromise of 1850, and the Nashville Convention," *Mississippi Valley Historical Review,* II. 336, 337.

the eleventh resolution, which embodied Benning's idea of offering the Missouri line as the maximum concession of southern rights in the territories, and the twenty-eighth, which provided that a second session of the convention should meet about six weeks after the adjournment of Congress.

The "Address to the Southern People," which accompanied the resolutions, reviewed northern aggressions in the fashion then orthodox in southern "addresses." It then proceeded to condemn the Clay Omnibus in general and in detail. The California bill, it declared, applied the Proviso; the Texas Boundary bill "partitioned" Texas; the abolition of the slave trade in the District was a step towards the abolition of slavery therein; and the Fugitive Slave bill was inefficient and not in any real sense a concession by the North. In this way, the Address stated the chief objections to the Omnibus and supplied the southern-rights men with an indictment which would be useful in opposing that plan.[24]

The attitude of most of the Georgia delegates towards the Address was well expressed by Colquitt, who remarked that "it was indeed tame enough" and added that he would advise the southern states to prepare munitions of war and to get ready for final resistance.[25] A formal protest entered against the Address by the Alabama Whig delegates was not signed by any of the Georgia delegation.

[24] For the Resolutions and Address see *Resolutions, Address and Journal of the Proceedings of the Southern Convention*, p. 51 ff. See also Ames, *State Documents*, pp. 263-269; M. W. Cluskey, *Political Text Book* (1857), gives the first thirteen of the resolutions. For further notes and references to the sources for the convention, see foot notes to Sioussat, *op. cit.*, especially note 64.

[25] Washington *Republic*, June 17, 1850; see also Ames, "John C. Calhoun," *University of Pennsylvania Public Lectures*, 1917-1918, p. 127.

On June 12 the convention adjourned to await the action of Congress. It had created some excitement in the North, where it was accused of fomenting treason,[26] and where a report had spread that President Taylor would suppress it with troops. It was generally agreed, however, that the "Disunionists in Session" had proved an unrepresentative group and had accomplished nothing.

Apparently undisturbed by such opinions, the delegates wended homeward to appeal for the support of their own states. When the Carolinians reached home, Rhett made a violent disunion speech, which openly proclaimed the real purpose of the secessionists. This was dangerous, as it was sure to bring violent condemnation from the Union-loving masses outside of South Carolina.[27] It was apt to convince some in Georgia, hitherto doubtful, that "secession *per se*" was indeed the purpose of "Palmettodom."

The Georgia delegation was more tactful upon its return, but set to work with the other extremist leaders to organize public sentiment in favor of the late convention. Their problem was a difficult one, but they were resourceful men, and a plan of campaign was already at hand in the move proposed by Benning at Nashville. The March elections had indicated that not only almost all the Whigs, but the majority of the Democrats as well, were either indifferent or opposed to secession for any causes then known. This meant that many Democrats who could be termed "southern-rights" men in the sense that they favored southern

[26] Many of the northern papers compared the Nashville proceedings with those of the "Hartford Convention" of 1815.

[27] For Rhett's speech and Clay's violent condemnation of it, see the Washington *Union*, July 24, 25, 1850. Hammond, though sharing Rhett's views, bitterly condemned his indiscretion in openly proclaiming them, see Merritt, *James H. Hammond*, p. 97.

political unity against the North, were not yet prepared to support a secession movement. This group,
however, as has been suggested, could probably be
counted upon to support the Missouri line principle,
in the belief that such support represented an honest
effort at compromise. If the secessionists could but
persuade the South to demand the Missouri line as an
ultimatum, the North was certain to reject it, and the
South would then have no alternative but to secede.[28]
How soon it would be expedient for the extremists in
Georgia to come out for secession would then be determined by circumstances.

At the same time that the secessionists were anxious to arouse sentiment in favor of the Nashville convention and its Missouri-line ultimatum, they were naturally desirous that the Clay compromise should be
condemned. It was necessary, if the Georgia people
were ever to be aroused, that an energetic campaign
directed towards these ends be inaugurated immediately upon the return of the Nashville delegation.

This renewed radical campaign of the summer was
opened, naturally enough, by the southern-rights editors. The radical press did not immediately come out
openly for secession, but urged that the Clay plan was
"no compromise"; that it was insulting to the South;
that Congress should therefore adjourn; that the
South should unite on the Missouri-line ultimatum of
the late convention and then make this the chief issue

[28] That this was probably the real intention of the secessionists is
indicated by the private views of such leaders as Benning and Hammond,
already noted; by the sudden shift in the policy of the Georgia extremists
in 1850 from opposing the Missouri line in the legislature, to favoring
it at Nashville, and later at home; and by the shrewd analyses of their
purpose made by the Union Democrats, especially those of John H.
Lumpkin and Dr. Richard Arnold, to be noted below. See, e.g., W. H.
Morton to Cobb, July 10; John H. Lumpkin to Cobb, July 21; *Toombs,
Stephens, and Cobb Correspondence*, pp. 194, 206; Arnold to Forney,
December 18, 1850, Arnold MSS., etc.

in the coming congressional elections. There was general agreement in approving the Nashville convention and all its works.[29]

Editorials were then supplemented by resort to another traditional method of arousing public sentiment. Appeals were made to the people to "get up" southern-rights meetings. The *Federal Union* was able to list by July 10 some thirteen counties in which southern-rights meetings had been held, most of them in connection, however, with the usual celebration of the Fourth of July. In nearly every case resolutions were adopted condemning the Clay plan and demanding the Nashville ultimatum. The chief speakers were the erstwhile delegates to the southern convention, McDonald, Colquitt, McWhertor, and A. H. Dawson, who went from one meeting to another upholding their cause. Associated with them, as before, was the vigorous "old Whig" editor, James Smythe, of Augusta. There was no open advocacy of secession, but A. H. Dawson revealed at Augusta the next step in the plan for organizing the extremist movement. This was that every county should form a "southern rights association" whose purpose would be to arouse local enthusiasm and to insure coöperation with similar associations throughout the state.[30] This plan may have been urged upon the Georgia delegates at Nashville by their colleagues from South Carolina, where such local associations had been formed more than a year before.[31] The plan for local organization would probably have met with a general response, as it did in South Carolina, had there been widespread and intense

[29] *Federal Union*, July 10, 17, 24, 31; *Georgian*, July 24, 25, 1850.

[30] *Federal Union*, July 10; Washington *Union*, June 24, July 17; Columbus (Georgia) *Times*, July 18, in Washington *Union*, July 27, 1850; *Georgian*, July 10, 1850.

[31] Hamer, *The Secession Movement in South Carolina*, p. 32.

excitement. In fact, it was taken up by some of the papers, but does not seem to have born much fruit in the state during the summer.[32]

The accounts of the July southern-rights meetings, as given by their friends, were enthusiastic ones. That held in Columbus on July 16 was the largest and probably the most important meeting, as Columbus was the home of an unusual number of extremists. Those in charge prepared, after the manner of the day, a large barbecue in order to attract both the town and country-folk to an all-day political outing. There were to be lots to eat and lots of excitement—food for both body and mind. The streets were crowded early by farmers coming into town, and it was claimed that by ten in the morning a crowd of three thousand had gathered at "Smith's spacious warehouse." Here hundreds could not reach the long tables spread for the feast and "ate their good Southern meat and bread without knife, fork, or plate." The affair lasted, with intermissions for meals, until midnight. There were ten speakers, most of them prominent local citizens, like Major J. H. Howard, "to whom was assigned the task of exposing the frauds of the Clay Compromise and whose execution of his trust was masterly." Some were from nearby counties, such as Porter Ingram, of Harris, "who, though a Northern man by birth, had imbibed all of Georgia's principles and boldly avowed he would fight for her rights." Three speakers came across the Chattahoochee from Barbour County, Alabama, and "the people seemed never weary of listening to them." All of these speakers claimed that the Clay compromise would lead to disunion "or to a result

---

[32] See, e.g., the *Georgian*, July 10, 1850. An association was formed in Camden County, and there may have been a few others which escaped general notice in the press.

still more deplorable—a servile war and the destruction of the white or black race throughout the South."[33] Both the emphasis on the race problem and the failure openly to advocate secession are worthy of note.

The accounts of southern-rights meetings as given by Union Democrats, of course, took on quite a different tone. "A meeting was held on the 4th day of July in Cobb," wrote John H. Lumpkin. "Fouche, Stiles, McDonald and Joe Brown were the only persons invited or who attended, and they had everything their own way. They studiously concealed from the people their ulterior purposes, and carefully arranged it so that no one opposed to them should be heard on that occasion."[34] The Saundersville *Central Georgian* made this charge general, stating that "almost all the meetings that had been called to approve the Nashville Convention were called only for those who favored it—others being excluded. In some counties, after general meetings proved moderate, a few radicals would withdraw and pass southern rights resolutions. No fair meeting in any city would favor the Nashville meeting."[35]

The evidence to be had indicates that these meetings were not usually the result of spontaneous popular demand, but were rather the result of studied effort by the small and able group of enthusiasts, who had in mind the ultimate purpose already discussed.[36] It was very evident, however, that the radical leaders were

[33] Columbus *Times*, July 18, in Washington *Union*, July 27, 1850. For similarly enthusiastic accounts of Georgia meetings see the Columbia *South Carolinian*, July 25, 1850.

[34] Lumpkin to Cobb, July 21, 1850, *Toombs, Stephens, and Cobb Correspondence*, p. 207.

[35] In *Chronicle*, July 27, 1850.

[36] See, *e.g.*, the account of efforts to arouse excitement in Athens, as described in a letter of W. H. Morton to Cobb, July 10, 1850, *Toombs, Stephens, and Cobb Correspondence*, p. 194.

thoroughly in earnest in their renewed effort to arouse extremist feeling.

The most dangerous groups among the extremists, from the Union Democrat's viewpoint, were, first, the "old nullifiers," who had left the Whig Party in 1840;[37] and, second, those who were of South Carolina origin and who had brought their Carolina views with them into the Georgia Democracy.[38] This last group was particularly strong in Savannah and in the counties "along the river." The two groups together made up the real "fire-eaters" of Georgia. In Savannah, Dr. Richard Arnold, several times mayor of the city and representative at Milledgeville, was convinced that the South Carolinians were at the bottom of the renewed radical agitation. Toward the end of June, while there was much debating of Clay's plan in Savannah, Arnold happened to defend that plan at a "wine party" he was attending. Much to his surprise, he was jeered and told that "both parties at the North were rotten on the subject of slavery—the South must look out for herself." He was indignant that Democrats could say this, but found the explanation in the fact that "half of those present were South Carolina men."[39]

The opinions of some of the conservative observers concerning public feeling in July are interesting and suggestive in the light of what had already occurred in the spring and what was to come later in the fall. Lamar wrote Cobb, July 3, from Macon, criticising severely the reckless and unrepresentative character

[37] See chapter iii.
[38] See chapter ii.
[39] Arnold to Forney, December 18, 1850, Arnold MSS. For notes on Forney's position in the northern Democracy see R. F. Nichols, *The Democratic Machine, 1850-1854*, pp. 33, 48, 64, 70, published in the *Columbia University Studies*, CXI, No. 1 (1923).

of the extremist journals, which has already been commented upon in connection with the April election. He said:

The Democratic press in middle Georgia is in the hands of those who are leading the party to the devil. Their audacious assertions have heretofore been treated as idle and harmless bravadoes; but as they are now doing mischief there seems to be a spirit rising among the people to speak out and let their representatives in Congress know what public sentiment really is. . . . The game played by some of the Democratic presses is to browbeat our representatives in Congress into the belief that the people are opposed desperately to the Senate Compromise. . . . It is queer how impudently they utter what everybody knows to be untrue. As an example, a press in this place[40] . . . italicized these words, "The Compromise has no friends in the South and never had," and a few hours after the appearance of the above alluded to a call of a meeting of the friends of the Compromise numbered over 100 highly respectable names. I can say . . . pay no attention to what the papers say. *The noise and bluster of a few presses in Georgia is no more the voice of the people than the delegates to the Nashville Convention were their representatives.*[41]

Another gentleman in Macon wrote in mid-July, "I am satisfied by a close observation of the opinions of the people in both political parties in this section that they are all for the Union is certain."[42] In a somewhat more cautious manner, the Macon *Journal* had observed late in June that, "seven tenths of the people are in favor of an adjustment and the action of the Nashville convention is increasing the number rapidly." The *Chronicle* reminded it that the majority which favored adjustment even before the convention met had also been "very large."[43] One conservative observer in Central Georgia did fear that the majority

[40] Probably the Macon *Telegraph*.

[41] J. B. Lamar to Cobb, July 3, 1850, *Toombs, Stephens, and Cobb Correspondence*, pp. 191, 192; the italics are my own.

[42] Quoted in *Republican* July 24, 1850.

[43] *Chronicle*, June 28, 1850.

of the Democrats in that section were in danger of being tricked into secession. This was Absolom H. Chappell, who wrote Cobb on July 10, also from Macon, that,

the Democratic party of this section of the state is becoming rapidly demoralized in reference to the great question of the preservation of the Union. The game of the destructives is to use the Missouri Compromise principle as a medium of defeating all adjustment and then to make the most of succeeding events . . . to infuriate the South and drive her into measures that must end in disunion.

Chappell believed, however, that "the Whigs are more united for . . . a proper course than the Democrats are against it," and declared that the "Ultraists" did not yet dare to come out openly for secession.[44]

John H. Lumpkin, reporting to Cobb on conditions in Upper Georgia in July, declared that all the Whigs there were for the compromise and that, while a majority of the Democrats might favor the Missouri line as a settlement of the territorial difficulty, they were, nevertheless, "for a settlement in good faith." The only danger was that unless warned they might be tricked by the "Ultraists" into an impracticable mode of adjustment. The only real secessionists were the "old Nullifyers" of 1832.[45] "You cannot imagine," wrote a friend in Eatonton to Cobb a month later, "how perfectly quiet the people are on the subject of all the stir and fuss at Washington, and they are heartily sick and disgusted with the pretended excitement there. Nobody at home, Whig or Democrat, believes

[44] Chappell to Cobb, July 10, 1850, *Toombs, Stephens, and Cobb Correspondence,* pp. 193, 194.
[45] J. H. Lumpkin to Cobb, Rome, July 21, 1850, *Toombs, Stephens, and Cobb Correspondence,* p. 207.

that any man there feels what he expresses of ultra-ism."[46]

In Coastal Georgia there was little evidence of excitement in July and August. The Whig planters who dominated this region[47] may have been excited in December, 1849, lest the Proviso pass, but they were now willing to accept the compromise. Only in Savannah was there some uncertainty, where the mixed nature of the population, which included numbers of South Carolinians, Yankees and European immigrants,[48] made an estimate of popular feeling difficult.

In spite of their optimism, the conservatives felt that the southern-rights meetings called for an answer which should both point out to the people the real purpose of the secessionists and at the same time demonstrate, as Lamar put it, the real feeling of the people. Hence Union meetings were held in the chief towns where the enemy had staged gatherings, and special appeals to the people were issued by leading Union men. In Macon the *Citizen,* a militant pro-Union paper edited by a man of northern origin, asked the opinion of ex-Congressman Absalom H. Chappell upon the great question. Chappell, who believed the spirit among the Democrats was dangerous, replied in a veritable essay, which occupied no less than seven columns in the Washington *Union.*[49] It was essentially an appeal to the southern Democrats to accept the Clay compromise and a plea for the preservation of "this glorious Union of ours, which now overshadows America from ocean to ocean, like a very

[46] J. A. Meriwether to Cobb, Aug. 24, 1850, *Toombs, Stephens, and Cobb Correspondence,* p. 211.

[47] The population of the shore area of these counties was from 75% to 90% Negro.

[48] See chapter ii.

[49] Macon *Citizen,* July 6, in the Washington *Union,* July 13, 1850.

heaven sent down to us undeservers by a too benign-
ant God!" Similar efforts to warn the people against
disunion were now made in addresses to their constituents by the Democrats, Cobb and Wellborn, at Washington.[50]

All the conservative meetings now began to emphasize, even more than had been the case in the
spring, this appeal for the Union, the power of which
in attracting the masses can hardly be exaggerated.
It may well have been an asset to those making the
Union appeal that a victorious war had been waged
but two years before with the usual accompaniment of
patriotic enthusiasm among the masses, though it was
the irony of fate that the very Whig leaders now emphasizing nation-wide patriotism had been opposed to
that war.

The Columbus Union meeting well illustrates the
appeal to traditional loyalties. It was held two days
after the radical Columbus meeting described, in an
effort to show that the majority of the people disagreed
with the principles expressed in that first gathering.
According to the *Enquirer,* it was "a large and enthusiastic meeting without distinction of party."
Strong resolutions were passed upholding the compromise as "fair and equitable" and declaring "that
the ultimatum of the Nashville convention is desperate
and revolutionary." The "Honorable Jas. E. Belser
of Alabama addressed the meeting for one and one-
half hours in an eloquent and patriotic strain that frequently brought forth long continued applause." A
local glee-club then sang the Star Spangled Banner,

[50] Address of M. J. Wellborn, *To the Voters of the Second Congressional District;* n.d., apparently August, 1850. It is notable that
Wellborn had displayed some sympathy for the southern movement and
that he represented Southwest, not Upper Georgia. For Cobb's lengthy
address see the *Toombs, Stephens, and Cobb Correspondence,* pp. 196-206.

and "the audience repaired to the warehouse of Ruse, Patten and Brice, where a sumptuous barbecue was prepared." After dinner, the Reverend A. H. Speer warned against the danger of political excitement and controversy. The glee-club again appeared upon the stage and sang the patriotic song, 'The Red, White and Blue,' and with three cheers for the Union the meeting adjourned *sine die*."[51]

The climax of the secessionist campaign promised to come late in August. There were two reasons for this; first, sufficient time would have elapsed by then to count upon the cumulative effects of months of energetic oratory and, second, the secessionists hoped to persuade the people to support soon thereafter a call for a state convention. As the prospects for the passage of the California bill in Congress improved, it began to be assumed that Governor Towns would summon a convention the moment the bill passed. If this body were called, Georgia would be the first southern state to proclaim officially its attitude towards the Clay compromise. This would mean that much of the success of the whole secession movement would depend upon her action at this critical moment. The "Ultraists" throughout the lower South could be expected to join in a desperate effort to prepare the Georgia people for the great decision.

Southern-rights meetings were held on August 6 in eight or ten counties, chiefly in Central Georgia, preparatory to a general state conclave, to be assembled at Macon on August 22. This was to be the grand demonstration at which Georgia would proclaim to the nation her readiness for secession. The secessionists of the lower South concentrated their atten-

[51] Columbus *Enquirer,* July 20, 1850.

tion upon it, and the nation was watching. Came Rhett from Carolina and Yancey from Alabama for the good of the cause. Elaborate preparations were made for a great barbecue, and delegates were invited from all over the state. The radical press called for an attendance of fifty thousand and claimed up to the last moment that at least fifteen thousand would actually be there.

Accounts varied widely, as usual, as to the number who were present when the great day dawned and as to the spirit that prevailed. Two of the Washington papers, the *Southern Press* (established in 1850 to represent the secessionists) and the *Daily Union,* arranged for direct telegraphic reports from the meeting.[52] The contrast between those received by the two papers was interesting. In comparing them, it should be remembered that the *Union* was itself a Democratic journal which had been generally sympathetic with the southern movement. The wire to the *Southern Press* read as follows:

> Our mass-meeting has just adjourned. It was one of the largest and most enthusiastic ever held in this state. It was addressed by Rhett, Yancey and Cochran of Alabama, and Colquitt, Stiles, Jones, Gibson, Raivley and Platt of Georgia. Resolutions were passed urging that if a state convention is called the Georgia delegates should at once leave Congress to consult and act with the people.[53]

The first wire to the *Union* was brief and to the point and was followed shortly by a second of similar tenor:

[52] Through telegraphic connection between Macon and Washington was first established in August, 1850, and was considered a very remarkable achievement.

[53] *Southern Press,* August 23, 1850.

Macon, 10:30 P.M.

Aug. 22:

The mass-meeting held by the disunionists of Georgia proves to be a failure. Not exceeding 1500 delegates at the meeting all told.

Macon, 10:55 P.M.

Mass-meeting is a failure. Not more than 1500 men in town, one-third Union men. Only 300 arrived by the railroads. Rhett, Yancey, Colquitt, chief speakers. Disunion openly avowed. Some delegates repudiate it. Rhett favors temporary secession.[54]

The question of the attendance at this meeting was considered important by the press of both sides, as it was considered to be indicative of popular feeling in the state. The *Southern Press,* on the basis of the telegram quoted, termed the affair a "tremendous out-pouring of the people." Nothing, it declared, could now keep Georgia in the Union! The Savannah *Republican,* on the other hand, completely disdained the entire meeting and agreed with the report to the *Union* that only from one thousand to fifteen hundred attended. This was the estimate of the other conservative papers in Georgia and was repeated by those of the North. A friend of Cobb reported the number present as eight hundred and termed the meeting "a stupendous failure so felt and so acknowledged." The *Georgian,* speaking for the local "Ultraists," went to the other extreme and claimed that there were no less than ten thousand present! No better illustration of the chronic unreliability of the southern-rights press in the state could be afforded than this exaggeration by the Savannah daily. The editor of the Savannah *News,* himself rather friendly to the southern movement, admitted that a gentleman returning direct from Macon told him that not more than three thousand were present. Such reports toned the estimates of the South Carolina papers down to "from three to five thousand."[55]

The significant thing about the Macon meeting was not only the relatively small attendance, but the fact that here for the first time in Georgia the "Ultraists" came out openly for secession. For this reason it represents one of the turning points in the secession movement in the state. In the first place, it was bound to further the division of the parties along the Union and secession lines, now that the issue was made clear, and to lead, therefore, to that practical realignment of parties which had been planned in the legislature as early as February. In the second place, the open approval of secession was bound to withdraw from the "Ultraists" the support of such Democrats as had been backing them up to this time in the mistaken belief that they were really seeking a compromise in the form of the Missouri principle. This defection of Democrats from the southern movement—once they realized that it was really a secession movement—also affected the Democratic press, notably in the cases of the Savannah *Georgian* and the Savannah *News*. Rhett had gone marching through Georgia only to spoil everything, just as Hammond had feared he would.

A specific illustration of reactions to the Macon meeting is afforded by the experience of Dr. Arnold, who wrote Forney:

[55] On the Macon mass-meeting see J. C. Butler, *Historical Records of Macon, Georgia*, (1878), pp. 194, 195; Washington *Southern Press*, Aug. 23; *Daily Union*, Aug. 24; *National Intelligencer*, Aug. 24; Philadelphia *Public Ledger*, Aug. 27; Milledgeville *Federal Union*, Aug. 28; Savannah *Georgian*, Aug. 23, 24; *Republican*, Aug. 23, 24; *News*, Aug. 23, 24; *Chronicle*, Aug. 23, 24; Columbia *South Carolinian*, Aug. 29; J. A. Meriwether to Cobb, Aug. 24, 1850, *Toombs, Stephens, and Cobb Correspondence*, p. 210.

At Macon the cry of dis-union was first raised, and the new parties had therefore to be formed. I and Ward decided that as all the Democratic papers had gone for the Ultras and we knew the people would not support this, the Whigs would swamp the Democrats unless those Democrats who were true to the Union made this entirely clear. . . . A meeting was called in Savannah. . . . One of the leaders was a young man, (drilled by a Carolina gentleman who was adjutant to Mr. Cheves) introduced resolutions, but I threw cold water on them. Some other ginger-pop lawyers drew up Southern rights resolutions which they intended to cram down the throats of the meeting. There was a great excitement when these were refused, and a call was made for all friends of the South to leave the hall! I was very angry and told one fellow that any man who said I, born and raised on the spot, was not in favor of Southern rights was a damned Liar!

The extremists then left the hall to adopt their own resolutions. With them, added Arnold, were the "Mayor and all twelve Aldermen. But four of these were South Carolinians and you have had experience with that kind of Democrats." The rest of the original body then adopted resolutions accepting the compromise but declaring it a last concession by the South.[56]

Arnold and his friend Ward now became active in Lower Georgia, building up a common organization of Union Democrats and Whigs. It may have been through their influence that the *Georgian* began to moderate its tone to such extent as to bring it into conflict with the *Federal Union*. On the other hand, the clarifying of the issue now made it possible for two actual secessionist papers, the Macon *Telegraph* and the Columbus *Sentinel,* to come out openly for disunion. Other southern-rights papers, such as the *Federal Union,* still refused to sanction disunion open-

[56] Arnold to Forney, December 18, 1850, Arnold MSS. *Cf. Georgian,* July 24, 25; *News,* July 31, 1850.

ly at the same time that they condemned the compromise. The editors of the *Georgian*, the *News*, and the *Federal Union* were either honestly opposed to secession, or else they possessed too healthy a respect for the feeling of the majority of the Democrats to demand it openly. In some cases this hesitancy was doubtless due to a sincere personal opposition to the final destruction of the Union, once the issue was divested of all the suggestive draperies of a southern-rights appeal, and there could be no question as to its real meaning.

The clarifying of the issue also made possible a more frank discussion of the secondary questions connected with secession. These were problems already debated to some extent in 1849, such as "the right of secession," the danger of civil war, the advantages and disadvantages of a southern confederacy, the extent of the spirit of southern nationalism then obtaining, and so on. The conservatives, Whigs and Democrats, assumed that there was some "right of secession," but were not yet clear as to its nature. The Whigs had already shown signs of a belief that it was revolutionary rather than constitutional in character,[57] while the Democrats were inclined to reverse this opinion[58]—a difference of viewpoint that was to involve their common candidate for the governorship in some difficulty during the ensuing year. Neither, however, desired the occasion for the exercise of the right, whatever its nature. The extremists usually viewed the right of secession as a constitutional one and desired the necessary occasion.

The "Ultraists" were inclined to believe that secession could be carried out peacefully, though they were

[57] Note the resolutions of the Columbus Union meeting, summarized above.

[58] See, *e.g.*, Rutherford to Cobb, April 16, 1850, *Toombs, Stephens, and Cobb Correspondence*, p. 190.

ready to force war if necessary.[59]   The conservatives, on the other hand, emphasized the danger of war and appealed to the economic motives naturally averse to it. The influence of the economic appeal for peace was probably more powerful in prosperous Georgia, which had much to lose by war and little to gain, than it was in economically decadent South Carolina, which had less to lose and—it was hoped—more to gain.[60] "Secession is bound to be followed by civil war if history tells us anything," wrote a Union Democrat, "and will begin with the first gun fired, a scene of discord and calamity the world before never beheld, involving our children and our children's children."[61] "The greatest blessings and unparalleled prosperity (we have enjoyed) have been secured by the Union of these states," wrote another Democrat, "let us abandon this Union *only when* it fails to secure a continuation of this prosperity."[62]   A franker appeal to economic interest and a better statement of the motivating idea that may have been in the minds of many conservatives at the time, can hardly be imagined.

Indeed, it was this discussion of the dangers of civil war that brought out most clearly contemporary opinions as to the conserving influences of economic prosperity.   It has been pointed out in a preceding chapter that the year 1850 marked a high point in prosperity in Georgia, a prosperity based upon rising cotton prices, the possession of relatively unused and promising soils in some parts of the state, a rapid increase in cotton manufacturing, an extensive railroad

[59] See, *e.g.*, W. H. Trescott, *The Position and Cause of the South* (Charleston, 1850), *passim*.

[60] See chapter i for a general discussion of this theme.

[61] Letter of James Clark, February 15, 1851, to the Committee, *Macon Union Celebration*, p. 14.

[62] Letter of Asbury Hull, February 15, 1851, *ibid.*, p. 22.

development, and the general stabilization of the state's finances. Most of these developments had been achieved in the short period between 1845 and 1850, and it was small wonder that the state had acquired a preëminent reputation among its southern sisters and that its own propertied citizens had become enthused with a spirit of "booster" optimism.[63] It was entirely natural, therefore, that the Georgian quoted above should have referred to the "unparalleled prosperity" that had been enjoyed, and that he should have added the remark that the Union should be abandoned *"only when* it fails to secure a continuation of this prosperity."* Some contemporary observers from without the state reached the conclusion during the fall of 1850 that it was this desire of the propertied classes to maintain a Union that had brought prosperity, and a desire to avoid the threat to that prosperity involved in the danger of civil war, which determined the state's conservative position in the crisis of 1850.

General James Hamilton of South Carolina, for instance, passed through Central Georgia during the fall of 1850, when the secession movement was supposed to be at its height. He found the state "in a condition of philosophic calm," since "thirteen cents a pound for cotton was a powerful contributor to make civil war and revolution exceedingly distasteful to her people."[64] In like manner, observers in South Carolina, seeking aid from Georgia, feared that the good times there would defeat their purpose. "Disunion feeling in Georgia," admitted the Columbia *South Carolinian,* "is neutralized by the high price of

---

[63] See chapter i for a discussion of this whole situation.

[64] Letter to the Charleston *Mercury,* published in the Washington *Republic,* December 2, 1850. Hamilton wrote from Texas, November 11, and probably passed through Georgia some time in October, 1850, *i.e.,* in the midst of the state convention campaign.

cotton."[65]   Governor Seabrook wrote Quitman of Mississippi, with reference to the South in general, that "prosperity makes the masses indifferent to the crisis."[66]   So, too, felt northern observers in Georgia. The Savannah correspondent of the Boston *Courier*, although taking the other side in the general political controversy from that held by the Carolina critics, reached just the same conclusions as to the economic forces at work. "It is very fortunate for this Union," he observed, "that cotton is thirteen to fourteen cents a pound, instead of four to five.   There is now a state of prosperity they do not care to disturb—but were it otherwise, all the depression in trade and prices would have been attributed to the burden of the Union and to the baneful effects of national legislation and northern agitation."[67]

Other problems besides those relating to prosperity, the right of secession, and the dangers of civil war, were discussed in the course of the general debate that was carried on through the summer and fall of 1850 and during the next year.   The years 1850 and 1851, indeed, constituted a time of education during which

[65] Columbia *South Carolinian,* June 21, 1849.   The Mobile *Daily Advertiser* made the same analysis of the situation in Alabama; see the *National Intelligencer,* Dec. 6, 1850.

[66] Seabrook to Quitman, July 15, 1850, Seabrook MSS.

[67] Such contemporary interpretations of the economic influences at work can hardly be ignored, in the light of all attending circumstances, even though the claims quoted may well have been exaggerated.   Nor is a partially economic interpretation of Georgia's conservatism in 1850 necessarily inconsistent with the fact of Georgia's radicalism in another period of prosperity; namely, 1860-1861.   Georgia did, to be sure, secede *despite* prosperity in this later period.   The election of 1860 was viewed in the South as an ultimate threat to all prosperity based upon the slave-labor system as well as a threat to the whole southern social order. Such a threat obviously overbalanced any interest in the preservation of the immediate prosperity of 1860.   In like manner, and for like reasons, the passage by Congress of the Proviso would probably have resulted in the secession of Georgia in 1850, despite the prosperity of that year.   In a word, prosperity did not incline Georgia to surrender, but it did incline her to compromise.

the people of the South first went to school to study all
those problems which they later attempted to solve during the tragic period of 1860-1865. There was, for instance, the problem of a "southern confederacy"; if
the South did secede from the old Union, what sort of a
government should be set up in its place? Some of the
Georgia secessionists believed, with Benning, that it
should be a "consolidated republic," in order that it
should protect propertied interests and possess the sta-
bility necessary to survive. Others who would have desired this, to be sure, did not believe that a "consolidated" government would ever be approved by a people devoted to "state rights." Such men feared that, if the
old Union could not survive, neither could a "United
States South." "Even if a Southern Confederacy
were well formed," wrote a Georgia planter, "there
would come internal quarrels, a second disunion, and
we should exhibit the melancholy aspect of a parcel
of little pitiful republics."[68] It was a similar fear, it
will be remembered, that Alexander Stephens said
kept him from advocating secession that year.[69]

Some extremists thought it would be wise for the
South to cultivate economic independence of the North
by means of a non-intercourse policy prior to demanding political independence, in case this economic
pressure brought no response from the North. This
was the opinion of Senator Berrien, as expressed in
his letters already quoted, and the same view was held
by a few other leading men, such as Governor Collier
of Alabama.[70] It never commanded a large popular

[68] Letter of Eli H. Baxter to the Committee, February 19, 1851, *The
Macon Union Celebration*, pp. 10, 11. For similar opinion in South
Carolina, see Philadelphia *Public Ledger*, November 9, 1850. *Cf.* J. C.
Reed, *The Brother's War*, p. 59.
[69] A. H. Stephens to L. Stephens, January 15, 1850, Johnston and
Browne, *Alexander Stephens*, p. 245.
[70] Philadelphia *Public Ledger*, November 12, 1850.

following in Georgia. The more typical view expressed by the extremists was that a southern confederacy would become at once a great economic success at the expense of northern interests.[71]

The conservatives predicted dire difficulties for a "United States South," and claimed that even the slavery problem would be complicated rather than solved by political separation from the North. Slave property, they urged, would be far more insecure in a southern "unconsolidated republic" than in the present Union.[72]

It is difficult to say how far a spirit of "southern nationalism" was developing in Georgia as a result of the general controversy, and no estimate whatever can be given without a definition of terms. It is no easy task to mark the point whereat a consciousness of sectional identity evolves into a consciousness of national identity. There had certainly been a consciousness of sectional identity in the South since about 1820 and probably even before that date. If the consciousness of national feeling is to be limited to those who, in 1850, desired immediate secession and a united southern confederacy, the number in Georgia was confined to a small group of able extremists, of whom Benning was the best type. These men were talking openly in 1850 about the "United States South," and, when they said "patriotism", they meant patriotism for the South.[73] Between such men and the old Alabaman who declared, "I do not wish to survive the Union!—My Country Now! My Country Forever!",[74] there was

[71] Augusta *Constitutionalist,* quoted in and approved by the Columbus *Times,* January 30, 1849.
[72] Eli H. Baxter to the Committee, *Macon Union Celebration,* p. 11.
[73] See Savannah *News,* February 2, 1850.
[74] Montgomery *Daily Alabama Journal,* December 16, 1850. Similarly passionate devotion in Georgia to the Union will be noted in connection with the state convention of December.

the great mass of the people, who held all shades of opinion varying from one extreme to the other. The sense of nationalism which animated the great majority of Georgians in 1850, however, was the old loyalty for the old Union.

One must remember that the majority of the Democrats in Central and Lower Georgia were, as has been noted, southern-rights men in the moderate sense that they favored southern political unity and were often excited in their denunciation of the North. That men were not secessionists did not mean that they lacked feeling in the whole matter. There was sectional feeling in plenty. In Savannah, early in August, a northern man expressed certain ideas "not altogether southern in sentiment," and handbills were promptly posted announcing the hour at which he would be tarred and feathered! The *News* cautioned against such sentiments "just now," and advised the gentleman concerned "to make a speedy return to his boasted clime of the North."[75]

The most interesting expression of popular indignation—or hysteria, as one wishes to view it—occurred at Macon in August, 1850. Here the *Citizen,* edited by one, Dr. L. F. W. Andrews, and established March 28 of that year, had been a bitter opponent of the southern-rights movement. In the middle of August, it greatly excited the people by publishing letters from a certain Hanleiter, of Atlanta, in which he condemned the domestic slave trade and expressed a hope that the slave sales depot there would be "razed to the ground." This brought forth the serious charge that the *Citizen* was an abolitionist paper, established secretly in Macon and subsidized by the northern socie-

[75] *South Carolinian,* August 15, 1850.

ties in connection with the political crisis then at hand. Just at this time occurred the radical Macon mass meeting of August 22, and the *Citizen* proceeded to denounce that meeting most scathingly. This was too much under the circumstances. A special nonpartisan meeting was called, and a committee of thirteen waited upon Andrews, the editor, demanding the name of his Atlanta correspondent. Meanwhile, a crowd gathered outside and threatened to lynch Andrews. Dr. Collins, of Macon, saved him from the mob only by eliciting the promise that he would close the paper and leave Macon within ten days. The *Chronicle* declared this episode a "high handed outrage" against the rights of a citizen and the freedom of the press, but the radical editors applauded it and intimated that the *Chronicle* itself should receive like treatment.[76] As a matter of fact, the *Citizen* resumed publication just a fortnight later.

Towards the end of August there was a temporary lull in the controversy in Georgia, as all eyes turned to Washington to watch the closing scenes of the congressional drama. After a long summer of debates, the separate bills of the "Omnibus" were now assured of acceptance—"the passengers would all arrive." Both moderates and secessionists in Georgia desired this, the first in order to have the compromise finally adopted; the latter, because the passage of one of the bills, that admitting California, would make it obligatory upon the Governor to call a state convention.

Towns was ready. Indeed, he had sent a special representative to Washington who was to bring him post haste an official copy of the California bill as soon

[76] The incident received much attention in both the North and the South; see the *Georgian,* August 24; the *South Carolinian,* August 29; the *Chronicle,* August 30; the Boston *Liberator,* September 20, 1850; etc.

as it passed. Things now happened quickly at the capitol, for the Texas and California bills passed September 7, the Utah measure September 9, and the fugitive slave bill September 12. The news of the California law reached Georgia on the tenth, and the *Federal Union* (generally viewed as Towns' organ) announced on the seventeenth that the Governor would issue a call for the convention as soon as his agent arrived with the official copy. This gentleman reached the Governor's home in Milledgeville on September 23, and Towns promptly issued the long awaited summons.

The proclamation repeated Towns' opinions on northern aggressions and the need for calm but determined action in Georgia. It called the convention, as provided for by law, to meet at the capitol on December 10. The elections were to be held on November 25, exactly as the usual elections for the legislature, save that the representation of each county was to be doubled.[77] "In the hour of danger," read the governor's appeal, "when your institutions are in jeopardy— your feelings wantonly outraged; your social organization derided; and the Federal Constitution violated by a series of aggressive measures, all tending to the consummation of one object, the abolition of slavery . . . it well becomes you to assemble, to deliberate, and counsel together for your mutual protection and safety."[78]

This proclamation was the opening gun in the final battle for secession, both in Georgia and in the lower South as a whole, and it was naturally followed by a volley from both sides. The entire proclamation of

[77] For text of the convention law see *Debates and Proceedings of the Georgia Convention,* 1850, p. 27.

[78] *Ibid.,* pp. 27, 28; Letter Books of the Georgia Governors, 1850; for Towns' plans for his proclamation, see Columbia *South Carolinian,* September 10, 1850.

over one thousand words was wired directly from Macon to Washington, where it was being anxiously awaited. The *Southern Press* immediately hailed it as the harbinger of final action. Georgia now showed, it declared, that "the point of endurance has been passed. The destiny of the South is decided. She will not submit. . . . The cotton states will all unite with Georgia. So will the rest of the slave-holding states. The North has a last chance to reconsider." The radical papers in South Carolina and the Gulf states reacted in a similar manner. The Columbia *South Carolinian* and the Charleston *News* believed that "the assembling of the Georgia Convention will probably be the first step in the vindication of Southern honor," and were sure that the conventions and legislatures soon to be called in South Carolina, Mississippi, and Alabama would follow her.[79] Rhett declared that Georgia would "lead off," while Hammond wrote Fouche that he believed Georgia was "entitled to lead the South because of her prompt action and because of her strength and position."[80] There was significant talk about holding the next session of the southern convention at Milledgeville.

Whig papers in the North generally derided Towns' call, declared that "we do not tremble in our boots in view of this new crisis got up by the Quattlebums of the South"; but some conservative Democratic papers were seriously worried and besought Georgia to pause and contemplate before acting.[81]

[79] *Southern Press*, in Washington *Union*, September 25; *South Carolinian*, September 27, 1850.

[80] Hammond to Fouche and Committee, Silver Bluff, South Carolina, September 26, 1850, Hammond MSS.

[81] Columbus *Ohio Statesman*, September 31; Washington *Union*, October 1, 1850.

Within Georgia, the more moderate of the southern-rights editors welcomed the Governor's call as a means of securing either concession in the North or secession in the South. The more extreme editors openly welcomed the coming convention as a means to disunion. "The continuance of the Union is no longer problematical," announced the Columbus *Times,* "it is now virtually dissolved. There is no time to be lost. Draw your swords and throw away your scabbards!"[82]

The response of the Georgia Whig and Union Democratic papers was vigorous and emphatic. The convention should "never have been called"; "it would be a farce"; "it would have nothing to do but adjourn"—such were the typical comments.[83] "The proclamation," declared Holsey in the Athens *Banner,* "is but a solemn mummery under the existing calm of public opinion."[84]

So in September, as during the preceding spring, the opposing editors differed widely in their published estimates of popular feeling in the state. The proclamation, which the *Times* announced had "virtually" dissolved the Union, was dismissed by the *Banner* as "a mummery under the existing calm of public opinion." The events of spring and summer had already shown that the more radical papers had little influence upon the public and were, therefore, not usually to be trusted in their estimates of public opinion. The conservative journals had proved more reliable in this respect and were, therefore, probably more to be trusted in their estimates of popular feeling in September.

[82] Columbus (Georgia) *Times,* in Washington *Union,* September 25, 1850.

[83] Opinions of several prominent Whig journals, as given in the *Chronicle,* October 29, 1850.

[84] Quoted in the *Chronicle,* September 28, 1850.

Since the editors in both camps, however, doubtless shared a natural desire to appear confident before the public, it is well to examine the estimates of public opinion exchanged in confidence between the leaders of each group.

In such private correspondence with others of their own party the politicians had little or no motive for exaggeration or distortion. The letters to Howell Cobb, written from Upper Georgia between August 24 and October 5, the period before the convention campaign had really begun, displayed complete confidence in a coming Union victory. Writing as early as August 24, Judge James Meriwether declared that if Towns called the Convention the disunionists "would not muster a corporal's guard." If they then attempted violence, he was ready to fight against them, and he was persuaded that this was "the sentiment of nine tenths of the Whigs and three fourths of the Democrats"[85] in his district. William Woods, of Dahlonega, wrote on September 15: "I have bin mixen amongst the people," and "I think the majority of my section . . . are willing to abide the action of Congress," though "nearly all the leading Democrats (are) opposed[86]. . . ." "The people are not ready to sacrifice the best government ever established," opined L. J. Glenn of McDonaugh on September 21, "to redress 'imaginary evils' existing in a distempered fancy at a distance of three thousand miles or more."[87] Cobb himself, upon surveying the whole field immediately after his return to the state, wrote Lamar that, while "we shall have a most exciting and angry contest in

[85] Meriwether to Cobb, August 24, 1850, *Toombs, Stephens, and Cobb Correspondence,* p. 211.
[86] Woods to Cobb, September 15, 1850, *Toombs, Stephens, and Cobb Correspondence,* pp. 212-213.
[87] L. J. Glenn to Cobb, September 21, 1850, *ibid.,* p. 213.

the state and in some sections a doubtful one . . . I
entertain no doubt that we shall have a large majority
of the convention. . . ."[88]

In contrast to this, there has been preserved an
interesting private correspondence between no lesser
leaders of the secessionist group than W. B. Seabrook,
governor of South Carolina, and G. W. Towns, governor of Georgia. South Carolina had come under the
control of the "coöperationists" by the fall of 1850,
and Seabrook was anxious to know just what chances
there were for assistance to his state in case she seceded. His chief hopes lay in Mississippi and in Georgia. On September 20, accordingly, Seabrook wrote
Towns asking what the prospects were that the coming
state convention would lead Georgia out of the Union
and declared that South Carolina was ready to go as
soon as her sister gave the sign.[89] The correspondence
was strictly secret. Towns replied from Milledgeville
on September 25, just two days after issuing his proclamation, and at the very time that such papers as the
Sentinel and the *Telegraph* were declaring that the
convention would dissolve the Union. He explained
to Seabrook the great difference between South Carolina and Georgia. "It is disgraceful," he admitted of
his own state, "that probably $^{19}\!/_{20}$ of the old states
rights group[90] are submissionists." These men, he
added, appeal to the old Union men,[91] and hence it
can be seen "how fearful the odds against which we
are struggling." Indeed, he had to confess that this
struggle in Georgia was "cheerless and discouraging."

---

[88] Howell Cobb to J. B. Lamar, Athens, October 10, 1850, *ibid.*,
p. 215.

[89] Seabrook to Towns, September 20, 1850, Seabrook MSS.

[90] The old Whig or Troup party of the thirties; see chapter iii.

[91] The old Democratic or Clark party of the thirties; see chapter iii.

Under the circumstances, he could but suggest that no action whatever be taken in South Carolina until after the election to the Georgia convention. Such action must be avoided, lest it increase the ever-present dislike of the Georgia people for their sister state and thus destroy what hope the faithful still have of coöperating with Carolina.[92]

The contrast between the blatant boasting of the radical papers at the time, and this private confession by a central leader of the Georgia secessionist group seems a significant one. It becomes even more significant when one recalls all the associated circumstances—the unreliable record of the radical press, the spring elections, the steady optimism of the conservatives, and, finally, the overwhelming victory of the Union men, which lay just ahead in the convention elections. The masses of the Georgia people continued to oppose or to be indifferent to the secessionist appeal during the summer and fall of 1850, as they had during the preceding winter and spring.

The remainder of Seabrook's correspondence relating to Georgia demonstrated not only his acceptance of Towns' estimate of sentiment there, but also the importance of the position which Georgia might see fit to take with regard to the whole sectional movement. Seabrook replied on October 8, assuring Towns that he would hold things back in South Carolina so as to "conciliate" Georgia, the while he "stimulated" the other states. He submitted to Towns his proposed proclamation calling the South Carolina legislature, desiring assurance before issuing it that it would not hurt the cause in Georgia.[93] Meanwhile, he had just

[92] Towns to Seabrook, September 25, 1850, Seabrook MSS.
[93] Seabrook to Towns, October 8, 1850, Seabrook MSS.

heard from Governor Quitman of Mississippi, who reported to headquarters, so to speak, that a convention would probably be called in that state to move for secession.[94] Prospects seemed good for Mississippi. Georgia, then, was the stumbling block. Seabrook was tactful and did not criticize in his letters to Towns, but he wrote a confidant that action waited upon Georgia and that she was most unreliable. "I shall wait the movement in Georgia and one or two other slave-holding states," he declared, "before I commit South Carolina. . . . As soon as it shall be known that our sister state has been seconded by Mississippi and Alabama, or Virginia and Florida, the period will have arrived for the Palmetto state to do her duty." But he added, "my word for it, that Georgia acts indecisively or makes a retrograde move."[95]

Seabrook had previously written Quitman in July expressing a belief that, if Mississippi and South Carolina both seceded, Georgia would be bound to be drawn into the movement;[96] but his September and October letters conveyed no such faith. Towns' letters had clearly declared that precipitate action in South Carolina would antagonize rather than invite coöperation from Georgia. So while extremist papers were loudly proclaiming that Georgia would "lead off," Georgia, as a matter of fact, seemed to the well informed secessionists a stumbling block in the way of those states already prepared to go.[97]

[94] Quitman to Seabrook, September 29, 1850, Seabrook MSS.

[95] Seabrook to T. A. Leland, September 18, 1850, Seabrook MSS.

[96] Seabrook to Quitman, July 15, 1850, Seabrook MSS.

[97] I. Seibels, of Montgomery, wrote Hammond to ask what South Carolina would do if Georgia "backed out." He thought that if Georgia would act "that would at once determine the course of Alabama, Mississippi and Florida." Seibels to Hammond, September 19, 1850, Hammond MSS.

Meanwhile, the convention campaign was on in the "Empire State." It was bound, as Cobb put it, to be fierce and exciting, both because of the importance of the issue and because the secessionists made up to some extent in ability, energy, and vociferousness for what they lacked in numbers. The conflict in Georgia became the center for all eyes in the Union. There was less interest taken in South Carolina, at least temporarily, because no one doubted the feeling there; and, while Mississippi shared with Georgia the critical and decisive position in the lower South, a special convention was to meet in Georgia at a time when only the regular legislature would be in session in the other state. The position of Georgia, moreover, was considered peculiarly important because of her apparent economic superiority to most of the other southern states.

All public expressions of opinion in South Carolina continued to declare great hope for the sister state and ofttimes recognized her economic importance to the southern movement. Uncertainty concerning her final stand, however, was sometimes publicly admitted. There was the Charleston official, for instance, who proposed the following toast at a dinner to General Hammond, at which Georgians were present:

Our noble sister, the state of Georgia, distinguished for her statesmen, famed for her extended agriculture, equally celebrated for wide-spread internal improvements and manufactures, foremost in advancing the mechanic arts:[98]—when called on to stand up in defense of Southern rights, *where will she be found?*

To which eulogy a Georgian present replied with the somewhat ambiguous toast:

South Carolina: Ever true—she need never be hasty.[99]

[98] For the economic basis of this praise, see chapter i.
[99] Washington *Republic,* November 28, 1850.

While Carolina continued her efforts at conciliation with the sister state, the old distrust of "Palmettodom" persisted and grew in Georgia in proportion to the growing intensity of the secession controversy. This distrust continued to embarrass the secessionists. Towns' warning to Seabrook that South
Carolina must be kept below the level of Georgia's
political horizon was a timely one. Conservative Georgians strongly suspected, from articles appearing in
the Charleston *Mercury*, that South Carolina was at
the bottom of the whole secession movement, and they
warned the people, as usual, not to allow "insolent
Palmettodom" to "make a cat's paw of Georgia." Indeed, the collusion of the governors was suspected at
the very time that they were exchanging the correspondence noted.[100]   The voters were reminded that
"our state has been treated *habitually* with the most
sovereign contempt by the chivalry, until they con-
curred recently in the idea of making *a subordinate
use of us.* Only then do they declare: 'The South
hangs her hope upon her as the Keynote State.' "[101]
Senator Butler of South Carolina urged Seabrook to
send representatives to the Georgia convention, and
added that "Surely, at this time, an unnatural jealousy
should not prevent these states . . . from acting together."[102]   Seabrook, however, was too well acquaint-
ed with the real situation in Georgia, by virtue of his
correspondence with Towns, to attempt to send such a
representative.   South Carolina had indeed sent a rep-

[100] See Macon *Journal* in the *Chronicle*, September 20, 1850.

[101] *Chronicle*, October 12; see also Macon *Journal* in the same, September 20; Letter of Eli Warren, February 14, 1851, to the Committee,
Macon Union Celebration, p. 16.

[102] A. P. Butler to Seabrook, October 22, 1850, Seabrook MSS.

resentative to the state convention of Mississippi the year before, but Georgia was another matter. Hammond, who was a keener observer than Butler, refused an invitation sent him by Samuel Ray to write articles for the Macon *Telegraph* during the state convention campaign. He based his refusal on the ground that it was unwise for any South Carolinian to "interfere" in Georgia politics.[103]

It was unfortunate for Carolina that the old trade rivalry between Charleston, on the one hand, and Macon and Savannah, on the other, which was perhaps the chief economic factor in the dislike for "Palmettodom," should have continued just at a time when the latter's political ambitions demanded conciliation with Georgia. Less than three years before had come the deliberate effort of Charleston to tap the Georgia Central Railroad above Savannah, an episode which had created considerable feeling in 1847.[104] Even at the height of the crisis in 1850, a Charleston editor, in reporting that Upper Georgia was warming up to his radical political appeals, added significantly that "now is the time for your direct tradesmen of Charleston to take advantage of this feeling."[105] Georgians returned this compliment by deliberately planning in some cases to divert most of the Charleston trade to Macon and Savannah the moment that South Carolina seceded. This could be done easily enough, it was believed, if the Carolina coast were to be blockaded by the federal naval forces. It was also hoped that Carolina currency could be driven out of the state, since Georgians would presumably not wish to hold it after

---

[103] Hammond to Ray, October 20, 1850, Hammond MSS.

[104] See chapter i.

[105] Charleston *News,* in the Columbia *South Carolinian,* August 31, 1850.

the other state had seceded.[106]   General James Hamilton and Bishop Capers, of the Methodist Church, both warned South Carolina of the seriousness of the intention to secure the Charleston trade. Indeed, the existence of this desire in parts of Georgia was generally recognized throughout the South.[107]

Editors outside of South Carolina and Georgia were generally convinced that a Union victory in Georgia was probable, if not certain. The importance of the result was also generally recognized. "The anxious eyes of the whole nation," declared the national organ of the Democracy in October, "are fixed upon Georgia and New York. These are the two great battlefields of southern and northern excitement."[108] The usual prediction as to the outcome in Georgia was that there would be much talk but no *action* looking towards disunion. "Georgia will cave in, back out, and swallow her big words of treason," wrote the Washington correspondent of a New York daily.[109]

Within Georgia itself, meanwhile, a number of interesting developments had taken place during the early fall. The beginning of the convention campaign was concomitant with the return of the state's congressional delegation. This brought Berrien and James W. Jackson to Savannah to urge "non-intercourse." It

[106] Marietta *Union*, in Savannah *News*, December 17, 1850. The *News* declared that the *Union* "gave some good hints."

[107] See, *e.g.*, Jackson (Mississippi) *Flag of the Union*, March 7, 1851; Richmond *Daily Whig*, December 17, 1850; Hamilton's warnings are in the Washington *Republic*, December 2, 1850.

[108] Washington *Union*, October 16, 1850. Three large northern dailies, the New York *Express*, the Baltimore *Sun*, and the Boston *Courier*, considered the situation in Georgia important enough to justify the maintenance of regular correspondents in Savannah through the fall.

[109] New York *Herald*, September 17; see also New York *Express* and New York *Evening Post* in Savannah *News*, October 2, October 10; Philadelphia *Public Ledger*, September 19, November 27; Columbus *Ohio State Journal*, November 5; Natchez (Mississippi) *Courier*, September 20, 1850, etc.

also brought Wellborn to Southwest Georgia, Cobb and Hackett to Upper Georgia, and Toombs and Stephens to Central Georgia—all to defend the compromise and to decry disunion. The districts represented by the last four named, however, were practically certain to remain conservative before they returned,—those of Cobb and Hackett being dominated by Union Democrats coöperating with the Whigs, and those of Toombs and Stephens always having a safe Whig majority, no matter what the Democrats might do. The only uncertain areas in the state were those in the strip of four or five Democratic counties lying athwart Central Georgia,[110] several counties in the Pine Barrens, and the cities of Columbus and Savannah. There was uncertainty about the first because these Democratic counties followed their leaders with a tenacity that transcended all ordinary economic influences,[111] and many of the leaders of the Democracy were secessionists. There were one or two counties in the Pine Barrens of which this also held true, and there was some uncertainty as to how the degraded and ignorant "piney-woods people" in this region would react to the violent anti-Yankee and anti-Negro appeal which would feature the radical campaign. There was uncertainty about Columbus because of the unusual number of extremists resident there; and uncertainty about Savannah because that city contained considerable numbers of South Carolinians and European immigrants. The Berrien element might also prove to have some strength in the Senator's home county, Chatham, which included Savannah.

[110] See Map No. 5, p. 109.
[111] See chapter iii.

Stated in terms of social classes,[112] an analysis of the campaign and its results reveals that the groups most apt to be swayed by the secessionist appeal were: (1) Democratic partisans who had never outgrown the old Georgia political habit of following personal leaders regardless of issues;[113] (2) the lower middle classes in the cities, who might own one or two slaves and who read local secessionist papers; (3) able lawyers, editors and politicians in the cities, who either felt that they "saw further" into the future than could the majority or, else, hoped to attain political prominence at the head of the new movement;[114] and (4) the other extreme in the social scale, the illiterate "poor whites" of the Pine Barrens belt, who, even if they could not read the papers, were apt to be most responsive to appeals against "Yankee" or "nigger."[115] The combined numbers of these uncertain elements was but a small fraction of the entire population.

The congressional leaders, Toombs and Stephens, immediately set to work with C. J. Jenkins, E. A. Nisbet and others already on the ground to organize an energetic Union campaign. Cobb likewise began to coöperate with Lumpkin and Judge Andrews in the up-country and with Arnold and Ward in Savannah. The Union leaders who really faced the most difficult situation were these Democrats, Arnold and

[112] See chapter ii.
[113] See chapter iii.
[114] It is a rather peculiar fact that, with the exception of Towns and Haralson, every one of the secessionist leaders was out of office in 1850.
[115] For a contemporary northern analysis of some phases of this situation, see, e.g., Philadelphia Public Ledger, November 26, 1850. "Singular as it may seem," observed the Oneida (New York) Herald, "crowds of those who do not and never expect to own a negro, are most influenced by pro-slavery nonsense. The inhabitants of . . . the uncultivated portions of Georgia, are the men whom the slavery champion can mould to his will"; quoted in Federal Union, October 30, 1849. The Public Ledger claimed that the urban classes were inclined to be radical. Cf. Weston, Progress of Slavery, p. 40.

Ward, who had to deal in Savannah with a combination of South Carolinians and Berrien Whigs; and who eventually triumphed largely by bringing to the support of the conservative "old Savannah families" the assistance of the patriotically inclined German and Irish immigrants. Thus the exigencies of the campaign brought together strange political bedfellows in Georgia,—the "poor white" coöperating with the city lawyer secessionist, while the Irish laborer consorted with "people of consequence."[116]

The Union campaign during the fall was featured, as might have been expected, by county meetings and addresses as well as by the confident appeals of the press. It was marked, as usual, by a defence of Clay's compromise as acceptable, though far from perfect; by a constant emphasis of the economic advantages of the Union and the economic disadvantages of disunion;[117] and by the fervent appeal to old loyalties. The call for the state convention was at times condemned.[118]

The extremist orators, on the other hand, featured news garnered from the abolitionist press in the North in order to excite the people. Such news was supplemented by direct appeals to race feeling. It was declared, for instance, that the Yankees "preferred niggers to poor white men" and that secession was the only possible alternative to the social and economic equality of the races.[119]

[116] There is an interesting analysis of this peculiar situation in Savannah in Arnold's long report to Forney, December 18, 1850, Arnold MSS.

[117] See, *e.g.,* Columbus *Enquirer,* in *Chronicle,* September 21, 1850.

[118] For typical resolutions of a county Union meeting see those of the Macon meeting early in October, in Washington *Union,* October 6, 1850.

[119] Banners to this effect were displayed at extremist meetings; see, *e.g.,* Augusta *Constitutionalist,* in the Columbia *South Carolinian,* October 6, 1850.

The secessionist campaign opened with violent condemnations of the Union, elicited from a few of the more extreme of the radical editors by the excitement attending the Governor's proclamation. These editorials have been much quoted, particularly the statements of the Columbus *Times* and the Columbus *Sentinel* that "we hate the Union as we do hell itself," and that "we are for open, unqualified secession, for war upon the government." The *Times* worked itself up to an extremely hysterical mood, urging the leaders to "Form clubs, enlighten the people, put arms in their hands . . . do anything and everything to save this state from recreancy and the eternal disgrace to herself from backing out."[120]

Other southern-rights papers hesitated, however, to advocate immediate secession, and by the latter part of October there was a noticeable moderation in the opinion of all the radical papers save one or two. At the same time, the southern-rights leaders ceased to counsel "secession" and came to speak only of "resistance to oppression." This "swing to the right" was the most noticeable and significant feature of the entire campaign. The secessionists at last had their ears to the ground, or—to mix the metaphors—they had at last seen the Union writing on the wall. It was patent to all that the extremists admitted at last that the masses were against them and that it would have been wiser never to have come out openly for secession. Papers which advocated secession in September were ready by the end of October to accept the

---

[120] Quoted in the *Chronicle*, September 20, 1850. The papers openly urging secession were the *Times*, the *Sentinel*, and the Macon *Telegraph*. The exact attitude of the Augusta *Constitutionalist* and the Augusta *Republic* has not been ascertained.

compromise.[121] Practically no speakers were advocating secession by the time November arrived. In traveling the road from secessionist to compromise positions, some of the papers stopped at the half-way point of "non-intercourse" or the demand for another southern convention, but many went all the way to the compromise.[122] By the beginning of 1851, the *Federal Union* was calmly announcing to the people that "there never was an organized disunion party in Georgia." There were "only a few who believed that the rights of the South will never be secure in the Union," and few or no disunionists, *per se*. It announced truthfully enough that at the time of the election to the state convention "there was not among the southern-rights candidates a single one who was not opposed to or pledged against disunion."[123]

The Union men met this retreat at times with irony and scorn, at other times with great caution. At one meeting an extremist advocating "resistance" was forced to say what he meant by the term. He finally declared that when he said he would "resist" he meant that he would "petition." "Great God!" said a bystander, "who ever heard of such a mode of resistance." Another turned away with the significant comment: "Barnum ought to have him!" On the other hand, Cobb and others steadily warned the people against the secessionist wolves who had now donned the sheep's clothing of the compromise.

It is difficult to ascribe the "back down" of the secessionists to any one particular factor that entered into the fall campaign. The energy infused into the

[121] Especially the Columbus *Times;* see the Washington *Union,* October 27, 1850.

[122] See the *Georgian,* October 31; *News,* October 25, November 8; *Federal Union* in Washington *Union,* November 5, 1850.

[123] *Federal Union,* January 21, 1851.

Union appeal by the returning congressional delegation may have been one factor involved, though just
what potency this had it is difficult to say. There
had been little favorable public response to the call
for secession from the moment of the first open appeal
at the Macon mass meeting in August. There had, on
the other hand, been definite evidences of hostility and
indifference to this appeal from that moment on. It is
probable that these reactions convinced many of the
secessionists that the August appeal had been premature—that the Georgia people were not yet prepared
for secession and that a return to the ambiguous and
less radical appeals of the spring and early summer was
indicated under the circumstances. It is doubtful if
the return of the congressmen altered this situation in
any fundamental manner.[124]

Indeed, one of the returning Union leaders was,
in certain respects, a liability rather than an asset to
the Union cause. In the course of their campaign the
Georgia extremists evinced great bitterness against
"Hamilcar Toombs," who—having declared that "This
cry of Union is the masked battery from which the
rights of the South are to be assailed"—was now
sounding that very cry himself. When Toombs, aggressive as usual, challenged the radicals to a joint
debate at Columbus, they failed to respond, though
there was some talk of bringing Yancey over from
Alabama to meet him. When Toombs came to Colum-

[124] Cf. R. P. Brooks, "Howell Cobb and the Crisis of 1850", *Mississippi Valley Historical Review*, IV. 289; Brooks, *History of Georgia*,
pp. 243, 244; A. C. Cole, *Whig Party in the South*, pp. 180, 181; H. D.
Foster, "Webster's Seventh of March Speech and the Secession Movement, 1850," *American Historical Review*, XXVII. 250, 251; L. L.
Knight, *Reminiscences of Famous Georgians*, pp. 107, 211; U. B. Phillips, *Georgia and State Rights*, p. 164; Phillips, *Robert Toombs*, pp.
95-99.

bus, however, the secessionists made things as unpleasant as possible. The *Times* declared that:

Toombs and Stephens have operated like sparks on a tinder box in this community. They have raised the very dander of our people. Toombs had not been in town two hours before he was hanged in effigy. This was not proper in the boys but the boys will get excited in exciting times. The crowd was a very firey one that sat under Toombs and Stephens—we deem it fortunate there was no serious accident to report.[125]

Toombs denied emphatically the charge of inconsistency, pointing out that none of the three measures he had declared would justify secession had been incorporated in the compromise, and reminded everyone that he had "always denounced this California Rebellion."[126]

One incident occurred during the campaign that temporarily raised the hopes of the "Ultraists." It happened that two slaves belonging to the same Dr. Collins of Macon who had saved the editor of the *Citizen* of that city, escaped during October to Boston. He thereupon sent friends to Boston to reclaim them. These agents, upon arriving at that city, were threatened with mob violence by the abolitionists, and there was much excitement. The incident might have made trouble for the Union cause in Georgia, as the moderates had accepted the compromise only in the belief that it would be observed in good faith by the North. The "Boston Excitement" implied that the fugitive slave law might not be enforced. The Macon *Journal* solemnly warned Boston that, "while we yield to the compromise measures of the late Congress, we are determined to require a faithful compliance with the Fugitive Slave Act, and in case of refusal shall take

[125] *Times,* in Columbia *South Carolinian,* November 12, 1850.
[126] *Chronicle,* October 9, 1850.

our redress in what manner we think best."[127]   Some
fear was expressed in the North that the episode might
turn the tide in Georgia back to secession.[128]

Fortunately for the Union cause, President Fil-
more seized the opportunity to make clear his own
position and the status of the fugitive slave law by
writing personally to Dr. Collins, assuring him that
the law would be enforced by the federal authorities.
This "Collins Letter" was printed all over the country
as well as in Georgia.   The conservative papers in the
latter state expressed great satisfaction with it, while
the radical papers condemned it as a presidential attempt to interfere in the struggle in the state.[129]

This incident, therefore, did not react unfavorably
upon the Union cause.   It did, however, serve to bring
out what the conservatives always claimed; namely,
that they were in no sense the "submissionists" the
enemy accused them of being.   Practically from the
time the compromise was clearly outlined, the feeling
had prevailed among the Unionists that it was unsatisfactory and should be accepted only as a last concession to the antislavery power.   The first able and
formal expression of this feeling was given at a meeting in Savannah in October, over which Arnold and
Ward presided and from which the extremists had
been forced to withdraw.   The "rump" meeting
adopted resolutions drawn up by Cuyler, a Savannah
Union man, which declared that the compromise should
be accepted as a last full measure of conciliation, but
that no further concessions would be made.   The South
should now draw finally the line beyond which the

---

[127] Macon *Journal,* in the Washington *Union,* November 12, 1850.

[128] Baltimore *Sun,* November 9; Columbus *Ohio Statesman,* November 23, 1850.

[129] See the Washington *Republic,* November 23; Columbus *Ohio
Statesman,* November 23; Savannah *News,* November 12, 1850, etc.

North should not go. These resolutions were widely quoted in the state and elsewhere as the "Chatham Platform," a platform upon which southern men could well unite to preserve at one and the same time the integrity of the Union and the rights of the South. Cuyler's resolutions were practically identical with those subsequently adopted by the state convention and which became nationally known as the "Georgia Platform."[130]

To the extent that the Union men were now making clear their opposition to further concessions, they made it somewhat easier for the extremists to accept the compromise position. In a sense, the two parties approached one another during October and November to agree upon the common basis of the "Chatham Platform." This involved the extremists, however, in some inconsistency and humiliation, whereas with the Union men it meant only a greater emphasis upon the ultimate character of the compromise they had advocated from the beginning.

There was one other group besides the Union men and the extremists to be heard from during the fall campaign. This was the Berrien following, which advocated economic resistance to the North. The movement for "non-intercourse" never commanded a large popular following in Georgia, probably because it was considered an impracticable, middle-of-the-road position that could not be long maintained between the Union on the one hand and secession on the other. Because of this, there was always some uncertainty as to the real meaning of "non-intercourse"

[130] For the "Chatham Platform" see Savannah *News,* October 24; *Republican,* October 24, 1850. The general view taken therein was becoming common in the South at the time. See, *e.g.,* Mobile *Daily Advertiser,* October 15; Savannah *Republican,* October 22; Columbus (Georgia) *Times,* in Washington *Union,* October 27, 1850.

and as to whether its advocates should be classified as southern-rights or Union men.[131] Generally speaking, they were claimed by the former, but the "non-intercourse" men themselves always opposed immediate secession. Senator Berrien continued to be the leader of this group in Georgia through the fall compaign, and his chief press support came from the Savannah *News*,[132] though he was encouraged by all the southern-rights journals.

Berrien's main thesis was that already noted in his summer letters;[133] that is, that there must be resistance *within* the Union and the Constitution—but that there must be *resistance*. Secession would, he held, be "impracticable" and "the worst of evils." "Non-intercourse," on the other hand, would encourage the economic life of the South and would bring pressure upon northern conservative business interests that might lead to further concessions, or, if this did not happen, would prepare the South for the final stand that would then be necessary against the North. In defining "non-intercourse," he admitted, as a constitutional lawyer, that some of the measures in the recent legislature looking towards that policy were unconstitutional, but he believed that the Supreme Court would permit a tax on goods entering the state. Such taxes should therefore be levied; only southern ports should be used in trading with Europe; the state should subsidize steamship companies and encourage local

---

[131] Senator Foote and the Jackson (Mississippi) *Southron* claimed that Berrien, the leader of the non-intercourse men in Georgia, was for the compromise. The *Federal Union* and the Jackson *Mississippian* denied this; see the *Mississippian*, November 22, 1850.

[132] See the *News*, November 6, 7, 1850.

[133] "Tybee", correspondent of the Baltimore *Sun*, thought that Berrien came home "hot" and was "cooled off" by Georgia opinion; see Baltimore *Sun*, October 19, 1850.

manufactures; and, in general, the South should make itself economically independent of the North.[134]

Such was the "Berrien Platform," as it came to be known in Georgia, when its author became active in the fall campaign. He received some support from the "old Whig" element which had bolted that party the year before and from some of the extremists, especially in the lower counties "along the river," where the South Carolina element was strong. One of the few "Southern Rights Associations" which had been formed was reported to have adopted the interesting resolution that:

> The members of this Association will not hereafter hold any intercourse, social or commercial, with any Northern man or foreigner from any non-slave-holding nation, or the children or grandchildren, or any collateral relation of such Northern man or foreigner, however remote.[135]

This was indeed building the "Chinese Wall" about the state, of which the Boston *Courier* had spoken the previous winter, but few Georgians desired to help in its construction. One or two merchants in Savannah declared they would cease trading with the North at once, but the movement was not general. As a matter of fact, when the state convention elections were held, just one county chose delegates pledged to the "Berrien Platform."[136]

[134] For the general economic background to such principles, see St. George L. Sioussat, "Co-operation for the Development of the Material Welfare of the South," *The South in the Building of the Nation*, IV. 173-179.

[135] *Chronicle*, October 8, 1850.

[136] This was Burke, on the Savannah river; see Macon *Journal*, November 29, in Philadelphia *North American*, December 7, 1850. For data on Berrien's part in the campaign (which practically ended his career) see Jackson *Mississippian*, November 22; Augusta *Constitutionalist*, in Washington *Republic*, November 16; Mobile *Daily Advertiser*, November 26; *Chronicle*, October 2, 6, November 6; Tallahassee *Floridian*, November 9, 1850; Natchez (Mississippi) *Courier*, November 22;

The elections to the state convention were to be held November 25, in the manner usual for elections to the legislature. Nominations had been made by each party in most of the counties, usually by a committee appointed by "county caucuses," which meetings also endorsed the committees' recommendations after they were made.[137] In some ten counties the extremists failed to make any nominations. As the great day approached when Georgia should proclaim her attitude to the nation, the press on each side made final statements and appeals. The appeal of most of the radical papers was in line with their recent moderation and was often nominally a plea for, rather than against, the Union. "Submission now," said the *Federal Union* on November 19, "is abolition and ultimate disunion. Resistance now, with the rights of the South, may save the Union." The Union papers, on the other hand, displayed great confidence in coming victory and were inclined to ridicule the "backsliding" southern-rights party. "Tybee," the able Savannah correspondent of the Baltimore *Sun,* estimated that of the ninety-three counties not more than eighteen would go for the extremists.[138] Much ridicule was heaped upon the already fallen foe, of which the following quotation is a fair and suggestive example, taken from Holsey's Athens *Banner.* The substance may have been intended as a mockery of Governor Towns' proclamation:

Boston *Courier,* November 26; Philadelphia *Public Ledger,* November 25; Baltimore *Sun,* November 16; Savannah *News,* November 6, 20, 1850.

[137] See description of nominating methods in *Chronicle,* October 12, 1850.

[138] Baltimore *Sun,* November 20. "Tybee's" accounts of the campaign are the best-connected ones to be found, and contain valuable observations on public opinion; see the *Sun* for October 3, 19, 28, November 4, 1850.

PROCLAMATION OF ABSOLOM TRICKUM

Attention, Invincibles! To the rescue, Chivalry! Fire-eaters to your tents! Up with your new lights and down with the Union! You are ordered to muster at once in revolutionary style, and with your appearance touched off with a tint of the terrible,—your mustaches 18 inches long, your finger nails 3 inches long and pointed for gouging, knapsack of the shape and capacity of a coffin[139] . . . For regimental flag: "United we fall—Divided we stand;" and for company flags: "Catspaws for South Carolina." Col. Hydrogen Gass will take command with Rhett-orical flourish, and lead you:

> Where hills and dales
> And Brooks that fail
> And Senator Hale so merrily sail
> On the ocean of wild disunion.

Finally each man will kill twenty Yankees apiece, and capture New York . . . where they will seize Barnum & Jenny Lind—and then for the spoils of a real ridotto![140]

When the election was held, on November 26, the result was to a large extent a repetition of the April election fiasco. The "Ultraists" were swept off their feet by a Union majority greater than any party had ever rolled up in the history of the state. Of the ninety-three counties, but ten chose southern-rights delegations to the convention, which meant that the Union party would have complete control of that body. The popular vote was about forty-six thousand for the Union candidates to some twenty-four thousand for their southern-rights opponents.[141] This meant that less than half of the Georgia Democrats[142] had been willing to vote for the southern-rights candidates even when these men were strenuously denying secession and claiming that they would save the Union. The

[139] The extremists had said they would "march up to the Missouri line with their coffins on their backs."

[140] Athens *Banner*, in the Boston *Bee*, November 26, 1850.

[141] For election results see *Chronicle*, November 24; *Georgian*, November 29; *Republican*, December 17, 1850.

[142] The normal Democratic vote at this time was about 50,000.

Union press claimed, with apparent justice, that had the radical leaders not "backed down" and disclaimed secession, they would have sent scarcely a man to the convention. An analysis of the county results, as given in the press and compared with the voting policy of the delegates when present later in the convention, reveals that only two sections of the state held to the extremist cause. These were the tier of Democratic counties in Central Georgia and the ring of counties around the outer edge of the Pine Barrens.[143] The explanation in the case of the Democratic tier has already been suggested; that is, the incurable habit therein of following leaders rather than principles. The explanation in the case of the Pine Barrens is not so simple. In the case of Bulloch county, it may have been due to the same factors that affected the Democratic tier in Central Georgia, while counties on the Savannah river may have been influenced by their contacts with Carolina. It is suggestive, however, that these Lower Georgia counties which went for the "Ultraists" did form a partial ring around the edge of the Pine Barrens area. It is probable that a large percentage of the "poor whites" living on the fringe of the plantation country voted extremist. It is also possible, though it cannot be proved, that this was due to their responsiveness to appeals against the Yankees and the Negroes. It has been pointed out that their degraded economic and mental condition made them particularly responsive to these very appeals, which had been featured in the southern-rights campaign.[144]

In several of these Pine Barrens counties a divided delegation was chosen, which the Macon *Jour-*

[143] See Map No. 7, p. 320.

[144] See chapter ii for a description of the "poor whites" and their prejudices.

MAP NO. 7

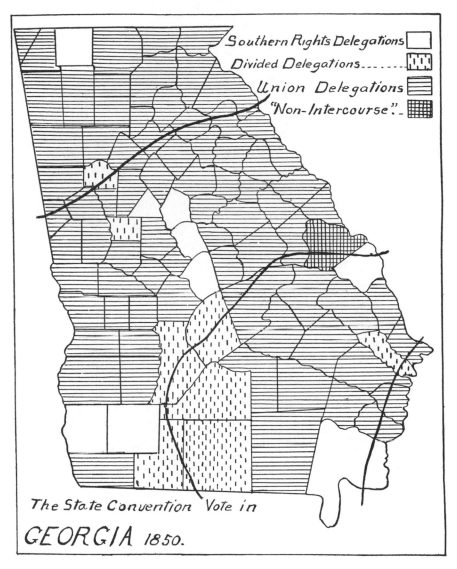

Southern Rights Delegations
Divided Delegations........
Union Delegations
"Non-Intercourse".

The State Convention Vote in
GEORGIA 1850.

nal said was due to the claim of the southern-rights candidates that they were as strongly for the Union as were their opponents.[145]   In ten counties the "Ultraists" offered no resistance whatever, but these were not concentrated in any one section.   In the one county already noted, Burke, a delegation pledged to the "Berrien Platform" was selected.

There were close contests in Columbus and Savannah, as had been anticipated.   In both cities the Union party was saved by the help of northern men and the foreign-born.   In Savannah the influence of the mayor and council was with the extremists, yet one hundred members of the city guards, most of whom were naturalized citizens, voted the Union ticket, despite threats from the local administration.   The same was true of the foreign shopkeepers.[146]   As it was, the Union men carried Savannah by a vote of only nine hundred and thirty to seven hundred and seventy.   Meanwhile in Columbus, declared the *Times,* "the Yankees, Foreigners and Traitors carried the Union ticket."[147]

In all other parts of the state, the Union forces won sweeping victories.   There was naturally great jubilation in the Union press of Georgia[148] and neighboring states, and also in the North.[149]   "Tybee" wrote North that "The Union men are astonished at the vastness of their victory.   They have carried the state by a majority that has no parallel in the history of this

[145] Macon *Journal,* in Mobile *Daily Advertiser,* December 10, 1850.

[146] Arnold to Forney, December 18, 1850, Arnold MSS.

[147] Columbus *Times,* in the *Chronicle,* December 6, 1850.

[148] *Chronicle,* November 27, 28; *Republican,* November 28, 1850.

[149] Mobile *Advertiser,* November 29; Montgomery *Daily Alabama Journal,* November 30; Jackson *Flag of the Union,* December 6; Natchez *Courier,* December 3; Aberdeen (Mississippi) *Independent,* December 7, 1850, etc.

country."[150]   The conservative press in all sections teemed with such phrases as "Pleasant Surprise"— "Glorious News," "Happy Omen," "Georgia has 'led off' nobly for the Union," and the like. The result was bound to influence all the lower South, it was thought, and thus play a great part in the national salvation.

The southern-rights press in Georgia, Alabama, and Mississippi varied in its reactions to the crushing defeat sustained. The Savannah *News* was moderate; it regretted the result, but "did not doubt the fidelity of the Union delegates to the South." The *Georgian* was bitter, declaring "we are beaten, but never was an election carried with such corruption." The Columbus *Times* was defeated, but not disheartened. "The Southern-Rights ticket is beaten," it declared, "but Southern rights are not conquered. From the thistle of defeat we will pluck the flower of victory! We entered the canvass under the banner of *secession* and *Southern Liberty*. We have kept it flying, and now nail it to the mast!"[151]

The effect of the election upon South Carolina was, of course, most important. Towns' fears and Seabrook's prediction had now been realized. Georgia had led off backwards, and, if South Carolina was to await coöperation, the opportunity for secession had ceased to exist. The day after the Georgia election Seabrook addressed the newly assembled South Carolina legislature, urging against precipitate action without

[150] Baltimore *Sun*, November 30; see also *National Intelligencer*, December 14; Philadelphia *Public Ledger*, November 29; New York *Tribune*, December 13, 1850; Columbus *Ohio State Journal*, December 2, 1851.

[151] *News*, November 27; *Georgian*, November 30; Columbus *Times* in the Columbia *South Carolinian*, November 29; see also the Tallahassee *Floridian*, November 30; Montgomery *Advertiser* in the Georgian, November 30, 1850.

the coöperation of the sister states.[152] It is clear from his secret letters to Towns that, had the Georgia election resulted in a southern-rights victory, his action would have been very different. Georgia had checked South Carolina.

It is true that some hope was expressed in the latter state that the Georgia convention could still be counted upon to take extreme action.[153] The more typical view of the Carolina coöperationists, however, was that expressed in the speech of B. F. Perry, representative from Greenville, in the South Carolina House. A fortnight after the elections in Georgia, Perry urged Carolina to await coöperation before seceding from the Union, and, in this connection, it was necessary to warn his colleagues of the situation in the sister states:

Mississippi (he declared) is more with South Carolina than any other state. But her interests are with the Mississippi Valley. I doubt very much whether Georgia and South Carolina can ever agree on anything, much less on the formation of an independent Republic. Two-thirds of Georgia is now opposed to the action of South Carolina. They would not support us even if we started the ball rolling.[154]

While the state convention campaign was still under way in Georgia, there had occurred a curious interlude that under other circumstances might have led to serious consequences; namely, the meeting of the second session of the southern convention at Nashville, on November 11. This assembly had been robbed of all *raison d'etre* by the passage of the compromise and the unmistakable tendency in the South to accept that ad-

---

[152] Savannah *News*, November 29, 1850.

[153] Charleston *News*, December 7, in the Washington *Union*, December 12, 1850.

[154] *Speech of B. F. Perry in the South Carolina House*, December 11, 1850, (pamphlet, Charleston, 1851).

justment. Hence there was probably less interest taken in it than there was in the Georgia election itself. Many delegates to the first session failed to attend the second. Only four of the original Georgia delegation returned to this meeting, Benning, McDonald, McWhertor, and Bledsoe, but the Governor appointed new representatives to take the places of those who refused to go.[155] Since Sharkey of Mississippi did not return, McDonald of Georgia was honored with the chair.

The Georgia delegation, like most of the others except that from Tennessee, was now purged of all but the most extreme members, and the secessionists therefore had things all their own way. President McDonald opened the session with an appeal for action, and various resolutions were introduced by members from several of the states, including Georgia, looking towards secession. McWhertor expressed the feelings of the Georgia delegation in the words: "Union and Slavery cannot exist together," while Cheves of South Carolina announced to a complacent nation: "Even now the Union is divided." After further oratory of this nature, the convention adjourned, leaving its members to wend their way southward once more, unhonored and unsung.

It is worthy of note, however, that the conservative Tennessee delegation adopted, in protest to the radical resolutions of the majority, the so-called "Tennessee Resolutions," which were of a conciliatory character. These declared the Clay compromise unsatisfactory, but accepted it with the distinct understanding that no

---

[155] For typical reasons for refusal to attend the second session, see the letter from ex-Governor Troup of Georgia, October 10, 1850, quoted in Harden, *G. M. Troup*, p. 529, note 1. For the list of actual Georgia delegates see the Nashville *Banner*, November 19, in Philadelphia *Public Ledger*, November 29; Washington *Republic*, November 26, 1850.

further concessions to the North were to be made. This was the same view which had been proclaimed in the "Chatham Platform" at Savannah on October 23, and which was being expressed elsewhere in the South at the same time. It received, of course, scant consideration at the Nashville meeting.[156]

The Georgia state convention assembled at Milledgeville on December 10, 1850. There were present some two hundred and sixty-four delegates, and, of these, a remarkably large number were able and influential men. More than half were slaveholders, owning from thirty to four hundred slaves each, and many were men of culture and education.[157] It was obviously a body representing the educated, propertied, and conservative classes, regardless of party. Among the delegates were such conservative leaders as Toombs, Alexander Stephens, Jenkins, Miller, W. B. Wofford, W. C. Dawson, Meriwether, Ward, and Arnold. The delegation from Chatham alone was sufficiently prominent to have afforded leadership for the whole body—Arnold, Ward, F. S. Bartow, and Cuyler, the last the author of the "Chatham Platform." Very few of the delegates had been members of the last legislature, whose personnel had been markedly inferior to that of the convention. Indeed, the contrast between legislature and convention in this respect recalls the contrast between the Congress of 1787 and the Constitutional Convention of that year. The only prominent leader among the handful of southern-rights delegates

[156] For descriptions of the second session, see Herndon, "The Nashville Convention", *Alabama Historical Society Publications*, V. 229-233; Sioussat, "Tennessee, the Compromise of 1850, and the Nashville Convention," *Mississippi Valley Historical Review*, II. 343-346. For the opinion held by the Georgia southern-rights group of the second session, see *Federal Union*, June 17, 1851.

[157] Macon *Journal* in the *Chronicle*, December 12, 1850.

was W. J. Lawton, who was assisted, however, by two relatively unknown extremists, J. L. Seward and R. W. McCune. The overwhelming majority of the Union members, numbering some two hundred and forty to twenty-three of the southern rights group, was impressive. The disproportion was so great that the convention served to all intents and purposes as the first Union party meeting in Georgia, deriving a peculiar significance from the fact that it represented the entire population.

On motion of Meriwether, the Honorable Thomas Spaulding, of McIntosh, was chosen president, that honor being accorded him as the last living signer of the state constitution.[158] Spaulding made a brief address upon taking the chair, thanking the convention for the honor which he felt was "perhaps a fitting termination for my long life. Perhaps," he continued, "the members may expect from me some expression of opinion on this occasion. . . . I must say that rather than have the Union under which we have enjoyed repose and happiness for sixty-three years destroyed, —rather than have the states separated—I should prefer to see myself and mine slumbering under the load of monumental clay."[159] This was hardly an auspicious beginning for the secessionists.

The state senate rules were then adopted as a basis of procedure, and a committee of thirty-three—three from each state judicial district—was appointed by the president to consider and report "action appropriate for the occasion." All the thirty-three appointed were Union men save two, W. J. Lawton, of Scriven, and J. M. Smith, of Camden. This brought an immediate protest from the southern-rights delegates, who felt

[158] *Chronicle*, December 20, 1850.
[159] *Debates and Proceedings of the Georgia Convention*, p. 2.

that the twenty-four thousand men who had voted their ticket were entitled to more than two out of thirty-three members on the committee.[160] These delegates considered it especially objectionable, moreover, that the only southern-rights men named were both of South Carolina origin, it being suspected that Spaulding thought this fact would discredit their party.[161] In other words, the feeling against South Carolinians was such that even the extremists in Georgia did not wish to be identified with them.

On December 11, a number of pro-Union resolutions were presented without being read and referred to the committee of thirty-three. Among them were those proposed by Bartow of Savannah, which in substance were probably like the "Chatham Platform."

On the next day the "Ultraists," apparently undeterred by their small numbers, took the initiative. Seward, of Thomas, began by introducing resolutions thanking Senator Berrien for his attitude on the California bill. The president thought that such matters should be referred at once to the committee, which, in view of the personnel of that body, would have been a simple way of burying all radical resolutions. It thus appeared that the Union majority was not even inclined to let the extremists be heard. This brought forth an energetic protest from McCune, of Butts, who had seconded Seward's resolution. McCune began to give his frank opinion of the whole convention:

[160] The lack of "proportional representation" meant, of course, that the southern-rights vote of twenty-four thousand was not represented in the convention in anything like a proportionate manner, *i.e.*, proportional representation, in the modern sense of the phrase, would have entitled them to about eighty-five seats. This lack of proportionate representation was typical of all American institutions, however.

[161] *Federal Union*, December 24, 1850.

I came here (he said), as a member of no particular party. I came here for the purpose of taking into consideration the action of the last Congress; and if possible of harmonizing the body for these matters. From what I have seen and heard since I have been here, I have come to the conclusion that there is a disposition in the majority not to harmonize, but to build up a great party. There should be no party in Georgia on this question, none in the South. As before remarked, I came here for the purpose of harmonizing . . . but, sir, I see a disposition to drive off members who are called "fire-eaters"—.

Here the President called him out of order. The Union "steam-roller" had begun to work![162]

Seward, not dismayed, immediately followed Mc-Cune with new resolutions accompanied by a long preamble. This preamble contained quotations from some of Toombs' most fiery utterances in the last Congress, an indictment of his want of fidelity to those utterances, and a declaration that his present policy was dangerous to the South and to the Union.[163] The resolutions repeated the demand made by the second Nashville meeting, that there should be no political coöperation with the North, and concluded with the declaration: "We are called upon to defend our honor, our property, and our country from the lawless rule of the North."[164] Seward read these statements in an excited manner, the while Toombs gazed upon him with what a reporter was pleased to call "the dignity of a lion."[165]

A motion to print these resolutions was lost amid some confusion. Seward was offended at the demonstration against him when the convention also refused

[162] *Debates and Proceedings*, p. 3.
[163] How far this solicitude for the Union was sincere it is difficult to say. It was typical of the new attitude assumed by the extremists during the fall.
[164] *Debates and Proceedings*, p. 4.
[165] Macon *Journal*, in *Chronicle*, December 29, 1850.

even to "take up" his resolutions. A Union member then demanded fair play, and votes were finally taken on the motion to take up the resolutions. Dr. Arnold of Savannah remarked that, "as the gentleman wishes to speak to Buncombe I will vote aye." The motion was defeated, one hundred and twenty-seven to fifty-seven. The extremists had gained nothing for their pains and felt, perhaps with some justice, that they were not receiving a consideration proportionate to the votes cast by their party.

On the thirteenth C. J. Jenkins presented to the convention the "Exposition and Resolutions" prepared by the committee of thirty-three. They had "carefully considered the papers referred to them," he reported, "and freely interchanged opinions" and now submitted the results of their deliberations. The "Exposition" was a remarkable document, and the resolutions appended were to become nationally famous as the "Georgia Platform." Authorship has usually been ascribed to Jenkins, who was chairman of the committee,[166] although Alexander Stephens later claimed that he wrote them,[167] and it has already been noted that the resolutions really followed in principle the "Chatham Platform" penned by Cuyler, the Savannah Union Democrat. The Georgia Platform owed its origin in principle, therefore, though not in exact wording, to the Union Democrats as well as to the Whigs.[168]

Jenkins, in reporting the preamble, was permitted to read it from the desk, which he did "in a clear, dis-

---

[166] C. C. Jones, *Life of Charles J. Jenkins,* (Pamphlet, Atlanta, 1884), p. 3; Stoval, *Toombs,* p. 93.

[167] Avary, *Recollections of A. H. Stephens,* p. 27.

[168] *Cf.* Cole, "The South and the Right of Secession," *Mississippi Valley Historical Review,* I. 382.

tinct, and manly tone." A Union party reporter, who was present, declared that

language would fail to describe the effect it produced. Many, many eyes were suffused with tears at one moment and all seemed to feel as if Georgia ought to be alike proud of her position and of her noble sons who framed such a report.[169]

The preamble began with a résumé of the difficulties in the last Congress and proceeded to the practical questions: "May Georgia *consistently with her honor* abide by the general scheme of pacification? If she may, then does her *interest* lie in adherence to it, or in resistance?" The answer was then given that it was consistent with Georgia's honor, for only the California law in any way violated even the demands of the last legislature. It was to Georgia's interest, moreover, to accept the Compromise, since the only conceivable form of resistance was secession, and secession would increase rather than decrease the state's difficulties. Georgia should therefore accept the adjustment. "To this course," it was added, "she is impelled by an earnest desire to perpetuate the American Union."

Here ended the first lesson of the preamble—that addressed to the people of Georgia. There followed one addressed to the "people of the sovereign states"— which meant, in large part, to the people of the North. This began with a review of the history of slavery and ended with a solemn warning to the northern conservatives. Georgia would say to the moderate northern patriots who were tolerating abolitionism in their midst:

[169] Milledgeville *Recorder,* in a special night extra, December 14, containing the resolutions and preamble, quoted in the Washington *Republic,* December 20, 1850. See also *Debates and Proceedings,* pp. 5-8; *Journal of the Georgia Convention,* 1850, pp. 11-19. For the Resolutions alone see Ames, *State Documents,* pp. 271, 272.

Be not deceived, the destiny of the Union is in your hands. Awake from your fatal dream of security. In the integrity of your patriotism rise up against this disorganizing heresy. Assemble in the venerated halls where *your* forefathers and *our* forefathers together signed the Constitution, and redeem the *City of Brotherly Love* from the reproach of nourishing its foe . . . Everywhere . . . decree its (abolitionism's) banishment from the high places of power. *You owe the country this lustration.* As for Georgia, her *choice* is fraternity and Union, with constitutional rights—her *alternative* self-preservation, by all the means which a favoring Providence may place at her disposal.[170]

The resolutions that followed the preamble were similar to it, in that they added to the acceptance of the compromise a warning to the North to maintain it. The resolutions, it was declared, were adopted in order "that the position of this state may be clearly apprehended by her confederates of the South and North, and in order that she may be blameless of all future consequences." The first three were general in character, declaring the necessity for the compromise and announcing that Georgia, "whilst she does not wholly approve, will abide by it as a permanent adjustment of this sectional controversy."

The fourth and fifth resolutions were the most vital ones, in that they clearly drew the line, beyond which the North must not go if the compromise was to be maintained:

The state of Georgia (declared the fourth resolution), will and ought to resist even (as a last resort) to a disruption of every tie that binds her to the Union, any action of Congress upon the subject of slavery in the District of Columbia, or in places subject to the jurisdiction of Congress, incompatible with the safety, and domestic tranquility, the rights and honor of the slave holding states, or any refusal to admit as a state any territory hereafter applying, because of the existence of slavery therein, or any act, prohibiting the introduction of slaves into

[170] *Debates and Proceedings,* pp. 7, 8.

the territories of Utah and New Mexico, or any act repealing or materially modifying the laws now in force for the recovery of fugitive slaves.

The fifth resolution declared, "That it is the deliberate opinion of this Convention that upon a faithful execution of the *Fugitive Slave Law* by the proper authorities depends the preservation of our much beloved Union."

Several statements in these resolutions are notable: first, that the compromise was viewed as "final"; second, that any infringement by the North might lead to the secession of Georgia; and, third, that each of a number of specific encroachments would be regarded as just cause for such secession.

As soon as the resolutions had been reported by Jenkins for the committee, Toombs moved that the entire report be accepted; but the "Ultraists" secured the right to consider the preamble and each resolution separately. As each resolution came up, the small opposition group usually attempted amendments and was as promptly voted down. When accused of "keeping up the agitation in this manner," Seward made the pointed retort that Toombs and Stephens had delayed the organization of the national House for weeks over the speakership, and "having got the people of Georgia to the point of resistance, they come home and ask [them] to submit to the injustice done them."[171]

The preamble was adopted on December 13, by two hundred and thirty-seven votes to twenty-three. On the same day, the first three resolutions were accepted without opposition. In other words, after all the condemnation heaped upon the compromise during the summer and fall campaign, not a single voice was

[171] *Debates and Proceedings,* p. 9.

raised in the convention against the resolutions accepting that compromise. On December 14, a long debate occurred on the fourth resolution, which dealt with the powers of Congress over slavery in the District of Columbia. Some differences developed between members of the Union party as to whether the consent of the slaveholders in the District would give Congress the right to abolish slavery therein. The question was also raised, whether the mere emancipation of four or five hundred slaves there would be a good cause for secession. The debate was notable for the statement of Bailey, an extremist, that, while the majority might ridicule them, the minority of twenty-three would again appeal these issues to the people. The end of the struggle was not yet![172]

This discussion of the fourth resolution also elicited the most fervent eulogies of the Union which the convention was to hear. An interesting illustration of this loyalty to the Union was afforded by the speech of Bartow, of Chatham. In a moment of haste he referred inadvertently to "our Southern confederacy," but immediately checked himself and exclaimed:

"I ask pardon, sir, of you and this House for using the expression, 'Southern Confederacy.' It inadvertently escaped my lips, for if there is any feeling of my heart more cherished than another it is that the day may never come when we shall have in this land a Southern Confederacy, or a Northern Confederacy, or any other Confederacy than the glorious Union in which we now live. May God preserve the Union of these states forever."

The fourth and fifth resolutions were finally adopted by the usual overwhelmnig majorities. New and radical resolutions proposed by W. J. Lawton, the same who had proposed similarly radical resolutions

[172] *Ibid.*, p. 17.

in the legislatures of both 1847 and 1849, were then promptly defeated. After accepting a resolution to inscribe the Georgia stone for the Washington Monument with the words "Georgia Convention, December, 1850,"[173] and brief congratulatory addresses by the presiding officers, the convention adjourned December 14, *sine die*.[174]

The assembling of delegates from all over the state, divided between the Union and the southern-rights groups, was naturally the occasion of the final organization of these groups into new political parties. Arnold, for instance, upon arriving as a delegate at Milledgeville, was surprised by the extent to which the new party lines had drawn fast. There was already, he found, an "impassable gulf" between the southern-rights and the Union Democrats. Campbell, an editor of the *Federal Union*, minimized this separation, remarking to Arnold, "Oh, we will all fall back into line"; but Arnold denied this. Upon taking dinner with Towns, he and Ward had a long, "personally friendly talk" with the Governor, but told him frankly that they and the other Union Democrats could no longer support him politically. Towns seemed "awfully cut" by the results of the late election and the character of the convention.[175]

During the sessions of the convention the Union men took advantage of their practical monopoly of the membership to meet several times in general caucus. The chief meeting held formally to organize the Union

---

[173] This resolution was never carried out, and as a result the radical inscription prescribed by Governor Towns ("The Constitution as it is, the Union as it was") was inscribed and remains on the Georgia stone to this day. See A. C. Cole, "Inscribed Stones in the Washington Monument," *History Teachers' Magazine*, III. 49.

[174] *Debates and Proceedings.* p. 25.

[175] Arnold to Forney, December 18, 1850, Arnold MSS.

party met in the House chamber on the evening of the eleventh, and Toombs made a great Union speech appropriate to the occasion.[176] He proclaimed the principles of the new Union party and made an inspiring appeal for its support.[177] Plans were subsequently made for a state-wide organization and for the usual machinery of party.

On the other hand, the Southern-rights party required no such spectacular manner of organization, as the elimination of the Union Democrats had left to the southern-rights group the majority of the leaders who controlled the old Democratic machine. In the course of the year that followed, the moderate policy of these leaders attracted back into the party some of the Democrats who had failed to support the Southern-rights ticket in the convention election. Hence the Southern-rights party was practically created by the negative process of eliminating the more conservative Union element rather than by the state-wide formation of the southern-rights societies, which had been originally suggested.

The new parties had now been finally formed; the convention had met; and the Union party, which controlled it, had declared for the compromise as a last

[176] For Toomb's speech and the other proceedings of the Union party caucus see Washington *Republic*, December 30, 1850. Toomb's opening words are suggestive of those of Lincoln's famous Gettysburg Address of later years. Toombs began with the declaration: "Sixty-three years ago our fathers joined together to form a more perfect Union, and to establish justice. . . . We have now met to put that government on trial. . . . In my opinion judgment the verdict is such as to give hope to the friends of liberty throughout the world."

[177] Toombs closing words in this great address were tragic ones in the light of his later irreconcilable attitude towards the Union government. "No man", he exclaimed, "rejoices more in the prosperity of his native state than I do, no man can be more jealous of her honor. But I am also an American. I am proud of every battlefield of the Revolution that reflects honor on my country—it is all, all my country! Let us then bind ourselves together and take counsel how we may best preserve our rights and the integrity of the Republic, now and forever!"

concession. Now that Georgia had taken official action, what response would that action meet with throughout the nation?

The chief significance of the convention, so far as Georgia itself was concerned, lay not only in the decision against disunion, but in the formal organization of the Union party. Two distinct reactions were to be noted in the southern-rights press of the state, the one from the moderate and the other from the more extreme papers. The moderate journals immediately accepted the "Platform" adopted. This was easy for them to do, because, as the *Federal Union* had early pointed out, the Union men had come to take a stronger stand against the North than had been anticipated.[178] The difference between the secessionist position and that of the Georgia Platform was only that the first meant secession at once; the second, secession upon the next serious provocation. This meant a vital difference in immediate action, but little variation in principle. The reaction of the *Georgian* was typical, when it declared it would accept the new Platform, but that all its pledges must be sacredly observed.[179]

The few out and out secessionist papers condemned the Georgia Platform. The Macon *Telegraph* declared it had "no spirit—it is too prudent to mean anything. A more objectionable paper was never written in Georgia."[180] "Georgia has backed down from her lofty resolves," observed the Columbus *Times*.[181] These same papers also sneered at the convention as having met only to form a Union party—a "Whiggery in disguise" that would provide offices for its leaders. Simi-

---

[178] *Federal Union*, November 12, 1850.
[179] *Savannah Georgian*, December 23, 1850.
[180] Macon *Telegraph*, in Savannah *News*, December 19, 1850.
[181] Columbus *Times*, in Charleston *Mercury*, February 27, 1851.

lar reactions obtained in the more extreme papers of the sister states.

The Union press in Georgia, of course, praised enthusiastically all three phases of the convention's work; first, the repudiation of disunion and the Georgia extremists; second, the warning to the North and the antislavery extremists; and, third, the foundation of a state Union party to carry on these excellent policies.[182]

The reaction in the Union press throughout the rest of the South was also an enthusiastic one. It was the general opinion that the "Georgia Platform" afforded the South a safe position between the "Ultraists" on the one hand and the abolitionists on the other —one upon which all conservative patriots, North and South, could unite to preserve the Union. The unanimity of these opinions was impressive.[183]

This reaction throughout the South led many observers to the conviction that the South would now unite on the Georgia Platform, and that to Georgia, therefore, belonged the credit for having saved the Union. The Union men of Georgia were sure of this. "Georgia was the first state that would accept or reject the Compromise," wrote Colonel John Milledge, of Augusta. "The eyes of the world were upon her, but calm and inflexible she came forth in the midst of unparalleled excitement, holding in her hands the destiny of this Empire. . . . Her voice was for peace and the Union. *She joined it in 1776 and she saved it in 1850.*"[184] Commenting on the state's geographical

[182] For typical praise see the *Chronicle,* December 15, 1850.

[183] See, *e.g..* Mobile *Daily Advertiser,* December 20; Richmond *Enquirer,* December 13, 24; Jackson *Flag of the Union,* December 27; Natchez *Courier,* January 14, 31, 1851; New Orleans *Picayune,* December 16, 1850; etc.

[184] John Milledge to the Committee, February 20, 1851, *Macon Union Celebration,* p. 20.

position, Washington Poe of Macon observed that:

Georgia was the connecting link between South Carolina and Alabama, so that a fire kindled in South Carolina would have spread to Alabama and Mississippi. But the Georgia State Convention stands firm. May not Georgia henceforth be termed the preserver of the Union?[185]

In the North, the press was convinced that the Georgia Platform was being accepted all over the South and that this meant the Union was to be preserved. The Philadelphia *Pennsylvanian* declared the Platform was "splendid,—a rallying ground for all friends of the Union."[186] "We have never hailed a victory with more satisfaction," exclaimed the New York *Express* of the Georgia Convention elections, "the Georgia victory, together with the Northern Union movement and the Texan acceptance of the Congressional proposal, show the Union is probably saved."[187] "The principles of the Platform," observed the New York *Tribune*, "are held throughout the South with great unanimity."[188]

Prominent political leaders at Washington were also of the opinion that the Georgia Platform would unite the South and save the Union. Senator Dawson wrote from Washington: "Her [Georgia's] Platform, as it has been called, will command the support of the majority of the people in the Union; . . . by it harmony has been in a great measure restored."[189] James Brooks, congressman from New York, wrote to the Georgia conservatives:

[185] *Ibid.*, p. 40.

[186] Philadelphia *Pennsylvanian*, in Washington *Union*, December 28, 1850.

[187] New York *Express*, in the Savannah *News*, December 4, 1850.

[188] New York *Tribune*, December 6, 1850. (Referring to the "Chatham Platform").

[189] W. C. Dawson to the Committee, February 17, 1851; *Macon Union Celebration*, pp. 8, 9.

I look upon your stand, considering the crisis, as the most important ever taken in the country, for while you resisted and overwhelmed disunion, you also marked out the true chart of the Union. Had Georgia taken the lead that was proffered I should have despaired of shutting the flood-gates of passion that were sure to open.[190]

Indeed, all the conservative leaders at the capital were greatly relieved and encouraged by Georgia's stand. "The name of Georgia is in everybody's mouth," wrote the correspondent of the Savannah *Republican*, "all praise the industry and patriotism that have placed her in her present proud position.[191] General Cass can scarcely talk of anything else. It is believed that Georgia has fought and won the battle at the South if the friends of the Union will only follow up her victory."[192] Probably the most interesting testimony to this effect, finally, was that given by the Great Compromiser himself. Writing to the Macon Union meeting during the following February, Henry Clay declared:

When the calm judgment of the people was to be passed upon the Compromise all eyes were turned to Georgia, and all hearts palpitated with intense anxiety as to her decision. Ultraism had concentrated its treasonable hopes upon that decision. I never doubted it. . . . I knew many of the prominent citizens and . . . their devotion to the Union. . . . At length Georgia announced her deliberate judgment. . . . It diffused inexpressible joy among the friends of the Union throughout the land. It crushed the spirit of discord, disunion and Civil War.[193]

[190] James Brooks, February 17, 1851, quoted in the Savannah *Republican*, March 7, 1851.

[191] The tendency to couple references to Georgia's "prosperity" with references to her "patriotism" is suggestive.

[192] *Republican*, January 3, 1851.

[193] Henry Clay, February 13, 1851, to the Committee, *Macon Union Celebration*, p. 3.

Such opinions suggest that the Union victory in Georgia was a prime factor in the preservation of the Union in 1850. This becomes clearer, when it is recalled that the decision of Georgia left but two states likely to secede, South Carolina and Mississippi. It was highly improbable that any combination of these twain could become effective so long as conservative Georgia and Alabama lay between. The secessionists thought at one time, as was pointed out in connection with Seabrook's correspondence, that if South Carolina only started, Georgia would follow. That illusion was well dissipated by December, 1850. The attitude of the conservatives in Georgia toward an independent secession movement in South Carolina was not to be mistaken. "If South Carolina secedes," declared the Macon *Journal*, "we must stand by the Union. . . . If a conflict of arms comes . . . we owe no allegiance to South Carolina but we do to the Union. It would be treasonable even for individuals to cooperate with South Carolina."[194]

Georgia was fairly credited, then, with having done much to save the Union. It was also credited with having done much to unite the South. There were some capable observers who believed this to be the case months and even years after the opinions already quoted had been expressed. Thus Bishop Capers, of the Methodist Church in South Carolina, warned that state in 1851 that the Georgia Platform voiced the opinion of the South.[195] No less an "Ultraist" than Yancey, of Alabama, expressed five years later the opinion that the South became almost united upon the

[194] Macon *Journal*, in Boston *Courier*, December 18, 1851. The fear that this would be the Georgia attitude was expressed in the South Carolina legislature that was deciding that state's final position.
[195] Columbia *South Carolinian*, March 7, 1851.

Georgia Platform, once the extremists had failed to carry immediate secession.[196] Within Georgia itself, as will be seen, many of the southern-rights group accepted it and considered themselves as well as the North to be bound by its principles. Not only did Cobb, the Union party governor from 1851 to 1853, hold to the Platform, but Herschel V. Johnson, Democratic governor from 1853 to 1857, continued to consider himself bound by it as late as 1860.[197]

Any evaluation of the influence exerted by the Georgia Platform in uniting the South must, of course, consider two facts limiting its significance. In the first place, the principles it embodied can hardly be said to have been peculiar to Georgia in 1850. To some extent, at least, the Platform simply expressed, rather than determined, feeling in the lower South. In the second place, the degree of unity achieved upon this Platform was limited by the fact that the sectional issue might eventually take forms which those who built the Platform did not and, indeed, could not anticipate. In case such unforeseen contingencies arose, southerners who agreed upon the Georgia resolutions might well disagree upon new problems.

Yet those who felt that the Platform had "unified" the South were probably correct in a measure. The very fact that it did give forceful expression to the half-formed convictions of many southern people, and the spectacular circumstances attending the formation of the Platform, were both calculated to exert some in-

---

[196] W. L. Yancey to W. H. Worthington, June 23, 1855, quoted in DuBose, *Yancey*, p. 295.

[197] Johnson, although he had been a leader of the state-rights element in the Georgia Democracy in 1849, held as late as 1860 that the state was "bound" by the Georgia Platform; see "From the Autobiography of Hershel V. Johnson," *American Historical Review*, XXX. 314, 318. The portions of this autobiography relating to the years prior to 1856 are, unfortunately, not yet available for examination.

fluence upon southern opinion. That there were contingencies in the future which the Platform could not be framed to meet, moreover, did not entirely divest of significance the fact that there were a number of specific contingencies for which it did provide. To the extent that the South accepted the Georgia Platform, it was united in proclaiming to the North that there were at least four specific acts which must not be attempted if the Union were to be preserved. These acts were the ones which the South most feared in 1850 would mark any further northern "encroachments" upon "southern rights." The measure of the influence of the Platform in the South was thus the measure of a defensive unity against such specific dangers as were then apprehended.[198]

The Georgia Union victory had done much to check the extremists of South Carolina. It had done something to unify the South against the extremists of the North. In the one way, as in the other, it played an important part in saving the Union of the states. There was some truth in Colonel Milledge's heroic declaration: *"She joined it in 1776 and she saved it in 1850."*

[198] *Cf.* C. S. Boucher, *"In Re* That Aggressive Slavocracy," *Mississippi Valley Historical Review,* VIII. 58, 59.

CHAPTER VIII

THE AFTERMATH, 1851-1852

The advent of the year 1851 found the political situation in Georgia unique in every respect but one; namely, that the new party alignments were as usual more or less unstable. The decision of the people to stand by the Union had apparently been proclaimed beyond question, but it was by no means certain just what turn political developments would take. To all appearances the party which had suffered the most as the result of the sectional storm was the Democratic, which had lost at least half its potential vote in the elections for the state convention; while the Whigs not only held to the new Union party most of their own vote, but had added to it a goodly share of that which normally belonged to their opponents. There was some poetic justice in this situation, to be sure, in view of the fact that the Democratic leaders had been the prime movers in demanding new party formations and had doubtless intended that the realignment should redound to their own advantage, in case it did not actually carry the state out of the Union. In a word, those Democratic leaders who had not so completely dedicated themselves to "secession *per se*" as to be truly above party had hoped that the Democracy, under the guise of "southern-rights," would swallow Whiggery. The actual outcome, however, had been that Whiggery, under the guise of the Union party, had nearly swallowed the Democracy.

The obvious remedy for this was for the latter to withdraw from the position which had so weakened it.

The Georgia people were evidently opposed to secession and just as evidently in favor of the Georgia Platform. Democratic editors, therefore, hastened during the winter that followed the state convention to deny that the southern-rights group ever had favored secession.[1] In addition to this, they promptly accepted the Platform as the will of the people—an acceptance which could be granted with a good countenance in view of the "southern spirit" of its resolutions.[2] Having accepted the convention resolutions and vehemently denied any intention to urge secession, the southern-rights Democrats next declared that, in view of these moves, there was no *raison d'etre* for a Union party in the state. Why a party in favor of the Union when no one was against it? They consequently invited all Union Democrats to return to the party fold. As the year progressed some of the editors even dropped the party appellation of "Southern-rights" and reassumed that of "Democratic."[3] This move was doubtless hastened by a desire to maintain contacts with the conservative northern Democracy.

The small group of out-and-out secessionists within the Georgia Democracy was, to be sure, disinclined to reëstablish the old party name and organization. The events of the fall could not change their conviction that the struggle between the sections was inevitable and that the sooner the South organized to meet it the better. "As was to have been expected," observed the Columbus *Sentinel,* "the storm which has just passed over our state has been succeeded by a calm. It is the calm of preparation, and not of peace; a cessation, not an end of the controversy. The recent election deter-

---

[1] *Federal Union,* January 14, 21, 1851.
[2] *Federal Union,* February 4; April 1, 1851.
[3] See, *e.g.,* Savannah *News,* December 3, 1850.

mines only a question of time. . . . The elements of that controversy are yet alive and they are destined yet to outlive the government. There is a feud between the North and the South which may be smothered, but never overcome."[4]

It was to such sentiments that the Whigs pointed when the Democrats inquired their reasons for maintaining the Union party. The small but active group of secessionists had not been converted by the fall elections, declared the Union men, but had been merely driven under cover; and some organization of the conservatives was necessary to keep them there. There was some truth in this declaration, and there is no question that it was made in all sincerity by the Union rank and file.[5]

On the other hand, it is to be remembered that the Georgia Whig leaders had no such hope of maintaining old contacts with the northern wing of their party as had the Georgia Democrats, and that it was therefore to Whig interests to maintain the new and popular Union party rather than to revert to the now impossible Whig organization. This situation lent at least some truth to the Democratic indictment of the Union party as "a mere Whiggery in disguise."[6]

The Union Democrats, meanwhile, were no more in a mood to reassume old party lines than were the Whigs. They distrusted the Southern-rights group for the same reasons as did the Whigs and were indeed inclined to feel more strongly in this matter than were

[4] Columbus *Sentinel* in the Charleston *Mercury*, January 23, 1851.

[5] For a typical statement of the Union position see Savannah *Republican*, January 6, 1851. See also Columbus *Enquirer* in the *Republican*, April 17, 1851.

[6] When the Macon *Journal* boasted that the Georgia Union party had the approval of the Fillmore administration, the *Federal Union* replied (February 11, 1851) that this proved that said party was simply the old Whig organization.

the latter. The years of intra-party strife which had preceded the final break in Democratic ranks had not inclined the conservative element to a hasty reconciliation, once the separation had been accomplished.[7] The Union Democrats had no intention of allowing their separation from the rest of the state party to cut them off from the national body. They naturally had to consider, however, the possibility of finding some national affiliation which would be acceptable to their new associates within the state. The obvious solution to this difficulty seemed to lie in the formation of a national Union party, which the conservative northern Democrats could join simultaneously with conservative Whigs and southern Democrats. The large Whig element in the Georgia Union party was more than willing to work for such a national organization because of that impossibility of a reunion with northern Whiggery, which has already been mentioned. There was much talk early in the winter of 1851, therefore, of the formation of a great national Union party.[8] This move received some support from northern conservatives, who still feared the danger of secession and civil war.[9]

As the months passed, however, it became apparent that the Union Democrats of Georgia were less interested in the projected national Union party than they were in preserving their old contacts with the safe northern Democracy. While Toombs and Stephens, for instance, were working in Congress for the formation of the new party, Cobb took the position that if both the old parties could be dominated by conserva-

[7] Athens *Banner,* in the Savannah *Republican,* March 13, 1851.
[8] See, *e.g.,* Macon *Journal,* in the *Chronicle,* December 28, 1850.
[9] See R. F. Nichols, *The Democratic Machine, 1850-1854,* pp. 26, 27.

tives, there was no necessity for a third organization.[10]
The lack of interest displayed by conservative
Democrats of both sections in the proposed national
coalition party was an important factor in the failure
of the southern Whigs, led in Congress by Clay,
Toombs, Stephens, and Foote, to establish a successful
organization. The Georgia Whigs greatly regretted
this failure, ostensibly and perhaps sincerely because
they feared the reversal to the old parties would mean
the reappearance of sectional strife.[11] It is no doubt
fair to assume, however, that their regret was also due
in no small measure to the failure of the proposed organization to afford them a place of safe national attachment.

This situation, while most embarrasing to the Georgia Whigs, was not without its difficulties for the
Union Democrats. They, to be sure, could trust the
northern wing of their party, but would that wing
trust them? In a word, if the national Democracy was
sufficiently conservative to be maintained, which faction of the old Georgia Democracy would this national
organization recognize as comprising the legitimate
state party? The Southern-rights party was certain
to claim exclusive legitimacy, basing its claim on the
undeniable fact that it possessed the majority of the
members of the old state organization. This claim was
bound to receive sympathetic consideration in some
quarters. Indeed, the winter had barely begun before
efforts were being made in the inner circles of the
national Democracy to reinstate the southern-rights
element throughout the South to full fellowship.[12]

[10] Cf., e.g., the letters of Cobb and Toombs in the Macon Union Celebration, pp. 6, 7.
[11] Savannah Republican, January 16, 1851.
[12] For an interesting letter illustrating this effort, see Duff Green to
L. S. Coryell, November 21, 1850, Coryell MSS.

The Georgia Union Democrats accordingly prepared to combat this claim of their local enemies to national recognition and to remind the party chieftains that it was but a few months since that the Southern-rights group in Georgia had urged the abandonment of both the old parties. The conservative Democrats, they claimed, were the only real Democrats.[13]

Such was the general party situation in Georgia during the winter of 1851. The Union and Southern-rights parties[14] were evidently organized to meet the exigencies of the state and sectional situation and just as obviously were not adapted to the national situation, once the conservative Whigs and Democrats had failed to expand their state organization into a national Union coalition. It was inevitable, therefore, that the state parties born of the 1850 struggle should be short-lived, their decease being certain as soon as the pressure of national political interests became greater than that of the local.

It happened, however, that no national campaign was due in 1851. This left the infant state parties this one year, during which the election of the governor and legislature were again in order, and when, therefore, state issues would be emphasized and the parties based thereon temporarily preserved.

The refusal of the Union Democrats to accept immediately the invitation for reunion extended by the southern-rights element was the first sign that the new parties were to persist throughout the year. The

[13] R. D. Arnold to J. W. Forney, June 17, 1851, Arnold MSS.

[14] These relatively simple names will be used here as a matter of convenience. As a matter of fact the formal names employed by the two organizations were confusingly (and deliberately) similar, made so by respective efforts to steal the thunder of one another's slogans. The Union party, *e.g.*, referred to itself at times as the "Union and Southern Rights Party," see Savannah *News,* December 3, 1850. Its more commonly used name was the "Constitutional Union" party.

second was to be observed in the determination of the Whig element in the state Union party to maintain that organization, despite the failure to connect it with a similar national machine. The two conservative groups openly proclaimed their intention to "carry on" for the Union at an elaborate affair held at Macon on Washington's birthday. This "Macon Union Celebration" proved a happy love-feast for the new allies. Many able Georgia men attended, and the national leaders who could not be present supplemented the speeches of the day with elaborate letters which were read to those assembled.[15] Perhaps the most significant of the numerous toasts drunk upon this exhilarating occasion was that which declared in the following words the new coalition's attitude toward the old parties:

> *The Old Parties:* The hot-beds in which are grown Abolitionists in the North and Ultraism in the South. It is vain for a rational people to quarrel about Whiggery and Democracy when they are in danger of having no government to which to apply their favorite theories.[16]

The southern-rights Democrats having failed to break up the Union coalition,[17] it was necessary for

---

[15] See *Union Celebration in Macon, Georgia, on the Anniversary of Washington's Birthday, February 22, 1851,* (herein cited as *Macon Union Celebration*), *passim.* See also U. B. Phillips, *Robert Toombs,* p. 100. The southern-rights press declared the meeting "a miserable failure"; *Federal Union,* February 25, 1851.

[16] Other typical toasts were the following: *"The Union Party of Georgia:* It has blotted out all party distinctions"; *"Robert Toombs, Howell Cobb and Alexander Stephens, the rising statesmen of the South:* A noble triumvirate of talent and true chivalry," etc. Not the least interesting was one which called attention to the importance of Georgia's economic position in connection with the general political controversy: *"Georgia, the Empire State of the South:* Her railroads and manufactures speak to the northern states in arguments . . . louder than the cannon's roar."

[17] The only exception to this statement is to be found in the fact that the Democrats did poll nearly their normal vote, running under their old name, in certain local elections, as *e.g.,* in that held in Savannah, December 2, 1850. See *Savannah News,* December 3, 1850.

both these groups to hold state conventions early in the summer of 1851 in order to nominate a ticket and to formulate a platform for the coming state campaign. The Southern-rights conclave assembled on May 28, and was naturally made up largely of Democrats. The little group of old state-rights Whigs was quite active, however, and James M. Smythe, their leader, served as president of the meeting.[18] State-rights resolutions were passed, but proved on the whole to be of a generally moderate character. The most significant resolution adopted was one proclaiming the "sovereign" (*i.e.*, the constitutional) right of a state to secede from the Union, when its people were acting in their "sovereign capacity." No desire to exercise this right in the immediate future, however, was expressed. Charles J. McDonald, sometime fire-eating president of the second session of the Nashville Convention, was nominated for the governorship without serious opposition.[19]

The resolutions adopted clearly indicated that the party's strategy would be characterized by a return to the policies of 1849. These policies had been successful in the latter year for the reason that they had featured the appeal for southern-rights—which proved a popular one—at the same time that they avoided the appeal for immediate secession—which proved in 1850 to be an unpopular one. The resolution declaring the merely abstract constitutional right of secession afforded an especially good illustration of this return to old policies, for it was one which would appeal to the people's southern sentiment and which at the same time would not offend their love of the Union. This self-

---

[18] Berrien, the other leader of this old Whig group, "accepted" the Georgia Platform, but refrained from active coöperation with the Union party.

[19] Savannah *Georgian*, May 30, 31; *Federal Union*, June 3, 1851.

same abstract right had indeed been urged by the southern-rights Democrats in 1849 to the embarrassment of the Whigs, who were inclined to deny it, but who feared popular disapproval for so doing. The extremists now revived it in 1851 with hopes of even greater success, since the Union Democrats were likely to disagree in this matter with the Whigs; and it was hoped that the allies could be split upon the issue.[20]

The Union party, meeting in convention early in June, was immediately confronted by this question of the right of secession. Some of the Union Democrats were inclined to defend the abstract "sovereign right," while most of the Whigs denied it and took the view that, if there were any "right," it was a revolutionary rather than a constitutional one. The convention at once realized that here was a divergence of opinion which could only redound to the advantage of the enemy, and, as a consequence, the subject was avoided in the resolutions adopted for the campaign. These declared that the Southern-rights party was still at heart a secession party which, having been defeated in the open, was continuing by divers and underhand methods to seek its disloyal ends. The fight to save the Union must be maintained. To lead this fight the convention then nominated Howell Cobb for the governorship.[21]

Both gubernatorial candidates issued formal letters of acceptance, which in each case anticipated the gen-

[20] The Southern-rights party also had other schemes for dividing the allies, e.g., they demanded that the Union convention declare its principles on the bank, the tariff, etc.—points upon which Whigs and Union Democrats would certainly have disagreed. The Union party press, however, would not walk into so obvious a trap. The reply was given that all such matters were now dead issues. Cf. the Savannah Georgian, June 18, with the Republican, June 19, 1851.

[21] Republican, June 10; Federal Union, June 10, 1851; Toombs to Howell Cobb, June 9, 1851, "Cobb Papers," Georgia Historical Quarterly, V. No. 3, pp. 45, 46.

eral positions that their parties were to take during
the summer campaign. Cobb emphasized the achieve-
ments of the Georgia Platform, but did not declare himself definitely upon the delicate subject of the right of
secession.[22] McDonald condemned the Clay compromise and specifically upheld the "sovereign right" of
secession. He did not make it clear that he approved
the Georgia Platform, though most of his party's journals had done so.[23]

Most of the essential features of the campaign that
followed have already been suggested. The Southern-
rights party exploited their advantage upon the right
of secession issue, profiting by their experience of
1849 and by the inability of the Union party allies to
agree upon the matter. Cobb, as spokesman for the
conservatives, was forced to straddle both views of
the nature of the right, and, while his utterances upon
the subject were marvels of sophistical ingenuity, they
were not entirely convincing.[24] The Union men, for
their part, continued their old appeal to "save the
Union," profiting by their experience of the preceding
year and practically repeating each argument which
they had urged at that time.[25] Thus the campaign
tactics of 1849, which had brought victory to the ex-

[22] *Republican,* June 30, 1851.

[23] *Federal Union,* June 17, 1851. The Clay compromise was never
approved by the Southern-rights group, even though they had usually
accepted the Georgia Platform which was itself an acceptance of the
compromise. The Savannah *Georgian, e.g.,* declared (June 7, 1851) that
the compromise was the "most outrageous wrong ever perpetrated in
legislation." *Cf.* Arnold to Forney, September 19, 1851, Arnold MSS.

[24] For Southern-rights ridicule of Cobb's inconsistencies see *Federal
Union,* July 8, August 19; *Georgian,* August 21, 1851. For his defence
see *Republican,* July 25, August 6, 1851. For constitutional arguments
pro and *con,* consult A. C. Cole, "The South and the Right of Secession," *Mississippi Valley Historical Review,* I. 388, ff. See also R. P.
Brooks, "Howell Cobb and the Crisis of 1850," *ibid.,* I. 291, ff.

[25] See, *e.g.,* issues of the *Chronicle* and *Republican* for July and August, 1851.

tremists, were pitted against the tactics of 1850, which had brought triumph to the conservatives.

McDonald, as spokesman for the radicals, was handicapped by his record as a secessionist leader in the Nashville convention sessions. This record was somewhat inconsistent with the fact that his party's editors were now denying that the southern-rights movement had ever been a secession movement. Here was a situation of which the Union men hastened to take advantage. Whenever their enemies embarrassed Cobb by asking what he *believed* with regard to the right of secession, the conservatives rejoined by asking McDonald what he desired to *do* about secession. The one question was almost as embarrassing, under the circumstances, as the other.[26]

The campaign was one of sound and fury. Toombs and Stephens, who had given their chief interest in Congress during the winter to the unsuccessful effort to organize a national Union party, returned during the summer to lend their support to Cobb in the state struggle. Stephens was kept out by illness, but Toombs outdid himself, filling both his own and some of Stephens' engagements. "Wherever the fire-eaters have a chance," he wrote, "they fight like the devil— though we shall whip them out all over the state."[27] Feeling was increased because southern-rights Democrats felt rather bitterly towards the Union Democrats as "deserters," while the mass of the Whigs felt similarly towards the old southern-rights wing of their party.[28]

[26] See *e.g.*, Athens *Banner* in Savannah *Republican*, July 1, 1851. The *Federal Union* denied that McDonald "had ever desired secession *now*."
[27] Toombs to General Eli Warren, August 19, 1851; letter in possession of Mr. Warren Grice, of Macon.
[28] R. D. Arnold to J. E. Ward, Savannah, September 1, 1851, Arnold MSS.

Throughout the year conservatives continued to point to the economic prosperity enjoyed within the Union as a cogent reason for maintaining that Union.[29] This economic appeal, in addition to the more sentimental arguments for preserving the old government, proved effective in maintaining the alliance of the conservatives, despite Cobb's difficulties in the constitutional debate. The preservation of the alliance, in turn, made inevitable a Union victory in the fall, for it meant that the Southern-rights party would remain but a part of the old Democratic machine. It also meant that the real issue of the campaign remained the Union issue, despite the efforts of the extremists to avoid it and to substitute for it that of the right of secession.

The state election was held early in October, 1851, and resulted in an overwhelming Union victory. Cobb carried all but twenty-one of the ninety-five counties in the state and had a majority in the popular vote of about eighteen thousand. His party also secured an unprecedented majority in the legislature and elected six out of the eight congressmen.[30] The county results indicated that as a rule only such counties in Central and Lower Georgia as habitually went Democratic had supported McDonald.[31] He received practically no support in any of the other sections of the state.

[29] See e.g., Dr. Robert Collins (of Macon) to the Committee, February 22, 1851, *Macon Union Celebration*, p. 44; Columbus *Times*, in Charleston *Mercury*, February 27, 1851. The Milledgeville *Southern Recorder* declared in September that Georgia's prosperity demanded the cessation of all agitation. See Savannah *Republican*, September 25, 1851.

[30] *Federal Union*, October 14; *Republican*, October 16, 1851.

[31] *Cf*. Maps nos. 5 and 7, pp. 109, 320, showing elections of 1848 and 1850, with map of election of 1851 given in Cole, *Whig Party in the South*.

Generally similar results obtained in the state elections held at about the same time in Alabama and Mississippi. In the former state the Union group, led by Hilliard, won a definite victory in the congressional election over the Southern-rights party led by the redoubtable Yancey.[32] In Mississippi, where the governor had duplicated Towns' procedure in summoning a state convention, the elections to this body were held in 1851 and resulted in a Union party victory, much as had the analogous election in Georgia during the preceding fall. As a result of all these circumstances, the state convention which met in South Carolina in the spring of 1852—the last of the state conventions called in the South to consider secession—decided that the Palmetto State would have to remain in the Union as a matter of expediency.[33]

The Union victories in Georgia and the Gulf states were therefore hailed by conservative papers throughout the country as final evidence that the Union was saved. This verdict was also accepted by the more moderate of the southern-rights papers, although some of these expressed both regret and bitterness at the undeniably decisive character of their defeat.[34] "The last two elections in Georgia," observed the *Federal Union*, "have twice definitely settled all practical questions in reference to the Compromise measures. . . . The South has pretty plainly shown that she will not secede from the Union."[35]

The fact that the election of 1851 finally confirmed the Union victory of 1850 did not mean, however, that

[32] G. F. Mellen, "Henry W. Hilliard and W. L. Yancey," *Sewanee Review*, XVII. 32-50.
[33] *Federal Union*, May 18, 1852.
[34] Mobile *Register*, in Mobile *Advertiser*, October 14, 1851.
[35] *Federal Union*, October 21, 1851.

the efforts of McDonald's supporters had been made
entirely in vain. They had at least continued the education of the Georgia people upon the various problems involved in the sectional controversy—a process
which they had now carried on for several years, and
which was to show results in the not very distant
future. Indeed, it is quite possible that they were successful in persuading a large part of the state's population of the truth of their chief contention; that is,
that the state had a legal right to secede if it so desired.
The Union leaders had not succeeded in defeating this
contention, they had only succeeded in subordinating it
to their own more practical demand; namely, that the
Union must be maintained at the time. In a word, the
extremists, in the process of losing the election of 1851,
had prepared the way for victory in 1861.

The very finality of the Union victory in the state,
moreover, foreordained the disintegration of the Union
party. As the *Federal Union* observed, no one could
believe that any large body of citizens still desired
immediate secession, and, if there was no such group
opposed to the Union, there was no longer any *raison
d'etre* for a party whose prime purpose had been to
defend it. Democratic editors therefore resumed in
1852, with an even greater gusto than they had displayed the preceding year, the invitation to the Union
Democrats to return to the old organization. This desire to reëstablish a unified state ,Democracy actually
led the southern-rights editors to emphasize their acceptance of the Georgia Platform and to decry any
further agitation of the sectional issue.[36]

This attitude immediately alarmed the Whigs of
the Union party, who feared that the return of their

[36] *Federal Union,* December 16, 1851.

Union Democratic associates to the old allegiance would leave Georgia Whiggery isolated, without party allies either in the North or in the state itself. It seemed a cruel irony of fate that, the agitation of the slavery issue having alienated the Whigs from their northern associates, the subsidence of that very agitation should now alienate them from their state associates. Whig editors, therefore, found themselves tempted to assume an attitude exactly the reverse of that which they had maintained for two years; that is, they actually began a mild agitation of the slavery issue. This seemed the only way in which to maintain that state of alarm among Union Democrats which would insure their continued allegiance to the conservative coalition. Southern-rights editors countered by reversing their attitude in turn. When the Milledgeville *Recorder,* for instance, displayed alarm over the discussions of slavery that arose in Congress in December, 1851, the *Federal Union* scoffed at its fears, held that all was well, and declared that the Whigs were simply agitating in order to remain in power.[37] Once again, at the call of party expediency, the state parties had reversed their fundamental attitudes towards the whole sectional controversy.

Meanwhile, 1852 was to be a presidential year, and here again fate favored the apparently defeated Democrats. The state parties must now adjust themselves to the national situation—an adjustment that had only been put off temporarily in 1851, and which, for reasons that have already been noted, was bound to redound to the benefit of the Democracy. There was only one national party which Georgians of any party could afford to support, and that was the Democratic.

[37] *Federal Union,* December 16, 23, 1851.

Northern Whiggery was "unsound" on the all-important slavery issue, and no national Union party had ever been organized. Both the Georgia Whigs and Union Democrats must choose between supporting the national Democracy and throwing their votes away upon some improvised and hopeless third-party ticket. The Union Democrats were not likely to abandon the national Democracy, in view of their persistent claim to recognition as the legitimate state branch of the party. It remained to be seen whether the Whigs would go with them into the Democracy, or whether they would prefer even isolation to such political apostasy.

The Whigs and Union Democrats had coöperated in the state legislature of 1851-52, the latter even sitting on the same side of the chambers with their associates.[38] They had combined with the Whigs to defeat the candidacy of Berrien for reëlection to the national Senate[39] and to grant that honor to Toombs.[40] As the winter waned, however, and the question of national presidential nominations loomed on the political horizon, it became increasingly difficult to maintain this coöperation.

The Union Democrats insisted upon sending delegates to the coming Democratic convention at Baltimore, for to abstain from representation therein would have simply meant the surrender of their claims to national recognition. There was talk of persuading the Whigs to join with them in sending a general Union party delegation, and some Whigs encouraged

[38] *Federal Union*, January 27, 1852.
[39] Berrien, after denying his candidacy, later indicated that he would accept re-election. His age, and his alienation from his party in 1850 and 1851, combined at this point to terminate his career.
[40] See Phillips, *Robert Toombs*, p. 105.

the suggestion. The Macon *Journal,* for instance, admitted that there was not much further need for a Union party in the state and advocated that its members affiliate with the Democracy and be represented at Baltimore.[41] This may be viewed as one of the first steps in the process that was to carry most of the Whigs over into the other party before the end of the decade.

It was a premature step, however, so far as most of the Whigs were concerned in 1852. The Union party met in state convention on April 22 and was promptly involved in a controversy between the Union Democrats, who wished to send a delegation to Baltimore, and the Whigs, who opposed such action. The debate ended in deadlock, whereupon the Union Democrats—nicknamed the "Tugalo Democrats" from the Tugalo river region in Upper Georgia—independently chose their own delegation to Baltimore. A small group of conservative Whigs then met at Milledgeville on June 7 and elected a delegation to the Whig national convention.

The southern-rights Democrats had, meanwhile, met in convention on March 31 and had duly chosen a delegation to the Democratic convention. When that body assembled, both this delegation and that selected by the Tugalo faction arrived to claim recognition as the legitimate representatives of Georgia. Neither group could be ignored, since the Tugalo element had strong support among the northern conservatives, who felt that it had been loyal to the national party when the southern-rights group had bolted in 1850;[42] while

[41] Macon *Journal,* January 14, 1852; cf. *Federal Union,* January 20, 1852.
[42] Cobb's influence at Washington had helped to retain the support of the Washington *Union* for the Union Democrats; and Arnold had used

the latter could not be snubbed in view of the simple fact that it now included nearly three fourths of the Democratic voters in the state.[43]   The convention solved this seeming dilemma by the simple expedient of admitting both delegations.   Spokesmen for both the state factions approved this action, and cheers greeted the apparent reconciliation within the Georgia Democracy.[44]   The convention nominated Franklin Pierce as a candidate who was sufficiently safe and sane to appeal to both sections.

Throughout the summer, however, both the Whigs and Union Democrats in Georgia showed signs of a lingering attachment to the fast disintegrating Union party organization.   When the state's southern-rights delegates at Baltimore, for instance, invited the Tugaloes to join with them in calling a general Pierce ratification meeting in Georgia, the latter declined, evidently in the hope that they could still persuade the Whigs to go with them in an independent support of the same candidate.

Meanwhile, the Whig national convention nominated General Scott, who was considered entirely "unsafe" by many of the Georgia members of the party.   The fact that this convention, like the Demo-

his influence with Forney to secure the support of so important a party paper as the Philadelphia *Pennsylvanian*. See Arnold to Forney, September 1, 1851, Arnold MSS.

[43] In the election of 1850 the southern-rights Democrats polled less than half of the normal Democratic vote. The moderation of the Southern-rights leaders in the campaign of 1851, however, attracted back many Democrats who would not vote for them when they had been stamped with the stigma of secessionism. As a result their party polled about three-fifths of the normal Democratic vote in 1851. They claimed by the spring of that year to have the support of three-fourths of the original party, i.e., that the Southern-rights party numbered some thirty-nine thousand voters, and the Tugalo element only thirteen thousand. See *Federal Union*, May 22, 1852.

[44] *Federal Union,* June 15, 1852.

cratic, formally approved the Clay compromise did not reassure such Whigs. While the more conservative Whigs, led by Senator Dawson and supported by such papers as the *Chronicle*,[45] accepted Scott's candidacy, the more radical members, led by Toombs and Stephens, supported a separate ticket headed by Daniel Webster.

This left the Tugaloes in an isolated position, since they had refused to go with the rest of the Democrats for Pierce; and now the Whigs were refusing to go for Pierce with them. In a last effort to hold the Union party together, they called a meeting of the same at Milledgeville on July 15. The Tugaloes comprised a majority of its membership, and, when they attempted to approve the nomination of the Pierce ticket, the Whig delegates bolted. The Tugalo rump was then forced to nominate an independent ticket of Pierce electors. The Union party had finally succumbed to the pressure of national issues, and the executive committee shortly thereafter declared its official dissolution.[46]

When the election was held in the fall, the southern-rights (now claiming to be the "regular") Democratic Pierce electors received 33,843 votes and were elected, while the Tugalo Pierce electors polled only 5733 votes.[47] The Scott ticket, which may be viewed as representing what was left of the "regular" Whig organization, received 15,789 and the Webster ticket 5289 votes. A ticket of the die-hard secessionists, who

[45] *Chronicle*, July 20, 1852.

[46] *Federal Union*, July 13, 20, 1852; Phillips, *Robert Toombs*, pp. 109, 110.

[47] This probably does not represent the normal strength of the Tugaloes, as there was little incentive for this group to vote when there was no possibility of election of their ticket.

had nominated Troup and Quitman, polled only 119 votes. This last was the first vote taken in the state which could be viewed as indicating specifically the number of secessionists, yet it was not a reliable test for the same in view of the fact that some secessionists may have not thought it worth voting under the circumstances.

The subsequent history of the state parties need not be pursued here. When the state election of 1853 was held, the Union Democrats coöperated with the southern-rights group in electing Herschel V. Johnson as governor,[48] and the reunited factions polled the normal party vote. The Whigs, still retaining the now meaningless appellation of the "Union party," also polled a normal vote and were consequently defeated by a narrow margin.[49] The crisis of 1850 was past; the events which led to the greater crisis of 1860 were yet to be.

Within Georgia the lull between the two storms was mistaken by many for the reality of permanent peace and calm. The "Empire State of the South" could now devote itself undisturbed, they felt, to the cultivation of progress and prosperity. Governor Cobb's final executive message, written just before he left office in 1853, was of the most optimistic character —a veritable benediction to a happy people. "The general character of our Federal relations," he declared, "presents a flattering prospect. Since the happy termination of those annoying sectional strifes, which for a time threatened our peace and quiet, the country has returned to a state of calm and repose, and all indica-

[48] There were, of course, some signs of lingering feeling between the two elements, especially of the extremists' dislike for Howell Cobb. See, e.g., W. H. Hull to Cobb, August 16, 1853, *Toombs, Stephens, and Cobb Correspondence*, pp. 334, 335.

[49] Phillips, *Georgia and State Rights*, pp. 168, 169.

tions of the present point to a happy, peaceful and prosperous future."[50] Perhaps, after all, it was well for the Georgia people that they could not know what this future really was to be.

[50] *Message of Governor Howell Cobb to the Legislature, November 8, 1853,* (pamphlet in the De Renne Library collection.)

BIBLIOGRAPHY

I—GUIDES

BROOKS, R. P., *A Preliminary Bibliography to Georgia History*, Athens, Ga., 1910.

FLISCH, JULIA, "Records of Richmond County" (Augusta), *American Historical Association, Annual Report*, 1906, II. 159, ff.

HARDEN, WILLIAM, "Georgia Newspaper Files in the Library of the Georgia Historical Society," *Gulf States Historical Magazine*, I. 348, ff.

HULL, A. E., "Georgia Newspaper Files in the Library of the University of Georgia," *Gulf States Historical Magazine*, I. 205, ff.

JACK, T. H., "Historiography in Georgia," *Georgia Historical Association, Annual Proceedings*, I. 21-31.

JACK, T. H., "Files in the Emory College Library, Oxford, Georgia," *Gulf States Historical Magazine*, II. 194, ff.

KNIGHT, L. L. and COBB, M., "The Condition of Georgia's Archives," *Georgia Historical Association, Annual Proceedings*, I. 32-35 (1917).

KENNEDY, J. C. G., "Catalogue of the Newspapers and Periodicals Published in the United States, 1850." (Included as appendix to John Livingston's *Law Register for 1852*, New York, 1852. Gives lists of papers in each state, with party affiliations and circulation figures.)

MACKALL, L. I.., "The W. J. De Renne Georgia Library," *Georgia Historical Quarterly*, II. 63, ff. (June, 1908.)

OWEN, T. M., "Georgia Newspaper Files in the Carnegie Library, Atlanta," *Gulf States Historical Magazine*, I. 423, ff.

PHILLIPS, U. B., "Public Archives of Georgia," *American Historical Association, Annual Report*, 1903, I. 439, ff.

PHILLIPS, U. B., "Georgia Local Archives," *American Historical Association, Annual Report*, 1904.

"State Histories, Check List of, in the New York Public Library," *New York Public Library Bulletin*, No. 5 (New York, 1901).

WEGLEIN, O., *Materials for Georgia History in the Library of W. J. De Renne*, Savannah, 1911.

II—UNPUBLISHED SOURCES

Unless otherwise noted the manuscripts listed below are in the Library of Congress.

Arnold MSS. A collection of the letter-books of Dr. Richard Arnold of Savannah, containing correspondence from c. 1840 to 1870, in possession of his granddaughter, Miss Margaret Cosens, of Savannah. (Letters from the Savannah Democratic leader, dealing with personal, professional, and political matters. Those of a political nature are valuable here, as they contain periodical analyses of political conditions in the state from the viewpoint of the union Democrats. These were sent by Arnold to his friend Forney, the Pennsylvania Democrat. The letters give especially vivid details of party struggles in Savannah. They contain material for the history of Georgia in the Civil War and Reconstruction periods, but this has not as yet been examined.)

Berrien MSS. A few letters of Senator John McPherson Berrien. (Important for Berrien's political position in 1848-1850.)

Calhoun Papers. Unpublished letters of J. C. Calhoun, in possession of the American Historical Association, preparatory to publication. (Contain c. 15 letters from Georgia extremists to Calhoun, 1847-1850. Important for the connection between Calhoun and the secession movement in Georgia.)

Crittendon MSS. A large collection of 28 volumes of great value for the general history of the Southern Whigs. (Useful here in connection with Toombs and Stephens, though most of this material has been printed in the *Toombs, Stephens, and Cobb Correspondence.* A calendar by C. N. Feamster (1913) makes the manuscripts readily accessible.)

Hammond MSS. (A large collection of the letters of the South Carolina Governor, James H. Hammond, dealing with personal and political matters, slavery, etc.)

Stephens MSS. (About twenty papers of Alex. H. Stephens, including a few Toombs letters.)

Seabrook MSS. (Political letters to and from Governor W. B. Seabrook of South Carolina, 1849-1850. Valuable for the

relationship between South Carolina and the secession movement in Georgia and Mississippi. Contains several letters from
Governor G. W. Towns of Georgia to Seabrook, in 1850, which
are of great importance.)

Georgia Executive Department, Letter Books of: in the
Department of Archives, Atlanta. (Relate largely to routine
matters, but are occasionally suggestive.)

Georgia Executive Department, Minutes of: in Department
of Archives, Atlanta. (Contains executive proclamations.)

III—Contemporary Writings

Brooks, R. P. (Ed.), "The Howell Cobb Papers," *Georgia
Historical Quarterly*, V. Numbers 1, 2 and 3. (March, June,
September, 1921.)

Jameson, F. P. (Ed.), "The Correspondence of John C. Calhoun," *American Historical Association, Annual Report,*
1899, II.

Johnston, R. M. and Browne, W. H., *Life of Alexander H.
Stephens,* Philadelphia, 1878. (Largely a collection of excerpts from Stephens' letters.)

Phillips, U. B. (Ed.), "Toombs, Stephens, and Cobb Correspondence," *American Historical Association, Annual Report,* 1911, II.

Quaife, M. M. (Ed.), *The Diary of James K. Polk,* Chicago,
1910.

Rowland, Dunbar (Ed.), *Jefferson Davis, Constitutionalist:
His Letters, Papers and Speeches,* Jackson, 1923.

IV—Memoirs and Reminiscences

Andrews, Garnett, *Reminiscences of an old Georgia Lawyer,*
Atlanta, 1870.

Avary, M. L., *Recollections of Alexander H. Stephens,* New
York, 1910. (Contains Stephens' letter reviewing his own
career.)

Benton, T. H., *Thirty Years View,* New York, 1854, 1856.

Burke, Emily, *Reminiscences of Georgia,* Oberlin, Ohio, 1850.
(Interesting observations on social and economic life, from
a northern point of view.)

Davis, Mrs. V. H., *Jefferson Davis, A Memoir,* New York,
1890. (Interesting observations on the slavery issue in
1850.)

FELTON, MRS. W. H. (R. L.), *Country Life in Georgia in the Days of My Youth*, Atlanta, 1919.

GIDDINGS, JOSHUA R., *History of the Rebellion*, New York, 1864. (Largely a memoir useful for the abolitionist point of view in 1850.)

KEMBLE, FRANCES A., *Journal of a Residence on a Georgia Plantation in 1838-1839*, New York, 1863.

LUMPKIN, JOSEPH H., "Memoirs," *United States Law Magazine*, July and August, 1851 (Chiefly legal).

MALLARD, R. Q., *Plantation Life Before Emancipation*, Richmond (Va.), 1897. (Accounts of slavery in Georgia.)

PIKE, J. S., *First Blows of the Civil War*, New York, 1879. (Recollections and opinions of a Taylor Whig.)

STEPHENS, A. H., *A Constitutional View of the Late War between the States*, Philadelphia, 1868-70.

SCOT, W. J., *Seventy-One Years in Georgia: An Autobiography*, Atlanta, 1897.

WYLIE, L. B., *Memoirs of Richard H. Clark*, Atlanta, 1898. (Relates chiefly to Savannah.)

V—BIOGRAPHY

AMES, H. V., "Calhoun and the Secession Movement of 1850," *University of Pennsylvania, Public Lectures*, 1917-1918. (An excellent brief account of Calhoun's leadership.)

BOYKIN, SAMUEL, *A Memorial Volume of Howell Cobb*, Philadelphia, 1870. (Brief biography, eulogistic and unsatisfactory.)

CANDLER, A. D. and EVANS, C. A., *Cyclopedia of Georgia*, Atlanta, 1907. (Contains laudatory biographical sketches.)

CHAPPELL, A. H., *Miscellanies of Georgia*, Atlanta (Ga.), 1874. (Miscellaneous collection of biographical and historical sketches.)

CLEVELAND, H., *Alexander H. Stephens*, Philadelphia, 1866.

FIELDER, HERBERT, *Life and Times and Speeches of Joseph E. Brown*, Springfield (Mass.), 1883. (Contains interesting comments on Georgia politicians.)

GILMER, G. R., *Sketches of Some of the First Settlers of Upper Georgia*, New York, 1855.

HARDEN, E. J., *The Life of George M. Troup*, Savannah, 1859.

HOLSEY, HOPKINS, "George W. Towns," in the Milledgeville *Federal Union*, July 13, 1847.

JOHNSTON, R. M. and BROWNE, W. H., *Life of Alexander H. Stephens*, Philadelphia, 1878.

JONES, C. C., *John McPherson Berrien*, Atlanta, 1891. (Address before the Georgia Bar Association, 1891—eulogistic.)

JONES, C. C., *Life and Services of Ex-Governor C. J. Jenkins*, Atlanta, 1884. (Memorial Address to the Georgia Legislature, 1883—laudatory.)

KNIGHT, L. L., *A Standard History of Georgia and Georgians*, New York, 1917. (Of the 6 volumes, volumes IV-VI. inclusive, are biographical.)

KNIGHT, L. L., *Reminisences of Famous Georgians*, Atlanta, 1907-08.

Memoirs of Georgia, the Southern Historical Association, Atlanta, 1895. (Contains convenient biographical sketches.)

MERRITT, ELIZABETH, *James Henry Hammond, 1807-1864*, Baltimore, Johns Hopkins University Press, 1923.

MILLER, S. F., *Bench and Bar of Georgia*, Philadelphia, 1858. (Contains valuable biographical sketches, by a contemporary politician, of both Whig and Democratic leaders.)

MITCHELL, B., "Frederick Law Olmsted," *Johns Hopkins University Sudies in Political and Social Science*, Series XLII, No. 2, Baltimore, 1924.

NORTHERN, W. J., *Men of Mark in Georgia*, Atlanta, 1907-12.

NORTON, F. H., *Life of Alexander Stephens*, Alden, N. Y., 1883. (An early biography, superseded by Pendleton.)

PENDLETON, L. B., *Alexander Stephens*, Philadelphia, 1907.

PHILLIPS, U. B., *The Life of Robert Toombs*, New York, 1913.

SHURZ, CARL, *Henry Clay*, Boston, 1887.

STOVALL, P. A., *Robert Toombs*, New York, 1892. (Superseded by Phillips' *Toombs*, but contains some interesting material.)

TURNER, J. A., "William C. Dawson," *The Plantation*, I. No. 1, pp. 71-100 (1860).

TURNER, J. A., "Herschel V. Johnson," *ibid.*, pp. 62-70.

WADDELL, J. D., *Linton Stephens*, Atlanta, 1877.

WADE, JOHN D., *Augustus Baldwin Longstreet*, New York, 1924. (Useful for the social history of Georgia in the antebellum period.)

VI—Newspapers

GEORGIA

ATHENS, CLARK COUNTY

Southern Whig, Weekly, Whig. Library of Congress—
June-December, 1849. (Typically conservative Whig
Journal, not of great value. Circulation—700.)[1]

Southern Banner, Weekly, Democratic. Library of University of Georgia, 1833-1846. (Most militant journal of
the Union Democrats. Hopkins Holsey, Editor. Usually
considered the organ of Howell Cobb. Circulation—700.)

AGUSTA, RICHMOND COUNTY

Constitutionalist, Daily, tri-weekly and weekly, Democratic.
Office of the Augusta *Chronicle.* Complete files to 1860.
These damaged by fire, 1921. Present condition confused. (Militant Democratic journal. Became a southern-rights paper in 1849. Gardner, J. R., Editor. Circulation, weekly edition—3,000.)

Chronicle and Sentinel, Daily, tri-weekly, and weekly, Whig.
(1) Library of Congress, March, 1849-December, 1854.
(2) Complete files in the *Chronicle* office, damaged by fire,
1921. Present condition confused. (3) Library of the
Western Reserve Historical Society, Cleveland, Ohio—
1855, 1857, 1859. (Conservative Whig organ, expressing
remarkably independent views of the most conservative
Whig group. Especially interesting for its constitutional
principles and views on slavery. Strongly anti-Carolina.
Dr. Daniel Lee, Editor. Largest circulation in the state—
among political papers. Weekly edition, 5,350.)

Republic, Tri-weekly and weekly, Independent Whig. No
files located. (A vigorous independent Whig paper; favored Clay in 1848 and southern-rights in 1850. Founded
1848, perhaps to back Clay. Smythe, J., Editor. Circulation, weekly edition—2,950.)

COLUMBUS, MUSCOGEE COUNTY

Enquirer, Weekly, Whig. (1) Office of the *Enquirer,* 1828
to date. (2) In possession of Mr. J. J. Gilbert, of Colum-

---

[1] Facts given are for 1850, unless otherwise stated.

bus—1874 to date. (3) Office of the Ordinary, Harris County, Georgia, 1856-1860. (Conservative Whig. No circulation figures.)

Times, Tri-weekly and weekly, Democratic. (1) Library of Congress—January, 1847-May, 1848; January-June, 1849. (2) In possession of J. J. Gilbert, Columbus, 1847 to 1860. (An able Democratic journal, became favorable to southern-rights, 1849, after James N. Bethune was replaced by John Forsyth as editor. No circulation figures.)

Muscogee Democrat, Weekly, Democratic. No files found. (A consistently southern-rights paper. In 1850 became the *Sentinel,* and advocated "secession *per se."* Radical statements attracted attention in the North, but no indication in Georgia press that it was so important as the *Times.* Circulation probably small. No figures.)

Daily Sun, Daily, Whig. In possession of J. J. Gilbert, Columbus—1853-1874, when it merged with the *Enquirer.* (Of value for years just prior to the Civil War.)

MACON, BIBB COUNTY

Georgia Messenger, Weekly, Whig. Emory College Library (Oxford, Georgia), 1830-1847, when it merged with the *Journal and Messenger.* (Conservative Whig.)

Georgia Journal and Messenger, Weekly, Whig. (1) Georgia Historical Society, 1847-1849. (2) Files in the office of the Macon *Telegraph,* partly destroyed by fire, 1910—files preserved relate largely to the Reconstruction period. (3) Emory College Library—1851-1857, 1858-1860. (4) Western Reserve Historical Society, 1856-1857, 1858. (A typically conservative Whig paper. Circulation—3,200.)

Georgia Telegraph, Weekly, Democratic. (1) Files in its own office largely destroyed by fire, 1910. (See above.) (2) Office of the Court of Ordinary of Jones County (Grey, Georgia), complete from May, 1852, on. (3) Western Reserve Historical Society—1856. (An interesting and militant southern-rights journal. Was the first in Georgia to assume this position, after Sam J. Ray succeeded O. H. Prince as editor in 1847. See Savannah *Georgian,* April 15, 1847.)

Georgia Citizen, Weekly, Whig. No files found. (A militant pro-Union paper, expressing the most violent condemnation of the southern movement offered in the state. Its editor, L. F. W. Andrews, was seriously accused of being an abolitionist, and the paper temporarily suppressed, July, 1850, after he was driven from Macon. Circulation —1,000; in 1851 became the Macon *Union Banner.* For reference to latter see Pendleton, *A. H. Stephens,* p. 109.)
Southern Tribune, Weekly, Democratic. No files found. (Character unknown. For reference to, see Savannah *Georgian,* July 9, 1850.)

MILLEDGEVILLE, BALDWIN COUNTY

Federal Union, Weekly, Democratic. (1) Complete files in the *Union Recorder* office, Milledgeville. (2) Library of Congress—January, 1847-November, 1849. (3) Office of the Court of Ordinary, Jones County (Grey, Georgia), May, 1852, on. (4) The De Renne Library. (The central organ of the Georgia Democracy; an able and vigorous journal. Favored the southern movement after 1848. R. W. Flournoy, Editor. Circulation—3,000.)
Southern Recorder, Weekly, Whig. (1) Library of Congress, 1851. (2) In private possession, Milledgeville, 1820-1868. (The central organ of Georgia Whiggery, but not so important a paper as the Augusta *Chronicle* or the Savannah *Republican.* A typical conservative, pro-Union journal. Circulation—2,705.)

SAVANNAH, CHATHAM COUNTY[2]

Daily Georgian, Daily, Democratic. (1) Library of Congress—1847-August, 1849. (2) Georgia Historical Society—1818-1854. (An able Democratic daily. Strongly anti-Calhoun and anti-Carolina. Mildly favored southern-rights movement, but tended generally towards conservatism. Circulation—650. Daily circulation always much smaller than weekly. W. H. Bulloch and H. R. Jackson, editors.)
Daily Republican, Daily, Whig. (1) Library of Congress—

---

[2] There is a collection of scrap-books prepared by Dr. Richard Arnold, containing valuable excerpts, chiefly from the Savannah newspapers between 1840 and 1870, in possession of Miss Margaret Cosens, of Savannah.

Complete files for this period. (2) Georgia Historical Society—1844-1846. (Ranked with the Augusta *Chronicle* as an able, conservative Whig newspaper. Less independent and original, however, than the *Chronicle*. Strongly anti-Calhoun and anti-Carolina. Francis Winters and J. W. Locke, Editors. Circulation—900.)

Daily News, Daily, independent. Office of the *News*, 1850 to date. (An independent paper, with mild leanings toward southern-rights. Established 1850 as the first cheap newspaper, and had a phenomenally rapid growth. One month after establishment claimed to have largest circulation in Savannah. See Savannah *News*, January 30, 1850. Well conducted by Col. W. T. Thompson, its first editor, and the only ante-bellum Savannah paper surviving today. Circulation—1,020. For its history see the *Savannah News, its History*. Pamphlet, Georgia Historical Society, n.d., apparently written 1880-1890.)[3]

OTHER STATES

ALABAMA

Mobile *Daily Advertiser*, Daily, Whig.[4]
Montgomery *Daily Alabama Journal*, Daily, Whig.

DISTRICT OF COLUMBIA

Daily National Intelligencer, Daily, Whig.
Daily Union, Daily, Democratic.
Daily Republic, Daily, Whig.
Niles' Weekly Register, Weekly, Whig.
Southern Press, Weekly, "Southern-rights."

FLORIDA

Pensacola *Gazette*, Daily, Whig.

---

[3] For a nearly complete list of all the remaining papers in the state, with their political affiliations and circulations, see Kennedy, J. C. J., *Catalogue of the Newspapers and Periodicals Published in the United States* (See *Guides*.) The following papers are not listed therein:
Marietta *Helicon*, Weekly, Whig.
Graffin *Whig*, Weekly, Whig.
Griffin *Georgia Jeffersonian*, Weekly, Democratic.
Eufaula *Democrat*, Weekly, Democratic.
Dahlonega *Watchman*, Weekly, Democratic.
Dalton *Eagle*, Weekly, Whig.
[4] Type of edition used is here given, *e.g.*, weekly, daily, etc.

LOUISIANA

New Orleans *Picayune,* Daily, Whig.

MARYLAND

Baltimore *Sun,* Daily, Democratic.

MASSACHUSETTS

Boston *Bee,* Daily, Democratic.
Boston *Courier,* Daily, Whig.
Boston *Liberator,* Weekly, Abolitionist.

MISSISSIPPI

Aberdeen *Independent,* Weekly, Whig.
Jackson *Mississippian,* Weekly, Democratic.
Jackson *Southron,* Weeky, Whig. (Became *Flag of the Union* in 1850.)
Natchez *Courier,* Weekly, Whig.

NEW YORK

New York *Herald,* Daily, Democratic.
New York *Tribune,* Daily, Whig (antislavery).

OHIO

Akron *Summit Beacon,* Weekly, Whig.
Cincinnati, *Enquirer,* Daily, Democratic.
Cleveland *Plain Dealer,* Daily, Democratic.
Columbus *Ohio State Journal,* Daily, Whig.

PENNSYLVANIA

Philadelphia *Evening Bulletin,* Daily, Independent.
Philadelphia *Pennsylvanian,* Daily, Democratic.
Philadelphia *North American,* Daily, Whig.
Philadelphia *Public Ledger,* Daily, Independent.

SOUTH CAROLINA

Charleston *Daily Courier,* Daily, "Southern-rights."
Charleston *Mercury,* Daily, "Southern-rights."
Columbia *South Carolinian,* Tri-weekly, "Southern-rights."

VIRGINIA

Richmond *Daily Whig,* Daily, Whig.
Richmond *Enquirer,* Daily, Democratic.

VII—PERIODICALS

American Whig Review, New York, 1845-1852.
DeBow's Commercial Review, New Orleans, 1846-1864.
Hunt's Merchants' Magazine and Commercial Review, New York, 1839-1870.
Harpers New Monthly Magazine, New York, 1850, on. (Useful for monthly summaries of current news.)
The Plantation, Elberton, Georgia, 1860. (A literary and political periodical. Its few numbers contain some interesting descriptions of Georgia politics and politicians.)
Southern Cultivator, Augusta, Georgia, 1848, on. (Important for agricultural conditions in Georgia. Had the largest circulation of any periodical in the state.)
United States Magazine and Democratic Review, Washington, D. C., 1838-1859.

VIII—PAMPHLETS

(Unless otherwise noted these pamphlets are in the De Renne Library, or the Georgia Historical Society Library, in Savannah.)
Address of the Executive Committee to the Constitutional Union Party of Georgia, Milledgeville, 1852. (Sent out in July, 1852, chiefly by Whig members, advising a dissolution of the Union party.)
Address of a Portion of the Executive Committee of the Constitutional Union Party, to the Union Democrats and Union Whigs, Friends of Pierce and King. (Sent out in July, 1852, chiefly by Democratic members, advising the preservaion of the Union party, and its support of Pierce and King.)
ARNOLD, RICHARD D., *Remarks on the Report of the Committee on the State of the Republic* (Georgia Senate) *in Relation to the Honorable John McPherson Berrien,* Savannah, 1843. (Speech in the Georgia Senate, December 19, 1842, concerning Berrien's attitude towards the tariff and senatorial responsibility.)
CAMPBELL, L. D., *Kansas and Nebraska,* Washington, 1855. (Reprint in pamphlet form of speech made in House of Representatives, December 14, 1854. Contains Campbell's analysis of A. H. Stephen's economic comparison of Georgia and Ohio.)

CHAPPELL, A. H. (Editor), *Pamphlets of Georgia History.* Columbus, Georgia, 1873, and Atlanta, 1896. (Of miscellaneous character and indirect value. Pennsylvania Historical Society.)

CLARK, JOHN, *Considerations on the Principles of William Crawford,* Augusta, Georgia, 1819. (Clark's own account of the personalities which precipitated the differentiation of the Clark and Troup parties.)

COBB, HOWELL, *Message to the Georgia Legislature,* November 8, 1853, Milledgeville, 1853. (Urging political harmony in the state and declaring the crisis of 1850 safely past.)

COBB, HOWELL, *To Our Constituents,* Washington, D. C., 1849. (The "Minority Address," of 1849, signed by Cobb, John H. Lumpkin, B. Boyd, and B. L. Ciark.)

COLQUITT, W. T., *Circular to the People of Georgia and especially to the States Rights Party,* Milledgeville, 1840. (Appeal to the party to abandon the national Whigs and unite with the Democrats.)

DEBOW, J. D. B., *The Interest in Slavery of the Southern Non-Slaveholder,* 1860 Association, Tract No. 5, Charleston, S. C., 1860. University of Pennsylvania Library. (Written to prove the antithesis of Helper's argument. Contains interesting conclusions based upon the census of 1850.)

EUBANK, THOMAS, *Inorganic Forces, Ordained to Supersede Human Slavery,* New York, 1860. Included in *Democratic Opinions of Slavery,* 1776-1863. (A volume of pamphlets, New York Public Library. That by Eubank gives an economic interpretation of the history of slavery, predicting peaceful emancipation for economic reasons.)

FISHER, SIDNEY G., *The Laws of Race as Connected with Slavery,* Philadelphia, 1860, University of Pennsylvania Library. (Interesting as an early effort to prove the slavery question incidental to the race problem.)

FISHER, ELWOOD, *The North and the South,* Address to the Young Men's Mercantile Association of Cincinnati; Charleston, South Carolina, 1849. (An economic comparison of the two sections, denying northern superiority. Popular in the South in 1850.)

FREE NEGROISM, (n.d.) Included in *Democratic Opinions on Slavery,* New York Public Library. (Apparently written by a southerner, 1860-1863. Interesting opinions on slavery and emancipation.)

GREEN, G. E., Translator's Preface to A. G. de Cassagnac's *History of the Working and Burgher Classes*, Philadelphia, 1872. (An unusual essay claiming that the interests of southern capital and northern labor were identical, that northern capital forced the Civil War to divide these two, and that slavery greatly improved the social status of the poor, non-slaveholding whites.)

Incidents of a Journey from Abbeville, South Carolina, to Ocola, Florida, by an Observer of Small Things, Edgefield, South Carolina, 1852. New York Public Library. (Interesting observations upon political conditions in Augusta and Savannah.)

Inquiry into the Condition and Prospects of the African Race in the United States, by an American, Philadelphia, 1839, University of Pennsylvania Library. (Candid, fair, and discerning. Deals with the race problems in slavery.)

JONES, A. SEABORN, *Speed the Plough: An Essay on the Tariff, by a Georgia Planter*, Athens, Georgia, 1845. (Expresses opposition of the conservative Georgia planter to the protective tariff and the introduction of manufacturing.)

KING, JOHN P., *Letter to a Whig Planter*, September 15, 1844. (Able argument by Georgia Democrat against the tariff.)

LONGSTREET, A. B., *Voice from the South, or Letters from Georgia to Massachusetts and to the Southern States*, with an appendix containing an article from the Charleston *Mercury* on the Wilmot Proviso, together with the fourth article of the Constitution, the Law of Congress, the Nullification Law of Pennsylvania, the Resolutions of Ten of the Free States, the Resolutions of Virginia, Georgia and Alabama, and Mr. Calhoun's resolutions in the Senate of the United States, with an introduction by the editor of the Baltimore *Western Continent*, Baltimore, 1847. (Copy in Yale University Library, in the Pennsylvania Historical Society, in possession of Dr. U. B. Phillips. An interesting and valuable résumé of the history of Georgia and Massachusetts with relationship to slavery, from the Georgia point of view. Some comment on current conditions in Georgia. An appeal to the south to join the southern movement. The pamphlet was probably the first important bit of propaganda literature favoring that movement in the state. Notes on authorship, influence, etc. are in Wade, J. D., *Longstreet*, pp. 286, 287; Phillips, U. B., "Literary Movement for Secession," *W. A. Dunning Studies in Southern History*, p. 35.)

MCALLISTER, M. H., *Address of, of Georgia, to the Georgia Democratic-Republican Convention*, July 4, 1840. Milledgeville, 1840. (Made upon joining the party in 1840. Largely an appeal by the former Whig leader to the rest of the State-rights men to abandon the national Whig party.)

PERRY B. F., *Speech in the South Carolina House, December 11, 1850, on Federal Relations*, Charleston, S. C. (The co-operationists' attitude towards Georgia.)

State-Rights Party of Georgia, Proceedings of, November 13, 1833, Savannah, 1833. (Favoring nullification and South Carolina.)

STEPHENS, ALEXANDER H., *More of Georgia and Ohio*, Washington, D. C., 1855. (Speech in national House, continuing his reply to Campbell of Ohio, and comparing the economic condition of the two states, to the advantage of Georgia.)

TOWNSEND, JOHN, *The Southern States, Their Present Peril*, Charleston, South Carolina, 1850. (Able statement of the secessionist view and a detailed calculation of the possibilities concerning civil war.)

TREASCOTT, W. H., *The Position and Cause of the South*, Charleston, 1850. (A secessionist reply to Toombs and the Georgia advocates of compromise.)

The Union, Being a Condemnation of Mr. Helper's Scheme, With a Plan for the Settlement of the Irresistable Conflict, n.d. (Included in *Democratic Opinions on Slavery, 1776-1860*. New York Public Library. Title descriptive.)

Union Celebration in Macon, Georgia, February 22, 1851; Macon, 1851. (Copy in possession of Mr. Warren Grice, Macon, Georgia. Copy in possession of Dr. U. B. Phillips. A valuable pamphlet, containing important letters sent the local committee of the Georgia Union party, especially by Union Democrats, but also by Whigs and northern political leaders of both parties. Contains important comments on the history of political parties in Georgia, on the slavery problem, and on the significance of the Union victory in the state.)

WESTON, G. M., *Poor Whites of the South,* Washington, 1856. (Harvard University Library.)

WELLBORN, M. J., *To the Voters of the Second Congressional District,* n.d., probably August or September, 1850, copy in the Library of the University of Michigan, *Pamphlets on American Slavery,* IV. No. 18. (Address by the Democratic congressman from the second district of Georgia urging his constituents to accept the Clay Compromise.)

YEADON, RICHARD, *Speech of Mr. Richard Yeadon of Charleston to the Madison Georgia Whig Convention,* July 31, 1844. Charleston, S. C., 1844. (Relations between Georgia and South Carolina Whigs.)

IX—PUBLIC RECORDS AND PROCEEDINGS

Congressional Globe, for 1847-1851, inclusive, especially for the twenty-ninth Congress, second session, and the thirty-first Congress.

Journal of a General Convention of the State of Georgia, 1833. (A constitutional convention which considered the problem of the "white basis" of representation in the state legislature. Copy in Columbia University Library.)

Journal of the Convention to Reduce and Equalize the Representation of the General Assembly of the State of Georgia, 1839. (Copy in Columbia University Library.)

Journals of the Georgia Senate, 1847-1848, and 1849-1850.

Journals of the Georgia House of Representatives, 1847-1848, and 1849-1850.

Acts of Georgia, 1847-1848, and 1849-1850.

COBB, T. R. R., *Digest of the Statute Laws of Georgia, in Force Prior to 1851,* Athens, Georgia, 1851.

COBB, T. R. R., *Reports of the Georgia Supreme Court.* (Vol. XIV. 499, ff. contains account of the important case of Padelford, Fay, and Co., v. City of Savannah, which throws much light on the constitutional theories of Judge H. L. Benning, the Georgia secessionist leader, and upon Georgia's relations with the federal Supreme Court.)

Debates and Proceedings of the Georgia Convention, 1850, Milledgeville, 1850. (Copies in Georgia Historical Society

380   GEORGIA AND THE UNION IN 1850

Library, University of Pennsylvania Library, University of
Chicago Library, Yale University Library, also in *Federal
Union*, issues of December 17, and December 24, 1850. Reported by A. E. Marshall, of that journal, and printed by its
press. Essential for the study of the state convention of
1850. Also contains executive proclamation calling the convention.)
Journal of the Georgia Convention, 1850, Milledgeville, 1850.
(University of Pennsylvania Library.)
*Resolutions, Address and Journal of Proceedings of the South-
ern Convention*, Nashville, 1850. (Copy in Harvard University Library. Directly useful for its record of the Georgia
members of the "Nashville Convention.")
*Resolutions and Address of the Southern Convention, Published
by Order of the Convention*, Nashville, 1850. (Copy in
Georgia Historical Society Library. A useful pamphlet,
since the complete resolutions are difficult to find elsewhere.)

X—SOURCE COLLECTIONS

AMES, H. V., *State Documents on Federal Relations*, Phila-
delphia, 1911.
CLUSKEY, M. W., *The Democratic Hand Book*, New York,
1856. (Material on party platforms, etc., largely for 1851-
1856.)
CLUSKEY, M. W., *The Political Text Book*, Philadelphia, 1859.
(Useful for sources not available elsewhere.)
Democratic Textbook, The, By "G. H. H.," New York and
Philadelphia, 1848. (Copy in New York Public Library.
Much material concerning the attitude of both major parties
toward the Mexican War.)
GREELY, H. and CLEVELAND, J. F., *A Political Text Book for
1860*, New York, 1860. (Includes national platforms, etc.,
1850-1860. New York Public Library.)
PHILLIPS, U. B., *Plantation and Frontier*. (Vols. I and II in
Commons, J. R. [Ed.] *A Documentary History of American
Industrial Society*, Cleveland, 1910-1911.)

XI—STATISTICAL COLLECTIONS

American Almanac, Boston, 1830-1861.
The Seventh Census of the United States, Washington, D. C.,
1850. Bancroft, J., *Census of the City of Savannah*, Savannah, 1848. DeBow, J. D. B., *Historical View of the United*

States, Compendium of the Seventh Census, Washington, 1854.

DEBOW, J. D. B., *The Industrial Resources of the Southern and Western States,* New Orleans, 1852. (Valuable collection of contemporary essays and surveys containing statistical data.)

Georgia, Statistics of, an abstract of the State of Georgia, compiled by authority of the Legislature, from the Census of 1850, Milledgeville, 1851. (Copy in Pennsylvania Historical Society.)

SHERWOOD, ADIEL, *A Gazetteer of the State of Georgia,* Washington, D. C., 1829, 1837, Atlanta, 1860. (Some interesting statistical and historical data. Sherwood preceded White in the statistical study of his state, and regarded the latter as an interloper.)

WHITE, G. M., *Statistics of the State of Georgia,* Savannah, 1849. (Contains some statistics, as well as much contemporary description, and map of the state for 1849. Useful surveys of the counties.)

WHITE, G. M., *Historical Collections of Georgia,* New York, 1854. (A work difficult to classify, containing statistical, biographical, and historical data. Not so useful as the above.)

XII—GEOGRAPHICAL DESCRIPTIONS AND MAPS

SHERWOOD, ADIEL, *Gazetteer of Georgia,* Washington, 1837, 2nd edition. Contains four maps for the fourth decade. (For others in this decade see those of Wellborn, Tanner and Mitchell, listed by Phillips, U. B., *Georgia and State Rights,* p. 218.)

TANNER, H. S., *Map of Georgia and Alabama,* 1846. (Copy in Georgia Historical Society. Shows roads and railroads.)

BONNER, W. G., *Map of Georgia,* 1861. (A large wall map.)

Neueste Karte von Georgia mit seinem Strassen, Eisenbahnen, u. Entfernungen, 1845, Bibliographischen Instituts zu Hildburghavsen, Amsterdam, Paris u. Philadelphia. (Copy in Pennsylvania Historical Society. A German equivalent of Tanner's map of 1846.)

WILLIAMS, W. T., *Map of Georgia, with its Geological Features,* in White, G. M., *Statistics of Georgia,* 1849. (Shows the usual as well as the geological features.)

XIII—Special Studies—Contemporary and
Non-Contemporary

For practical convenience a distinction is made between
"Contemporary" and "Non-Contemporary Studies." For this
purpose the date 1880 is arbitrarily selected as a dividing
point, those titles published prior to that year being listed as
"Contemporary." The supposition is that most of such works
were written by those who participated in the activities of 1847-
1852.

CONTEMPORARY STUDIES

Adams, Nehemiah, *A Southside View of Slavery,* 2nd edition, Boston, 1855. (Favorable view of slavery in Georgia,
by a Massachusetts man.)

Cobb, T. R. R., *Law of Negro Slavery,* Philadelphia, 1858.
(Contains historical sketch of slavery from the viewpoint of
a Georgia planter-lawyer.)

Christy, David, *Cotton Is King,* Cincinnati, 1855. (An economic analysis of slavery and the tariff.)

Cairnes, J. E., *The Slave Power,* London, 1862, 1863. (The
anti-slavery view.)

Fowler, W. C., *The Sectional Controversy, or Passages in the
Political History of the United States,* New York, 1863.
(Written in the fifties. Critical and well documented.)

Fitzhugh, George, *Cannibals All,* Richmond, 1857. (The
apotheosis of slavery.)

Fitzhugh, George, *Sociology for the South,* Richmond, 1854.
(See above.)

Giddings, J. R., *History of the Rebellion,* New York, 1864.
(The abolitionist view of the Congressional struggle, 1849-
1850.)

Goodloe, D. R., *An Inquiry Into the Causes which have
Retarded the Accumulation of Wealth and Increase in Population of the Southern States,* Washington, 1846.

Helper, H. R., *The Impending Crisis of the South,* New
York, 1860.

Hundley, D. R., *Social Relations in our Southern States,* New
York, 1860. (A rare and valuable study of social classes in
the South by a southerner familiar with both the North and
the South.)

KETTELL, T. P., *Southern Wealth and Northern Profits as exhibited in Statistical Facts and Official Figures*, New York, 1860.

LYELL, SIR CHARLES, *A Second Visit to the United States*, New York, 1849. (Incidental observations on Georgia society.)

LANMAN, CHARLES, *Letters from the Allegheny Mountains*, New York, 1849.

OLMSTED, F. L., *The Cotton Kingdom*, 2nd Ed., New York, 1862.

OLMSTED, F. L., *Journey in the Seaboard Slave States*, New York, 1856.

PARSONS, C. G., *Inside View of Slavery or Tour among the Planters*, with an introduction by Mrs. H. B. Stowe, Boston, 1855. (Impressions of Georgia by a professional man of strong anti-slavery opinions.)

PAINE, L. W., *Six Years in a Georgia Prison*, Boston, 1852. (Personal narrative of a Northern mechanic and teacher of abolitionist views. Interesting comment on social and economic conditions.)

RUFFIN, EDMUND, *The Political Economy of Slavery*, Richmond, 1857.

RUSSELL, ROBERT, *North America, Its Agriculture and Climate*, Edinburgh, 1857. (Includes a study of slavery economics.)

VAN EVRIE, J. H., *Negroes and Negro Slavery*, New York, 1853. (Pro-slavery Anthropology.)

WESTON, GEORGE M., *The Progress of Slavery in the United States*, Washington, D. C., 1857. (A keen contemporary analysis of the economic and political phenomena associated with slavery. Calls attention to the often unrecognized conservatism of the planter class in the sectional struggle. Moderately anti-slavery in opinion.)

RECENT STUDIES

AMES, H. V., "Calhoun and the Secession Movement of 1850," *University of Pennsylvania Public Lectures*, 1917-1918.

BOUCHER, C. S., "The Ante-Bellum Attitude of South Carolina Towards Manufacturing and Agriculture," *Washington University Studies*, III. Pt. II. *Humanistic Series*, No. 2.

BOUCHER, C. S., "The Secession and Coöperation Movements in South Carolina, 1848-1852," *Washington University Studies*, V., *Humanistic Series*, Pt. II, No. 2.

BOUCHER, C. S., *"In Re* That Aggressive Slavocracy," *Mississippi Valley Historical Review*, VIII. Nos. 1 and 2 (June-September, 1921). (An emphatic refutation of the traditional northern thesis.)

BRAWLEY, B., *A Social History of the American Negro*, New York, 1921. (Considers the slavery question incidental to the race problem.)

BROOKS, R. P., "Howell Cobb and the Crisis of 1850," *Mississippi Valley Historical Review*, IV. No. 3 (December, 1917). Also printed as *Bulletin of the University of Georgia*, XVIII. No. 2. (A brief study by the best informed student of Cobb's career. Especially good for the events of 1851.)

BROOKS, R. P., "A Local Study of the Race Problem, Race Relations in the Eastern Piedmont Region of Georgia," *Political Science Quarterly*, XXVI. 193-221.

BROOKS, R. P., "The Agrarian Revolution in Georgia," *Bulletin, University of Wisconsin*, No. 639, *History series*, V. 3, No. 3, Madison, Wis., 1914.

BROWN, G. W., *The Lower South in American History*, New York, 1903.

CLARK, V., *History of Manufactures in the United States*, Washington, D. C., 1916.

COLE, A. C., *The Whig Party in the South*, American Historical Association Prize Essay, 1912.

COLE, A. C., "The South and the Right of Secession in the Early Fifties," *Mississippi Valley Historical Review*, I. No. 3 (December, 1914).

COLLINS, W. H., *The Domestic Slave Trade of the Southern States*, New York, 1904.

COTTERILL, R. S., "Southern Railroads and Western Trade, 1840-1850," *Mississippi Historical Review*, III., 427-441.

COULTER, E. M., "The Nullification Movement in Georgia," *Georgia Historical Quarterly*, V. No. 2 (March, 1921). (An able account.)

COULTER, E. M., "A Georgia Educational Movement During the Eighteen Hundred Fifties," *Georgia Historical Quarterly*, IX. No. 1, pp. 1-33. (December, 1924.)

EMBRY, M. A., *A Study of the Secession Movement in Georgia*, M. A. Thesis, University of Chicago, 1916 (bound manuscript, University of Chicago Library. Relates to both the 1850 and 1860 periods. Useful only as a summary of several secondary accounts.)

FLEMING, W. L., "Immigration to the Southern States," *Political Science Quarterly*, XX., 276-297.

FOSTER, H. D., "Webster's Seventh of March Speech and the Secession Movement, 1850," *American Historical Rveiew*, XXVII., 250 ff. (January, 1922). (Able presentation of the influence of Webster and the Compromise in averting danger of secession in the South. Exaggerates, however, the degree of secessionist spirit in Georgia prior to March 4, 1850, and the danger of actual secession thereafter.)

GARNER, J. W., "The First Struggle Over Secession in Mississippi," *Mississippi Historical Society Publications*, IV., 89 ff. (Superseded by Miss Hearon's study.)

HAMER, P. M., *The Secession Movement in South Carolina*, Allentown, (Pa.) 1918.

HAMMOND, M. B., "The Cotton Industry," Ithaca, N. Y., 1897, *American Economic Association Publications, New Series,* No. 1.

HARPER, R. M., "Development of Agriculture in Upper Georgia, 1850 to 1880," *Georgia Historical Quarterly*, VI., No. 1, 1-27.

HERNDON, D. T., "The Nashville Convention," *Alabama Historical Society Publications*, V. 203, ff. (1904). (Based upon newspapers but generally reliable.)

HEARON, CLEO, *Mississippi and Compromise of 1850*, Oxford, Miss., 1913.

INGLE, EDWARD, *Southern Sidelights, A Picture of Social and Economic Life in the South a Generation before the War*, New York, 1896.

JERVEY, T. D., *The Slave Trade, Slavery and Color*, Charleston, S. C., 1925.

JONES, C. E., *Education in Georgia*, in *Contributions to American Educational History*, ed. H. B. Adams. *United States Bureau of Education Monographs*, No. 5, 1889. (Not based on extensive research but gives a general account of the main features of educational evolution.)

LAWTON, ALEXANDER R., *Judicial Controversies on Federal Appellate Jurisdiction*, President's Address, 38th Annual Meeting of the Georgia Bar Association, Tybee, Ga., 1921. (A valuable survey of the relations of Georgia to the Federal Supreme Court, which is especially useful for its study of the constitutional theories of H. L. Benning, the Georgia secessionist leader.)

MACY, JESSE, *Political Parties in the United States, 1846-1861,* New York, 1900.

McLENDON, S. G., *History of the Public Domain of Georgia,* Atlanta, 1924.

MEYER, B. H., *History of Transportation in the United States before 1860,* Washington, 1917.

MERRITT, ELIZABETH, "James H. Hammond," *Johns Hopkins University Studies,* Series XLI., No. 4 (1923).

MELLEN, G. F., "H. W. Hilliard and W. E. Yancy," *Sewanee Review,* XVII. 32-50.

MITCHELL, BROADUS, "The Rise of Cotton Mills in the South," *Johns Hopkins University, Studies in History and Political Science,* XXXIX. No. 2, Baltimore, 1921. (An able study. Exhibits somewhat unsympathetic attitude towards the antebellum South, and misunderstands certain phases of antebellum manufacturing. Contradicts Clark's thesis that there was continuity between the ante- and post-bellum industries.)

NEWBERRY, F., "The Nashville Convention," *South Atlantic Quarterly,* XI. (1912), No. 3, p. 259, ff.

NICHOLS, R. F., "The Democratic Machine, 1850-1854," *Columbia University Studies in History, Economics and Public Law,* CXI., No. 1, Whole No. 248, 1923.

PERSINGER, C. E., "The Bargain of 1844 as the Origin of the Wilmot Proviso," *American Historical Association Report,* 1911, II.

PHILLIPS, U. B., *American Negro Slavery,* New York, 1918.

PHILLIPS, U. B., "The Decadence of the Plantation System," *Annals of the American Academy of Political and Social Science,* XXXV. 37-41.

PHILLIPS, U. B., "An American State Owned Railroad" (The Western and Atlantic), *Yale Review,* XV., No. 3, pp. 259-282 (Old Series).

PHILLIPS, U. B., "The Economic Cost of Slave-Holding," *Political Science Quarterly*, XX. 257-275.

PHILLIPS, U. B., "Georgia and State Rights," *American Historical Association Report*, 1901, II.

PHILLIPS, U. B., "The Literary Movement for Secession," in *W. A. Dunning Studies in Southern History and Politics*, Chapter II, Columbia University Press, 1914.

PHILLIPS, U. B., "The Origin and Growth of the Southern Black Belts," *American Historical Review*, XI. 798-816.

PHILLIPS, U. B., "Plantations with Slave Labor and Free," *American Historical Review*, XXX. 738-753.

PHILLIPS, U. B., "The Southern Whigs," in the *Turner Essays*, New York, 1910.

PHILLIPS, U. B., "Transportation in the *Ante-Bellum* South, An Economic Analysis," *Quarterly Journal of Economics*, XIX. 434-451.

PHILLIPS, U. B., *A History of Transportation in the Eastern Cotton Belt to 1860*, New York, 1908.

POWELL, EDWARD P., *Nullification and Secession in the United States: A History of the Six Attempts During the First Century of the Republic*, New York, 1897.

REED, J. C., *The Brother's War*, Boston, 1905.

RUSSEL, R. R., "Economic Aspects of Southern Sectionalism, 1840-1861," *University of Illinois Studies in the Social Sciences*, XI. Nos. 1-2.

SIOUSSAT, ST. G. L., "Coöperation for the Development of the Material Welfare of the South," *The South in the Building of the Nation*, IV. 173-179.

SIOUSSAT, ST. G. L., "Tennessee, the Compromise of 1850, and the Nashville Convention," *Mississippi Valley Historical Review*, II. 259 ff., December, 1915.

SMITH, JUSTIN, *The War With Mexico*, 2 Vols., New York, 1919.

STONE, A. H., "Some Problems of Southern Economic History," *American Historical Review*, XIII. 779-797.

STONE, A. H., "The Cotton Factorage System of the Southern States," *American Historical Review*, XX. 557-565.

STONE, A. H., *Studies in the American Race Problem*, New York, 1908.

TAYLOR, A. A., "Movement of Negroes to the Gulf States," *Journal of Negro History*, III, No. 4, pp. 367-383. (November, 1923.)

TILLINGHAST, J. A., *The Negro in Africa and America*, New York, 1902.

WAGSTAFF, H. McG., "State Rights and Political Parties in North Carolina, 1776-1861," *Johns Hopkins University Studies in History and Political Science*, XXIV, (1906).

WHITE, M. J., *The Secession Movement in the United States, 1847-1852*, New Orleans, 1916. (Of relatively little value for Georgia.)

XIV—STATE HISTORIES

State Histories: Like most American states, Georgia lacks a critical and comprehensive history. Few of the state histories come down so far in time as 1850. As exceptions to this, note: *The History of Georgia*, in *The South in the Building of the Nation*, II. 122-242. (The only critical survey of the state's entire history. It is necessarily brief and contains chapters of varying merit.)

AVERY, I. W., *History of Georgia*, 1850-1881, New York, 1881. (Suggestive but uncritical. Only chapter iii is pertinent here.)

BROOKS, R. P., *History of Georgia*, Chicago, 1913. (A brief text book, but written from the modern critical point of view.)

KNIGHT, L. L., *A Standard History of Georgia and Georgians*, New York, 1917. (Vols. I-II, inc., deal with state history, Vols. IV-VI, inc., with biography.)

SMITH, C. H., *The Story of Georgia and the Georgia People*, 1736-1860, Macon, 1900.

XV—LOCAL HISTORIES

Georgia local histories, like the majority of such works, are usually laudatory and uncritical, and reflect the interests of the antiquarian rather than of the historian. Note as exceptions:

BUTLER, J. C., *Historical Records of Macon, Georgia*, Macon, 1879. (Shows interest in important historical developments and contains some source material.)

CHAPPEL, A. H., *Miscellanies of Georgia*, Atlanta (Ga.), 1874. (Contains miscellaneous collections of facts concerning towns and counties which are occasionally useful.)

DUTCHER, S. and JONES, C. C., *History of Augusta*, Syracuse, New York, 1890. (Rather superior to the ordinary local history and deals with an unusually interesting city.)

FORT, KATE H., *The Fort and Fanin Families*, Chattanooga, Tenn., 1903. (A reliable picture of social life in Middle Georgia.)

GAMBLE, THOMAS, JR., *A History of the City Government of Savannah, Georgia, From 1790-1901*, Savannah, 1901. (Drawn from the Savannah archives, important for social and economic conditions.)

WYLLY, C. S., *Annals of Glynn County, Georgia*, Brunswick, Georgia, 1897. (Deals with an unusually interesting county, the only one in Georgia in 1850 which possessed a very large majority of Negro population).

XVI—GENERAL HISTORIES

CHANNING, EDWARD, *History of the United States*, VI. New York, 1925.

DODD, WILLIAM E., *The Cotton Kingdom*, New Haven, 1921. (*The Chronicles of America*, Vol. 27.)

DODD, WILLIAM E., *Expansion and Conflict*, New York, 1915. (*Riverside Historical Series*, III.)

GARRISON, G. P., *Western Extension*, New York, 1906. (*The American Nation: A History*, Vol. 17.)

McMASTER, J. B., *A History of the People of the United States*, VII. and VIII., New York, 1914, 1919.

SMITH, T. C., *Parties and Slavery*, New York, 1906. (*The American Nation: A History*, Vol. 18.)

STEPHENSON, N. W., *Texas and the Mexican War*, New Haven, 1921. (*The Chronicles of America*, Vol. 24.)

INDEX